PRAISE FOR *RAW DEAL*

"A provocative, remedy-based perspective on the joint complexities of economic stability and ever expanding technology."

—*Kirkus Reviews*

"Hill's scathing critique will give readers pause before checking their smartphones for their next vacation rental or ride to the airport, as he develops the image of a well-educated Uber driver earning less than minimum wage while her bedroom is Airbnb'd to a tourist."

—*Publishers Weekly*

"*Raw Deal* is a must read for those concerned about how technology is disrupting the way we work and eroding the social safety net and how policy makers should respond. Hill delineates a promising new policy remedy: the creation of Individual Security Accounts to ensure that the growing number of workers in the 'gig' economy have adequate safety-net protections and benefits."

—Laura D'Andrea Tyson, Professor of Business Administration and Economics, University of California-Berkeley and former Chair of the US President's Council of Economic Advisers

"In *Raw Deal,* Steven Hill documents in frightening detail the ways in which new forms of work promise to plunge US workers and their families into further economic hardship, risk-assumption, and instability. Fortunately, Hill does not simply anticipate catastrophe; he closes the book with an informed call for institutional reforms that would lessen the negative consequences of these novel yet potentially dangerous forms of work. Anyone concerned with US working conditions – whether American workers, worker advocates, labor market scholars, or policy-makers – must read this book."

—Janet C. Gornick, Professor of Political Science and Sociology, Graduate Center, City University of New York, Director, LIS: Cross-National Data Center in Luxembourg

"*Raw Deal* is a compelling work—a stockpile of empirical analyses, anecdotes, and primary sourcing—laying out the evidence of the incredibly detrimental, yet often-disregarded downsides of many of the most talked-about 21st century business models. Steven Hill's work is by far the most forceful case I've read describing the tragedy of the commons that is the 'sharing economy,' and provides a much needed reality check for investors, civil libertarians, and everyone who cares about the American dream. At its heart, Raw Deal is a necessary catalyst that encourages us to explore the dark side of Silicon Valley, presenting not only an in-depth critique, but a wealth of proactive solutions that could prevent the pending decimation of America's working class."

—Sascha Meinrath, Director of X-Lab, Palmer Chair,
Penn State University

"Steven Hill's *Raw Deal* is an important book that will help shape the debate on the 'sharing economy.' It raises fundamental issues about the extent to which the sharing economy is largely an effort to evade crucial regulations which serve important public goals."

—Dean Baker, Co-Director,
Center for Economic and Policy Research,
publisher, *Beat the Press* economic blog

"Steven Hill's groundbreaking book on the part-time, unstable 'Uber Economy' shows how a new sub-economy becomes a work of law-flouting regress undermining full-time work. Remote corporate algorithms run riot!"

—Ralph Nader, consumer advocate

"Steven Hill has written a timely and important book that raises all the right questions about the future of the 1099 economy. From ground zero in San Francisco, he has the perfect vantage point to see where the technologies and business innovations shaping our world are going. *Raw Deal* should be required reading for every policy maker trying to make sense of how we ensure the sharing economy benefits are shared by all and not captured by a small group of disruptors."

—Lenny Mendonca, Director Emeritus,
McKinsey and Company

"For many years, Steven Hill's analysis, commentary and activism have helped shape our understanding of the U.S. political economy. His latest book, *Raw Deal* is a riveting expose that shows with alarming lucidity what Americans stand to lose if we don't figure out how to rein in the technological giants that are threatening the American Dream."

—Katrina vanden Heuvel, Editor and Publisher of *The Nation*

"We love to talk about technological innovation and disruption, yet rarely do we understand and discuss the actual consequences across broader society. Steven Hill's *Raw Deal* is superb. It is the best book I've read about the consequences of such 'creative destruction' as the future hurtles toward us at breakneck speed."

—Peter Sims, Co-founder and Managing Director,
Silicon Guild and author of
Little Bets: How Breakthrough Ideas
Emerge from Small Discoveries

"Steven Hill's impressive *Raw Deal* exposes the so called 'sharing economy.' As Hill explains, the new insecurity of workers produces wealth that is shared mainly with the top one percent using new forms of predatory capitalism. *Raw Deal* is a much needed antidote to a lot of hype about how insecurity is supposedly the ticket to prosperity."

—Robert Kuttner, Coeditor of *The American Prospect,*
author of *Debtors' Prison: The Politics of Austerity Versus Possibility*

"The best takedown yet of how capitalism's 'share' economy is only another shareholder one. Brilliant."

—Joel Rogers, Professor at UW-Madison, author
of *American Society: How It Really Works*

ALSO BY STEVEN HILL

Europe's Promise: Why the European Way Is the Best Hope in an Insecure Age
(www.EuropesPromise.org)

10 Steps to Repair American Democracy
(www.10Steps.net)

Fixing Elections: The Failure of America's Winner Take All Politics
(www.FixingElections.org)

Whose Vote Counts? (with Robert Richie)

Author's website: www.Steven-Hill.com;
Facebook: StevenHill01 Twitter: @StevenHill1776

RAW DEAL

HOW THE "UBER ECONOMY" AND RUNAWAY CAPITALISM ARE SCREWING AMERICAN WORKERS

STEVEN HILL

St. Martin's Press

New York

All lawsuits and criminal cases mentioned in the book were, except as noted in the text, still pending at the time that the book was completed. All quotations in the book from individuals are based upon secondary sources unless the text specifically states that they are from interviews conducted by the author.

www.stmartins.com

Library of Congress Cataloging-in-Publication Data

Hill, Steven, 1958-
Raw deal : how the "Uber economy" and runaway capitalism are screwing American workers / Steven Hill.
pages cm
ISBN 978-1-250-07158-3 (hardback)
1. Information technology—Economic aspects—United States. 2. New business enterprises—United States. 3. Entrepreneurship—Moral and ethical aspects—United States. 4. Working class—United States. 5. Labor—United States. 6. United States—Economic conditions—2009- I. Title.
HC110.I55H55 2015
331.10973—dc23

2015014664

ISBN 978-1-250-07158-3 (hardcover)
ISBN 978-1-4668-8272-0 (e-book)

Our books may be purchased in bulk for promotional, educational, or business use. Please contact your local bookseller or the Macmillan Corporate and Premium Sales Department at (800) 221-7945, extension 5442, or by e-mail at MacmillanSpecialMarkets@macmillan.com.

Design by Letra Libre, Inc.

First edition: October 2015

10 9 8 7 6 5 4 3 2 1

Printed in the United States of America.

To Maria Fernandes, former Dunkin' Donuts worker and now a star in the sky, showing us what we stand to lose; to my nieces and nephews, in the hope that the world you inherit will still provide as good a life as your parents and grandparents knew; and of course to Lucy, always to Lucy.

CONTENTS

INTRODUCTION
EARTHQUAKE IN SAN FRANCISCO

"How do we eradicate the barriers which separate substantial minorities of our citizens from access to education and employment on equal terms with the rest? How, in sum, can we make our free economy work at full capacity–that is, provide adequate profits for enterprise, adequate wages for labor, and opportunity for all?"

—President John F. Kennedy, 1962[1]

I'M SITTING IN SAN FRANCISCO, LOOKING OUT MY WINDOW INTO THE CHILLY, grey fingers of fog threading through the upper red spans of the Golden Gate Bridge. I'm watching the world change before my eyes. The number of revolutionary inventions and innovations emanating from the Bay Area is astonishing: Google eyeglasses that turn your head into a mobile computer and surveillance camera; self-steering cars that don't need a driver; search engines that track your personal interests (whether you want them to or not); robots that use increasingly sophisticated software and algorithms to take on tasks once considered exclusively human; stem cell research and regenerative medicine that, like Dr. Frankenstein, seek to transform living tissue.

Of course, already ubiquitous are the wireless Harry Potter wands that put in the palm of our hands everything from a communications revolution (phone/text/email/tweets) to an information revolution (24/7 news/weather/entertainment) to a creativity revolution (camera/video/audio/apps) to a powerful GPS system that makes it virtually impossible to get lost. We have unprecedented capacity to record, publish and mythologize our every waking moment in our bid for our 900 billion nanoseconds (i.e., 15 minutes) of fame. As we became seduced by the iPhone and Android's charms, few of us realized that those same devices would provide the means for the government, as well as corporations, to spy on us in ways the Nazi Gestapo or Stalin's NKVD could never have imagined. And now these devices have spread outward from the tech nirvana in the Bay Area to every corner of the world. The genie has been let out of the bottle, with seemingly no way to stuff it back.

The Bay Area long has been an epicenter of disruption and revolution, whether the source was the mad gold diggers of '49, the Beat poets, woman's lib, gay marriage, the Black Panthers, antiwar protests, the free-speech movement, free love, hippie flower power, LSD or psychedelic music. In trendsetting San Francisco, the future has always been now. But today the "revolution" is of a decidedly different nature. Brand names like Google, Apple, Oracle, Facebook and Twitter dominate the accelerating digital arena, their companies synonymous with business innovation, creativity and commercial success. Upstart companies are finding ways to load software and algorithms into just about everything, from automobiles to wristwatches, from drones to home appliances, from music to movies, from hospitals to the Pentagon, from agriculture to the assembly line floor. Robots and automation are boosting productivity to unimaginable levels—and human redundancy along with it, as the machines threaten to replace the humans.

In short, the science fiction of yesterday is racing up and down Highway 101 between Silicon Valley and the City, like a high-tech steamroller cruising at Indy 500 speeds. The tidal wave of innovation and GDP maximizers sweeping the country seeks nothing less than to transform the ways we work, communicate, create, inform, educate, entertain, shop and travel. The sweep of the disrupters is historic; their ambitions are total. Tech trendsetter and venture capitalist Marc Andreessen says, quite simply, "Software is eating the world."[2]

Now from the techno-wizards comes the latest groundbreaking trend, which appears destined to further reshape the ways we work and live. It's called the "sharing economy," sometimes referred to as the "peer-to-peer," "collaborative-consumption" or "on-demand" economy. The sharing economy is hot, a darling of venture capitalist investors as well as the media, which reports in rapturous tones on its every new development, including astounding company valuations in the tens of billions of dollars for companies that have yet to make a penny of profit. Its signature companies like Uber, Airbnb, TaskRabbit, Elance-Upwork, Lyft, Zaarly, Etsy, Washio, Postmates and dozens more, which have all incubated in the San Francisco Bay Area, are being hyped as the new avatars of the way things will be. These Internet-based companies deploy online Web- and app-based platforms to directly connect buyers and sellers of goods, labor and services, cutting out any middle person in a way that has never been possible before. Amazon and eBay pioneered this type of technology initially for selling books and used stuff; now the sharing economy companies are extending this powerful capability into the selling of dozens more services, goods and labor.

But its revolution is more than merely commercial—its leading visionaries say that the sharing economy offers a viable alternative to laboring in the trenches of Corporate America. Instead of selling your soul to the Man, you will be able to work for yourself as your own microentrepreneur. With no middle man between you and your customers, the work will come directly to your computer, via the Web or via apps on your smartphone—all you have to do is wait and check your app feed for the next paying gig. You will no longer be a lowly grunt, climbing the ladder to enrich someone else—you will run your own microbusiness, able to work when you want, doing what you want. This is why it's also called the DIY (do-it-yourself) economy, replacing the old postindustrial economy by "liberating workers" to become "independent" and "work for ourselves," with promises that each of us can become the "CEOs of our own freelancing business."

Yes, according to the techno-visionaries, there's gold in them thar hills. Brian Chesky, a former bodybuilder who is Airbnb's young 34-year-old billionaire cofounder and CEO, likes to cast his company as saving the world. "I think we're in the midst of a revolution," he told a conference in San Francisco.[3] Travis Kalanick, CEO and founder of the ridesharing company Uber, also known for his rhetorical boldness, has boasted that his company will "make car ownership a thing of the past."[4] Not to be outdone, Leah Busque, founder and CEO of TaskRabbit, trumpets that all she wants to do is, well, "revolutionize how people work."[5] And media outlets like *The Economist, Forbes, Fast Company, TechCrunch* and *Wired* beat the drum for the changing of the guard.[6]

Sitting here in San Francisco, I have a front-row seat at the epicenter of this latest earthquake. But as the future that the tech geniuses have planned for us comes slowly into view, it looks increasingly alarming. It's not just the many people evicted, including elderly and disabled tenants, to clear entire apartment buildings to make rooms available for tourists via Airbnb, even as Airbnb has disputed its obligation to pay local hotel taxes; or the desperate workers scrambling like low-rent *braceros*—"arms for hire"—on jobs found via TaskRabbit, Elance-Upwork, CrowdFlower and other job brokerage websites, sometimes for less than minimum wage (according to some workers); or the middle- and low-income households being forced to leave the Bay Area in a tech-driven "Trail of Tears" because they no longer can afford the escalating costs; or that Uber, which is valued at $51 billion—larger than Delta or United Airlines, and approaching General Motors and Ford—has incorporated more than 30 different foreign subsidiaries, many of them no more than mailboxes in the Caribbean, as low-tax havens to greatly reduce its U.S. tax obligations.[7]

No, the impact of the sharing economy goes way beyond that. The new economy visionaries—a new genus that I have taken to calling the *techno sapiens*—have conceived of nothing less than a wholesale redesign of the U.S. workforce, the quality of employment and the ways we live and work.

Of course, they will admit when pressed, there will be short-term disruption and dislocation. Schumpeterian "creative destruction" is their quasi-religious creed, and already the new economy has overturned numerous housing, labor, transportation and other laws and regulations in the San Francisco Bay Area, New York City, Los Angeles and virtually everywhere else its tornado has set down. As it spreads from the "left coast" across America, from blue to red country, it is becoming increasingly clear that it offers to most Americans a raw deal to replace the New Deal that created the middle class and made the United States not only the envy of the world but the most powerful nation in the post–World War II era. Much is at stake in the navigation of these turbulent forces and trends.

In this book, I will challenge conventional thinking that is celebrating this new economy by showing why the vision that the *techno sapiens* have planned for us is a dead end for U.S. workers, as well as for the national economy. This book will provide an exposé showing that the so-called sharing economy is just the tip of an iceberg, looming ever closer; the iceberg itself is what I call the "freelance society," with the sharing economy increasingly central to this brave new world.

THE CREEPING ONSET OF THE FREELANCE SOCIETY

In the aftermath of the Great Recession of 2008, both the right and the left agree at least on one thing: the American workforce has become more vulnerable. Wages are lower, workers have less security and the safety net is disappearing. Alarmingly, income inequality is now as bad as it was in 1928,[8] just before the Great Depression, with the top one-tenth of 1 percent of Americans—a mere 160,000 families[9]—now owning nearly a quarter of the nation's wealth, a share that has doubled over the last few decades. The Federal Reserve's Survey of Consumer Finances in 2013 found that the top 10 percent of families own 75.3 percent of the nation's wealth, while the share of wealth held by the bottom 50 percent of families has fallen to just 1.1 percent.[10] Incredibly, the share of wealth held by the bottom 90 percent is no higher today than during our grandparents' time.[11] It's as if the New Deal, the package of government programs enacted by the Franklin Roosevelt administration in the 1930s to alleviate vast inequality in the midst of the Great Depression, had never existed.

And future prospects do not look much brighter. Unlike previous economic recoveries, the latest "recovery" has made little difference for the vast majority of people. Even though corporations have seen a 30 percent rise in profits since the Great Recession in 2008, and in 2013 pocketed an all-time high of $2.1 trillion, they have quit investing in the United States.[12] The *Wall Street Journal* reports that U.S. multinational corporations, the marquee companies that provide employment for a fifth of all U.S. workers, have been cutting jobs at home while hiring overseas, slashing their American workforces by 2.9 million while increasing employment abroad by 2.4 million from 2000 to 2010.[13] In the two years from 2010 to 2012, more than three-fourths of the jobs created by 35 of the biggest U.S. companies were overseas.[14] That's a major shift from the 1990s, when they added 4.4 million jobs in the U.S., as well as 2.7 million abroad.

Besides axing U.S. workers, these "artful dodger" corporations have found numerous loopholes and foreign tax havens to reduce their tax liabilities.[15] On their $2.1 trillion in profit, they paid just $419 billion in corporate taxes, an effective tax rate of just under 20 percent[16]—one of the lowest rates since 1931, only a third of the rate that corporations paid in the 1960s and less than the rate paid by most middle-class people.[17] The share of federal tax revenues paid by U.S. corporations has declined dramatically from 33 percent in 1952 to a mere 11 percent today.[18] "American" corporations have forgotten where they came from.

Even as corporate profits have climbed and tax receipts plummeted, wages as a share of national income fell to their lowest point since after World War II.[19] Real median household income now is 8 percent lower than it was in 2007.[20] Many of the jobs that were lost during the Great Recession of 2008 were what used to be considered "good jobs"—they offered decent pay, health care, retirement, a safety net, with a measure of job security. Now, without new corporate investment in plants, factories and workplaces, the quality of jobs is atrophying. Nearly half of the new jobs created in the so-called recovery pay only a bit more than minimum wage. Six years into the recovery, the economy had nearly 2 million fewer jobs in mid- and higher-wage industries than before the recession and 1.85 million more jobs in lower-wage industries.[21] Indeed, a report from the U.S. Conference of Mayors found that the average annual wage for new jobs is 23 percent less than the average annual wage of jobs lost during the recession.[22]

If this book were a Broadway play, those numbers and figures would serve as the backdrop—the painted landscape and scenery—to what is going to unfold center stage. The actors on stage would be drawn from the ranks of the vast and growing army of freelancers, contractors, temp workers and part-timers that increasingly are assuming leading roles in the freelance society. A significant factor in the decline of the quality of jobs has been employers' increasing reliance on these "non-regular" employees. This practice has given rise to the term "1099 economy" since these employees don't file W-2 income tax forms like any regular, permanent employee. Instead, they file the 1099-MISC form for an IRS classification known as "independent contractor" ("MISC" is short for Miscellaneous Income).[23] The advantage for a business using 1099 workers over W-2 wage-earners is obvious: an employer usually can lower its labor costs dramatically, often by 30 percent or more, since it is not responsible for a 1099 worker's health benefits, retirement, unemployment or injured workers compensation, lunch breaks, overtime, disability, paid sick, holiday or vacation leave and more. In addition, contract workers are paid only for the specific number of hours they spend providing labor, which increasingly is being reduced to shorter and shorter "micro-gigs."

Outsourcing to these 1099 workers has become the preferred method for America's business leaders to cut costs and maximize profits. One new economy booster clarified employers' new strategy: "Companies today want a workforce they can switch on and off as needed"[24]—like one can turn off a faucet or a radio.

So Corporate America, once the anchor of the "good-jobs" economy that came out of the New Deal era, is increasingly relying on an army of 1099 workers. Indeed, a 2014 study commissioned by the Freelancers Union found that more than one in three workers—53 million Americans—are now freelancing. "Freelancing is the new normal," says Sara Horowitz, executive director of the Freelancers Union.[25] Other estimates predict that within 10 years nearly half of the 145 million employed Americans—around 65 million workers—will find themselves on similar grounds, turned into so-called independent workers: freelancers, temps, contractors, day laborers, microentrepreneurs, gig-preneurs, solo-preneurs, contingent labor, permalancers, perma-temps. It's practically a new taxonomy for a workforce that has become segmented into a dizzying assortment of labor categories.[26] Even many full-time, professional jobs and occupations are experiencing this precarious shift.

In a sense, employers and employees used to be married to each other, and there was a sense of commitment and a joined destiny. Now, employers just want a bunch of one-night stands with their employees, a promiscuousness that promises to be not only fleeting but destabilizing to the broader macroeconomy. Set to replace the crumbling New Deal society is a darker world in which wealthy and powerful economic elites—not only in San Francisco but across the nation—are collaborating with their political cronies to erect the policy edifice that allows them to mold their proprietary workforce into one composed of a disjointed collection of 1099 employees. Employers have called off the marriage with their employees, preferring a series of on-again, off-again affairs. This is a direct threat to the nation's future, as well as to what has been lionized around the world as the "American Dream."

Welcome to the Freelance Society.

Beyond the road paved with the many categories of gig-preneurs and other roadkill of the 1099 economy lies the outer reaches of town where the "greys" reside. An increasing number of "discouraged" workers are dropping out of the labor force entirely. Many of them work under the table and have semi-permanently drifted into the underground or "grey" economy, which is one of the fastest growing cohorts of the freelance society. Grey economy workers live at the edge of the American Dream, one foot in a growing dusk of unreality. The forces driving people to work under the table are formidable, and the numbers have reached such a magnitude that they are wreaking havoc with national unemployment statistics and tax revenue. A declining *unemployment* rate is occurring simultaneously with a declining *employment* rate, which in normal times is impossible, say labor market experts. Unemployment and employment rates are supposed to be inversely related: when one goes up, the other goes down, like a seesaw. Not so today. That's because the multitudes of workers drifting into the grey economy are not counted in official employment statistics, and the numbers have grown large enough that the unemployment rate appears to be declining.

But more and more experts are realizing that the unemployment figures don't reflect reality. Even Federal Reserve chief Janet Yellen, whose job is to sound as upbeat as possible about the economy, had to admit in February 2015 before the Senate Banking Committee that the overall picture is "less rosy" than the declining unemployment rate indicates. That's because of the surge of "marginally attached and discouraged workers," as well as "an unusually large number of individuals who are working part-time who would like full-time jobs," she testified. Indeed, the U.S. Bureau of Labor Statistics estimates that 12 million fewer Americans are participating in the workforce, compared to before the onset of the Great Recession. And that's probably an undercount.[27]

Beyond the road paved with the "greys" lies even more outer reaches of town, where the sharing economy meets its dark side. In the murky "breaking bad" outskirts of the freelance society, the faceless purchase of services and goods over these Web- and app-based brokerages makes exploitation all so anonymous. The "sharing" economy becomes a strange and seedy continuum that, past a certain point, slides into nefarious and illegal activities, led by websites such as Silk Road—an eBay for vice and illicit activities and goods. Until it was smashed by the feds (though multiple websites have sprung up to take its place), the story of Silk Road further revealed the tendency of the sharing economy to go off the rails if not regulated properly: across the transom of a faceless website you can hire a task rabbit to trim your hedges, or hire a Spinlister bike or an Uber car—or buy illegal drugs, hire a prostitute or rent a semiautomatic rifle. Or worse, one could even hire hit men in the "on-demand economy" that was available via Silk Road. Faceless technology meets working stiffs who badly need money.

Adding to the growing list of anxious concerns, even as millions of American workers are becoming little more than disposable workers, the faceless technology is about to get even more faceless. Job automation, robots, increasingly "smart" devices and artificial intelligence already have been replacing many humans in the workplace—but leading experts say this process is about to accelerate. An Oxford University study of over 700 occupations has estimated that "47 percent of existing U.S. jobs are at risk from computerization" over the next twenty years[28]—that's 60 million jobs threatened by "technological unemployment," as economist John Maynard Keynes once called it.[29] Technology boosters like Erik Brynjolfsson and Andrew McAfee, in their best seller *The Second Machine Age,* maintain that as human jobs are destroyed, new ones will be created by the technology, just as occurred in the past whenever new machines and technologies were introduced.[30] But Mark Nall, a program manager for NASA, observes, "Unlike previous disruptions, such as when farming machinery displaced farm workers but created factory jobs making the machines, robotics and AI are different. Due to their versatility and growing capabilities, not just a few economic sectors will be affected, but whole swaths will be."[31] With that level of penetration, nearly every neighborhood, town and city, nearly every industry and workplace, eventually will experience the impacts, as increasingly sophisticated software and computer algorithms take over tasks that previously only humans could do. *New York Times* technology reporter Farhad Manjoo writes that "artificial intelligence machines are getting so good, so quickly, that they're poised to replace humans" across a much wider range of industries than machines have ever done before.[32]

So the "invisible hand" now has a robotic arm, and it's not in a sharing mood. The benign view that new jobs will somehow magically appear in unforeseen ways seems shaky and blindly faith-based. The sheer volume of jobs turning over will be daunting, as the Oxford study indicates. If the crystal ball gazers are wrong, the cumulative "jobs gap" will be devastating. Disturbing signs of this reality are already appearing: in 2010 the *Washington Post* reported that the first decade of the 21st century resulted in zero net job creation in the United States.[33] It was a lost decade for American workers and job creation. Since World War II, no decade has had job growth of less than 20 percent, including the 1970s, a decade of stagflation and ongoing energy crises, yet one that still saw a jobs increase of 27 percent.

The sharing economy does nothing to reverse these disturbing trends. In fact it exacerbates the worst tendencies because, as we will see, it turns "opportunity for all" into a race to the bottom for U.S. workers.

CANARIES IN THE MINESHAFT

I've experienced the vagaries of this new working life myself. After working for many years in the Washington, D.C.–based think-tank world, the program that I directed lost most of its funding and was shut down shortly thereafter. All my employees, myself included, were laid off. I was promoting my latest book that had been published a few months before, so I surfed that wave for many more months. For a while, all seemed normal and natural, but without realizing it I had stepped off the safe and secure boat of having what is known as a "good job," with a steady paycheck, secure employment and a comprehensive safety net, into the cold, deep waters of being a freelance journalist.

Suddenly I was responsible for paying for my own health care, arranging for my own IRAs and saving for my own retirement. I also had to pay the employer's half of the Social Security payroll tax, as well as Medicare—nearly an extra 8 percent deducted from my income. The costs for my health-care premiums zoomed out of sight, since I was no longer part of a large health-care pool that could negotiate favorable rates. But that's not all. Suddenly not only was the pay per article or lecture not particularly lucrative, but I didn't get paid for those many hours in which I had to query the editors for the *next* article or lecture, or conduct research and interviews. It was as if I had become an assembly-line worker who was paid on a per-piece rate; the "extraneous" parts of my working day—rest and bathroom breaks, staff meetings or time at the water cooler, usually paid time in a "good" job—had been stripped to the bone. Not to mention I no longer had paid vacations, sick days, holidays, nor could I benefit from unemployment or injured workers compensation. Instead of receiving a paycheck from a single employer, now I had to track my many and varied sources of income, making sure that unscrupulous editors didn't stiff me.

In short, I had to juggle, juggle, juggle, while simultaneously running uphill—my life had been upended in ways that I had never anticipated. And I began discovering that I was not alone. Many other friends and colleagues—including Pulitzer Prize–winning journalists, professionals and intellectuals, as well as many friends in pink-, white- and blue-collar jobs—also had become 1099 workers. They found themselves increasingly faced with similar challenges, each in his or her own profession, industry or trade. In short, we had entered the world of what is known as "precarious" work, most of us wholly unprepared.

Not to worry. The sharing economy visionaries—who like Dr. Pangloss in Voltaire's *Candide* always see "the best of all possible worlds"—had a plan in place for us. We could "monetize" our assets—rent out our house, our car, our labor, our driveway and other personal possessions—using any number of brokerage websites and mobile apps like TaskRabbit, Airbnb, SnapGoods, the ridesharing companies Uber and Lyft and more.

For example, Frederic Larson enjoyed a successful thirty-year career as a staff photographer with the daily newspaper *San Francisco Chronicle,* during which time he won numerous awards, including being a Pulitzer Prize finalist. In his early sixties and with two children in college, he suddenly became a victim of the economic collapse when the *Chronicle*—which had been hemorrhaging readers, losing nearly half its readership in a few short years—downsized and laid him off in 2009. He picked up some part-time work teaching photography at an art school and as an occasional lecturer, but this income was inadequate and no longer came with any safety net attached. He had gone from having steady work and a "good job" to the precarious working life of a freelancer. His worth in the free marketplace had taken a major hit, his world turned upside down. He was not financially set enough to retire early, and too old to start over.

So what to do? He *monetized.*

He owned a nice home in verdant Marin County (just across the Golden Gate Bridge from San Francisco), so using Airbnb's online brokerage service he rented out his home for 12 days per month at $100 a night. A source of income, true, but the income was miniscule compared to his previous employment. And besides that, hosting via Airbnb had turned a professional photographer into an innkeeper—in his own home. Adding insult to injury, for those nights when he had guests, he had to endure the indignity of shuttering himself in one cordoned-off room of his house and showering at the local gym. Now for 12 nights per month—40 percent of his life—he stays in a rabbit hole inside his own home while complete strangers have the run of the place.

But hey, it's income, so what other "asset" could he "monetize"? Well, how about his spiffy Prius? Four nights a week he transformed his auto into a taxi via the ridesharing service Lyft (which advertises itself as "Your friend with a car," and is easily identified by its gonzo pink mustaches on the front of its commandeered autos). Now, many nights of the week this professional photographer is a taxi driver—in his own car. His former career on hold, if not over, he also started looking at websites like SnapGoods to rent out some of his expensive camera equipment.[34]

Welcome to the sharing economy. This award-winning ex-photographer and millions more like him increasingly will be forced to scramble to find any asset, anything of value, to bring in income. More and more Americans will be forced to "monetize"—to use one of the new economy gurus' favorite words—not just their homes and cars but their very lives to see what parts they can rent out. The pro-business magazine *Forbes,* a sharing economy booster, waxes exuberantly about the prospects: "A few dozen square feet in a driveway can now produce income via Parking Panda. A pooch-friendly room in your house is suddenly a pet penthouse via DogVacay. On SnapGoods, a drill lying fallow in a garage can become a $10-a-day income source from a homeowner who just needs to put up some quick drywall. On Liquid, an unused bicycle becomes a way for a traveler to cheaply get around while visiting town for $20 a day."[35]

Fred Larson was one of the luckier ones. He had enjoyed a successful career, and so had a few valuable assets to monetize. What about those who have only one thing to rent out—their labor?

For them, the sharing economy leaders have devised something else altogether—and it is practically medieval in its impact. Companies like Upwork, Elance, TaskRabbit and Freelancer.com have created "labor brokerage" websites and mobile apps that allow vulnerable workers to bid against each other for work, driving down wages to that of the lowest bid. These workers now have the "opportunity" to throw themselves onto the hard cold slab of the labor market—via an online auction—in an effort to attract buyers of their services. Since the Internet is global in its reach, some of these labor brokerage websites put U.S. workers into direct competition with workers in the Philippines, India, Thailand and other locations. The result is predictable: cheap, Third World labor undercuts developed-world wages.

One scrappy microentrepreneur who tried to make a go of it utilizing TaskRabbit and other websites found himself running like a hamster on a wheel, going faster and faster. "I tried out some online gig sites, and the wages offered look decent at first until you realize that you spend at least half your time commuting [from micro-gig to micro-gig] and/or dealing with flakes, neither of which is paid. Add in the 15 percent self-employment tax, the cut that the sites take [usually 10–20 percent of each gig], and for some jobs competition from third world countries, and it really starts to suck."[36]

Another "gig-preneur," a Fulbright Scholar who had just finished her MBA, set up a bunch of micro-gigs on Fiverr to keep herself afloat while she looked for a permanent job. Fiverr is an online job brokerage that connects buyers to sellers of numerous tasks and services, which pay as little as $5 per job (hence, its name). After fulfilling a total of 27 orders, she found that she had made a grand total of $176. "I've seen panhandlers get more money outside of the 7–11," she said.[37]

Lest one think these are just lethargic or disgruntled 1099 workers, Lukas Biewald, cofounder and CEO of CrowdFlower, yet another San Francisco–based "labor on demand" company, provided the company frame: "We end up paying people about $2 to $3 per hour," he said in an interview.

"It really depends on the level of quality that you need."[38] So workers hoping to make the minimum wage need not apply.

Thousands of sharing economy refugees have similar stories in the "turn 'em on, turn 'em off" economy. The prospects are so dim that even some of the customers have noticed. One TaskRabbit customer, a *San Francisco Chronicle* columnist who hired a rabbit (yes, that's what the TaskRabbit workers have been called) for a household chore, was surprised at how low the bids were from all the rabbits that responded to her advertisement. Apparently, she wrote, they "are frantic to work for less money per hour than I made as a teenager, babysitting."[39] She compared the process of her inbox filling up with lower and lower bids from desperate rabbits looking for work to watching contestants on *The Price Is Right.*

But this is no game show, and these are not game-show contestants. These are 1099 workers—task rabbits, contractors, temps, day laborers, gigpreneurs, practically a new form of indentured labor. What makes the situation frighteningly unfamiliar is that for the most part these are not teenagers or retired housewives looking for extra cash—these are *highly educated* rabbits who are under- or unemployed: 70 percent have at least a bachelor's degree, 20 percent a master's degree and 5 percent a PhD.[40] That's an education level you normally would expect to find among staff people and professionals working at a university or on Wall Street. Many of these dislocated workers formerly had "good" jobs and now have become tumbleweeds blowing in the labor market. And of course none of these "arms for hire" receive health care, retirement or other safety-net benefits—or labor union representation, either.

There has been a surge in companies like TaskRabbit, CrowdFlower, Elance-Upwork, Freelancer.com, Guru, Zaarly, Fiverr and many more using this lucrative model, based on vulnerable 1099 workers who auction themselves off for ever smaller jobs and smaller amounts of money. Many freelancers are barely better off than lowly paid *braceros,* offering their services in naked competition against each other. The customers can take the lowest bids, which are guaranteed to keep the bids low for the future. It is no coincidence that these online brokerage businesses gained major traction during the deepest economic downturn in nearly a century, with the condition of the most vulnerable workers now putting downward pressure on even the least vulnerable. The evangelists of the sharing economy present themselves as alternatives to the ongoing degradation of the U.S. workforce, but in reality their alternative is frighteningly grim. One Uber driver who I interviewed scoffed at the notion that this is the "sharing" economy. "More like the 'share the crumbs' economy," he said.

Defenders of the sharing economy say that Uber, Airbnb, TaskRabbit, Lyft and other venture-capitalized companies are providing low-price, widely available services that benefit consumers, as well as a source of income for dislocated workers in a difficult economy. There is a certain degree of truth to that claim, but the same can be said of Walmart—at what cost to the overall economy and society? It's as if the sharing economy leaders are saying, "You may not have health care from your job anymore, or unemployment, retirement or sick days, but hey, you are your own boss now. Congratulations." When we add up all the different types of employee classifications in which jobs have become increasingly precarious, and stir into that steaming cauldron the impacts of job automation and robots replacing millions of human jobs, we arrive at an alarmingly volatile landscape that is shifting beneath the feet of American workers.

This is the new economy: contracted, freelanced, "shared," automated, Uber-ized, "1099-ed." In essence, the purveyors of the new economy are forging an economic system in which those with money will be able to use faceless, anonymous interactions via brokerage websites and mobile apps to hire those without money by forcing an online bidding war to see who will charge the least for their labor, or to rent out their home, their car or other personal property. Websites like Uber, Elance-Upwork, TaskRabbit, Airbnb, Lyft and others are taking the Amazon/eBay model to the next logical step. They benefit from an aura that seems to combine convenience with a patina of revolution; convenience *as* revolution. The idea of a "sharing" economy sounds so groovy—environmentally correct, politically neutral, anticonsumerist and all of it wrapped in the warm, fuzzy vocabulary of "sharing." The vision has a utopian spin that is incredibly seductive in a world where both government and big business have let us down by leading us into the biggest economic crash since the Great Depression.

But if the "sharing" economy's app- and Web-based technologies have made it so incredibly easy to hire freelancers, temps, contractors and part-timers, why won't every employer eventually lay off all the regular, W-2 employees and hire 1099 workers? Any business owner would be foolish not to, as he or she watches his or her competitors shave their labor costs by 30 percent (by escaping having to pay for an employee's safety net and other benefits). As we will see, that is exactly the strategy that an increasing number of employers are adopting. Indeed, the so-called new economy looks an awful lot like the old, pre-New Deal economy—with "jobs" amounting to a series of low-paid micro-gigs and offering little empowerment for average workers, families or communities. We're losing decades of progress, apparently for no other reason than because these on-demand companies conduct their business over the Internet and apps and somehow that makes them "special." Technology has been granted a privileged and indulged place where the usual rules, laws and policies often are not applied.

If the practice becomes too widespread, you can say good-bye to the good jobs that have supported American families, good-bye to the middle class and adios to the way of life that made the United States the leading power of the world.

STARING INTO THE ABYSS OF THE ECONOMIC SINGULARITY

Whenever I attend tech conferences in Silicon Valley, or converse with any of the new-economy self-promoters, or overhear their conversations in San Francisco cafés (which increasingly are teeming with young, wide-eyed, free-market techno-fundamentalists), I'm always struck by how much they are committed to remaking the world in ways they sincerely believe will be overwhelmingly positive—and at the same time will put millions of dollars into their own pockets. They are blessed with, if nothing else, a blind sense of their own certainty and entitlement. The new economy *techno sapiens* feel righteously justified by their credo of Ayn Rand utopian libertarianism, even as the new economy rips open a widening "jobs gap"—a discrepancy between the number and quality of jobs needed for full employment, and the number and quality of "jobs for humans" being produced by the economy.

But if the fate of employment continues to decline, and if the aggregate wages and salaries no longer provide consumers with adequate income to buy up all the products and services that U.S. companies produce, the economy could reach a dangerous disequilibrium—unceasing downward economic pressure that will make the Great Recession of 2008 a recurring event. At some point we could well face the prospect of having too few viable consumers with enough purchasing power to continue driving economic growth in our mass-market economy. Already the top 5 percent of households are responsible for 30 percent of consumer spending, up from 23 percent in 1992.[41] And the latest data shows that this shift is accelerating. With inequality so great and growing, at some point not enough people will have sufficient cash in their wallets and ATM accounts to buy. As these disturbing trends become entrenched, they will result in additional severe consequences for the broader macroeconomy.

Tech geeks and wide-eyed futurists like to fantasize about what they call the "Technological Singularity"—a future period predicted to occur around 2045 when the current "artificial-intelligence explosion" will result in machines achieving true intelligence, and even surpassing their human inventors as they design ever-smarter versions of themselves, causing a runaway effect that radically alters civilization in an event called the "singularity." In *Raw Deal,* I will write about another horizon just as disturbing, what I call the "Economic Singularity"—the tipping point at which our economy implodes from too little consumer demand because the wealth has been captured by a small number of powerful economic players who extract the best of our nation for their own private use. Everyone else will be left to scramble for the scraps via the sharing economy. Indeed, these two singularities may end up being two facets of the same future, a kind of techno-feudalism that threatens nearly everything good and true about the American Dream and that made America special in the world.

As economist Thomas Piketty demonstrated in his book *Capital in the Twenty-First Century,* this trend of "elite magnification" is near-certain to continue and even accelerate without sensible policy intervention. A strong American middle class has been part of the allure of the U.S. model of development and a core part of America's superpower status. But the onset of the freelance society is slowly severing the connective tissue that made the middle-class society such an inspiration to the world.

As these forces gain momentum, increasingly the competitive pressures of the global economy and the internal logic of the U.S.-style "Wall Street capitalism" are pushing American businesses to cannibalize their own workforces.[42] For decades the goal of the U.S. Chamber of Commerce and business leaders has been to break the back of labor unions, and they have greatly succeeded; now their goal seems to be to break the workforce itself. But that effort ultimately will backfire, resulting in the specter of an Economic Singularity.

Those trends are already apparent, and the pressures are growing. It's like some malevolent force is unraveling over two centuries of progress toward a more fair and egalitarian society and turning back the clock to a previous era when the monarchs and aristocrats of old lorded over the peasants and serfs. Indeed, economist Juliet Schor has called the sharing economy and freelance society the "post-industrial peasant model."[43] Some have compared the current techno-feudalism trajectory to turning back the clock's hands to the Gilded Age of the late 19th century. During that era, the level of inequality was shocking, workers had few rights, safety net or job security, and robber barons like railroad tycoon Jay Gould could boast, "I can hire one-half of the working class to kill the other half." If Gould were alive today, no doubt he would use some of the dozens of online, on-demand sharing economy services to do it.

This is the type of pre–New Deal world that Americans thought we had left behind in the rearview mirror. Suddenly, like the disembodied evil Lord Voldemort of *Harry Potter* fame who refuses to die—it's back.

But as the new economy evangelists try to take everyone backward, it's time that we ask ourselves: What do we want from work, and in what kind of society do we want to live? Is the future we are heading toward, spurred on by the sharing economy, automation/robotization and other technological shocks, destined to be one of declining *quantity* as well as *quality* of jobs? Might the current trajectory of the new economy toward a freelance society manned by millions of 1099 workers fundamentally disrupt the very foundation of the middle-class society that so many—my parents and grandparents, your parents and grandparents and now ourselves—have benefited from? The answers to these fundamental questions suddenly are up for grabs, as are many of the assumptions and values we have lived by since the dawn of the New Deal.

Yet there is nothing ordained or inevitable about the onset of the freelance society or the "share-the-crumbs" economy. Indeed, as we will see, the sharing economy holds potential if steered in the right direction. The current trajectory is the consequence of certain laws, regulations, institutions and practices, all of which are human-created, any of which can be modified and changed. In chapter 10, I propose a new social contract and safety net for the new economy, and in chapter 11, I propose other reforms that will move our political economy forward. *Raw Deal* will help us understand what laws and regulations are essential to ensure that the ongoing transformation will launch us in the right direction of History's Arrow.

Indeed, we can let history be our guide. In the mid-19th century, when the new industrial working class began to organize against dreadful conditions, the threat of revolution that Karl Marx and others predicted was mitigated by politicians who wisely enlarged political and economic rights, began regulating corporations and fashioned the beginnings of a safety net and social insurance. "In effect, they reinvented capitalism to make it more inclusive and to give workers a stake in the system," says Princeton economist Dani Rodrik.[44]

Today's challenging moment calls for a similar reinvention of the political economy—guided by the "visible hand" of government and representative democracy. The potential benefits of new digital technologies, Web- and app-based platforms, smart machines, robotics, biotechnology and other areas are apparent to all. But who will benefit from their encroaching preeminence in our nation's economy? That is the outstanding question of our age. The central dilemma of this brave new world can be illustrated by a simple thought experiment: What if smart machines and robots could perform every single job there is to do, and sharing economy websites could deliver all the services and goods, so that no human had to work at a job anymore? Who would reap the benefit of this unimaginably enormous productivity increase? Would it be a handful of "Masters of the Universe," such as the chief entrepreneurs and investors? Or would the gains be broadly distributed to the general public?

Nobody's crystal ball can tell us the answer, but what we do know is this: over the last several decades, the economy has been restructured so that the wealth gains from higher productivity and new technology have flowed into the pockets of a small minority of one-percenters. We also know that wages have stagnated despite sizable increases in corporate profits. So our nation's recent economic history shows all too vividly that the general public is in no way guaranteed to benefit from technological innovations and productivity gains. Quite the contrary.

Indeed, the answer to this question is a political one. It depends greatly on what policies and politics are pursued during this interregnum, before our society begins edging closer to this very uncertain future. Like a giant comet from another galaxy, this future is arriving more rapidly than the public or the politicians realize. We are heading toward a head-on collision with it.

U.S. Supreme Court Justice Louis Brandeis once said, "We may have democracy, or we may have wealth concentrated in the hands of the few, but we cannot have both."[45] It seems we are destined to live through an experiment to test if he was right. The United States is standing at a fork in the road, staring into the distance of an unfamiliar landscape. And I've got a front row seat to it all, right here in the gold rush city of San Francisco.

ONE

BACK TO THE FUTURE IN THE 1099 ECONOMY

IT'S A WARMISH YET WET APRIL FOOLS' DAY 2014 IN SAN FRANCISCO. I'M standing at the corner of 24th and Valencia, in the longtime Latino but increasingly gentrified Mission District, watching an unusual cast of acrobats. There are half a dozen of them, dressed in bright yellow and blue-striped silken leotards, with big goggle eyes like frogs, moving gracefully across the damp pavement of the early morning street. Something about their elongated movements reminds me of Picasso's *Family of Saltimbanques.*

But these "saltimbanques" are not here to juggle. Instead, along with a crowd of another 25 people, they are blocking traffic. Specifically, they are blocking what is known as a "Google bus," which is a privately chartered, cushy luxury liner hired by Google to transport its San Francisco–residing employees the 40 miles south to the Googleplex campus in Mountain View, at the heart of Silicon Valley. Facebook, Apple, Genentech and other Silicon Valley companies also charter their own private shuttles for their employees. Much has been written about these "pirate shuttles"—the fact that they sit like sultans at hundreds of city bus stops waiting for their 14,000 daily passengers, arrogantly blocking city buses and everyday San Franciscans trying to get to work;[1] the fact that a University of California, Berkeley study found that rents around the tech shuttle stops have increased by 20 percent, as has displacement of long-term tenants, forced out by greedy landlords who have jacked up rents to a level affordable only to the highly paid tech workers;[2] the fact that, for this privilege of everyday disruption, Google, Facebook and others pay the city of San Francisco the princely sum of one dollar—yes, that's $1—per bus stop per day (private autos that block public bus stops incur a

$271 fine, but the shuttles receive mostly a free pass from tech-enamored city officials).[3]

The sheer arrogance of avarice exhibited by the Lords of Silicon Valley has inspired dozens of protests, as well as several (unsuccessful) legislative attempts to regulate and charge higher fees for the hogging of city bus stops. (Finally, after much outcry, Google agreed to donate $6.8 million to the cash-strapped local bus and transit agency.[4]) Rebecca Solnit, a San Francisco–based writer, struck a chord when she called the buses "the spaceships on which our alien overlords have landed to rule us."[5]

The Google buses and protests attracted beaucoup media attention, both locally and across the country, as a sign of something gone badly wrong in the city of St. Francis. (Ironically St. Francis, one of the most venerated of Catholic religious figures and the namesake of current Pope Francis I, took an oath of poverty and made his ministry out of serving the poor.) But on the morning of the acrobat protest at the corner of 24th and Valencia, there was one person caught in the middle that no one seemed to care much about: the driver of the Google bus. He was an African American male, dressed more like the crowd of protesters than the young tech scions he was transporting. The protesters, caught up in their passion, got in his face and generally gave him a rough time, practically accusing him of being a Judas. He reacted with anger, and I suspect a fair amount of fear, toward the mostly white protesters.

But not necessarily out of any great allegiance to his job or employer. It turns out that the drivers of these pirate shuttles are themselves victims of the Silicon Valley two-tier way of doing business, and his own job security is fragile. Few of the drivers work for the tech giants themselves, but instead are employed by outside contractors. The disparities in pay, benefits and working conditions between the regular tech company employees and the service workers who pamper them, including not only the shuttle drivers but also security guards, janitors and landscapers, are substantial. The drivers and other service workers are part of the invisible labor force that literally makes Silicon Valley run, yet as we will see, receive less than livable wages and work under conditions that are semi-feudal.[6]

Meet Jimmy Maerina, a bus driver who shuttles Facebook employees the 37 miles from San Francisco, where they live, to the company's Menlo Park, California, headquarters.[7] Jimmy's passengers work exclusively for Facebook, but Jimmy and the other 90 or so Facebook bus drivers actually work for an independent contractor, called Loop Transportation. Besides not being paid high enough wages by Loop to support their families and afford to live decently in the high-priced Bay Area, Jimmy and his fellow drivers also work a punishing schedule. They start their day at 5:30 a.m., arriving at the main bus depot near Facebook's campus, and finish their hellishly long day at 8:45

p.m. That's over a 15-hour day, which clearly stretches the labor laws, so Loop Transportation (aptly named) found a loophole—it forces the drivers to take five to six *unpaid* hours off in the middle of the day. Not only that, Jimmy and the other drivers are prohibited from finding other employment during the period between their split shifts. And unfortunately, many of them live too far away from the lot to commute all the way home and return for their second work shift, so instead they must hang around and wait.

Loop Transportation responds to charges of unfair labor practices by saying that it generously provides a rest trailer—which is true. But it only has four beds and one bathroom for dozens of drivers, plus it lacks heat or air conditioning. Consequently most of the drivers are forced to rest or sleep in their cars between shifts. Silicon Valley is a sunny area so there's not much shade, necessitating that the drivers hang blankets in their car windows to keep the sun out and run the air conditioning or the heat, depending on the season. "You are basically being held hostage in that parking lot," says Jimmy. "And you are not being paid."[8]

Given these Dickensian-length hours, Jimmy complains that he barely sees his family. "When I leave the house at 5:30 each morning for my morning route, my kids are asleep. And by the time I make it home around 9, they are getting ready to turn in for the night. I miss family dinners, helping with homework—all the little things that a family is supposed to do together."[9]

Driven by his increasing sense of unfairness and fury, Jimmy launched a unionizing drive among his fellow workers. That led to intimidation of drivers by Loop and threats to fire Jimmy, while Facebook conveniently looked the other way. Tearing a page from a tried and true anti-union playbook, Loop sent representatives to Facebook's campus to "inform" the drivers that a union actually would hurt their own self-interest. When Jimmy took his and his fellow drivers' grievances to the public in a story published by *USA Today,* Facebook was embarrassed.[10] Teamsters representative Rome Aloise wrote a public letter to Facebook CEO Mark Zuckerberg, saying, "It is reminiscent of a time when noblemen were driven around in their coaches by their servants. Frankly, little has changed; except the noblemen are your employees, and the servants are the bus drivers who carry them back and forth each day."[11]

Finally the tech giant—which has a market capitalization of $206 billion—told Loop to give the drivers a raise: a whopping $0.75 per hour. If that generosity was supposed to persuade the drivers that they did not need a union, it didn't work. On November 19, 2014, the 87 drivers voted in favor of representation by the Teamsters.[12]

This is just one tale out of many that reveals how two-tiered Silicon Valley treats the invisible workforce that toils in the shadows of its mansions, Maseratis and Moët & Chandon.

In 2005, when the first tech buses were making runs up Van Ness Avenue and Valencia Street in San Francisco, approximately 23,300 households in the city reported annual income above $200,000, according to the U.S. Census' American Community Survey.[13] By 2012, the number of "200k households" in San Francisco had nearly doubled, to 46,200. The gap between Silicon Valley's high and low earners has widened dramatically, to the point where a region that lays claim to some of the world's wealthiest companies has hit a 10-year high in food stamp participation and a 20 percent increase in homelessness, according to Joint Venture Silicon Valley, a business-friendly consultancy that publishes an annual report card on the region.[14] Moreover, even as average per-capita incomes have zoomed due to escalating salaries for the high-tech workers, the *median* household incomes have fallen several years in a row. That kind of statistical anomaly indicates one thing—a huge overall rise in inequality. The Bay Area has become a region dominated by HNWIs and UHNWIs—high net worth individuals and ultra-high net worth individuals—not only in the sheer numbers of wealthier households but also in the political and free-market gunpower they are amassing to shape the region's future.

Desperate times call for desperate measures, and so one driver filed a class-action lawsuit against Google's shuttle contractor, WeDriveU, claiming it too had failed to compensate drivers for downtime between split shifts, provide legally required rest breaks, and other alleged violations.[15] But the billionaire titans that control America's best-name companies are happy to let the private contractors do the exploiting, whether in China where contractors like Foxconn build the iPhone, iPad, Xbox, Kindle and other tech gadgets (and where 150 Foxconn employees threatened to commit mass suicide in protest over the horrible working conditions) or right in their own backyards.[16]

MANUFACTURING PERMA-TEMPS AND INDIES

But Silicon Valley is not the only place that resorts to such tactics in the United States. In fact, as the freelance society takes deeper root, outsourcing to "1099 contractors" increasingly has become the way businesses cut costs in their never-ending pursuit of greater profits. Manufacturing companies in particular have increasingly relied on private contractors to hire temps, freelancers and other categories of 1099 employees, switching them on and off as needed.

Meet Chris Young, an assembly-line worker at Nissan's manufacturing plant in Smyrna, Tennessee. Chris works alongside dozens of other employees, everybody doing more or less the same job. But Chris doesn't get to wear the coveted Nissan jersey that many of his fellow workers wear—because he doesn't work for Nissan.[17]

Instead, he is what is known as a "perma-temp." He works for Yates Services, a private contractor who now provides a majority of Nissan's workers. Chris says, "I build the same Infiniti SUV" as the Nissan workers, but he and other Yates employees receive half the salary (Yates pays between $10 and $18 an hour), less job security and way fewer safety-net benefits. Like Silicon Valley, auto manufacturers increasingly rely on a two-tiered system, and being in the lower tier means Chris can't say no to overtime, can't take a sick day and doesn't receive long-term disability, nor does he enjoy the privilege of leasing a company vehicle. With wages so low, he can't afford a new car (his own car is a 2001 Cavalier with 200,000 miles on it), get a mortgage or save for retirement, and he can barely make ends meet for his family of four children.

Sometimes he has to work seven days a week, with 10-hour shifts on Saturdays and Sundays—despite experiencing severe wrist pain from the repetitive nature of the work (exacerbated by a motorcycle accident that occurred long ago). "No one's really worried about the fact that you're so exhausted from working seven days a week, you're dependent on some drug to stay awake, or dependent on some drug to go asleep, or for pain," he says. "Everybody I work with has some type of pain, whether it's hands, fingers, back, feet, something. . . . If you don't want to do it, you clean out your locker and go somewhere else."

The *Washington Post* reports that Nissan, one of several foreign automakers to establish operations in Tennessee, has blazed a path in the corporate business world. Companies from Dell to Amazon have outsourced significant parts of their operations, including call centers and warehouses, to hundreds of staffing agencies that have set up shop in the "right-to-work" region. Tennessee has one of the lowest levels of unionized workers in the nation, only 6 percent (compared to a national average of 11 percent). According to the Bureau of Labor Statistics, Tennessee saw a dramatic 56 percent increase in temporary workers, from 51,867 temps in 2009 to 80,990 in 2012, even as median wages stayed flat. That temp worker explosion was responsible for almost all of Tennessee's job growth since the Great Recession, resulting in temp jobs comprising over 3 percent of all jobs in the state, one of the highest percentages in the nation.

After Nissan's brush with bankruptcy in 2001, it started introducing temps into front-office positions at its plants, and by 2008 had reduced its permanent workforce by about a third. Following the Great Recession, as consumer demand returned for automobiles, Nissan began to fill production jobs with employees hired by outside private contractors. The company refuses to say how many of its 7,000-person workforce have been placed by staffing agencies, but many current and former employees say it's easily a majority, according to the *Post.*

Nationwide, the U.S. Department of Labor reports that the nation has more temp workers than ever before, approximately 2.8 million, representing 2 percent of total jobs.[18] And factoring in the high rate of worker turnover among temps, the American Staffing Association (the temp industry's trade group) reports that more than 12 million people worked at a temp agency for a period of time in 2013. It's now called "domestic outsourcing"—instead of outsourcing jobs overseas we are outsourcing them domestically, from permanent full- and part-time positions to temporary 1099 employees. Overall, the temp sector has provided nearly a fifth of the total job growth since the recession ended, according to federal data. But the American Staffing Association says the number is even greater. With the economy continuing to drag along unevenly, temp work has galloped back 10 times faster than private-sector employment—a pace "exceeding even the dramatic run-up of the early 1990s."[19]

And the industry is no longer just supplying office assistants—the vast majority of that growth has come in blue-collar positions in warehouses and factories, with more than 1 in 20 blue-collar workers in 2012 being a temp. Auto and other manufacturing jobs used to be part of the backbone of the American economy, offering high wages, job security and a ticket to the American Dream. The middle class was built upon such jobs, as was the comfortable consumer society that became the envy of the world. Now an increasing number of autoworkers toil away as temps in downwardly mobile McJobs that can barely provide a living wage.

While temp work has become one of the fastest-growing sectors of the economy, an investigation by ProPublica has documented an array of problems. Increasingly the temps aren't very temporary. Some workers originally hired as "temps" have been employed at the same company for as long as 11 years, never getting moved into a full-time position—hence the new term "perma-temp," an oxymoron if ever there was one.[20] And the pay is low; the median wages of temps are a whopping 22 percent below that of all workers, regardless of industry.[21] Making matters worse, companies assign temps to the most dangerous jobs; nationwide, temps are far more likely to find jobs in dangerous blue-collar occupations like manufacturing and warehousing. In several states, temps suffer triple the number of amputations on the job, compared to regular workers.[22] And even some of the nation's largest and most successful companies have used the services of immigrant labor brokers and fly-by-night temp agencies that have defrauded workers of their wages.[23]

Temps, perma-temps, perma-lancers—these are a few of the new categories of workers that are becoming enduring fixtures in the labor force. Treated like just another resource to be fed into the industrial machine, they join another exploited category known as "independent contractors," or "indies."

Take the case of Fritz Elienberg, who worked for five years as a full-time employee installing cable and Internet service for RCN Corporation in Boston. According to the *New York Times*, on six mornings a week, shortly after 6:30 a.m., he and a dozen other employees arrived at the RCN office where they received their schedule for the day's installations. On a frequent basis, Elienberg worked long days—10 to 14 hours—yet he never received the overtime rate of time-and-a-half. Then when a ladder fell on his foot and seriously injured it, workers' compensation would not cover his medical bills. Why? Because it turns out he was hired as an independent contractor, meaning RCN did not consider him to be one of its regular employees. For all intents and purposes, according to RCN, Elienberg was his own boss, his own CEO, in business for himself—and not employed by RCN.[24]

Oftentimes these "independent" contractors are treated like regular employees, even provided desks and phone lines. When Elienberg worked a separate job for Comcast as an independent contractor, he says that he drove a van and wore a shirt inscribed with "Comcast"; he installed the cable providers' equipment, and customers paid Comcast for his work.[25] But he and his fellow "indies" had a lower status than regular employees, which many contractors are reluctant to challenge, given the tough job market. When Elienberg injured his foot and discovered that, as a contractor, he wasn't covered by workers' compensation, that was the final straw. He sued RCN for overtime pay and the value of lost benefits.

"I didn't feel like an independent contractor," Mr. Elienberg said of his job working at RCN. "I didn't feel like my own boss. I always believed I was an employee. It's a win-win situation for them and a lose-lose for us. We didn't get overtime, sick days, vacations, health insurance or pensions."[26] Nor did he get to keep his job: Elienberg was fired by RCN after he filed his lawsuit, adding retaliation to his list of grievances.

The deployment of independent contractors began in a handful of occupations, such as janitors and security guards, but now it has become pervasive. Evidence is rampant that employers are taking advantage of both precariously employed workers and the tax system by misclassifying regular employees as independent contractors. David Weil, author of *The Fissured Workplace: Why Work Became So Bad for So Many and What Can Be Done to Improve It* and who was appointed by President Barack Obama to run the Department of Labor's Wage and Hour Division, told a *Wall Street Journal* reporter, "There are violations of our standard labor laws that are almost jaw-dropping," particularly in the area of misclassification of workers. "There are companies out there that aren't complying because they don't want to or don't feel they need to."[27] Companies that can get away with misclassifying employees as independent contractors avoid paying Social Security, Medicare and unemployment and injured worker compensation for those workers; they also circumvent paying overtime, holidays, vacation or sick pay.

"It's a very significant problem," says Ohio's former attorney general, Richard Cordray. "Misclassifying can mean a 20 or 30 percent cost difference per worker."[28]

Paying 20 to 30 percent less for a worker's salary and benefits adds up to a lot more profit for the company. One survey in California of 300,000 contractors found that two out of three responded that they had no direct employees.[29] A federal study concluded that employers illegally "disguised" 3.4 million regular workers as contractors, while the U.S. Department of Labor estimates that up to 30 percent of companies misclassify employees.[30] Not only do these businesses reduce their labor-related costs by 30 percent, but they also find it to be a useful tactic for union-busting—the presence of indies working alongside regular employees doing the same jobs not only puts downward pressure on wages and benefits but also sends a warning to the regulars—"This too could be you, if you aren't careful."

Examples abound of companies laying off all or most of their workers, and then rehiring the same workers—but as independent contractors, a clear abuse of this legal loophole. Merck, one of the world's largest pharmaceutical companies, was a pioneer of this underhanded strategy. When it came under pressure to cut costs, it sold its Philadelphia factory to a company that fired all 400 employees and then rehired them as independent contractors. Merck then contracted with the company to carry on making antibiotics for them, using the exact same employees.[31] An Arizona public-relations firm, LP&G, fired 88 percent of its staff, and then rehired them as freelancers working out of their homes, with no benefits.[32] Even *Out* magazine, the most-read gay monthly in the U.S., laid off its entire editorial staff and then rehired most of them as freelancers, but without benefits and with salary cuts.

Once enough companies are engaged in these practices, it unleashes a race to the bottom with systemic consequences. As more businesses cut costs by using 1099 freelancers, temps and contractors, every other business in that industry feels a market squeeze to do the same or face declining market share as well as profits. Just like the steroid scandals in sports, these practices become the steroids of the economy—once one competitor is doing it and gains a competitive edge, the other competitors don't dare not do it.

Misclassification has another severe impact: the IRS estimates that in one year alone, the practice deprived the government of $1.6 billion in tax revenue (since companies are not responsible for withholding income taxes from 1099 workers' paychecks, and many of those indies never remit taxes to the IRS).[33] Another study by the National Employment Law Project found that "state and federal governments lose billions in revenues annually as a result" of worker misclassification.[34] When he was attorney general, California's governor Jerry Brown sued two companies for misclassifying 300 janitors as contractors rather than regular employees and not paying minimum wage and overtime. The companies' practices resulted in cheating the state out of payroll taxes, and Brown won a $13 million judgment against the companies. Like Comcast workers, room cleaners and desk clerks at many leading hotel chains like Hilton and Marriot actually work for contractor companies, not for the hotels. Receptionists and guards in government buildings in many cases are not government employees, but the low-wage hires of a private security contractor. Technical support call centers for most major U.S. corporations are answered by the familiar lilting English of Indian workers in Bangalore or somewhere-else India, none of whom work directly for the corporation. When a factory fire at Rana Plaza in Bangladesh killed more than 1,100 garment workers, companies like Benetton and Tommy Hilfiger blamed the unsafe conditions on their subcontractors. Apple, which employs some 63,000 workers directly, employs over 10 times more—more than 750,000—via a variety of private contract relationships. That's what allowed Apple—one of the world's most hands-on companies when it comes to technical quality—to deflect blame when cruel and exploitative working conditions were revealed at the Foxconn plant in China that makes iPhones and iPads. Apple just blamed the contractor.[35]

A "see-no-evil, hear-no-evil-until-a-journalist-catches-us" attitude has become pervasive in the land of Corporate America and its wicked twin, the shadowy cabal of private company contractors. The increasing uncertainty over who is responsible for adherence to labor standards is muddying the waters and complicating enforcement. About one in three workers are hired today, not by the corporation identified with its brand-name products, but by someone else—a subcontracting business, a franchise, a third-party outsourcer, a temp agency. This has led to an increasing number of lawsuits, such as the one filed on behalf of FedEx workers that drive the company's trucks and wear its uniforms but were not considered company employees.[36] In August 2014 a ruling by a federal appeals court found that 2,300 FedEx delivery drivers had been misclassified as independent contractors, since FedEx exercised broad control over their schedules and methods, including forcing them to "wear FedEx uniforms, drive FedEx-approved vehicles, and groom themselves according to FedEx's appearance standards," said Judge William Fletcher. The three-judge panel ultimately ruled that since the contractors were being treated like employees, they were entitled to employee benefits such as overtime pay and reimbursement of expenses.[37]

But with the legal route a slow, tortuous remedy, the connection between employer and employee has become "fissured" as large corporations try to have it both ways. Employment is becoming fragmented into increasingly complex levels of contractors, subcontractors and sub-subcontractors, making it harder and harder to track.[38] Many corporations in Silicon Valley are particularly enamored with fissuring, since they like to think of themselves as "virtual" and so resist direct hiring of employees. Billion-dollar startups have a relatively small number of salaried employees who are augmented with huge numbers of temps, contractors, freelancers and other types of 1099 workers, says Robert Kuttner, author and coeditor of the *American Prospect*.[39]

Yet as Katherine Stone points out in her book *From Widgets to Digits,* the entire structure of worker protections and benefits that began with the New Deal—virtually all of the rights legislated since the 1930s—are predicated on the assumption that the employee is on the payroll of the company that makes the product.[40] With that relationship melting away like the polar ice caps, contractors and contingency workers have ended up with fewer rights. Compared to regular workers, they are more likely to experience wage theft, subminimum wages, overtime violations and working conditions that violate health and safety laws. And they have less practical recourse to legal remedies. "The modern employment relationship," Weil writes in *The Fissured Workplace,* "bears little resemblance to that assumed in our core workplace regulations."[41]

Proponents and apologists for this deteriorating state of the U.S. workforce claim that in the new economy of this globalized age, we have to accept this kind of collateral damage as the price for remaining internationally competitive and an economic leader. Indeed, at the TechCrunch Disrupt conference in San Francisco in September 2014, the term "1099 economy" was praised as a core component of the "innovative labor practices" of businesses today, especially Silicon Valley startups.[42] A recent study by venture-capital firm SherpaVentures, which has invested in many Silicon Valley startups, including from the sharing economy, predicts that the "freelance marketplace" labor models used by these companies will transform industries like law, health care and investment banking, as those industries become flooded with 1099 employees. Consequently fewer people will have traditional full-time or part-time jobs—a good thing, according to Sherpa's report, since "perpetual, hourly employment is often deeply inefficient for all parties involved."[43]

While hundreds of U.S. companies are hiring more and more of these 1099 employees, many other countries have responded to similar abuses by adopting laws to protect the growing number of temps, perma-temps, freelancers and indies in their workforces. These include extending safety-net benefits to 1099 employees, limiting the duration of temporary assignments, guaranteeing equal pay for equal work, extending a degree of legal parity between 1099 workers and their regularly employed counterparts and forbidding companies from hiring temps for dangerous tasks. Almost half of the 43 countries that the Organization for Economic Cooperation and Development (OECD) collects data on restrict the duration of temp assignments. In Germany, temps and indies are guaranteed the same wages and working conditions as employees hired directly by the company. In South Korea, any temp job has a two-year limit, and then the company must hire that worker as a regular employee or end the contract. In Brazil, temp jobs and independent contracts are limited to three months, unless an extension is received from the ministry of labor. In Italy and Japan there is a three-year limit, and in the Czech Republic, the limit for temp jobs is 12 months.[44]

But in the United States, temp workers often hold such jobs for years. The U.S. has some of the weakest protections and benefit floors for temp, freelancing and indie workers in the developed world, according to data compiled by the OECD.[45]

There is no question that the increasing drift of the U.S. economy away from its New Deal moorings is not simply the result of U.S. companies responding to global economic pressures, since companies in Europe, Japan and elsewhere are subject to the same pressures. Instead, this troubling direction is the result of specific homegrown laws, policies and regulations passed in the United States, which many other nations are choosing not to endorse.

GOOD-BYE 9-TO-5, HELLO 9-TO-GRAVE

Jobs in the manufacturing, transportation and telecom sectors used to be good, stable jobs that allowed hardworking Americans like Fritz Elienberg, Chris Young, Jimmy Maerina and their families to enjoy a decent middle-class existence. If even workers in these occupations are struggling in today's new economy, imagine how it must be for low-wage workers toiling away in the fast-food industry, hotel sector and other service jobs. It's becoming increasingly difficult to put on a Ronald McDonald smile as these workers come to grips with their dwindling chances of making it on the yellow brick road of the American Dream.

Meet Maria Fernandes, a 32-year-old single woman and fast-food worker. She's a bubbly personality who worries about her weight, and she adores Michael Jackson and his music. Kindhearted, she feeds bits of bagels and bread to the birds in her neighborhood, and she regularly pays for coffee and doughnuts for a homeless man, even when she falls behind on her own bills. Born in Massachusetts to Portuguese-born immigrants, Maria does not have a college education and hopes to become a beautician and hair stylist if she can ever raise enough money for cosmetology school.[46]

But Maria will never realize her dream of cosmetology school because—well—she's dead. Killed, in the opinion of many, by the miserable working conditions of her fast-food worker life.

Maria couldn't make it financially on one fast-food job, since she earned little more than New Jersey's minimum wage of $8.25 an hour. So she worked three jobs, all at different Dunkin' Donuts stores in northern New Jersey. She worked afternoons in Newark, overnights in Linden (about a 30-minute drive away) and weekends in Harrison, shuttling from one place to another. Despite her grueling schedule, Maria's managers described her as a "model" employee. But she hardly slept at home—to juggle her schedule she often had to sleep in her car at a rest stop or parking lot—two hours here, three hours there.

As explained in a lengthy *New York Times* article, while she slept she often kept the engine running, to keep the interior cool with air conditioning during the summer and warmed by the car's heater during cooler months. Maria slept in her car so often that she started keeping a container full of gasoline in the back, because she didn't want to run the risk of waking up to an empty tank and not being able to get to her next shift. Her boyfriend warned her that this wasn't safe. But Maria said she was afraid to miss even a single shift. With such low wages, she struggled to pay rent on her $550-per-month apartment, missing her payment on a couple of occasions—for an apartment she rarely slept in—and so had turned her auto into her "home on wheels."

After working an overnight shift in Linden, Maria pulled over for a nap in the early morning hours of August 25, 2014, in the parking lot of a Wawa convenience store in Elizabeth, New Jersey, about halfway back to Newark where her afternoon shift awaited. The store's surveillance camera videotaped her arrival in their parking lot behind the store at 6:27 a.m. She reclined in the driver's seat and closed her eyes. Not long after, a Wawa employee noticed Maria in her car as he arrived for work. He thought she was sleeping and went inside. Hours later, when he finished his shift around 3:30 p.m., the Wawa employee noticed that Maria was still lying there, but now she was foaming at the mouth. He told his manager who called 911. Emergency responders found the gas can overturned in the back, and the car filled with heavy fumes. A police investigation found that Maria had been asphyxiated by a deadly dose of carbon monoxide fumes from the overturned gasoline container. When Maria was pronounced dead at 5:56 p.m., she was still in her Dunkin' Donuts uniform.

Maria Fernandes's death ignited a national outpouring of emotion, as the country examined its soul over the type of society we seem to be creating. In a bout of soul-searching reminiscent of that in China following an incident where a toddler was left to die after a hit-and-run accident,[47] many people asked how the United States, where the middle class was born, could reach such a point of decline that any American would have to work three hectic jobs to scrape by. Maria was seen as a symbol of the hardships facing our nation's corps of low-wage workers, and for some the general decline in the quality of jobs over the last several decades.

But others thought there were a lot of unanswered questions: Why did Maria sleep with the engine on? Why did she have a gasoline can in her car? Why didn't she at least crack her windows? If she was so broke and had to work three jobs, how could she afford to leave the engine running? One commenter on the *New York Times* website, disputing that there was any lesson here about low-wage workers, wrote, "Sleeping in a car with the motor running is foolish, and that is what killed Ms. Fernandes." Another commenter wrote, "Perhaps poor judgement, not low wages, was the culprit here."

Certainly it was a tragic miscalculation to have had fuel in the vehicle, but it's not surprising that someone so underslept and overextended would make an error in judgment. As one commentator retorted to the critics, "If I don't sleep 6 hours straight, I can barely write my name, and this is with one 9–5 sedentary job." Another defender of Maria, with the benefit of personal experience, wrote: "I am poor and often sleep in my car. . . . If [the critics] had experience living in modern poverty, they would understand some of its finer points, such as the common practice of sleeping in a car. Readers who fault her for such financially wasteful gas usage (for running her car's AC) also slept in an air conditioned bedroom."

So yes, Maria could have made some better choices, but that misses the point. As a low-wage perma-lancer, scrambling to make ends meet, the narrow range of her choices left her with little margin for error. New Jersey has tens of thousands of people like Maria working multiple jobs, says Carl Van Horn, director of the John J. Heldrich Center for Workforce Development at Rutgers University in New Brunswick. "These are folks who would like to work full-time but they can't find the jobs. They wind up in these circumstances in which they are exhausted. More commonly it creates just an enormous amount of stress," he said.[48]

Meanwhile, Dunkin' Donuts in 2013 had $9.3 billion in sales, and CEO Nigel Travis received $4.2 million in pay, stock options and perks, up 120 percent from 2012.[49] He gained another $21 million exercising stock options, according to the company's annual proxy.[50] Dunkin', owned by Mitt Romney's old firm Bain Capital, has profited handsomely off its army of low-wage workers.[51] Maria Fernandes is collateral damage from "business as usual" in the new economy. Low-wage workers like her have reached a level of desperation that this country thought it had mostly left behind. That we *ought* to have left behind.

Instead, the captains of commerce continue to invent new ways to wring every drop of life and vitality out of their low-wage workforce. It's well known that many Walmart workers must receive public assistance to make ends meet, and recently Marriott Hotels beseeched its clients to tip its maids—apparently the hotel chain's wages are too low to provide a decent standard of living. Now the profiteers have come up with another travesty—it's called "just-in-time scheduling."[52]

Employers increasingly require that their employees remain constantly on call and give them little advance notice about schedules. Large retail employers have begun using digital scheduling systems that tailor employees' work hours to the precise times when customers are most likely to shop. Increasingly, part-time workers don't know what hours they are scheduled until they show up to punch in.[53] Or an employee shows up for a scheduled shift and is told to go home. That happened to Mary Coleman in Milwaukee. She arrived at her scheduled job at Popeyes after an hour-long bus commute, and her boss told her he didn't need her that day. She received no pay for her aborted shift.[54]

Instead of using this technology to make life easier and more predictable for everyone, employers are using it to maximize profits at their employees' expense. The resulting constant precariousness deprives low-wage employees of the ability to plan their lives, to figure out child care, to schedule classes (for students) or second (or third) jobs, attend family events or take care of their own health. It more easily facilitates employers hiring a number of part-time workers instead of fewer workers full time (and for which they might have to pay additional safety-net benefits). That means many workers like Maria Fernandes do not get to work enough hours at one job to make ends meet, and so must work multiple jobs, opening the door to other abuses and dangers. In short, just-in-time scheduling makes it impossible for employees to live normal lives.

This unpredictability of work is especially problematic for the 27 million Americans who work part time.[55] Some of the part-timers are 1099 workers, others like Maria Fernandes are regular W-2 employees. But pretty much all of them are losing ground. The number of part-timers who would prefer to work full time has almost doubled since 2007, to 7.5 million, particularly in the aftermath of the Great Recession, and remains high.[56] Part-time workers are significantly less likely to have access to any form of health insurance or paid leave.[57] Nearly 30 percent of Americans say they have work schedules with daily start and stop times that vary, and according to the Bureau of Labor Statistics, 47 percent of part-time hourly workers between the ages of 26 and 32 are given a week or less of advance notice about their work schedule.[58] Two professors from the University of Chicago found that bosses decreed the work schedules for about half of young adults without any input from the employee at all .[59] Another study by Demos found that women, African Americans and Latinos are disproportionately impacted by just-in-time scheduling.[60]

Fast-food workers are some of the most prone to just-in-time scheduling, working an average of only 24 hours a week; nearly 70 percent of low-income workers do not have the option of changing their scheduled start or stop time if needed.[61] They earn a median wage of $8.94, with many making much less.[62] Consequently, more than half of fast-food workers receive public assistance, at a cost to taxpayers of $7 billion a year.[63] Besides being drastically underpaid and pressed into compulsory flexibility, another study found that 89 percent of fast-food workers have been denied breaks, pressured to do off-the-books work, and in some cases even have been cheated out of wages, especially overtime pay.[64] Meanwhile, fast-food CEOs earned on average $26.7 million in 2012, resulting in a CEO-to-worker pay gap of 1,200 to 1, which is by far the highest of any industry.[65]

Fast-food leaders like McDonald's (which costs taxpayers $1.2 billion per year for public assistance to its workers[66]) certainly can afford to pay a living wage, yet McDonald's implies that it shouldn't have to because it has this self-serving belief that its workers are predominantly young people working their first jobs and McDonald's is merely an entry-level pathway to a young person's career. But in truth, half of the fast-food industry's workers are over 28 years old.[67] McDonald's also has tried to wiggle out of violations of labor and wage laws by saying the employees do not work for them but for one of their 14,000-plus franchises—so the mother ship isn't responsible (even though McDonald's requires those franchises to adhere to hundreds of rules about everything else that goes on inside or outside their restaurants, including food quality, appearance, even the design of the napkins).[68]

Like McDonald's, Walmart, which costs taxpayers $6.2 billion per year for providing public assistance to its workers, will accept no criticism of its exploitative business practices.[69] The Walmart driver who hit comedian Tracy Morgan in June 2014, killing his companion, had not slept in twenty-four hours, according to police; he'd already been working for thirteen and a half hours (with a federal cap of fourteen hours) and was probably rushing to make his final delivery rather than taking the nap he so urgently needed.[70] Even as founder Sam Walton's heirs—three children and one daughter-in-law—are worth collectively over $140 *billion* and ranked 6, 7, 9 and 10 on *Forbes* list of wealthiest Americans,[71] Walmart officials insist that just-in-time scheduling is central to its business model and has been essential to its success.[72] It is used throughout its operation, including in its warehouse distribution and manufacturing.

But Rep. George Miller (Democrat-California) asks if just-in-time scheduling "really is critical to [Walmart's] being a successful business, or is it critical for them to be able to extract the maximum amount of money out of that business? Those two things are not necessarily the same. If the purpose of the just-in-time scheduling and a contingent work force is so that the Walmart family, the richest people in the United States, can continue extracting billions of dollars rather than sharing some of the productivity of their workers with those same employees, then we've lost any kind of sense of economic justice in this country." Representative Miller cosponsored the Schedules That Work Act, which would mandate that workers who are summoned to work on short notice be paid extra, and would require employers to pay a minimum of four hours' pay to a worker who is sent home after coming to work.[73] While this legislation has little chance of passing at the federal level, San Francisco and Vermont have passed versions of it. A national campaign called the Fair Workweek Initiative is pushing for legislation to limit these practices in various places, including Milwaukee, New York, Santa Clara, California and more. The battle has only recently been joined.

In the meantime, there are signs that low-wage workers are beginning to fight back. In the past couple of years, protests by fast-food workers over poverty wages and the right to organize a union without retaliation have spread.[74] Strikes have taken place in more than 150 U.S. cities. In May 2014 at the McDonald's shareholders meeting, nearly a hundred workers were arrested protesting their unfair treatment, and 2,000 protesters, including several hundred McDonald's workers in uniform, marched through the company's headquarters in Oak Brook, Illinois.[75]

And in July 2014, more than 1,000 fast-food workers traveled from all over the country for a first-ever nationwide convention to organize how to escalate their demands, including a $15-an-hour minimum wage and the right to form a union without retaliation. One of the conference organizers wrote, "I've worked at McDonald's for 10 years and still make $7.35 an hour—only pennies above the federal minimum wage. My four girls deserve better. I deserve better. McDonald's and the other fast-food companies are going to learn that when you aren't paid enough to survive, you're willing to do whatever it takes, for as long as it takes, until you are treated fairly."[76]

Finally in December 2014, the National Labor Relations Board issued a decision that named McDonald's Corp. as a "joint employer" of workers at its franchisees, making the parent company responsible for hundreds of complaints for underpaid wages and violations of law by its franchises. This raised an outcry from many businesses and trade organizations, saying it struck "at the heart of the franchise system" used for many years by corporate businesses.[77] But David Weil from the U.S. Department of Labor's Wage and Hour Division pointed out the obvious contradiction in the employers' position: "The companies at the top dictate quality standards and exactly what the end product or service should be. But, if any labor problems arise, that's when they say, 'these aren't my employees.' Can you really have it both ways?"[78]

While low-wage and fast-food workers have made modest gains, another victory for working people was achieved when, in February 2015, Jimmy Maerina and the Facebook drivers that had voted in the Teamsters union agreed to a contract with their employer, Loop Transportation. The contract provided a sizable across-the-board wage increase of nearly 20 percent, an additional pay increase for drivers who work split shifts, a six-hour minimum for drivers who do not want to work split shifts, more paid vacation and sick leave, and health-care and pension benefits for workers and families of full-time employees. The victory of the Facebook drivers in turn has spurred new levels of organizing among drivers for other Silicon Valley companies. When workers join together and present a clear and compelling case of unfairness and injustice, they can still win.[79]

Still, there are many Maria Fernandeses all around us, yet they are invisible. They are everyday heroes trying to stay optimistic about life despite the challenges they face, struggling against employers who have lost all sense of the wise and inspiring—yet fading—message of President Franklin Roosevelt, who said, "The test of our progress is not whether we add more to the abundance of those who have much; it is whether we provide enough for those who have too little."[80]

MIDDLE-CLASS SERFS

For many people, it's not surprising—and even somewhat acceptable—that the quality of jobs in the fast-food industry is subpar. Such jobs are viewed as something you do only if you must, and only until you find something better. But increasingly more middle-class professionals are also feeling the bite of sporadic income and a diminishing safety net. Many individuals aspiring to the ranks of the intellectual and creative elite are becoming little more than cogs in a highly educated contingent workforce of 1099 employees.

There are the journalists, many of whom have won awards for leading newspapers, yet were laid off (some possibly replaced by prose-writing robots—see chapter 6) and now are journeymen writing for peanuts for any publication that will toss them a bone. There are the graphic designers and webpage developers who go from job to job, always scrambling to find the next paying gig. There are the increasing legions of freelance tech workers who hire themselves out to the barons of Silicon Valley and other tech capitals, trying to keep their heads above water. There are the adjunct professors who are hired as "intellectual temps," wondering if they'll ever gain a tenure track or must continue to be wandering academic gypsies (known as "freeway flyers") going from university to university for the rest of their careers.[81] There are the college graduates with dim prospects, the skills and education they gained at school of little use for manning the espresso maker at the coffee shops where they are finding jobs. There are freelance filmmakers, screenwriters, photographers, copy editors and translators who must spend inordinate hours looking for the next job, time for which they do not get paid.

Imagine being a secretary for a Wall Street financial or law firm who got laid off in the wreckage of the financial crisis, and during the "recovery" found a job as a menial clerk for a local accounting firm that said it couldn't afford to provide health or retirement benefits. Imagine being an editor at Random House, let go on "Black Wednesday" during a sweeping reorganization aimed at trimming costs following the plummeting of book sales, now faced with a precarious working life as a freelancing literary agent.[82]

Or who can forget the emergency landing of U.S. Airways flight 1548 on the Hudson River by Capt. Chesley Sullenberger on January 15, 2009. "Sully" Sullenberger became an instant national hero, yet a month later, there he was testifying before Congress about the drastic reductions in pilot pay, pensions and other benefits that were driving experienced pilots out of the industry and threatening passenger safety. Captain Sullenberger told the House aviation subcommittee that his pay had been cut 40 percent in recent years and his pension had been terminated.[83] The reduced compensation has placed "pilots and their families in an untenable financial situation," Sullenberger said. Without experienced pilots "we will see negative consequences to the flying public."[84]

His testimony was not just conjecture: less than two weeks earlier the nation was gripped by the most tragic airline crash in many years, Colgan Air Flight 3407. Flight 3407 was a regional commuter flight, but it was marketed as a Continental Airlines flight, with whom it has a partnership for flying regional routes. Unbelievably, pilots who fly for regional airlines earn as little as $12.50 per hour, less than the hourly wage of a New York City taxi driver.[85] Often they are allowed an inadequate number of sick days and have to commute hundreds and even thousands of miles to get from their homes to their regional base, leaving too many of them flying while they are overtired, run down and ill.[86] This is no small matter. Regional pilots fly roughly half of all scheduled flights in the U.S., carrying 160 million American passengers every year. When Colgan/Continental Flight 3407 crashed into a house on February 12, 2009, near Buffalo, New York, killing everyone on board and a homeowner on the ground, the copilot was earning a salary of just $16,200. In fact, the copilot moonlighted part time, working in a coffee shop to supplement her meager salary, and had pulled an all-nighter to commute from her home in Seattle to get to work at Colgan's operation in Newark.[87] The captain of the flight also had commuted the previous evening from his faraway Florida home. On the cockpit voice recorder, both pilots could be heard yawning during the course of the flight.

The crash of Flight 3407 and Captain Sullenberger's riveting testimony cast a spotlight on working conditions for a highly skilled position such as commercial airline pilots, but as the horror stories became public they sounded all too familiar because we already had heard them coming from so many other occupations and industries. And we had heard similar stories coming from our own families, friends and associates.

Things have gotten so topsy-turvy across most industries and occupations that even Tina Brown, the flamboyant media mogul and former high-octane editor of *Vanity Fair,* the *New Yorker* and the *Daily Beast,* has noticed with disbelief the impact on her own associates and friends.

"Now that everyone has a project-to-project freelance career, everyone is a hustler. No one I know has a job anymore. They've got gigs," she says. For a while "the downsized people I know went around pretending they enjoyed the 'freedom' and 'variety' of doing 'a whole lot of interesting things.' Twelve months later, nobody bothers with that cover story anymore."[88]

Sounding like working-class blokes Fritz Elienberg, Chris Young and Jimmy Maerina, Brown decried how "everyone knows what it actually feels like, this penny-ante slog of working three times as hard for the same amount of money (if you're lucky) or a lot less (if you're not). Minus benefits, of course. . . . Doing three things badly is the name of the game. . . . With so many part-time people on—and not on—the job, corporate America has started to feel like it's on a permanent maternity leave."

Formerly known for throwing extravagant bashes attended by A-listers from her personal Rolodex, suddenly Tina Brown is sounding like a nascent union leader. "The folks at the bottom of the greasy pole have been living with the anxieties, uncertainties, and indignities of Gigwork (it used to be called piecework) for a long time," she says. "Now that people nearer the top are learning firsthand about the wonders of 'individual initiative' and 'self-reliance,' a little more sympathy—maybe even solidarity—with those the meritocracy dismissed as losers may be in order. . . . With the economy in free fall, the American workplace is changing and now the top tiers are hustling. . . . Today's hustler looks much swankier."

What Brown is perceptively picking up on is that, for all those Americans who lost their "good" jobs and have entered the disordered world of 1099 work, many of them now exist on a job-to-job basis, contracting with a variety of clients and earning lower pay than before with little job security. Indeed, many now must track income from multiple sources, perhaps a dozen or more per year; they must locate and pay for their own health insurance and save for their retirement without the benefit of an employer-sponsored pension or 401(k) plan, nor employer matches of employees' contributions; they must deduct their own income tax and mail it to the IRS, and as a 1099 employee they are now doubly taxed for Social Security and Medicare, treated as both an employer and an employee. They need to become their own bookkeepers and accountants, a skill set most do not naturally have. And there is a lot of overlap between all the various employee categories—many workers will pass from part time to full time to temp to perma-temp to indie to contractor to freelance to gig-preneur and back again, throughout their working careers.

Even those workers who make sufficient income to afford some middle-class niceties live with the nagging insecurity of wondering where their next job will come from, and how long they can keep juggling so many balls in the air. Many aspects of their lives that were once relatively straightforward are now infinitely more complicated, as more and more workers must navigate the shifting ground with skill sets that seem to be increasingly ill-suited for our times.

BRACEROS BY ANOTHER NAME

So from the lowliest fast-food worker to the top-tier rarified air of Tina Brown's soirée world, nearly everyone is feeling the pinch. It's happening everywhere, high and low, in every quarter, in every geographic region, among all ages and demographics. It's an epidemic. The stories of the struggling people introduced in this chapter are just a small slice of the downsizing experienced by millions of American workers in recent years, with no end in sight. The numbers show quite clearly that, for the vast majority of these people, if they have been able to find work again following the Great Recession, that employment is less secure, pays less money and has virtually no safety net attached. If previously they were embedded in the reciprocal embrace of an employer-employee relationship, now they are on their own. Over the last two decades the workforce has become increasingly more vulnerable, with declining expectations. And now the Great Recession has completed that transition. Businesses have capitalized on the crisis to accelerate their use of all sorts of quasi-legal loopholes and third-party operations to "1099" and/or part-time their employees. It's all part of the same strategy, a way for parent companies to evade responsibility for providing a decent, middle-class wage and safety net for their employees. The parent companies have cleverly figured out a way to let the third-party agencies play the role of the bad guy.

In short, it's a brave new world in which great uncertainty and risk are becoming the norm, and work—along with personal lives—has become "precarious." The millions of Americans who already are experiencing this overturned reality are the "canaries in the mineshaft," a harbinger of what is coming for tens of millions of U.S. workers, as well as millions more around the world. Adding to the looming sense of crisis, a recent study found that three-fourths of Americans are living paycheck to paycheck, with little to no emergency savings to tide them over if they lose their source of income.[89] These are the new *braceros* of the workforce, part of the new tide of "workforce migrants" who are being forced by an overwhelming economic tide to shift from job to job, employer to employer, with little safety net to catch them if they fall off the narrowing path. The new predicament of U.S. workers prompted authors Marion Crain and Michael Sherraden to write in their book *Working and Living in the Shadow of Economic Fragility,* "A silent crisis is underway, with huge social and economic costs for the nation."[90]

The United States is not the only place where these workforce pressures and trends are emerging, but among developed nations it is happening here fastest. Increases in precarious jobs, including part-time, temporary, contract and freelance, have appeared in other advanced economies, like the UK, Germany, Japan and Spain—not to the same extent as in the U.S., in part because many of the workplace protections and safety-net supports provided to regular workers in other developed countries are by law also extended to non-regular and 1099-type workers. But the global trajectory is troubling.[91]

Welcome to the Freelance Society. Huge swaths of workers are becoming freelanced, contracted and temp-ed, and even many regularly employed, full-time workers are being slowly squeezed, feeling the ground shifting beneath their feet. Millions of Americans are being left to their own devices, stranded on their own island of survival. Due to circumstances beyond their control, all of these different categories of workers now are being shoveled like ore into the roaring furnaces of what has been rosily dubbed the "sharing" economy (a gross misnomer, as we shall see in the next several chapters).

TWO

AIRBNB AND THE SHARING ECONOMY

ECONOMIC SAVIOR OR . . . DEAD END?

LIKE THE MARVELS OF THE WORLD WIDE WEB, EMAIL, TWEETS, "FRIENDS," followers, "pins," search engines, "smart" phones and other new-economy fixtures, the "sharing economy" has entered the nation's lexicon as yet another innovative wave at the nexus of technology, the economy and the future. But what exactly is the "sharing economy"?

The sharing economy includes a vast array of companies spread across many industries and occupations. Those companies are engaged in activities as diverse as transport (taxi alternatives like Uber and Lyft and, in Europe, Hailo and BlaBlaCar), delivery (Postmates and Instacart), day labor (TaskRabbit, Upwork, Elance, Washio, Homejoy), personal property sales, rental and exchange (Etsy, Peerby, Parking Panda, Yerdle), home rental (Airbnb, VRBO, DogVacay—yup, dogs stay in your home while their owners are on vacation) and more. Some of the companies are explicitly commercial and profit-making in nature, others are projects of idealists and environmentalists aiming to reduce waste and consumption by creating a portal for swapping goods and services, with minimal money exchanged.

But despite their differences in vocation or industry, all of the sharing economy companies have the same dominant feature: an innovative use of Web- and app-based platforms to connect buyers and sellers (and swappers for noncommercial transactions) of goods, labor and services. The transactions often are called "peer to peer"—between you and another individual—rather than "peer to business," between you and a store or business.[1] The company running the platform charges a fee for its matchmaker service (anywhere from 10 to 25 percent of the cash value of the transaction between buyers and sellers, depending on the company). The genius of this Web- and app-based platform is that you can summon an Uber car, or a TaskRabbit to assemble your IKEA furniture, or rent an Airbnb room or a Spinlister bicycle or get your laundry Washio washed, and have it show up at your door without ever dealing with a live human sales clerk or intermediary. Just a flick of your computer mouse, a tap of your app, and presto! Virtual stores, open for business 24–7, available all over the world. "Workers of the world, turn on your smartphones," says technology analyst Evgeny Morozov.[2]

This digital space, which has dramatically lowered what are known as "transaction costs," was pioneered originally by websites such as eBay and Amazon, all of whose founders ended up fabulously wealthy. A key component of the digital technologies that those companies passed on to the sharing economy is the idea of rating sellers and buyers: that information on their reliability can be crowdsourced—accumulated from the collective wisdom of thousands and even millions of transactions—thereby providing "Internet gossip" on sellers' reputations. This feature, called "reputation analytics," is intended to foster trust and reduce the risks of transacting with strangers. The ease with which strangers all over the world now can connect, buy, sell and swap for commercial or noncommercial purposes is truly a game changer.

But the nature of this technology also means that these transactions are impersonal and faceless. You don't get to know the local shopkeeper anymore or chat with the sales clerk. The online marketplace has lost nearly all vestiges of personal relations and Robert Putnam–like social capital—consumers and purveyors of goods and services are "buying and selling alone." Capitalism already has a strong tendency toward impersonal commodification of all that it touches; as we will see, the digital technologies at the core of the "sharing" economy amplify these atomistic tendencies in a way that is not only "disruptive," as tech enthusiasts like to boast, but also unleashes disturbing elements.

Salivating to build upon the success of Amazon, eBay, Facebook and Twitter, venture capitalists have been pouring billions of dollars in investment capital into many of these sharing economy companies. Visionaries on both the left and the right, whether business boosters or small-is-beautiful enviros, trumpet the sharing economy as the answer to what ails our nation, each for his or her own reasons (more on that left-right dynamic in chapter 8). With so much momentum and money lining up behind it, the sharing economy has come to occupy a unique and even unusual place in the U.S. economy: corporate capitalism on the one hand, but also decentralized and grassroots on the other. As the freelance society comes closer into view, the sharing economy visionaries are positioning their brain-child as the economic engine that will allow tens of millions of U.S. workers (like the types of workers we met in chapter 1) to plug into the post–New Deal economy.

No question, their vision is full of a perky techno-optimism, sometimes wrapped in the alluring values of environmental sustainability and decentralization. To its true-blue believers, the sharing economy is revolutionary, and to the more idealistic, it has the potential to remake capitalism into a kinder, gentler version. Supposedly it will empower workers to become their own microentrepreneurs, CEOs of their own businesses—whether as handymen, cleaning ladies, Uber drivers or landlords of their own homes—monetizing their own personal assets. Undimmed by facts and figures about economic and workforce decline, the sharing economy gurus have a vision—to their credit a very human-centered vision—that aspires to give people more power over their lives. More than a vision, they also have a burning ambition to tear up and transform "the old economy, the last economy,"[3] as they call it, like historical heirs of Marx's dialectic disruptors, with marketing strategies targeting all the millions of anxious Americans who suddenly find themselves facing insecure times. But paradoxically, the best-known sharing economy companies are courting—and attracting—billions of dollars in venture capital. Can you tear down the edifice of the old boss while still using the boss's methods? Or, in the process, do you become the new boss?

THE TORNADO OF AIRBNB

More than any other company, Airbnb has come to personify the sharing economy ethos. As one of the movement's most successful and recognizable faces, Airbnb keeps its sharing philosophy at the forefront of its marketing strategy. "Belonging is the idea that defines Airbnb," says its 34-year-old CEO and founder Brian Chesky.[4] "Really, we're about home. You see, a house is just a space, but a home is where you belong. That is the idea at the core of our company: belonging." In a confusing, topsy-turvy world, his words sound reassuring, and Chesky in his many interviews comes across as sincerely believing it.

Truly a modern business miracle, Airbnb was started in San Francisco rather haphazardly by a couple of twentysomethings, Chesky and his roommate Joe Gebbia, both graduates of the Rhode Island School of Design. Unemployed in 2007 and having difficulty paying their rent, and noting the lack of available hotel space for attendees to an industrial design conference, Chesky and Gebbia threw air mattresses on their living room floor (hence, the name "air" bnb), turning their apartment on Rausch Street in the South of Market area into a cross between a flophouse and a short-term bed-and-breakfast. With that quick money in their pockets, they expanded by focusing first on conferences and events where lodging was scarce. They drew in friends who wanted to make a few extra dollars subrenting their apartment for a few nights. They added computer programmer Nathan Blecharczyk as a cofounder to build a website, and the whole enterprise took off like a rocket.

They tapped into a rich vein of people, at first in urban areas in the U.S. but eventually all over the world, who grasped for the financial benefits of hosting travelers. Those hosts in turn filled a niche for travelers looking for low-cost accommodations, particularly during high-season times when hotel vacancies were scarce. Airbnb has become an impressive commercial empire, yet its appeal has been authentically grassroots.

The young entrepreneurs had no idea what they had wrapped their arms around. Now, less than eight years later, Airbnb is a global success story, valued at $25 *billion*—the same as the 100-year-old Hyatt chain—and self-reporting a mind boggling 25 million nights booked since its inception, with a million current listings across 34,000 cities and 192 countries.[5] It employs a thousand people around the world, and has become not only an economic but also a cultural phenomenon, already an iconic company in its short life. Its young founders have become wide-eyed billionaires who at times seem to barely believe their good fortune in stumbling upon a fabulous new innovation in global hospitality and travel.

But in San Francisco, New York City, Los Angeles and elsewhere, the legacy of their gold rush has been decidedly mixed. Airbnb is not merely a "community-driven hospitality company," as its founders like to say, but also a catalyst for massive lawbreaking, a tax rogue and, tragically, an impetus for the eviction of longtime tenants, including the elderly, the disabled, children, even people with life-threatening illnesses. Other short-term rental brokerages such as VRBO, FlipKey, Roomorama and Home Away, while much smaller in size, have followed the Airbnb model. For reasons that will be elaborated below, many cities have been left reeling from the bitter disruption of entire neighborhoods, as well as from poisoned landlord-tenant relations that were based on laws that had been stitched together over decades, yet now are being flushed as Airbnb's investors and local real estate interests rush to cash in. If "belonging" is the idea that defines Airbnb, it depends a lot on whether or not you belong to the right club.

To understand the whirlwind of Airbnb, let's meet the faces of three San Francisco residents who represent its promise and its peril. First, there is Mr. Brian Chesky himself, Airbnb's young CEO, cofounder, former bodybuilder, newly minted billionaire and ideological guru of his company's "trust and share" ethos that struggles to maintain its sincerity amidst the intense profit-seeking desires of his venture-capitalist backers.

Second, there is Cathryn "Catbird" Blum, one of the Airbnb hosts—or "sharers," as they like to call themselves—trying to make ends meet by offering up a room for rent in her Potrero Hill home to the global travelers for whom San Francisco is a magnet destination.

And third, there is Theresa Flandrich, a retired nurse who has lived for 30 years and raised her son in a two-bedroom, rent-controlled apartment on North Beach's Lombard Street—and now is desperately fighting eviction as a greedy landlord tries to remove her (and other tenants in her building) to make room for Airbnb-ing her apartment (yes, Airbnb has become a verb, with nasty connotations).

Like the conflicted actors in a Sam Shepard play (Shepard once was a resident playwright in San Francisco, writing some of his best work here), these three faces are being buffeted by forces they don't always understand, with a clashing momentum that so far has meant they can't all win. Therein lies the heart of a tragedy.

ACT I—DOWN AND OUT IN NORTH BEACH

Theresa Flandrich gives me a tour around her North Beach neighborhood. North Beach is one of San Francisco's most historic and loved districts, also known as "Little Italy" because it was the borough where many Italian immigrants settled in the early 20th century. Seeking opportunity in the wave of European immigration that flooded America, the Italians opened shops, built homes and churches and, with North Beach abutting Fisherman's Wharf, anchored the then-thriving fishing industry.[6] Joe DiMaggio's father was a fisherman in the Bay Area, and Joltin' Joe married Marilyn Monroe at San Francisco City Hall; Joe DiMaggio Playground is located a block from Theresa's apartment. The North Beach neighborhood was a multigenerational place, where families thrived and kids played stickball in the streets, with grandparents in close proximity to their extended families. Neighbors knew and helped each other and felt a measure of post–World War II security. "It was a real neighborhood," says Theresa.

But now things look very different. Just on her street alone, on a single block, Theresa can point to five buildings (including her own) where all the tenants have received eviction notices. Around the corner there are several more buildings with threatened tenants. "Most of these buildings," says Theresa, "were owned by the old Italians who took care of their community. They kept rents reasonable, and didn't mind rent control because, well, we were all *neighbors.*" That word says a lot to Theresa. "They wanted to help each other, and as a nurse when they needed medical care I helped them. Everybody took care of each other."

But then the Italian patriarchs grew old and died, and many of their kids didn't live in San Francisco anymore and so, for one reason or another, they wanted to sell. A new breed of landlords bought the buildings. Owners like Peter Iskandar of Bubble Realty (yes, that's really his real estate company's name), a speculator from Indonesia who saw this neighborhood as his personal gold rush. Like a Monopoly game board, he purchased property after property and began evicting tenants—often using questionable means—so that he could get them out of their rent-controlled apartments. Then he would jack up the rents, sell them as condominiums or, more recently, Airbnb them. The Anti-Eviction Mapping Project shows Mr. Iskandar as having bought at least 10 buildings in the neighborhood.[7] To make way for his ambitions, he has evicted a 68-year-old woman with breast cancer; Carlo Tarrone, in his seventies and using a walker, who had lived in his apartment for 56 years; and Sandy Bishop, who is 70 and has lung cancer. "I can't even find a place to live because I don't make enough money," Bishop said. "Maybe I should just stay and let the sheriff carry me out."[8] Iskandar is a one-man wrecking ball, demolishing the lives of elderly and sick people, seemingly targeting the most vulnerable. Some have accused him of bending the rules to commit naked acts of what amounts to "elderly cleansing."

Just down the street, Theresa shows me a four-unit building that is accessed via a quaint, brick alleyway, reminiscent of the honey-hive maze around Piazza Navona in Rome. All the tenants have been evicted and now, she points out, four lockboxes are visible on the banister outside the front entryway for the apartments—the telltale sign that this building has been Airbnb-ed. The constant carousel of new faces coming and going can check themselves in and out of each apartment, accessing the key via the lockbox for which they are given the combination, without ever meeting the landlord or manager. The transaction can be completed anonymously, facelessly, over the Airbnb website. Where before this building housed families who were part of the neighborhood, now it's an Airbnb tourist hotel.

Across the street is another building that has suffered through a similar fate. Two doors down, still another. A few blocks away, Chinatown, with its vulnerable population of English-limited elderly, has been targeted by landlords taking advantage of language and cultural barriers to evict immigrant families and seniors who are ill-equipped to defend themselves.[9] Around the corner, Theresa's 80-year-old friend Diego Deleo is also in the process of being evicted. Diego came to the U.S. at age 17 from Bari, Italy, working as a laborer with bricklayers. "Theresa, I helped build this city, and now they want to force me out," he tells her. He has lived in North Beach for over 40 years, the past 30 in his apartment on Chestnut Street, where his wife, Josie, died a few years ago. The memories of his life with her are in the walls of his home, he says. "North Beach is my life. At my age, [the eviction notice] is a death sentence."[10]

Theresa's building has met with a similar fate, though the circumstances are somewhat different. The owner of her building died at 96 years old. "She and I were close," says Theresa, "I used to help her take her medications." Everyone in the four-apartment building was close, including the Palestinian shopkeepers who run a small grocery store on the street level. "They let the neighbors run a tab; if you had a short month, they would let you pay the next month. It was close knit," says Theresa.

The deceased owner had willed the property to her niece who lives in faraway Laguna Beach, in Southern California. Within a week after getting her hands on the deed, the niece served notice to everyone in the building to clear out, including a man in advanced stages of Parkinson's disease. The niece claimed she was going to invoke a legal loophole called an "owner-occupied move-in"—moving in members of her family, including herself, none of whom actually lived in San Francisco.

"Seven o'clock in the morning on April 11th, the doorbell rang. And, there was a server," says Theresa. "My son answered the door and he was just given the papers. I was offended. I was hurt. I was shocked. My son had to go off to work. And he said, the first thing he said was, 'Oh my God. This is the only home I've ever known. I didn't expect to live here all my life. But I expected you to be here, Mom. This is where we'd continue to celebrate all our holidays and the neighborhood.'"[11]

According to a report by San Francisco's Rent Board, nearly 2,000 units were evicted in 2013, a 13 percent increase from 2012.[12] Since most rented locations house more than one person (San Francisco is too expensive for most people to have their own private place), housing experts have estimated that figure represents at least 5,000 people evicted in 2013. The landlords have been relentless in using different tactics, some of them illegal, to evict, such as claiming they're going to rehabilitate their building.[13] The landlords know that, by law, tenants have the right to move back into their unit at the same rent after the rehab is completed. But the tenants don't know that, and the landlord usually does not tell them because their goal is to remove these tenants from their rent-controlled apartments. They offer them a few thousand dollars to move out, telling the tenants they have no choice, and the tenants—especially when they are elderly, disabled, ill or language-challenged—often don't have the will or tenacity to fight back. After a few take the buyout and leave, the landlord can really put the squeeze on any that refuse. They harass and threaten them, they cut off garbage service, they refuse to do repairs . . . suddenly water or electricity becomes unreliable.

Property owners also have ramped up their use of "gotcha evictions" to remove tenants from their rent-controlled apartments—trumped-up, petty violations for alleged "nuisances," such as carrying your bicycle through a common hallway, painting the walls of your apartment or leaving a baby stroller in the common area. In Chinatown, tenants have been threatened with eviction for hanging laundry outside their windows and displaying Chinese New Year decorations in the hallways. Since there is no clear legal standard for what constitutes a "nuisance," the landlord issues an eviction notice, initiating a legal battle that most tenants are ill-positioned to wage.

In 2014, more than a thousand San Francisco tenants were intimidated out of their homes over these kinds of trumped-up charges. Breach of lease and nuisance violations have become the leading causes of evictions in San Francisco. Most tenants, especially seniors, do not know their rights or are afraid to assert them.[14] Once evicted, most move out of the city because, having been ousted from their rent-controlled apartment, they can't afford to remain when the median monthly rent for a one-bedroom apartment zoomed in 2015 to nearly $3,500 (up from $2,795 in 2013), and a two-bedroom apartment to $4,500.[15] Under this kind of price pressure, the San Francisco Controller's Office estimates that the city lost 1,017 rent-controlled housing units in 2013.[16] "When this happens year after year, as it has for many years in a row," says Sara Shortt from the Housing Rights Committee of San Francisco, "the very fabric of our neighborhoods, our communities and our city is ripped apart."[17]

But Theresa has successfully fought her eviction by organizing her building and her neighbors. They formed the North Beach Tenants Committee, and at the first meeting the turnout was strong, over 100 people. She has helped Diego resist his eviction, and other people are fighting back. Joe Tobener, a local San Francisco attorney, has represented many tenants against greedy landlords and their illegal evictions. Tobener is a straight-talking people's lawyer who grew up poor, raised by a single mom with six kids on a cashier's salary. "I feel like Robin Hood sometimes," he told me, defending so many vulnerable tenants against the wealthy interests behind these Airbnb-fueled evictions. "We get about 60 calls a week," many of them from tenants being illegally displaced so landlords can use Airbnb, VRBO, Roomorama, FlipKey or other services to rent to tourists. "There's so little enforcement, it's like the Third World," he says. "Airbnb is contributing to the displacement of long-term tenants in San Francisco."[18]

San Francisco, like New York City and other major urban areas, has a complicated code of laws and regulations that oversee real estate and landlord-tenant relations. One of the laws prohibits the renting of apartments or homes for fewer than 30 days, to prevent exactly the type of shenanigans that afflict

Theresa and her neighbors—property owners who decide it's more lucrative to turn their property into tourist hotels, thereby reducing the supply of housing available for local people who need permanent residence. That practice is called "illegal hoteling" and was banned decades ago by the Apartment Conversion Ordinance.

Property owners have always tried to skirt this law, but even when Craigslist became the first online service to facilitate short-term rentals, the small number of lawbreakers was ignorable. Now, Airbnb and other short-term rental brokerages, with their sophisticated Web- and app-based portals, have made it super easy for virtually anyone with property to find a short-term tourist to rent to. They have facilitated lawbreaking on a massive scale, and an investigation in May 2014 by the *San Francisco Chronicle* found 4,798 properties listed on the Airbnb website, and another 1,200 properties on the VRBO site.[19] A colorful map showing the location of each listing was produced, and the thousands of dots covering the map (especially the eastern half of the city) made San Francisco look like it was being swarmed by insects.[20]

Says San Francisco Planning Commissioner Hisashi Sugaya, "Short-term rentals have been around a long time. It hasn't been a big to-do. But these companies have shoved it back in the city's face by enhancing the ability of people to break the law."[21] In a city where almost two-thirds of residents are renters (compared to a national average of one-third renters), yet property owners and developers wield tremendous political and economic clout, the longtime balance between tenants and real estate interests has been completely overturned within a few short years. The Airbnb-ing of San Francisco has led to what Tenderloin Housing director Randy Shaw has called a "massive rezoning of the entire city for tourist use."[22] Ted Gullicksen, director of the San Francisco Tenants Union, said, "We call it the 'hotelization' of San Francisco. Seniors, families and low-income tenants are being pushed out."[23]

Airbnb has disavowed responsibility for any of this, claiming they are merely a booking agent, an anonymous intermediary facilitating commercial transactions between two parties. But this is disingenuous. It's like a rumbling jetliner flying low overhead that doesn't want to be blamed for its noise. Besides, Airbnb has fought, with all the lawyers and lobbyists that a billion-dollar company can buy, any attempts to regulate their business model, not only in San Francisco but everywhere else. That includes the regulation that requires hotels such as the Hyatt and Sheraton to pay a hotel and occupancy tax for each guest. That tax is typically levied by cities to cover costs of public services and amenities used by out-of-towners. The treasurer of San Francisco estimated that Airbnb owed the city $25 million in back taxes, which Airbnb refused to pay for over three years.[24] Airbnb griped about the difficulty of collecting taxes from 5,000 hosts, but critics pointed out that Airbnb's platform easily handles charging millions of guests a 6 to 12 percent service fee upon booking, then charges another 3 percent to the hosts, revenue that flows into Airbnb's pocket (and has quickly made it a billion-dollar company). If Airbnb can smoothly handle those transactions, why should it be so difficult to charge hosts and guests a hotel tax? It seems that the sharing-est of sharing economy companies doesn't want to go out of its way to share its good fortune and instead displays some very un-sharing behavior.

Finally, with the threat of a populist backlash in the form of an anti-Airbnb voter initiative hanging over its head, in February 2015 Airbnb agreed to pay up its back taxes and began collecting the hotel tax from its San Francisco hosts going forward. It turns out it wasn't such a difficult thing to do after all. Yet Airbnb continues to refuse to collect or pay hotel taxes in most of the 34,000 cities around the world where the company claims it is in operation.

In the meantime, much damage has been done to the fabric of San Francisco. Not the least because Theresa and her neighbors have received little help from City Hall. Indeed, San Francisco mayor Ed Lee's chief financial benefactor, Ron Conway, is a Silicon Valley venture capitalist with a significant financial stake in Airbnb. And Conway is not the only local investor banking on Airbnb. Tech investor billionaire Peter Thiel, a politically connected San Francisco resident who cofounded PayPal and owns a big chunk of Airbnb (as well as Facebook), saw his net worth in 2013 shoot up from $1.4 billion to $2.2 billion, as Airbnb's value steadily climbed.[25] Tragically, while the new sharing economy service offered by Airbnb is lucrative for a small number of people, it is forcing out longtime San Franciscans and pushing up rents by shrinking the supply of available housing, particularly rent-controlled apartments, from the permanent housing stock. This is what life has become in a gold rush city, where regulations to protect longtime tenants are not enforced because public officials are in thrall to the *techno sapien* gurus of Silicon Valley.

ACT II—HOMEOWNERS ALONE, MAKING ENDS MEET

The second actor in our drama, Cathryn Blum, I met at San Francisco's City Hall, at a government hearing over what to do about Airbnb's local impact. Inside the massively domed basilica structure that resembles St. Peter's in Rome, the Board of Supervisors (the name for San Francisco's city council) was weighing whether to legalize or crack down on Airbnb hosting in the city. Known as "Catbird," Cathryn is a pleasant, bright-eyed and engaging 60-year-old who makes her living as a "location scout"—if you want to film a movie or TV show in the city, and you need some specific locations for background—a zoo, the ocean or the Golden Gate Bridge—you hire someone like Catbird to scout out your locations. She not only is an expert at locating the right spots but also helps with permit and management services.

Catbird Scouts is the name of her small company, and the nature of her work is freelance—she doesn't always know when and from where the next job will come. She owns her home, a three-floor townhouse with a spectacular view of the San Francisco Bay from the top of Potrero Hill, just south of downtown, so Airbnb has provided a way for her to add another revenue stream to her income. "Airbnb has been a godsend," she tells me. It has allowed her to "monetize" her home, with the revenue from the tourists who stay with her sometimes amounting to thousands of dollars per month. Catbird says this revenue is crucial to her being able to afford to remain living in stratospherically expensive San Francisco.[26]

Homeowners and even some renters using short-term rentals to help pay their mortgage or rent is a point that Airbnb often emphasizes. "For thousands of families, Airbnb makes San Francisco more affordable," spokesperson Nick Papas says, citing a company survey that "56 percent of hosts use their Airbnb income to help pay their mortgage or rent."[27]

But a full-time renter would do that for Catbird and other hosts just as well. With such a critical housing shortage, why not rent out a room to a permanent renter who needs housing, instead of to tourists via Airbnb?

Catbird Blum says that having a full-time housemate has its drawbacks. For example, you can have a bad tenant, and it can be hard to get rid of her or him. She also likes to keep her guestroom vacant sometimes for visiting friends or family. Besides that, says Catbird, Airbnb fits her lifestyle better. She really values meeting visitors from around the world and helping to show them little-known aspects of San Francisco.

She sees a number of other upsides. "It's invigorated a lot of the neighborhoods that tourists might not come and visit," she says. Many parts of the city have no hotels at all, since most of them are concentrated in the downtown area. "We're not competing with the hotels . . . the hotels don't provide our kind of experience."[28]

I asked Catbird about Theresa Flandrich and Diego—what about them? Catbird didn't try to defend the practice of evicting entire buildings, but she did defend her own rights. "My house is my private property. Why shouldn't I be able to do what I want with it?" Private property rights have a strong cultural pull in the U.S., and homeownership is a core part of the American Dream (much more so than in places like Germany and Switzerland, where homeownership rates are around 40–50 percent compared to 64 percent in the U.S.).[29] Home-owning Americans feel entitled to do with their property as they see fit—even if that means denying its use for San Francisco locals who are badly hurt by a chronic shortage of affordable housing. Catbird's attitude is easy to condemn when it's espoused by big landlords evicting entire buildings of elderly and disabled tenants, but when that attitude is coming from homeowners like Catbird, trying to maximize their most important financial asset in order to survive and maintain their lives, things become more complicated.

Catbird and dozens of her fellow Airbnb hosts crowded into the Board of Supervisors chambers. When one supervisor introduced legislation aimed at cracking down on Airbnb for failure to abide by current laws and pay its taxes, Catbird (along with political organizers hired by Airbnb) became a leader of the very vocal opposition. She and others organized themselves into a coalition called Fair to Share comprised of Airbnb, Peers (a nationwide organizing group, initiated by Airbnb, that fights regulations aimed at the sharing economy) and her fellow Airbnb hosts, now rebranded as "homesharers." I sat in the Board of Supervisors' magisterial chambers, surrounded by 360 degrees of golden honey wood paneling carved nearly a century ago of rare Manchurian Oak, listening to speaker after speaker who waited in a long line that bent around the back of the chamber and stretched out the door. Passions were high, much was at stake. Someone remarked about the plaster work above the public speaking area, which includes four demon-like heads. Local legend has it they represent how the public is always making trouble for elected officials.[30]

Today was no exception. Airbnb organizers had rallied the troops, and Catbird and her associates came to praise and defend their brand of "homesharing." They displayed an impressive "Airbnb hosts of the world, unite!" determination, but notably none of them admitted that, like Airbnb, they had not been paying their local hotel taxes as hosts. Nor could Catbird and her fellow homesharers acknowledge that their own personal gain is the flipside of the troubles suffered by Theresa Flandrich and her neighbors. Theresa and some of her group, as well as the tenants union and other housing-justice advocates, also came to the hearing, but they could not match the resources of a billion-dollar company. It's hard to get evicted seniors and disabled people to show up at a City Hall hearing.

Consequently, the testimony that public officials heard was vastly different from reality. Virtually every one of the "homesharers" told the same basic story: that they are just "regular people" who own and live in their home, and occasionally rent out spare rooms to help make ends meet. Under Airbnb's watchful eye, they presented themselves as the face of the company, just everyday San Franciscans who are trying to bring in a few extra bucks in these difficult times. What could be wrong with that?

Here's what's wrong with that: data analysis of Airbnb usage in San Francisco tells a decidedly different story. Although Airbnb refuses to "share" its numbers, a data analysis commissioned by the *San Francisco Chronicle* found that of the nearly 5,000 San Francisco homes, apartments and private or shared rooms for rent via Airbnb, two-thirds are entire houses or apartments with no owner present during the rental period; and almost a third of Airbnb rentals are controlled by people with two or more listings.[31] A separate study conducted by data specialist Tom Slee found results similar to the *Chronicle* study and in addition found that about 70 percent of Airbnb revenue comes from hosts who are renting out an entire home or apartment (as opposed to a private room or shared room in their home or apartment), and 40 percent of revenue comes from Airbnb hosts with multiple listings.[32] In other words, a huge amount of Airbnb revenue in San Francisco does not come from the listings of "regular people" like Catbird who own and live in their homes and are merely renting out a spare room. Instead, an increasing amount comes from the types of professional landlords that are removing housing from the market for local residents, making it exclusively available for tourists. In the process, many of these landlords are getting rid of rent-controlled housing, and even evicting thousands of people like Theresa Flandrich and her neighbors.[33]

An Airbnb representative that I spoke with at length disputes the interpretation of these numbers, saying that just because a listing is for a whole home or apartment and has no owner present doesn't mean it's a listing from a professional landlord. Some people travel a lot for work, he stated, or spend many nights at the home of a girlfriend or boyfriend, and Airbnb their place when they are away for extra income. Airbnb also claims that with San Francisco having 220,000 rental units, the company's 5,000 or so hosts represent too small of a footprint to make a difference on the overall housing market. That sounds reasonable until you realize that, with a vacancy rate in San Francisco of a mere 2.9 percent—around 6,400 units across the entire city—Airbnb is devouring a huge chunk of the city's available vacancies.[34] It is the straw that is breaking the camel's back.

And since Airbnb absolutely refuses to supply any of its own numbers about its hosts and fights all requests for data—unless they are subpoenaed, as in New York (more on that below)—it leaves itself vulnerable to others' interpretations. With the number of Airbnb listings tripling in only two years, the evidence points to, as the *Chronicle* report concluded, "how far Airbnb has come from its couch-surfer origins, contradicting its portrayal as a service for people who rent out a spare room and interact with guests." A significant number of entire homes or apartments are being rented full time or had heavy and constant visitor traffic, "giving weight to arguments that the service is allowing landlords to flout strict rental laws."[35]

If "regular people" as hosts is not the biggest source of revenue for Airbnb, who is? Who are these "nonregular people" hosts on Airbnb?

They are professionals like Annette Fajardo. She is actually a property manager handling Airbnb rentals on behalf of home and condo owners who just want to receive a check for the jacked-up rents without the hassle. So they hire someone like Fajardo to manage their tourist rentals. Demand for Fajardo's business, SF Holiday Rentals, has exploded in recent years. Her team of assistants and accountants manages more than 40 furnished units that guests can book on Airbnb, Roomorama, VRBO, HomeAway, TripAdvisor and Craigslist. She receives about 100 inquiries on her managed properties every day, about half via Airbnb.

"We got Google, Apple—you've got the buses running here all the time," Fajardo told a reporter from the local weekly *Bay Guardian,* from the dining room of a Castro flat she lists for $350 per night on Airbnb. "I get Google people all the time and they spend big bucks."[36] Her clients are owners offering full homes or apartments—all units that have been permanently withdrawn from the local residential rental market. Clearly Fajardo is a very different type of Airbnb "host" than Catbird Blum; she is not the casual homeowner supplementing her income by renting a spare room (and neither are her absentee clients)—she is a professional real estate operative. Not surprisingly, Airbnb does not try to portray her as the face of its business. Indeed, the professionals did not show up at the Board of Supervisors hearing.

Annette Fajardo isn't the only person creating a full-time business out of managing short-term property rentals. Tech entrepreneur Sean Conway created Airenvy, which lists 59 Airbnb properties in San Francisco, has 15 employees and takes a 12 percent cut for handling everything from cleaning to keys.[37] One Airbnb host named Jesse has 85 listings. Casa Buena Vista Rental shows 76 properties on its website.[38] Another host named Bernat has 48 Airbnb listings, which also appear on Come2SF.com. Gaylord Suites, a Tenderloin apartment complex, lists on Airbnb's site at least seven different apartments in the same building. An advertisement in the local *BizJournals* commercial real estate "Hotels & Motels" section offered for sale a modest 1,500-square-foot home in the Outer Sunset neighborhood as an "income producing home" that "grossed $71,452 in 2013, and is solidly booked with increased daily vacation rentals for 2014," said the advert.[39] From the outside, this home is indistinguishable from all the other middle-class homes on the street.

Many of San Francisco's absentee home and condo owners renting their whole-home properties on Airbnb and other websites are wealthy Silicon Valley tech entrepreneurs, Marin County lawyers and doctors and Bay Area executives from ritzy zip codes like Los Altos Hills, Sausalito, Palo Alto, Menlo Park, Hillsborough, Atherton and Lafayette. Some live as far away as New

York City, Hawaii and Hong Kong. Some of their San Francisco homes and condos were listed for short-term rent on Airbnb and VRBO for breathtaking amounts—as much as $7,000 a night.[40] Using data from the Airbnb site, my own investigation found that just over 500 of the nearly 5,000 listings rented for $300 per night or higher—hardly the type of homes lived in by "regular people." In a dense, space-constrained city like San Francisco, these empty condominiums and luxury homes provide plenty of lucrative opportunities for Airbnb, even as they devour precious space that could be used for affordable housing.

Compounding the misery, City Hall utterly failed to anticipate or plan for this housing crisis, a study by the *San Francisco Examiner* revealed. Mayor Ed Lee, as well as previous mayors Gavin Newsom and Willie Brown, buried their heads in the sand while the housing market tilted toward the wealthy under their watches. From 2007 to 2014, over 19,000 new housing units were built in San Francisco, but two-thirds (nearly 13,000) of them sold at prices only affordable to the rich. Five thousand of them (28 percent) were priced for the poor, and only 1,213 (6 percent) were priced for the middle class (middle-class people are ineligible to move into subsidized lower-income housing).[41] Left to its own devices by City Hall's laissez-faire policies, the private housing market became whacked out, badly distorting price signals and resulting in supply failing to meet demand.

The lackadaisical policies also failed to mobilize city regulators as Airbnb's hotelization wave slowly spread across the city. Documents obtained by the 48 Hills investigative website through a Public Records Act request found that regulators had known about the increasing number of illegal rentals since 2011 yet did nothing about it.[42] It should have been a simple matter to look on the Airbnb or VRBO websites and see who the violators were; their websites were virtual advertisements for hosts' criminality (and possibly their own), with homes brightly photographed and openly displayed. But city officials declined to "troll" (as one city memo called it) the websites and adopted an inexplicable hands-off policy of only responding when someone filed a complaint. Despite the fact that thousands of violations were occurring every week, a city planning staffer's memo dated April 4, 2014, noted that only three cases had been sent violation letters, and only 15 cases had been closed since 2012. Could the stunning level of willful complicity have been the result of political interference, many began to wonder? Apparently so. The 48 Hills investigation found a smoking gun of phone calls made from Mayor Ed Lee's office to regulators, with an apparent intent of exerting influence on the regulators.[43]

Finally in April 2014, city attorney Dennis Herrera filed a lawsuit against two property owners accused of evicting longtime tenants, two of them disabled, so the owners could illegally convert the residential buildings into pricey tourist hotels.[44] But it was too little too late. With city government handcuffed by the pressure from real estate developers and Airbnb investors who have reached into the highest levels of government, San Francisco's middle class is being steamrolled and now is embarking on an exodus from the city to less pricey locations across the bay, like Oakland, Berkeley, San Leandro and Richmond. What's left behind in the City of St. Francis increasingly are the rich and what remains of the everyday people who are holding on by their fingernails to a runaway train.[45]

Despite this grim reality, at the Board of Supervisors hearing none of the "regular people" homesharers were willing to cop to owning multiple units that are rented out entirely as hotel rooms, or to renting out whole homes instead of a spare room. Instead, they sang as a chorus, repeating the hit tune of "fair to share" and "homesharers." Airbnb had cleverly maneuvered to make them—not Theresa Flandrich and her neighbors, or Annette Fajardo and Sean Conway—the face of Airbnb that certain gullible elected officials took pity on. Tim Redmond, editor of the 48 Hills blog, commented, "The hearing was almost a farce on one level—the term 'sharing' was bandied around so much that you could almost believe, if this wasn't a huge, lucrative, real-estate operation, that you were at a latter-day hippie convention where the talk was all about peace, love, and international harmony."[46]

The Board of Supervisors eventually passed legislation to legalize Airbnb in San Francisco. They attached a few conditions that hosts will have to follow, including a generous limit on the number of days per year a unit may be short-term rented. But most observers believe that the annual limit will be extremely difficult, if not impossible, to enforce, particularly since the legislation inexplicably failed to require Airbnb to provide the data that would allow enforcement. A San Francisco housing inspector told me, "The Board allocated no new funds or resources for enforcement, and the Planning Commission which was assigned enforcement responsibility is not set up to do this. They don't even *want* to do it." No doubt a major reason that the Planning Commission already had displayed stunning levels of incompetence. One of the new law's requirements said that homesharing hosts had to register with the city, but two months after the deadline a mere 9 percent of Airbnb and VRBO hosts had done so (in part due to insufficient staffing and resources for the registration process).[47] The lobbyists and insider influence in City Hall had prevailed, even as Mayor Ed Lee, the Polonius of Silicon Valley money, trumpeted perversely in his 2015 State of the City address about "unprecedented economic opportunity and prosperity for our City . . . our neighborhoods bustle again with young families."[48]

Mayor Lee had left out the part about Airbnb morphing into a giant loophole for professional real estate operatives, allowing them to weasel out of long-standing city laws that previously had protected the local housing stock by banning short-term tourist rentals. As Bob Dylan once sang, "Money doesn't talk, it swears."

"IT'S UP TO YOU . . . NEW YORK . . . NEW YOOOORKK"

With San Francisco having cowered before the path of the Airbnb tornado, the battle now has shifted to other locales. For it's not just San Francisco where the Airbnb-ing of the local housing market has caused an uproar. Airbnb has been fined in Barcelona (for violating local laws), pilloried in London, its hosts subjected to unannounced inspections in Paris (for being illegal rentals) and finally banned under most circumstances in Berlin (to protect the city's housing stock).[49] In New York, where city and state officials have not rolled over like they did in San Francisco, a battle royal has ensued.

The office of New York state attorney general Eric Schneiderman launched an investigation in New York City, including subpoenaing data from Airbnb and taking them to court. His investigation found that almost half of Airbnb's $1.45 million in revenue came from hosts who had at least three listings on the site.[50] In a story similar to San Francisco's, many Airbnb "hosts" are not in fact "regular people" homeowners merely looking to rent out a spare room; they are professional operators who took on multiple leases in desirable locations, resulting in what the *New York Times* has called the "professionalization" of short-term rental hosting.[51]

Airbnb has about 20,000 listings in New York City (according to data pulled from the Airbnb site). Once it's up and running, an Airbnb rental network can become seriously lucrative. One operation with 272 listings booked $6.8 million in revenue from 2010 through 2014, charging an average of $358 a night. Another signed leases on former factory spaces in Lower Manhattan, renovating them into a beehive of apartments and listing them on Airbnb. The attorney general's report said Airbnb was dominated by large-scale operators, finding that 6 percent of the hosts made 37 percent of the revenue, a whopping $168 million.[52] The number of units the professionals administered ranged from 3 to 272. More worrisome from an affordable housing perspective, the report found that nearly 2,000 units were rented for more than half the year in 2013, taking them effectively off the market for local residents.[53] These rentals accounted for 38 percent of all revenues. The reality is that the market created by the short-term rental services had attracted "a class of well-heeled professional operators who outperform the amateurs," concluded the attorney general's report.

One of those operators, Robert "Toshi" Chan, became an infamous jetsetter as the Airbnb "host" of over 200 apartments in dozens of different buildings known collectively as Hotel Toshi. He leased the apartments from landlords for 20 percent over market rate and then re-rented them as illegal short-term rentals for fabulous amounts on Airbnb. His enterprise was so lucrative that landlords began begging to do business with him.

"I had no idea that the landlords were evicting all of their tenants to give me the space," Toshi claims. "Landlords were coming to me and saying we want you to rent the entire building" because they could get more money from Toshi than from traditional tenants.[54] It was a sleazy operation and his apartments were tourist traps, with complaints mounting on sites like Yelp and TripAdvisor that there were problems with lack of heat, bedbugs, false advertising and rude customer service. As one Yelp reviewer put it, "DO NOT stay here!! This was the worst place I have ever stayed in my life—it's a slum."[55] Eventually Toshi's illegal operation was uncovered and he was shut down and agreed to pay a $1 million settlement for not having proper hotel permits or insurance.[56]

The attorney general's report exposed that nearly three-quarters of all Airbnb rentals in New York City were illegal, violating zoning and other laws, particularly municipal law forbidding short-term rentals of 30 days or less.[57] Confirming the attorney general's report, another study from tech analyst Tom Slee estimated that almost three-quarters of Airbnb's business in New York City comes from whole-home rentals, where the host is absent during the rental period.[58] The attorney general concluded that Airbnb had raked in nearly $40 million on illegal listings that violated zoning laws, cheated the city out of millions of hotel tax dollars and made a select few property owners very wealthy.[59]

Airbnb has tried to defend its practices by ignoring the facts and doubling down with its spin machine, saying that New York City, San Francisco and other uncooperative cities are operating under an "old business model." In a June 2014 interview on national TV with host Katie Couric, CEO Brian Chesky complained that a "lot of the laws are 20th century laws, or sometimes even 19th century laws, in the 21st century."[60] Just as in San Francisco, Airbnb in New York tried to make "regular people" the face of its business, claiming that it "allows longtime residents to stay in their homes by earning just a little extra money to help make ends meet."[61] Like Catbird Blum and others, Airbnb also claimed that it provides rental spaces where hotels are lacking, saying that only 18 percent of its New York rentals are "where the hotels are" (Midtown), while the other 82 percent are "outside of traditional tourist zones." But again, the attorney general's investigation found a different story: just three areas in Manhattan—Lower East Side/Chinatown, Chelsea/Hell's Kitchen and Greenwich Village/SoHo—accounted for 40 percent of revenue, or $187 million, while reservations in outlying boroughs

Queens, Staten Island and the Bronx accounted for only 3 percent, or $12 million.

After a city council hearing in January 2015, New York state assemblywoman Linda Rosenthal, who represents the Upper West Side of Manhattan, blasted Airbnb, saying, "This company is trying to create a 'sharing economy' . . . one in which their hosts contribute to the loss of affordable housing while the company 'shares' in the profits of its illegal enterprise. Like a marauding army, Airbnb is flooding the market in this city and cities across the country with illegal units, and after its incursion is complete, it comes to the government claiming ignorance and begs to be carved out of the laws that protect tenants and affordable housing."[62]

Complicating the New York City housing landscape, roughly 75 percent of the Manhattan housing inventory is comprised of co-ops that, unlike a condo or apartment, are owned by a corporation composed of its members. The history of housing co-ops in New York City goes back to at least the 1920s, when many were sponsored by trade unions such as the Amalgamated Clothing Workers of America. They are serious about protecting affordable housing for their members, and so the rules for co-op buildings are significantly more intensive than for condos or apartments.[63] Generally, guests are limited to immediate friends and family, and subletting is not permitted. Co-ops have near-universally come out against allowing Airbnb rentals within their buildings and have been laying down the law and writing warning memos.

One co-op resident who had hoped to Airbnb his apartment while on vacation complained that he received "a two-page letter under the door forbidding its tenants and shareholders from becoming Airbnb hosts." To drive home the point, his co-op threatened serious consequences: a $1,000 fine, eviction, and even jail time for contempt of court. That might sound harsh, but the rationale of his co-op board reads like a manifesto of why so many neighborhoods all across the country are vehemently opposed to Airbnb hotels in their proximity: "This building is our home and not meant to be treated as a hotel, B&B or weekend getaway for others . . . illegal subletting to strangers not only compromises the safety and environment of our building, it is unfair to fellow shareholders who follow the rules."[64] Many co-ops have begun actively monitoring Airbnb's website to identify rule breakers, as well as tightening building security, asking doormen to scrutinize visitors and requiring residents to sign authorization forms for guests.[65]

Housing co-ops can be a powerful political force in New York politics, so the politicians feel more emboldened than in San Francisco. At a press conference, Attorney General Schneiderman dismissed Airbnb's public-relations spin, saying that it presents itself as a useful and virtuous company helping "regular people," but the reality is far less benign. Unlike San Francisco officials, who rolled over and refused to enforce the law despite massive numbers of violations, Schneiderman pledged a crackdown saying, "a slick advertising campaign doesn't change the fact that this is illegal activity."[66] Councilman Mark Levine agreed, adding, "Despite whatever claims Airbnb has made that resident hosts are the majority of rental listings, this is 100 percent false."[67]

So the raw data in both New York City and San Francisco decisively refute the "regular people" portrayal of Airbnb by either company PR flaks or its defenders like the well-meaning Catbird Blum and her associates. But what about other U.S. cities? How has the Airbnb tornado worked out there?

In Los Angeles, a study of Airbnb listings by the Los Angeles Alliance for a New Economy (LAANE) found that while a majority of the 8,400 hosts were the mythical "regular people" renting a spare room in their home, those rentals generated just 11 percent of the company's Los Angeles revenue. The other 89 percent was generated by professional landlords and agencies and those renting out an entire home or apartment rather than a spare room.[68] One apartment building with 227 units in downtown Los Angeles had 20 percent of its units listed on Airbnb; "Danielle and Lexi," two young women hosts with an Airbnb "verified ID" and a photo and personal note, turned out to be a front for Ghc vacation property rentals.[69]

The LAANE study found that more than 7,000 houses and apartments had been removed from the rental market in metro Los Angeles for use as short-term rentals. Touristy Hollywood, Santa Monica and hipster beach town Venice have been particularly devastated. A *Los Angeles Times* data analysis of Airbnb's website found that in Venice, Hollywood and other tourist-magnet neighborhoods, Airbnb listings accounted for anywhere from 4 to 7 percent of all housing units, concluding that this was "worsening a housing shortage." The Venice Neighborhood Council sent a letter to city officials saying that the number of short-term rentals in Venice had tripled in only a year, condemning the "Gold Rush mentality" among investors. "It's making places like Santa Monica and Venice totally priced out. Silver Lake is impossible," complained a frustrated tenant trying to find a long-term rental.[70] Undermining Airbnb's typical claim that it "distributes economic impacts to neighborhoods that have not traditionally benefited from tourism spending," the LAANE report found that in fact Airbnb hosts were concentrated in just nine of the city's 95 neighborhoods, generating 73 percent of the company's LA revenue, with 23 percent generated in hard-hit Venice alone.[71] And of course, all of these Airbnb and other short-term rental listings are illegal, since they violate LA's laws against short-term residential rentals and pay no hotel tax.

Finally Santa Monica officials, fed up with the rampant hotelization of their beach town by the Airbnb-ing professionals, passed a law explicitly outlawing rentals of less than 30 days, though permitting the renting of a spare room as long as hosts followed certain licensing requirements and paid the city's 14 percent hotel tax.[72]

Similar problems were discovered in a study of Airbnb in Portland, Oregon, and show how resistant the company is to compliance with regulations. The Portland city council had worked with Airbnb to pass a law legalizing much of its activity, but requiring hosts to register for a license to operate and submit to fire and safety inspections. But like in San Francisco, a month after the deadline, only 6 percent of Portland's 1,959 hosts had registered, according to the local newspaper *Willamette Week*. An investigative report that scraped the Airbnb website for data found that 39 percent of Airbnb hosts had multiple listings and that 75 percent of hosts made their entire homes or apartments available for at least half the year, a clear violation of Portland's new law (which allowed hosts to Airbnb their homes if they reside in them for at least nine months per year).[73] Another study found that in Chicago, San Diego and Los Angeles, about half of guest visits as well as revenue came from hosts with multiple listings—not "regular-people" hosts, but professionals.[74]

How about cities outside the U.S., in Airbnb's far-flung global operation? Using the same statistical methods from his San Francisco and New York studies, Tom Slee collected data on over 90,000 hosts and 125,000 listings—about a fifth of Airbnb's total at the time—from 18 major cities all over the world, to draw a portrait of Airbnb's global business.[75] His findings are illuminating and follow the pattern found in San Francisco, New York City, Los Angeles, Portland and other U.S. cities. Forty-four percent of Airbnb's revenue and 45 percent of guest visits in these 18 cities came from hosts with multiple listings. In certain cities, including Rome, Barcelona, Tokyo, Mexico City, Rio de Janeiro and others, 60 percent or more of guest visits came from hosts with multiple listings, with London and Berlin showing a 50–50 split. In addition, more than half of Airbnb's revenue in these 18 cities came from whole-home rentals, instead of from rentals of spare rooms. In certain cities—Paris, London and others—70 to 80 percent of revenue was coming from whole-home rentals.[76]

The evidence from all over the world, San Francisco to New York to Paris to Berlin, is compellingly clear: Airbnb has offered as the face of its company this "regular people" standard, those who host guests in their spare rooms or on couches to make some extra money. Yet the data does not support this view. Quite the opposite, it shows how far Airbnb has drifted from its "origin myth" of couch surfing and extra-room renting. Slee concluded, "It turns out there is an element of wishful thinking in the [self] portraits of Airbnb," which he accused of being "consistently economical with the truth." There is "a lot more business coming from multiple-listing owners than they let on," which "casts further doubt on the company's claim to be a new class of business." In actual fact, Airbnb has become "much more like HomeAway and other vacation rental businesses." The "couch-surfing" narrative often used by the media to describe Airbnb's business is no longer accurate.

Not only is it not accurate, but Airbnb has its own data crunchers and is surely aware of the trajectory of its business. That means Airbnb strategists are cynically deploying the heartwarming stories of a few of its "regular-people" hosts as the cover for what increasingly is its real business: enabling professional landlords and multiproperty agents who displace tenants, undermine rent-control laws and gobble up affordable housing for permanent residents, thereby turning cities into broken patchworks of tourist hotels that avoid municipal regulations around safety, fire inspections, taxes and zoning.

And what about Catbird and all her fellow "homesharers"? On the one hand, I have sympathy for their attempts to do what they think they must to make ends meet. American homeowners are understandably very proprietary and protective of their biggest capital investment. And yet, on the other hand, they have become very vocal participants in a form of class warfare. People with property seeking to rent to tourists—even the little guys and gals like Catbird—are being pitted against those without property—renters and permanent residents—in a city like San Francisco that is composed of two-thirds renters, as well as in New York, LA and all across the world.

It's crucially important to recognize that if the only hosts were people like Catbird who owned and lived in their own home and occasionally rented out a room in that home, nobody would object that much. But that would make Airbnb much less valuable to investors waiting for a mammoth IPO to bust this out into a bigger success story than Facebook. After all, says San Francisco tenant attorney Joe Tobener, Airbnb has all the data from its website to figure out who the professional landlords and agents are—which ones are renting out multiple units, which ones are renting out entire houses. "They could pull this data and tell us, but they don't."[77] With one stroke of the computer mouse, Airbnb even could "evict the evictors"—proactively expel the professional landlords, tourist hotels and multiproperty agents from its website. But that would wipe out a large part of its business model and growth market. In New York City they finally did this to a few of the most egregious offenders, but only after the attorney general subpoenaed the company's records. Most of the time the company has displayed a clear pattern of foot-dragging, doing as little as possible and only when pushed by regulators and public outcry over its behavior. Brian Chesky can preach all he wants about sharing, trust and belonging, but he and his investors have shown no willingness to kill their golden goose, despite the damage that greedy professional landlords and multiproperty agents are causing to the very fabric of the cities where they operate.

That's not "sharing." It's just raw, naked capitalism.

IS AIRBNB WHO THEY SAY THEY ARE?

Besides bending the law, usually avoiding tax payments and catalyzing the disruption of the local housing market and eviction of vulnerable tenants, Airbnb and other short-term rental brokerages raise other issues of safety, whether in neighborhoods or with its customers. Hotels are inspected for fire and safety code compliance, but Airbnb's hosts' homes are not. When asked about this by Katie Couric, Brian Chesky responded, not by discussing procedures for verification and compliance, but by claiming that . . . Airbnb offers free smoke and carbon monoxide detectors to hosts. "We want to be a gold standard," he said, managing to keep a straight face. But when Couric pushed a bit further about how Airbnb ensures that hosts comply with fire and safety regulations, Chesky hemmed and hawed and talked about their "self-administered" system. Then he not-so-deftly changed the topic, saying, "We want to make sure that the codes and regulations are modernized, so that [regulators] recognize that people's homes are not hotels. These are not hotels, they should be regulated like houses."[78]

But like so many of the company's other PR bromides, this one was only so much mouthwash. As an "undercover" Airbnb host—see more on that below—I decided to take Chesky up on his "gold standard" offer of receiving a free and "self-administered" smoke and carbon monoxide detector. I requested one via the Airbnb website, and my query received the briefest of email responses directing me to a particular Airbnb webpage.[79] But on that page, instead of offering me a free detector it offered me a free "Emergency Safety Card," saying I could use it to "list emergency numbers, exit routes, and other resources" for my guests. Apparently the offer for a free smoke detector had expired—though the Airbnb representative didn't bother mentioning that.[80] Nor did the fast-talking Brian Chesky mention an expiration date in his interview with Katie Couric. Apparently Airbnb's fire and safety compliance program for its hosts also has expired.

Airbnb also has refused to take responsibility for the "creep factor"—it is such an open platform, anyone can register their living space as a rental. Sex offenders, pedophiles, serial rapists—there are no background checks for hosts and no inspections of rental properties. "We do not attempt to confirm, and do not confirm, any Member's purported identity," Airbnb states in its terms of service. "You are responsible for determining the identity and suitability of others." Its competitor Roomorama, which has a model similar to

Airbnb, has instituted a formal host verification process. "Our host verification is very tight," explained CEO Jia En Teo to the *Bay Guardian*. "When a host is listed on our site, they don't go live immediately. They go through a quality control and validation process. We have a team that will call the host and ask for utility bills and ID. We do due diligence."[81]

Chesky told Katie Couric that it has 100 employees devoted exclusively to trust and safety[82] and that "hosts verify their IDs by connecting to their social networks and scanning their official ID or confirming personal details."[83] So to test Airbnb's system, I signed up as a host. I took a few photos of my house, inside and out, and within 15 minutes my place was "live" as an Airbnb rental. No background check, no verifying my ID, no confirming my personal details, no questions asked. Not even any contact with a real human from their trust and safety team. Nothing. I could have been the next San Francisco Zodiac psychopath, signing up as a host. I could have used photos of my neighbor's house, or even photos saved from the website of *Better Homes and Gardens*. Within an hour, I had my first inquiry from a potential guest. Within a couple of months, I had over a dozen reservation requests that would have netted me over $4,000 in short-term rental income. I was both impressed and appalled at how easy Airbnb's website made it.

Besides the hosts, Airbnb has no quality control over the types of guests. Neighbors suddenly find themselves living next door to a short-term rental where complete strangers are traipsing in and out, keeping tourist hours, in close proximity to children, seniors and other vulnerable populations. That's true of hotels as well, but hotels generally exist in areas that have been zoned for such activity. With Airbnb and short-term rentals, strangers are now lodging in neighborhoods throughout the city.

Not surprisingly, neighbors regularly complain about noise and nuisance from an ongoing parade of complete strangers living next door. Some of those guests have engaged in rather unneighborly behavior, such as prostitution rings, orgies, meth addict parties, assaults, property theft, identity theft, ransacked apartments, apartments fraudulently rented out from under the real owner and other criminal acts.[84] Other guests arrive to their Airbnb rental only to discover that the gorgeous photos on the website hardly match reality. In most cases, requests for help from Airbnb by the abused party—whether a guest or a host—elicits a slow, begrudging response, if any. In some cases, Airbnb has provided some site credit, but complainants find that Airbnb leaders seem to be more concerned about the bad publicity from these incidents than either making restitution or instituting better policies. In one high-profile case, an Airbnb customer whose home was destroyed and looted by a guest found Airbnb to be mostly unresponsive to her appalling experience until she started to blog about it.[85] Then, she says, CEO Brian Chesky himself personally phoned her—only to try and pressure her to delete her post about her nightmare experience because of the negative impact it might have on the perception of his company, which could affect its growth and potential fundraising.[86]

After many public complaints, as well as concerns from public officials, the company finally began providing a $1 million "Host Guarantee" backed by Lloyd's of London. But in a now-familiar Airbnb style, that insurance comes with many conditions and a vague disclaimer that it "should not be considered as a replacement or stand-in for homeowners or renters insurance. The Host Guarantee does not cover: cash and securities, collectibles, rare artwork, jewelry, pets, personal liability."[87] It's not actually clear what it *does* cover. Also it is "secondary," meaning hosts have to make initial claims to their own insurers, even though many insurance companies forbid commercial activity and even have threatened to cancel the policies of homeowners who turn their homes into a hotel. Finally, Airbnb's liability coverage doesn't extend outside the United States, which became a major problem for Mike Silverman, a 58-year-old American whose arm got severely mauled in Argentina by a host's Rottweiler, resulting in a six-square-inch gash that ripped open the artery and tendons and required a two-night stay in a hospital.

Silverman contacted Airbnb, requesting reimbursement for his medical bills and additional lodging costs. All he received was the typical email response denying fault and offering to refund money for his stay. "Unfortunately, per our terms of service, we are unable to consider any request for compensation in a liability scenario such as this." But, the company assured him, it valued him as a guest and wished him well in his recovery.

However, when a *New York Times* reporter contacted Airbnb about this incident, and the possibility of bad press loomed, suddenly Airbnb interpreted its "terms of service" quite differently. The company offered to cover Silverman's medical bills and other incurred expenses. The badly injured guest, a technology and strategy consultant who had used Airbnb many times and previously had praised the service, suddenly understood why a hospitality company like Airbnb should include protection for both their hosts and for the guests. "They seem to want to deny that they are in the business that they are in," said Silverman. In the hundreds of reader comments accompanying the *Times* article, numerous readers testified to having problems with an Airbnb rental, including having their valuable property like laptops stolen, only to have Airbnb give them the same "not in our terms of service" kiss-off.[88]

Of course, even the limp Host Guarantee doesn't cover the impact done to neighborhoods. Neighbors used to have a reasonable expectation that they had the right not to be living next door to a hotel with strange guests coming and going. That's one of the reasons cities have zoning laws and restrictions. But Airbnb and other short-term rental agencies have disrupted the peace and tranquility of these hotelized neighborhoods, and that of the families and residents who live in them.

ACT III—THE CEO OF TRUST AND BELONGING

Which brings us to the third actor in this passion play, Mr. Brian Chesky himself. A former bodybuilder and graduate of the Rhode Island School of Design, Chesky's rise has been remarkable. A video floating around online of Chesky's commencement speech that he gave at his college graduation shows, if nothing else, major amounts of chutzpah. The future cofounder and CEO of Airbnb struts on stage in full cap and gown to the throbbing bass line of Michael Jackson's "Billie Jean" and proceeds to rip off his black graduation gown, revealing a white tuxedo underneath. He starts clumsily moonwalking and crotch-grabbing to the beat, before delivering his address to his classmates, families and faculty. His speech is more entertaining than profound, mixing quips, funny one-liners and even occasional bodybuilder flexes with a 22-year-old's version of wisdom. The young man in the video is working hard to be liked, is slightly grandiose but also self-aware enough to say that he is uncertain of his future (with an art and design degree, after all), and confident enough to relish his moment on the graduation stage. He displays definite leadership qualities, kind of like a head cheerleader urging on his homies at their final big hurrah.[89]

That was in 2004, and now in his new role, the chutzpah, leadership and cheerleading have remained and come to the fore. When Chesky spoke at a hospitality conference sponsored by the University of San Francisco in April 2014, he offered no acknowledgment of the complexities, much less the downsides, of his business model. People like Theresa Flandrich and her neighbors are not on his radar. Instead, rather unbelievably, he cast his company into another role in this script—that of the blue helmets saving the world.

"It's like the United Nations at every kitchen table. It's very powerful," said Chesky.[90] In the masthead of his company, Chesky has assumed the role of Ideologist-in-Chief. His early interviews as CEO, viewable on YouTube, show an awkward young man, wide-eyed, hands flailing, who scarcely can believe his and his cofounders' good fortune. He has an "aw shucks" charm so that when he says, in response to some difficult questions, "We understand that's a problem, we're looking into it, we still haven't figured that out, we're still a new company," he conveys a ring of naïve authenticity. But several years later, as the same old questions became more pointed and specific, Chesky's vague responses come off as evasive.

It's not just that Airbnb refuses to be responsive to the increasingly wide path of destruction it is hewing. It's also that Chesky wraps it all into a New Age-y kind of rap about trust, sharing, community and belonging. In early 2014, Chesky and his cofounders took a deep breath from their incredible success story to reconsider their mission; that led to the launch of a new symbol and branding for their company in July 2014. Chesky posted his thoughts about the newly revamped Airbnb, an 1,100-word sermon to his public translated into eight different languages that, like his college graduation speech, was another revealing moment into the character and fiber of this young phenom.

"Joe, Nate, and I did some soul-searching over the last year," wrote Chesky. "We asked ourselves, 'What is our mission? What is the big idea that truly defines Airbnb?' It turns out the answer was right in front of us. People thought Airbnb was about renting houses. But really, we're about home. You see, a house is just a space, but a home is where you belong. And what makes this global community so special is that for the very first time, you can belong anywhere. That is the idea at the core of our company: belonging."[91]

Like that young, slightly presumptuous college speaker holding forth at center stage, Chesky then goes on to wrap his company's growing commercial empire in a grandiose vision that he positions as a solution to a civilization gone awry, indeed as a reaction to the wrongful drift of history.

"We used to take belonging for granted. Cities used to be villages," wrote Chesky. "Everyone knew each other, and everyone knew they had a place to call home. But after the mechanization and Industrial Revolution of the last century, those feelings of trust and belonging were displaced by mass-produced and impersonal travel experiences. We also stopped trusting each other. And in doing so, we lost something essential about what it means to be a community."

Like a newly converted evangelical, Chesky explicitly tries to tap into a rich, red vein filled with the loneliness and isolation of this modern life. He does this as a bid to position his company as more than simply a hospitality business: it's a vehicle for building a global movement, a community of trust and sharing. But not of spiritual renewal or to provide humanitarian aid, or to end human rights abuses, as previous visionaries have tried to do—no, Brian Chesky's revolutionary act is . . . a commercial transaction . . . providing short-term rentals to tourists.

"Like us, you may have started out thinking you were just renting out a room to help pay the bills . . . the rewards you get from Airbnb aren't just financial—they're personal—for hosts and guests alike. At a time when new technologies have made it easier to keep each other at a distance, you're using them to bring people together. And you're tapping into the universal human yearning to belong—the desire to feel welcomed, respected, and appreciated for who you are, no matter where you might be. Belonging is the idea that defines Airbnb. . . . Airbnb is returning us to a place where everyone can feel they belong."

Chesky ends his Hallmark greeting card homily by signing off humbly with his first name: "I look forward to starting the next chapter of this improbable journey with the idea that first set it in motion—the belief that belonging can take us anywhere.—Brian"

It's akin to channeling John Lennon's "Imagine" and merging it with a hotel business. It's even more audacious than Nike's "Just Do It" or Apple's "Think Different." It simultaneously attempts to mine feelings of loneliness and isolation, a longing for community, a sense of history and an economy gone off the rails, as well as the desire for travel to exotic places—and merge all that with a real and growing financial need among Airbnb hosts in difficult economic times to use their own property—their home—to make money. To "monetize" their lives and their loneliness. It certainly is one of the most brilliant marketing pitches ever conceived.

Like any true evangelical, Brian Chesky seems to sincerely believe his newfound faith. But like so many fundamentalists of one kind or another, he is blinded by it. He deletes from his picture whatever fact or story doesn't fit. In his talk at the University of San Francisco conference, Chesky crowed, "For us to win, no one has to lose," and like that college commencement speaker he champions his "on-message" message with such a boyishly good-natured enthusiasm that audience members key into the hipness and coolness of his rosy version of the world. Yet sadly, Chesky has rendered invisible all those people like Theresa Flandrich and so many others across the city—across the world—who in fact are not winning and are being evicted under the housing pressures that Airbnb is contributing to. He ignores all the upset neighbors who have some pretty strong feelings about the hotelization of their neighborhoods. He slickly hides the fact that, increasingly, "regular people" are not the core of his business; in fact the core comes from professional landlords and multiproperty agents who rent vacation rentals to tourists and convert entire residential apartment buildings to tourist hotels, even if they have to evict elderly and sick people to do it. Indeed, he ignores all the disappearing apartments and housing stock and rising rents, not all of it attributable to Airbnb, but his company has become a key catalytic factor.

Brian Chesky and the rest of Airbnb's executives and venture-capitalist backers seem to feel little responsibility for upending so many people's lives. They are either oblivious to the destruction, or they have rationalized it away as the necessary collateral damage for their "sharing revolution." The contradiction between his professed revolutionary mission and his investors' demands seems not to have dawned on him—that a true community breaks down as it scales and grows larger, until finally it reaches the point where it makes a mockery of what it believes and the reasons for which it was founded.

Perhaps the biggest tragedy in all this is that at the core of Airbnb is a really good idea—it has cleverly used Web- and app-based technology to bust open a global market that connects tourists with financially strapped homeowners. After interviewing some of Airbnb's "regular-people" hosts, I'm convinced that this service legitimately does help them make ends meet. But by taking such a hands-off, laissez-faire attitude toward the professionalization of hosting by greedy commercial landlords and multiproperty agents, Airbnb has become its own worst enemy. As the number of victims piles up, it undermines its own "sharing and trust" ethos.

If Airbnb and Chesky really believed in that ethos, the company could partner with local governments and tenants associations to draft laws that take account of this new business model, saying, "Look, here's model legislation for how to regulate this so that the professionals are shut out and the 'regular people' are empowered." Chesky could delist the professional landlords and multiproperty agents from the Airbnb site, severely limiting their ability to turn badly needed housing into tourist hotels. He could forbid any professional agency from listing or managing the listing of another person on the Airbnb website, which would crack down on absentee hosts; he could cooperate with cities who require hosts to register by delisting any unregistered hosts; his company could pay hotel taxes in all 34,000 cities in which it operates, or collect it from the hosts, and supply the anonymized data that cities need to enforce regulations and taxation, including how many nights and rates have been charged by each host. This is not rocket science; all that's needed is the will. But Chesky doesn't do any of that because doing so would cut into his core business.[92]

Airbnb is not the only short-term rental service causing this disruption, but it is by far the largest, and therefore the greatest beneficiary of the regulatory chaos. No competitor comes close to Airbnb's market share.[93] And for those cities and places where there is not such a severe housing crisis, particularly those that are not such magnets for tourists, the urgency might not be as great as for cities like San Francisco, New York, Paris, London, Barcelona, Los Angeles and more. So that further narrows the scope of what Airbnb must do and where it must target its efforts to redeem its business model and reputation. It really wouldn't take very much for Brian Chesky and Airbnb to prove wrong the critics like Steve Jones, former editor of the progressive weekly *San Francisco Bay Guardian,* who has bluntly stated, "Airbnb and its young founders just don't seem to give a fuck."[94]

At this point, it's just feral capitalism, and there is little "sharing" about it. Casting even more skepticism on Airbnb's and its boosters' "sharing" claims is the fact that, before there was Airbnb with its $25 billion in market valuation there was the noncommercial platform Couch Surfing, where individuals host each other in their own homes with no money exchanged, and it was a nonprofit that provided a valuable coordination service. And today there is Love Swap Home, which facilitates vacation swaps between people with attractive homes and others they meet on the website. Founder Debbie Wosskow says their business model is "like online dating for homes," contrasting it with Airbnb's profit-making by saying, "We're swapping purists. . . . I was less interested in turning my home into a money-making machine than moving my home to places around the world."[95]

Indeed, we know Airbnb understands how to follow a truly "sharing" model, because when Superstorm Sandy devastated New York City, Airbnb partnered with Mayor Michael Bloomberg to offer free housing for many displaced New Yorkers. Airbnb built a dedicated website for this effort, where victims registered for housing and got connected with property owners offering free housing. Airbnb says that 1,400 hosts opened their doors and cooked meals for those left stranded.[96] Airbnb was so impressed with its own nonprofit effort that it repeated it in San Diego in response to major fires; in Toronto and Atlanta following severe ice storms; in Serbia, Bosnia, Croatia, London, Sardinia and Colorado after serious flooding; and in the Philippines following Typhoon Haiyan.[97]

These and other examples show that you can use these Web- and app-based platforms to do something truly "sharing" and useful when no one has a primary motivation of making gobs of profit. It shows that a true sharing economy with communitarian benefits does not require injections of massive amounts of cash from venture capitalists. Real experiences with these still-new platforms are showing us that there are "good" sharing economy companies and there are "bad" ones.

Unquestionably, Airbnb's rise from its humble beginnings in Brian Chesky and Joe Gebbia's apartment living room is a remarkable story, a made-in-America rags-to-riches fable. But it's clear that Airbnb, like Uber and Lyft (which we will consider in the next chapter) and other venture-funded "sharing economy" companies, has a different goal entirely besides "sharing." It's called profit—they want you to share *your* home or *your* car with paying guests, while they skim off the top a sizable amount of each and every transaction, all the while keeping their overhead low and providing relatively few jobs (a thousand employees worldwide is miniscule for a company with a $25 billion valuation—Hyatt Hotels employs about 45,000 people worldwide).[98] It may seem like a typically winning formula, but investors beware: Airbnb is a ticking time bomb of contradictions, promoting illegal rentals and tax avoidance that at some point may blow up.

Airbnb and the other short-term rental brokerages are hardly businesses that will help smooth the transition of the U.S. workforce to a progressive version of a freelance society. Just the opposite, they have become another merchant of rentier capitalism, siphoning off profit from the property and labor of others while increasing the anxiety and crisis of many working- and middle-class people. Airbnb's disruption of the hospitality industry has pushed down prices for tourists but at the cost of hurting those "regular people" too vulnerable to defend themselves. Apparently for Brian Chesky and his cofounder Joe Gebbia, making some tweaks to their business model—in a true spirit of sharing and caring, and of leading a *real* sharing and belonging economy—is incompatible with what they believe is necessary to lead a large company locked into a single-minded focus on revenue growth and market share. That's because an IPO still awaits, and global market share is paramount in that drive. Airbnb is focused on expansion, and the rentiers from the Rhode Island School of Design seem to care little about who is steamrolled in their path.

THREE

THE TICKING TIME BOMB OF UBER

IF AIRBNB IS THE "BELONGING" COMPANY OF THE SHARING ECONOMY, THE ridesharing business Uber is its "take-no-prisoners" counterpart. Uber also has become a global as well as a grassroots phenomenon, its impressive growth in a few short years to some 300 cities and 58 countries striking fear into the hearts of taxi companies everywhere. Occasionally a CEO comes along—Steve Jobs, Bill Gates, Larry Ellison—whose personality so imprints his (or rarely, her) company that the two become inseparable in the public's mind, as well as within the culture of the company. Uber founder and now-billionaire Travis Kalanick is such a CEO—for better and worse. He is the reigning bad boy of "wild west" capitalism, breaking livery laws, raiding competitors and spouting controversy wherever he goes. As one entrepreneur who has worked with him says, "Travis is ego personified." Others have described him more pointedly: "He's an asshole."[1]

But he has driven his company to the top of something remarkable—though no one is quite sure yet what that something is. Kalanick sees himself as a kind of Ayn Randian revolutionary and has said he thinks that Uber isn't just competing against taxis and other ridesharing companies, but against private car ownership itself. He aims to make Uber's network of drivers—and eventually, he hopes, driverless cars—a revolutionary logistics platform on which businesses could send packages, food and other products. It's about making "car ownership a thing of the past,"[2] says Kalanick.

But that's still down the road a ways, and in the meantime, Uber—like Airbnb—already is reaching legendary icon status, becoming a household name and a new verb and noun in our vocabulary. The company is being hailed by many free marketeers as the new "disruptive" kid on the block, overturning conventional business models, in this case the corrupt monopoly of Big Taxi, and bringing innovation to the important transportation sector.

It has grown at an astonishing pace since its launch in San Francisco in 2009, and with big backers like Goldman Sachs, Blackrock, Amazon's Jeff Bezos and Google Ventures, it has succeeded in attracting one of the largest direct investments in a startup company in U.S. history. In the murky world of Silicon Valley, where hype and "vaporware" often substitute for substance, Uber has been assessed a jaw-dropping market valuation of $51 billion—to put that in perspective, that's higher than Facebook's valuation at a similar point in its growth, is greater than Delta ($39 billion) and United Airlines ($26 billion), and has nearly overtaken the king itself, General Motors, the largest U.S. automaker ($52.6 billion value). Not bad for a company that doesn't actually *make* anything or own any cars or directly employ any drivers (since the drivers are all treated as independent contractors).

But as we will see, like the villain Harvey "Two-Face" Dent in the *Batman* comics, there is a dark, scabbish side to Uber's pretty face. Driven by Kalanick's pedal-to-the-metal tactics, Uber has lurched from scandal to scandal, which not only has undermined its popularity but also has served to obscure the merits of the ridesharing industry. So far, the ridesharing business is not nearly as disruptive to society as is Airbnb's ravaging of entire urban neighborhoods and real estate markets, and therein lies Uber's advantage. Few people are going to shed tears over a torpedoing of the taxi industry, since it has long been known for cartelism, political payola and lousy service.

In fact, as the U.S. plunges headlong toward a freelance society, and average Americans start casting around for any kind of reliable way to "monetize" their lives and bring in some income, peer-to-peer ridesharing holds potential—but only if it's done the right way. As Kalanick fully knows, the supply of drivers and cars on the road is the bottleneck in this industry, and those drivers' needs are in direct conflict with Kalanick's ambitions. Uber's business model seems to depend on driver exploitation and legal loopholes. As one fed-up ex-Uber driver said, the company does everything it can "to distance themselves from what they created," which is "an app-based taxi service for non-professional, unregulated and underinsured drivers."[3] But drivers won't have to form unions to win concessions—the software makes it possible for drivers to easily shift to other ridesharing companies, or, as the ridesharing software becomes commonplace, for groupings of them even to start their own companies.[4] Even as Uber pugnaciously fights any type of common-sense regulation, this ridesharing service is crying out for well-targeted oversight that minimizes exploitation of drivers, ensures the safety of the public, reduces price gouging and cracks down on abuse of the new ridesharing technology and its surveillance capabilities.

Yet all the warning signs indicate that Travis Kalanick is not interested in building such a company. His Uber is not about empowering either its drivers or the 1099 perma-lancers of the freelance society, and he is dismissive of concerns about privacy or public safety. Instead, this "sharing" economy company is about maximizing market share in its greed-grab to wipe out all competitors and achieve global domination of the ridesharing industry. Like Airbnb, Uber is polishing its gloss in preparation for a high-flying IPO, and it doesn't seem to care how many laws are broken in the process. Indeed, Uber's CEO has been criminally charged in South Korea with operating an illegal taxi service, and officials have threatened to seek an arrest warrant against him; in Amsterdam, Uber's European headquarters, the authorities raided the taxi app's office in March 2015, and Uber has been fined and banned.[5] Around the world and across the U.S., Uber has hit major regulatory obstacles. Despite its astounding early success, Uber is becoming its own bubble that seems likely to burst. The company is walking a tightrope, led by its notorious CEO, Travis Kalanick.

THE TASMANIAN DEVIL OF TAXIS

When I exit the Uber car that is dropping me off in downtown San Francisco—the first time I have ridden in an Uber car, as research for this book—a couple of impressions strike me. The car is clean, and the driver is polite with a youthful swagger. He looks to be in his late twenties, sporting Van Dyke facial hair and an "I'm the bass player in a rock band" kind of hip. When I met him at the base of my stairway leading to the street, he had been kicking a hackie sack while waiting for me to emerge from my home. On our journey he tells me that he drives part time, and Uber has been a good gig for making extra money. (He's not in a rock band, but he is studying graphic design and hopes to be an artist or illustrator one day.)

Secondly, the drive experience is pretty much identical to being driven by a taxi. I'm being chauffeured, I'm being charged per mile, San Francisco's sun-dappled, multicolored neighborhoods are whizzing by. The car does not have a meter, where I can watch the price racking up, which I've always kind of liked, but that's okay because the app has provided me an estimate of what it will likely cost (unless it's a time of peak demand, when prices can spike tenfold—more on that later). The app has a nice feature, in that when I am waiting for a car to arrive, I can track its progress on a map on my smartphone and see it heading my way. But in the age of smartphones, Google maps and instant GPS, that seems like a given these days, and taxi companies also are starting to incorporate that feature. One clear difference is that I summoned Uber with an iPhone app instead of calling a dispatch. But all in all, I conclude, yep, Uber is a taxi. This new "revolutionary" industry has just swapped an app for a telephone. No big deal.

But Travis Kalanick doesn't like it when journalists call Uber just another taxi company. The taxi industry is heavily regulated, and the prickly Kalanick has no use for regulations or paying taxes. "I'm in the technology industry,"[6] he told the *Boston Globe,* and the tech industry has always seen itself as a meritocracy where innovation and "getting there first" win, and government bureaucracy and rust are evil. At 39 years of age, and a UCLA dropout with perennial stubble and Marine-style salt-and-pepper hair, Kalanick is a laissez-faire capitalist who once chose the cover of Ayn Rand's *The Fountainhead* as his Twitter profile picture. His "Travis Shrugged"[7] persona projects a jet-setting, frat-house boyishness that switches easily from talking about the self-styled transportation revolution he believes he is fomenting to Twitter photos of him partying with rapper Snoop Dogg,[8] or bragging about his newfound billionaire's ability to bag nubile hotties as easily as he can summon an Uber car: "Yeah, we call that Boob-er," he told *GQ.*[9]

Welcome to Travis's World.

It's true that Uber is not in the taxi business, at least not in the conventional sense. It does not own any cabs, and has no cab drivers as direct employees (Uber drivers are classified as 1099 contractors, though there are several pending lawsuits from drivers challenging their status as contractors rather than employees). Uber and other ridesharing companies like Lyft and Sidecar play the role of matchmaker, connecting a driver and car with a customer looking for a ride, and then taking a cut of the fare for providing the service (an amount that has been steadily escalating from the original 5 percent of every fare to now more like 20–25 percent or higher). Its value comes from being a bit less expensive than a conventional taxi,[10] and also more convenient—tap your app, and the closest Uber driver to your location shows up anywhere from five to 15 minutes later. Which is a relief to anyone like this author, who has waited up to 45 minutes for a taxi in San Francisco. Kalanick is driven—some might say obsessed—by a mission to have enough roaming drivers who are within minutes of any potential passenger, increasing coverage and reducing wait times.

Uber's value also comes from its alleged screening of its drivers and cars, to ensure both safety and comfort. On Uber's website, the company trumpets that "every ridesharing and livery driver is thoroughly screened through a rigorous process," which includes "a three-step criminal background screening."[11] In fact, Uber charges every customer an extra $1.00 "Safe Rides" fee to pay for those checks. It sounds impressive.

But not to the district attorneys of Los Angeles and San Francisco. In December 2014 they jointly filed a consumer protection lawsuit against Uber, alleging that it misleads customers about the service's safety. The lawsuit also claimed that Uber overcharges customers and often thumbs its nose at the law.[12] At a news conference, San Francisco district attorney George Gascon accused Uber of making false statements about how it protects consumers. Gascon says that because Uber (as well as its leading ridesharing competitor Lyft) does not fingerprint its drivers, the company's criminal checks are "completely worthless."[13] Uber doesn't do what is known as a Live Scan (which includes fingerprinting), the highest standard of background check that most taxi companies in California are required by law to do.[14] Indeed, the FBI says Uber's method, called a "name-based criminal background check," has a 43 percent error rate.[15] "The company repeats this misleading statement," said Gascon, "giving consumers a false sense of security when deciding whether to get into a stranger's car."

Kalanick and his other Uber operatives reacted with howls of victimization over "big government" overreach. But they could hardly have been surprised. This issue had been building steam for some time. Only a week before, Uber had gained international notoriety when in New Delhi, India, an Uber driver was arrested for allegedly raping a passenger. The female passenger fell asleep during the ride, and when she awoke she found that the driver had taken her to a secluded area. He then stopped the car and assaulted her, according to the woman's testimony.[16] Police said that Uber did not conduct an adequate background check on the driver, who it turns out had been arrested at least twice before for alleged sex crimes.[17] The Delhi state government immediately banned Uber from operating there. Other Indian states quickly followed suit.

In the United States, Uber drivers also have faced a slew of charges. In Boston, three women reported (in separate incidents) being sexually assaulted by Uber drivers.[18] In Los Angeles, an Uber driver was arrested for allegedly kidnapping a drunk female passenger; she awoke in a motel room, after having been carried there unconscious by the driver, according to motel surveillance cameras.[19] In Washington, D.C., another Uber driver was accused of rape. In Brooklyn, an Uber driver was arrested for allegedly stealing $5,000 worth of jewelry from two passengers.[20] Other charges and complaints have regularly surfaced of assault, harassment and another kidnapping.[21] In one assault case the driver had a prior felony conviction, yet had passed Uber's background test;[22] in another case a passenger was allegedly bludgeoned by an Uber driver with a hammer, resulting in a fractured skull.[23] Numerous episodes have popped up of drivers who apparently obtained female passenger phone numbers from the Uber database, and continued to contact them, seeking dates and other forms of attention.[24]

A month earlier than the New Delhi incident, in November 2014, an Uber driver in Chicago was arrested for sexual assault. The charges were later dropped, but it turns out the driver was not even authorized to pick up passengers for the ridesharing company—he was using an account registered in his wife's name.[25] In Los Angeles, an Uber driver told about how easy it was to game Uber's background checks by handing off an approved driver's account to another driver. Some drivers actually share accounts. The company knows and looks the other way, claimed the driver, because "it's harder to find drivers than you'd imagine. The company just wants someone in that car."[26]

Practically admitting the failure of their background check system, an Uber spokeswoman could not explain how the discrepancy in Chicago could have been missed. But she then went on the offensive and blamed riders, a consistent Uber tactic used for deflecting criticism.

"There is a responsibility for the rider to make sure that when they get into an Uber that they're checking the license plate and they're checking the driver's face and making sure all that matches up," she said.[27] That was a first—a new safety procedure of checking the driver's face, as well as the license plate, amid the company's blandly reassuring words about the safety of its service. Following a previous incident in which a passenger—a former lecturer at Howard University—claimed to have been choked by an Uber driver (who denied the charge), Kalanick quickly dismissed the allegation, stating that "these incidents aren't even real in the first place."[28]

As many of Uber's defenders have pointed out, assaults and other bad things happen from taxi drivers as well. Uber tries to claim that their background checks are more thorough than those used in the taxi industry, even though the facts—as well an academic study of Uber's background checks, conducted by researchers at the City University of New York[29]—tell a different story. As one Uber driver said, "I've been a taxi driver in Massachusetts, Florida and California. You have to provide a 10 year driving history from the DMV dated within 30 days, pass a drug and alcohol test, go to the police department and get fingerprinted. Uber requires none of this." Uber's claims that its screening process is more rigorous than those taxi drivers go through, he says, "is an outright lie."[30]

Uber feels self-righteously justified in disclaiming any responsibility for its drivers' bad behaviors because of its insistence that it is not a taxi company but merely a Web- and app-based matchmaker between a driver and a passenger. According to Uber, the driver is a private contractor who is in fact not an employee, so the company has no liability. It's kind of an outrageous claim for a company valued at $51 billion to make, with all the clout that its high-priced lawyers bring to this discussion.

Yet that's exactly what Uber did when, on New Year's Eve 2013 at 8 p.m., one of its drivers in San Francisco hit and killed six-year-old Sofia Liu.

Sofia, her mother and brother were leisurely crossing the street in a crosswalk when Syed Muzaffar, an Uber driver in a Honda sport utility vehicle, turned into all three of them. Sofia was killed instantly, her mother and brother badly injured. Muzaffar was arrested and charged with vehicular manslaughter. But Uber immediately denied fault, claiming that Muzaffar was an independent contractor, not a direct employee, and besides he was not carrying a passenger or driving to pick up a passenger, and so technically he was not "on the clock." Uber "did not cause this tragic accident," said its attorney, and therefore had no legal liability.[31]

The girl's family sued both Muzaffar and Uber for wrongful death, alleging that Muzaffar was logged on to the UberX app when he fatally struck Sofia, waiting to receive his next ride request. The driver's attorney also stipulated that his client was awaiting his next fare assignment.[32] It also turned out that Muzaffar already had a reckless-driving record in Florida, including being arrested for driving 100 mph into oncoming traffic while trying to pass another car—something Uber's screening process did not uncover.[33]

The previous year, the California Public Utilities Commission had begun requiring that ridesharing companies carry commercial liability insurance that covers its drivers, particularly since drivers are legally forbidden to invoke their own personal auto insurance if the car is being used for commercial purposes (commercial auto insurance is a separate type and costs 3 to 10 times more than personal insurance). The new law mandated a minimum $1 million of coverage per incident, which Uber had complied with—but ambiguity in the law made it unclear who is responsible if the driver is logged in to the Uber app but has no passenger or is not on their way to pick up a passenger.[34] That was the "insurance gap" that Uber was trying to exploit to evade responsibility for the killing of young Sofia Liu.

Yet that distinction defies industry standards. Chris Dolan, attorney at Dolan Law Firm representing Sofia Liu's family, called Uber a "pirate" operation. "Pizza delivery drivers? They have insurance on the pizza car. From the minute it gets turned on until the minute it gets turned off. Everybody else who's driving vehicles on the road, whether they are full or empty, carries commercial insurance 24–7." Taxi drivers, for example, are covered by the company's commercial insurance for as long as they are in the car. He calls the ridesharing business "a tragedy waiting to happen. They [Uber] want to be exempt—because they're special. They're 'technology,' so they shouldn't have to follow the rules."[35]

This pattern of evading responsibility by any means necessary has become a frequent Uber tactic. The hard-charging company seems to care little about who is being trampled by its extremely narrow legal interpretations. Finally, yielding to the pressure of public opinion—and no doubt from legal advisors and investors, concerned about the company's reputation—Travis Kalanick announced with great fanfare that Uber would cover the "insurance gap."[36] But the fine print revealed that the coverage was minimal, far less than the $1 million required by law for the more clear-cut situations when there is a passenger in the car. This displayed yet another Uber pattern of nickel-and-diming whenever possible, despite its being a multi-billion-dollar-valued company.

THE UBER "CREEP FACTOR"

Inadequate background checks, evasion of responsibility, belligerent dismissal of victims—these have become the hallmarks of Travis's World. Uber's CEO regularly rails against a whole list of perceived enemies, including anti-innovation government bureaucrats, Big Taxi and ridesharing competitors like Lyft and Sidecar.[37] All of those enemies are fair game in the brass-knuckled world of "sharing" economy startups. But Uber stepped one giant leap over the line when it targeted another enemy—media critics.

In November 2014, Uber senior executive Emil Michael must have been having a bad day/week/month when he unloaded at a swanky private dinner party in Manhattan. The party was attended by an A-list crowd, including actor Edward Norton; author and publisher Arianna Huffington; Mort Zuckerman, owner of New York's *Daily News;* British political insider Ian Osborne and others. Travis Kalanick was also in attendance. Uber had been reeling from a series of recent news stories about its latest scandals, and Emil Michael, who is Uber's senior vice president of business and also sits on a board that advises the Department of Defense, floated an unsettling idea: that Uber should hire its own hit team of journalists to dig up dirt on its critics in the media.

Ben Smith, editor-in-chief of *Buzzfeed* who attended the dinner, relayed the play-by-play: "Over dinner, [Michael] outlined the notion of spending 'a million dollars' to hire four top opposition researchers and journalists" to help Uber fight back against hostile media—they'd look into "your personal lives, your families," expose private details and "give the media a taste of its own medicine," he said.[38] Stalk the critics, in other words.

Michael specifically targeted one journalist, Sarah Lacy, the CEO and editor of the Silicon Valley watchdog *PandoDaily,* who had been harshly critical of Uber and Kalanick. She has accused them of "sexism and misogyny" for a string of episodes, including victim-blaming after the incidents in which Uber drivers were charged with sexual assault. Lacy wrote that she no longer felt safe taking Uber cars and that she was deleting her Uber app and encouraged people to use ridesharing competitor Lyft. "I don't know how many more signals we need that the company simply doesn't respect [women] or prioritize our safety," she wrote.[39]

Over dinner, Michael expressed anger over Lacy's column and stated that Uber's dirt-diggers could expose Lacy and her personal life. According to Smith, one of the dinner partners suggested to Michael that a plan like that could become a problem for Uber if the public caught wind of it, but Michael—the executive with Defense Department connections—responded: "Nobody would know it was us."

When the story was reported by Smith, a new media firestorm erupted. Kalanick took to Twitter to issue an immediate disavowal—though not quite an apology—but declined to fire Emil Michael, as was widely demanded.

But that's just the beginning. With its Defense Department connections, Uber's creepiness has gone beyond rants about how to harass journalists and critics. It turns out that the Uber app gathers a lot of personal data on its passengers, and that data has been used to track some passengers—including its critics. The latter kind of activity can border on harassment and stalking.

Uber was once again caught flat-footed when it was reported that its general manager in New York City, Josh Mohrer, accessed the passenger logs of a *BuzzFeed News* reporter who had written critical articles about Uber, and used that information to track her physical location while in an Uber car.[40] A writer for *San Francisco Magazine* reported that, when she was writing a cover story about Uber, several friendly sources inside the company warned her that company higher-ups might monitor her rides and dig into her passenger logs.[41]

But in the most egregious incident, venture capitalist Peter Sims wrote in a blog post about being in an Uber car in Manhattan when he started receiving text messages from a woman he barely knew, telling him exactly where he was.[42] That person revealed to him that she was at an Uber launch party in Chicago, where Sims's movements were being tracked in real time on a large public screen while the audience in attendance watched. Besides Sims, the Uber rep tracked the location and movements of 30 Uber users in New York. Sims was on his way to Penn Station to catch a train to D.C., and this acquaintance in Chicago "continued to text with updates of my car's whereabouts," he says, which freaked him out.[43] When she revealed that his location was being broadcast at a public Uber party in Chicago, he was "outraged." His post about being publicly stalked by the company went viral, but Uber refused to comment.[44] Revealingly, the Uber presenter in Chicago jokingly titled the high-tech peep show the Creepy Stalker View.

Clearly Uber's reassurances about respecting privacy are no more trustworthy than its reassurances about background checks for its drivers. It turns out that Uber has a secret app called—wait for it—"God View," which can be used to track journalists and other surveillance targets, according to two former Uber employees. It's an internal company tool that shows the location of every Uber vehicle and customer who is riding in an Uber car. The two former Uber employees, both of whom worked at the company until spring 2014, said that God View was easily accessible to staff across the company (though the drivers did not have access to it).[45] Like whistleblower Edward Snowden's revelation that half a million private contractors have access to top security databases at the National Security Administration, Uber has allowed hundreds of staff to have access to the private details of its customers. And it does not inform those customers about their lack of privacy.

Jason Mick from the online magazine *Daily Tech* said that the Emil Michael incident exposed Uber's "deep seeded malicious streak . . . the world has caught a glimpse of the ugly side of Uber."[46]

Two-faced villain, indeed.

TRANSPORTATION REVOLUTIONARY OR . . . TAX CHEAT?

Like Airbnb, Uber also facilitates law-breaking and tax avoidance on a massive scale. Indeed, that's part of the "disruption" of traditional laws and norms that both companies say they are proud of. They believe that New York City, San Francisco and other uncooperative cities are operating under an "old business model" that should not be applied to their new innovative companies that are doing so much good for society and for people who are just trying to make a few extra bucks. Like Airbnb CEO Brian Chesky, Travis Kalanick portrays himself as fighting for the "regular people." And with so many underemployed Americans today, there is a degree of truth to their claims.

But like with Airbnb, closer inspection reveals an uglier side. The primary service provided by Uber is pretty similar to any taxi or limousine service: automotive transport of passengers to their destination, in exchange for money. But taxi companies and limousine services in most cities have to pay what are known as "livery taxes" and other related fees to local governments, which Uber has refused to pay. "Are we American Airlines or Expedia?" asked Kalanick, in an interview with the *Wall Street Journal.*[47] He maintains they are more like Expedia, merely a go-between connecting buyers and sellers. While Uber does pay federal corporate income tax on the earnings generated from its cut of each fare—sort of, since like Apple, Google and others it also has constructed a complex web of foreign subsidiaries and tax havens to greatly minimize its taxes in the U.S.[48]—it insists it should not have to pay the local livery taxes because they don't own any taxis or directly employ any drivers. Like its sharing economy brethren Airbnb, a major part of the Uber business model "disruption" is one that all Americans wish they could enjoy: tax avoidance.

But Uber's avoidance of laws and regulations does not end with taxes. Because they insist they are not a traditional taxi or limousine company, Kalanick believes that means they are free to operate without the usual taxi licenses. And they don't generally have to follow other regulations regarding safety, insurance and other requirements. In every location where the company has bumped up against regulations—which is pretty much everywhere—Uber has acted like a rogue operation that has refused to comply with local laws and tried to bully local officials. In many cases, it has been its own worst enemy, unwilling to make the least little compromise. The case of Birmingham, Alabama, was classic Uber.

Uber came to Birmingham city officials, saying it wanted to launch its service there. It put forward the idea of creating a separate classification for its type of business and engaged in tense negotiations with the city council. Uber had a few things going for it. Kim Rafferty, the councilwoman who headed the transportation committee, had used Uber in Washington, D.C., and said she liked it.[49] The local taxi industry wasn't really opposed; the president of Yellow Cab told the *Birmingham Business Journal* that he didn't mind the competition, but had concerns that Uber wouldn't play by the same rules or compete fairly.[50] Councilwoman Rafferty said ridesharing and taxis could complement each other. "In the end, the marketplace is going to decide who is successful and who is not," Rafferty said.[51]

So it seemed like the pieces were in place for an Uber win in Birmingham. Rafferty drafted legislation that would permit Uber to operate, but it also included certain safety and consumer protections, including that the ridesharing companies have full-time commercial insurance for all drivers using their personal cars for commercial work. Uber dug in its heels, saying it already had its own policies involving insurance, background checks and inspections. Councilwoman Rafferty expressed considerable frustration over what transpired.

"Uber pretty much told us they wanted no part of the transportation code. They felt that their drivers are small business, they should be allowed to operate however they want, with no regulatory oversight, government oversight whatsoever. That also includes no business license and no paying tax on their income revenue. We found that to be quite disturbing. Anything that required them to be in compliance with any law in general, they were totally against."[52]

The council passed the law it wanted, and Uber went ballistic. Its spokesperson Taylor Bennett lost all sense of decorum and released a statement attacking Rafferty. "Councilor Rafferty's true colors [have] shown through today. . . . She has made it explicitly clear that protecting big taxi and restricting competition is more important than providing a safe, reliable way to get around town. As we expected all along, this was indeed a backdoor rush job."[53]

Rafferty responded with incredulity, calling the company's statement an "unjustified personal attack." Uber demonstrated "disrespect for the very governmental regulatory measures we have in place to protect public safety and ensure fair play. . . . Uber made demands that we change codes and that we change it *now*, as well as make edits that would only benefit them. They asked me to do something unethical. I will not be bullied, pushed or rushed in the work that I produced."[54]

This is just one example of many in which Uber has tried to stampede local officials. But in Birmingham, they ran into a stone wall in the form of a tough city councilwoman who refused to buckle to the bullying culture that has been cultivated by Travis Kalanick. Not only did Uber's belligerence prevent it from operating in Birmingham, it backfired in other ways. Word got out, and it put the rest of the state of Alabama on alert. Caught in its own arrogance, Uber made the mistake of defiantly announcing it was setting up operations in Tuscaloosa and other Alabama college towns. A short time later, the Tuscaloosa police arrested two Uber drivers in a sting operation. One driver was arrested for operating a taxi without a business license after picking up two undercover police officers. Six other drivers received warning citations for hiring out their vehicles without the proper licenses and inspections.[55]

That kind of story has played out in numerous cities. Nevertheless, despite its arrogance and public-relations clumsiness, at the end of the day what Uber and the ridesharing industry have going for them is that virtually nowhere seems happy with existing taxi service. Taxi companies often exploit their drivers, with a typical cab driver's salary hovering around $30,000—practically poverty wages.[56] "The taxi medallion evil empire," as Kalanick rightfully fumes in numerous interviews, often is a small group of politically connected operatives who have been more than willing to flex their political clout to defend their monopoly.[57] They usually have influence at City Hall to muscle out any new competition and shut down advocates of a more open taxi market. "We're in this political campaign, and the candidate is Uber, and the opponent is an asshole named Taxi," Kalanick told the audience at one tech conference. "Nobody likes him, he's not a nice character, but he's so woven into the political fabric and machinery that a lot of people owe him favors."[58]

So along comes the brash, swaggering Travis Kalanick and his Uber baby, who has now turned his company into a highly connected firm of its own—one backed by Goldman Sachs, Google, Amazon's Jeff Bezos and billions of dollars from investors who are determined not to lose their money. Some investors have defended Kalanick by saying that it takes a personality like his to step on enough toes and break through the local fiefdoms. One of Uber's investors shrugs away Kalanick's belligerence: "It's hard to be a disrupter and not be an asshole."[59]

So it's asshole vs. asshole, and unfortunately caught in the middle of this battle royal are the drivers, the public and many local governments.

In many ways, this discussion is another version of an age-old argument about government regulation vs. deregulation and liberty vs. taxes. To understand how this applies to the taxi, limo and now ridesharing industries, it's instructive to briefly review the history of livery and rider-carrying services.

Commercial passenger transport of one kind or another has been regulated for centuries. Often what has driven regulatory interventions is the proliferation and resulting chaos of having too many vehicles on the road. For example, horse-drawn coaches for hire first appeared on the streets of Paris and London in the early 17th century. King Charles I of England ordered in 1635 that all these vehicles on the city's streets had to be licensed by the state "to restrain the multitude and promiscuous use of coaches."[60]

Centuries later in the United States, the Great Depression threw millions out of work, some of whom owned a car. Suddenly the number of "cars for hire" exploded. Uninsured drivers regularly got into accidents that injured passengers, unsavory drivers did criminal things, and it was difficult for the injured or aggrieved to receive compensation or justice. Moreover, the huge numbers of cars and competition shrank profit margins to the point where drivers were working long 16-hour days yet were barely squeezing out a living. In 1933, a U.S. Department of Transportation official wrote—sounding presciently familiar to today's situation—that "the excess supply of taxis led to fare wars, extortion, and a lack of insurance and financial responsibility among operators and drivers. Public officials and the press in cities across the country cried out for public control over the taxi industry."[61]

The response was that most major cities instituted regulations over licenses, fares, insurance and other parts of the rapidly evolving taxi service. Most importantly, they also imposed limits on the number of taxis permitted within a city. Constricting the taxi supply using a medallion system or some other method prevented the flooding of the market with operators, and became recognized as a legitimate way to ensure that drivers were able to earn a decent and consistent income. Over time, this approach also gave municipalities the ability to impose additional consumer and safety protections, like background checks and insurance requirements. Often the exactness of specific regulations has been the "path-dependent" end product of a fairly complex and drawn-out history, interacting with a particular culture over time. Despite the protestations of libertarians and free marketeers, most regulations usually are in place for some good reasons, developed over many years.

Uber and ridesharing's entry overturns all that history. Today, without the right regulations, it's not hard to imagine how the ridesharing technology could result in city after city returning to the "good ol' days" of too many drivers, not enough safety and inadequate accountability and consumer protection. "If Uber doesn't have to follow licensing laws, then neither does any Tom, Dick, or Harry who chooses to paint the word 'TAXI' on the side of his car, and start offering rides via the Internet," says Paul Carr, from the Silicon Valley watchdog *PandoDaily*. London often is plagued by rogue, unlicensed cabs, and it has been reported that 11 women a month are attacked in them; unlicensed drivers are responsible for a shocking 80 percent of all stranger rapes.[62]

Washington Post columnist Catherine Rampell points out two other obvious social costs that are even more pressing today in our mass societies: dense traffic and emissions pollution. "Medallions and other regulations capping the number of livery cars available are often derided as taxi cartel protectionism," she writes. "But they limit the number of empty cars driving around looking for passengers, snarling intersections and polluting the air. It's silly to assume cities can welcome ever-higher numbers of relatively unregulated quasi-taxis with no costs to consumers."[63]

So Travis Kalanick's ambition of putting as many Uber drivers on the road as possible tramples over many good public policy goals. With Uber (as well as other sharing economy companies like Lyft and Airbnb) also avoiding taxes and evading regulations, the company is providing dubious value to the economy and society, says economist Dean Baker from the Center for Economic Policy Research. "It is simply facilitating a bunch of rip-offs," taking business from other available services that do pay taxes. Dodging taxes and regulation isn't just disruptive—it's bad for the broader economy, says Baker.[64] If Uber and Lyft flood the market, they could harm all drivers' ability to earn even minimum wage (and there are signs that this is beginning to happen, despite Uber's claims to the contrary—more on that later). These services are undercutting poorly paid taxi drivers and unleashing a race to the bottom where the lowest wage will win.

Says Baker, "Many existing regulations should be changed, as they were originally designed to serve narrow interests and/or have outlived their usefulness. But it doesn't make sense to essentially exempt entire classes of business from safety regulations or taxes just because they provide their services over the Internet. . . . If these services are still viable when operating on a level playing field they will be providing real value to the economy. As it stands, they are hugely rewarding a small number of people"—especially the wealthy investors—"for finding a creative way to cheat the system."

Some former Uber executives have come to similar conclusions. Matt Kochman served as Uber's founding general manager in New York before he left in 2011. Kochman resigned because he got fed up with Uber's in-your-face attitude toward regulators. "Their strategy has been 'try and stop us, and if you try and stop us, then we'll cross that bridge when we come to it,'" said

Kochman. "Discounting the rules and regulations as a whole, just because you want to launch a product and you have a certain vision for things, that's just irresponsible."[65]

Another former employee says the company's model has been to launch first and wait for regulation to follow. "Uber is so well funded, profitable, and powerful in the marketplace that there's not a whole lot of incentive to play nice."[66]

No question, playing nice is not the Uber way. That includes when it comes to beating Big Taxi or its closest ridesharing competitors, Lyft and Sidecar. Uber has deployed various dirty tricks to gain an advantage, like trying to raid its competitors' drivers. Lyft has retaliated in kind. Watching all the tit-for-tat, the *Post*'s Rampell noted that "for all their bellyaching about the bullies of Big Taxi, Uber and Lyft are becoming pretty big bullies themselves."[67]

Meet the new boss, same as the old boss, she wrote. "Except less regulated."

UBER'S BIGGEST THREAT: ITS DRIVERS

Despite all its many outrageous behaviors, Uber's success or failure will hinge on one major "input" into its business: its drivers. That is the major bottleneck in its business model, at least until driverless cars come online (which, depending on who you talk to, is either just around the corner or will never be perfected enough to clear the regulatory and liability hurdles for everyday use). Without sufficient numbers of drivers, Uber's $51 billion valuation eventually will head south. Any smart investor should be asking, "How does Travis treat his drivers?"

In its promotions and public statements, Uber is fond of calling drivers its "partners." But the problem for Kalanick is that his company's self-interest clashes with that of his driver-partners. As the history of taxis show, drivers are better off when the number of cars is limited to some degree. But Kalanick wants to flood the streets with Uber drivers, creating (in Marxian terms) a large "reserve driver pool," not only to reduce customer wait times but also so he can swamp the competition, driving taxi and other ridesharing companies out of business. The fact that the CEO's interest and that of his drivers are in direct conflict is his Achilles' heel.

Already we are seeing the effects of this. Online message boards like UberPeople.net, where drivers chat about the ridesharing life, is filled with discussion from drivers who wait for hours without getting "pinged" for a ride. "I just realized why I'm not getting pinged," one disgruntled driver wrote, posting a picture of a cluster of idle Uber cars in Orange County, California. "We're all on top of each other, begging for pennies."[68]

As the company has grown exponentially, Uber says that it has hired tens of thousands of "partners"—though no one knows the true number. In January 2015, Uber released internal data and a commissioned survey of its drivers via a report coauthored by Princeton economist Alan Krueger, a former chairman of President Obama's Council of Economic Advisers.[69] That report claimed that Uber had over 163,000 drivers (as of December 2014), which if true meant the company was an über job juggernaut, to be sure. But in fact 80 percent of the drivers were part time, with over half of them driving fewer than 15 hours per week; indeed, only half the drivers remained active a year later. With Uber's own report showing that most of the "jobs" were temporary and extremely part time, Kalanick's boasts of being a champion job-creator were severely tarnished. *Slate*'s Alison Griswold wrote, "It seems disingenuous to trumpet signing up thousands of drivers a month—most of whom are part-time—in the same manner that a CEO might herald the addition of new factory jobs."[70]

But the Krueger report also inadvertently tripped up Kalanick in one of his other fantastical P. T. Barnum–like claims: that Uber drivers are highly paid, earning comfortable middle-class wages. Uber's CEO originally claimed in 2013 to the *Wall Street Journal* that Uber drivers were pulling in $100,000 per year.[71] An Uber ad I saw on Craigslist in August 2014 announced to prospective drivers "make over $1850 per week," which works out to over $96,000 on an annual basis. Despite the "doesn't pass the laugh test" quality of those figures, they were cited in the media for months. The *Washington Post* uncritically reported the median wage for an Uber driver as $90,766 a year, based on nothing more than an Uber blog post.[72] The *Post* headline even suggested Uber "could end the era of poorly paid cab drivers." If true, those figures would have meant a full-time Uber driver was making as much as most tech workers in San Francisco and New York—and was in the top 20 percent of income earners in the United States.

But the Krueger report, based on Uber's internal data, said the wage for drivers was on average $17 an hour in Los Angeles and Washington, D.C., $23 an hour in San Francisco and $30 an hour in New York.[73] If a driver in LA or Washington, D.C., earned those hourly rates, he or she would have to drive 5,800 hours per year—a minimum of 16 hours per day, 365 days of the year—and a driver in New York, 3,300 hours per year—at least nine hours per day, every day of the year—to reach $100,000 (a regular full-time worker, working a 40-hour week, averages about 2,000 hours per year). Working a full 40 hours per week at those hourly rates—which most Uber drivers don't do, since four out of five are part-timers—would yield gross annual earnings of only $34,000 in Los Angeles and Washington, D.C., and $60,000 in New York City.

That might seem like a decent wage, but inexplicably the numbers in the Krueger study did not take into account the Uber driver's expenses, such as the cost of gas, car maintenance, car payments, vehicle depreciation, tolls, insurance, car wash, traffic tickets and other payouts (a point the report mentioned, but buried deep inside one paragraph). Those costs are substantial; estimates have placed them anywhere from $7,000 to $10,000 per year.[74] If drivers are savvy enough, they can deduct some of these costs from their taxes as "business expenses," but there's no way the numbers add up to anything more than low wages for a full-time Uber driver. *Buzzfeed*'s Johana Bhuiyan took 11 rides with 11 randomly chosen Uber drivers in New York City and found that after subtracting the usual costs of driving in New York, Uber drivers don't earn much more than taxi drivers on an annual basis. Uber long has denigrated the taxi industry for its low driver wages, so another Uber myth bit the dust.

One of the drivers Bhuiyan followed around said, "When you look at expenses, you don't make anything for Uber. I work four days a week, the busy days which are Thursday, Friday, Saturday, Sunday. I work 14 to 17 hours a day just for those days. If I work about 10 hours, I'm rarely going to make anything after expenses; I'll only make $100 to $150. I work hard because I have to pay rent."[75] Shannon Liss-Riordan, a Boston-based attorney who filed two lawsuits on behalf of Uber and Lyft drivers for unfair labor practices, including misclassifying drivers as independent contractors instead of employees, said, "I don't see how they think the drivers are going to make more than taxi drivers when they are charging less than taxis and [the drivers] are having to pay all these expenses."[76]

When the Krueger report was released, and while the pliant media dutifully reported Uber's positive spin, the online chat boards of Uber drivers lit up with hundreds of sarcastic, derisive comments. "This is also why when a drug company tests its own drug you take the results with a big spoonful of salt," wrote one driver. Wrote another driver: "Uber is great, according to studies commissioned by Uber . . . *my* study says I make less than minimum wage." Another driver alertly pointed out that the data for the study had come from October 2014, but in January 2015 Uber cut its driver rates yet again in 48 cities, lowering "actual earnings by ~40%"—meaning the report's data was now obsolete, an obvious point that the media completely missed.[77] So the drivers themselves knew what a load of hooey the study was, several theorizing that it was probably released in time for Uber's self-promotion at the U.S. Conference of Mayors meeting as part of its campaign to expand to dozens of cities.

What was remarkable to me was that the media (not to mention Krueger himself, a renowned economist) was willing to accept Uber's numbers used for the report at face value. I have been continually surprised at how often the media has uncritically reported Uber's data for just about everything, given the many times the company has played fast and loose with the facts. Let's face it, believing Uber's numbers is about as sound as believing China's. Thirty dollars per hour to drive in New York City? Says who—Uber?

Beyond the poor wages, Uber feels entitled to suddenly and unilaterally change the drivers' split with the company of the income from each ride, as well as the rate charged to passengers. There's nothing contractual locking in these details between Uber and its drivers, and Kalanick has shown no willingness to dialogue, much less negotiate, with drivers. For example, in 2014 the company both slashed fares, in some locations by as much as 20 percent, and then increased its own take of each fare from 20 percent up to 25–28 percent (when Uber first began, it's take was only 5 percent).[78] One driver complained, in January 2014, "Just last night, right before the weekend rush, [Uber] sent out an email telling us they are immediately cutting our pay by almost 30% from $2.45 per mile to $1.80 per mile and tell us, don't worry, you can just do 30% more rides and make the same money, because we will be busier. Guess what? We weren't busier . . . because we were already busy enough."[79]

Uber cut prices again a year later, in January 2015 (just as the Krueger report was released), once again urging its drivers to make up for the loss by bagging more fares.[80] That's the Uber solution: work harder, drive longer, more fares, no breaks. There's a name for that: speed-up, usually applied to assembly-line workers. It's like Travis Kalanick expects his drivers to become behind-the-wheel automatons, strapped into their seats for many hours a day, week, month.

The net result of these unilateral price cuts is a significant slashing of drivers' net pay. Uber has done this regularly as part of its ongoing price war with taxis and ridesharing competitors like Lyft. Indeed, the company advertises that its service now costs less than the price of taking a taxi (and that claim at least appears to be correct, by about 10 to 20 percent on average).[81] Its strategy has been to steadily undercut its competitors' prices and drive them out of business, and they are willing to do that on the backs of their drivers. Not surprisingly, many drivers see themselves as collateral damage of a ruthless race to the bottom between Uber and its competitors. As one driver put it, in order to make up for a 20 percent price cut, not only do you have to work 20 percent more but "that means more mileage and more gas"—more expenses that *they* have to pay, not Uber. After the cut in fares, one Uber driver commented, "With the money I earn I can apply for food stamps, and that is no joke"—so it appears taxpayers may have to subsidize Uber's stinginess, just like they do with Walmart and McDonald's.[82]

Besides declining pay, more and more Uber drivers are complaining about other forms of unfair and disrespectful treatment. Across the country, drivers have complained about broken promises, deceitful payment policies and false promotions—such as promising a certain pay rate and then not paying it, unless the driver is willing to wrangle with Uber's faceless email bureaucracy over missing wages.[83] Uber has insisted that its drivers keep their cars shiny and polished, inside and out, and provide various amenities to their passengers, such as mints and bottles of water (and even advertised that its drivers provide these)—yet drivers have to pay for those out of their own pockets and then, adding insult to outrage, are not allowed to keep tips. (Uber tells its customers that tips are included in the fare, but drivers say they never see them. Some have sued Uber to get their tips, noting that Uber once added an option for passengers to include a donation to the No Kid Hungry campaign via its app—yet has refused to add a tip option.)[84] A multi-billion-dollar company is nickel-and-diming its working-class "partners" into a smoldering rebellion.

In addition, because Uber drivers are classified as independent contractors—1099 workers—they are not entitled to any health benefits, unemployment or injured workers compensation, paid sick or vacation leave or any other safety-net benefits. Some Uber drivers have gotten seriously injured while driving a fare, oftentimes by the passenger, including being assaulted, stabbed, choked and more. Yet they have never received a dime of support or lost wages from the multi-billion-dollar company. (In some states and cities, taxi drivers are provided injured workers' compensation even though they are independent contractors.[85] This is in recognition of the fact that federal statistics show that taxi drivers are 21 to 33 times more likely to be killed than other workers.[86])

Lyft has had some success positioning its company brand as the "nice" ridesharers, the anti-Uber, and while it's true that it has not been as consistently scheming, Lyft also has matched Uber's fare cuts and ripped off some of its drivers. For example, it launched a luxury service called Lyft Plus to compete with Uber's black car and SUV services, getting its drivers locked in—only to abruptly cancel it when the service failed to gain traction. But most of its drivers, who had been baited by Lyft with a promise of being paid higher rates for the luxury service, had ponied up $34,000 to purchase a tricked-out Lyft-branded SUV Ford Explorer to get into the driver pool. Many drivers had sold their existing cars and borrowed money from relatives to buy the luxury vehicle. So when Lyft suddenly pulled the plug only four months later, it left its Lyft Plus drivers high and dry. The drivers still had to pay off their loans for an expensive SUV gas-guzzler that burned 14 miles to the gallon. To its credit, Lyft offered to either help their drivers sell the vehicles or give them a $10,000 bonus (which was subject to income tax), but the bailout deal was woefully inadequate and resulted in a lot of angry drivers.[87]

Lyft and Uber have both argued that their drivers, as 1099 contractors, are small-business owners who assume the risk of running their own livery business. But in fact, both of these companies have used various ploys to rope in drivers and get them hooked. Travis Kalanick is so desperate to recruit more drivers and feed them into his furnace in order to grab more market share that Uber has waded into the murky business of lining up "subprime"-type loans for prospective drivers to buy new cars—ones they can hardly afford. According to discussions among drivers on Uberpeople.net, a chat board for drivers, the payments work out to an outrageous interest rate of 21 percent.[88] While Uber won't go out of its way to facilitate its drivers receiving tips, it has set up automatic car loan payments from its drivers, remitting them directly to the lender. Tellingly, Uber's financing program actually was the brainchild of a former commodities trader for Goldman Sachs, Andrew Chapin, now working for Uber.[89]

Nick Woodfield, an attorney with the Employment Law Group, has helped some of the victims of these sketchy practices. "The problem is you have a workforce that is naïve to the compensation arrangement they're in," he says. They think they are being offered flexible jobs and high wages, with low barriers to entry, which is a tantalizing offer to people who really need the money, or to people who aren't familiar with the challenges of being classified as an independent contractor. "You're introducing a number of people into an employment scenario that they don't understand."[90]

Even The Rideshare Guy, a.k.a. Harry Campbell, a former Uber driver who maintains a popular blog and is generally upbeat about the industry, has criticized Uber and Lyft for their unilateral cuts in wages and mistreatment of drivers. "Uber hasn't exactly gained a ton of favor with its drivers," says Campbell. "Given free reign [*sic*], companies like Uber have not shown a willingness to compromise with their drivers without upward pressure. Drivers can hope that guys like Travis Kalanick will do the right thing and come up with a better solution for drivers, but you don't get to be the head of a billion dollar company by doing the right thing."[91]

In other words, the ridesharing companies promise their driver-partners the moon and leave them with a grain of sand. These conditions and others have added fuel to driver complaints about decreasing pay and increasing mistreatment and indignity. Joseph De Wolf Sandoval, president of the California App-Based Drivers Association (CADA), an organization of drivers affiliated with the Teamsters union that has arisen to facilitate communication and education about their working conditions, says he's asked drivers all across the country, "Are you doing better now than you were six months ago?" "And not one single driver that we've spoken with, or one of our members, has been able to say, 'Yes, I am better off now than I was six months ago.' Unfortunately, they believe it's just going to be worse and worse."[92]

DRIVERS' REBELLION

It's hardly surprising then, that drivers have begun registering their complaints—loudly and visibly. In the summer and fall of 2014, Uber drivers around the world staged protests and work stoppages. In September 2014 in Los Angeles, 50 Uber drivers gathered in a parking lot to protest the ongoing cuts in their pay.[93] One driver said he had been through four fare cuts, going from $2.50 a mile to $1.10 a mile. In Santa Monica, 200 Uber drivers protested outside the company's office, saying they had been unfairly impacted by pay cuts and other conditions.[94] In New York City, 60 protesters showed up with signs reading things like "Uber: the most valuable asset is the drivers." One of the protesters said, "I've been driving for Uber for two years, and when I started, I loved it." But steep discounts in its battle with Lyft and yellow cabs are hurting Uber drivers, he said. "There's no union representing us, so we have to protest."[95]

A week earlier in Seattle, about 100 Uber drivers quit in protest over a fare reduction. The Seattle Ride-Share Drivers Association complained that drivers were losing money when you take into account expenses. Previously in San Francisco, about 100 Uber drivers rallied outside the company's global headquarters, demanding higher pay even as Uber announced another massive fare discount. On October 22, there were coordinated protests and pickets in cities across the country including Chicago, Seattle, San Francisco, Los Angeles, as well as in London, including some Uber drivers shutting off the app and refusing to serve customers. As previously mentioned, lawsuits and other labor grievances have been filed, including a class-action lawsuit claiming "job misclassification" that challenges Uber's insistence that the drivers are independent contractors rather than regular employees, and another lawsuit over Uber's confiscation of tips. One of the biggest blows to Uber's business model was the ruling in March 2015 by the California Labor Commissioner's Office in favor of a driver who claimed she should be considered an Uber employee and not an independent contractor (Uber has appealed that decision).[96]

And if any of the pending lawsuits are decided in favor of the driver-plaintiffs, and drivers are recognized as Uber and Lyft employees instead of indie contractors, the ridesharing business model will be busted. The companies would likely not only be on the hook for hundreds of millions of dollars to settle claims from tens of thousands of drivers but also suddenly required to pay for their employees' Social Security, Medicare, unemployment and injured workers compensation.

Pro-driver organizations are springing up, such as the California App-Based Drivers Association (CADA), Uber Drivers Network NYC (which maintains a Facebook page), the Seattle Ride-Share Drivers Association and others, as well as online chat forums, like UberPeople.net, many organized by city or region.[97] "It's not just a small group of disgruntled or unprofessional drivers, as Uber would like to cast us," De Wolf Sandoval of CADA says. "It's a nationwide feeling of general unhappiness and unease with policies and programs that are being promulgated by Uber without the drivers' input whatsoever."[98]

Uber drivers have begun to fight back in other, under-the-radar ways, taking advantage of one of Uber's goofiest features, called "surge pricing." That's Uber's method of raising fares when demand increases, in theory to attract more drivers to go "on shift," which is supposed to reduce waiting time for customers. Surge pricing is driven by a complicated computer algorithm based on the supply of both customers and drivers at any particular time. When passenger demand is higher—during large events, on weekend nights, around holidays (especially partying ones like New Year's Eve, July 4 or Halloween) or during public emergencies and disasters—fares can be wildly unpredictable, escalating to 10 times the normal rate. That has led to numerous episodes that have outraged the public and led to charges of price gouging.

For example, during Superstorm Sandy, Uber came under strong criticism for doubling prices when demand was high due to people trying to escape the storm. Even profit-maximizing Airbnb had the good sense to portray itself as the "good sharing company," facilitating free housing during that storm—but that's not how things work in Travis's World. Demand was way up, and the peculiar Uber algorithm automatically kicked in, and so prices soared. That outrage prompted New York attorney general Eric Schneiderman to go after the company under a 1979 price-gouging law, which forbids businesses from raising prices during crises.[99]

In Silicon Valley's Palo Alto, a train hit and killed a pedestrian and delayed all the trains, causing demand for Uber to spike—as did the price, to three times normal pricing.[100] During a blizzard in New York City in December 2013, comedian Jerry Seinfeld's wife, cookbook author Jessica Seinfeld, took an Uber and was shocked to discover at the end of her ride that she was charged $415 for the three-mile trip across Manhattan, eight times the normal price.[101]

But those incidents were just a warm-up for the worst outrage that (once again) sparked worldwide condemnation of Uber.

In Sydney, Australia, in December 2014, a gunman took customers hostage in a café, causing a horrific tragedy. The police and SWAT teams poured in, sealed off the area and initiated a siege, resulting in three deaths (including the gunman). As the public fled the area, Uber quadrupled its prices—setting fares at a minimum of $100 Australian (about U.S. $80).[102]

Besides surge pricing during disasters, other episodes have occurred during holidays, weekend nights and, well, just about any time there aren't enough drivers and the Uber algorithm wakes up—like automated stock market trading algorithms, which have triggered financial panics—and jacks up the price. Elliott Asbury was out partying on Halloween in Denver, and for an 18-mile ride home that normally costs $50 he was charged—wait for it—$539, more than seven times the usual fare.[103] Quite a shocking "trick or treat."

In Minneapolis, a woman was charged more than $400 for a 10.8-mile ride. In Los Angeles a woman was charged $357 for a 14-mile ride. In Durham, North Carolina, Gagandeep Bindra was charged $455.03 for a 15-mile trip on Halloween night; he had done that same Uber trip earlier in the evening, and it had cost him $44.25.[104] These are just a few of numerous travesties caused by surge pricing. All of the "rider victims" unfailingly say that it was not clear to them that their trip would cost so much; often it's not even clear to the driver why the surge pricing is kicking in. Said one aggrieved passenger, "The price surge policy is not transparent at all. They don't tell the rider the ride will cost hundreds of dollars. Instead, they tell them it is 9.8 times the base fare. But the base fare could be $5 for all the rider knows."

Many of these customers attempted to contact Uber, and in some cases Uber reduced the fair by a small amount. But often the customers don't even receive a response, adding to a smoldering sense that Uber is engaged in price gouging and taking advantage of its customers.

But here's where underpaid Uber drivers are seeing an opening for fighting back against their stingy Uber overlords. Some of these drivers have figured out how to game the system in a way that sparks episodes of surge pricing, driving up their wage. Uber and Lyft driver Kelly Dessaint, who wrote a blog about his experience called "Behind the Wheel: A Rideshare Confessional," laid out the strategy that has evolved as a result of the warped Uber incentives.

"As an Uber driver, you learn quickly that it doesn't pay to pick up passengers unless prices are surging. There are blogs and even driving coaches who offer to help new drivers figure out the best driving strategies. They all say the same thing: wait for the surge."[105]

Uber doesn't assign drivers to a time slot, drivers can drive whenever they wish, so in online forums drivers regularly discuss how to figure out when prices will surge. "So far, the only proven method to ensure getting a ride during a surge," says Dessaint, "is to stay offline and monitor the rider app. Once a part of town lights up, you race there in hopes of getting a higher fare." This is called "chasing the surge," and most drivers chase it, he writes. In short, surge pricing has introduced perverse incentives that are distorting the pricing mechanism because it encourages drivers to stay home and wait on the sidelines, artificially creating a shortage of drivers. That ignites the surge-pricing algorithm, driving up the prices for customers—SURGE.

It seems like a strange trick to play on your customers, and one study showed that it may be backfiring in other ways. That's because a price hike in one area means drivers relocate there by driving away from another area. "If someone in the newly underserved area now needs a car they wait longer. . . . Uber's surge pricing instead depletes drivers in adjacent areas."[106] Yet despite all the wild price fluctuations and bad publicity, Travis Kalanick stubbornly defends surge pricing on the basis of his rigid economic orthodoxy—it's supply and demand, free markets, "classic Econ 101," he told *Vanity Fair*.[107] But journalist Bob Sullivan, author of *Gotcha Capitalism,* commented on surge pricing saying, "Uber feels a lot more like a Third World economy with inflation so fast that this morning's taxi fare dollars can't pay for the evening's taxi ride home."[108] Kalanick apparently is unaware of how his drivers are manipulating the system, sitting on the sidelines and waiting for their pay to double or triple. If he's going to nickel-and-dime his "partners" in countless miserly ways, the drivers will fight back with the means at their disposal.

Lyft also uses a version of surge pricing it calls Prime Time, but another ride-hailing company called Gett has broken with this roller-coaster pricing model. Gett maintains the same price for customers even during periods of peak passenger demand. Yet it still pays its drivers a higher wage during busy times, to incentivize more of them getting on the road, with the additional money for the drivers coming out of Gett's pocket, instead of the passengers. Other ride-hailing services have discarded surge pricing, such as Via, which uses a two-tier flat fee service of $5 if you pay in advance or $7 otherwise.[109] These competitors show that surge pricing is not simply driven by "supply and demand" dynamics, but by Uber and Lyft's madcap policy that has little basis in economic fundamentals. Considering all the scandals and sensational headlines that Uber has generated, as well as the repeated lawbreaking, it's no surprise that some state and local governments have responded by shutting down Uber, Lyft and other ridesharing companies, or putting significant obstacles in their way until they comply with applicable laws. Uber has been closed down or partially curtailed in Virginia, Maryland, South Carolina, New York City, Nevada, Miami, Philadelphia, Chicago, Birmingham, New Orleans, San Antonio and many other places. Portland, Oregon, sought a court injunction to shut them down. Seattle initially placed a cap of 150 vehicles per company and instituted a $50,000 permit application fee (though it later lifted the cap after the companies agreed to certain regulations). In some places, cars have been impounded and drivers have been fined.[110]

Opposition has been even stronger in Europe and other parts of the world. In June 2014, many thousands of taxi drivers turned city centers into parking lots as protests swept across the continent. Previously in Paris, taxi drivers had smashed windows and slashed tires of Uber cars, and this time in Paris, London, Madrid, Berlin and elsewhere drivers blocked traffic to register their complaint against Uber and other app-based services.[111] Photos flashed around the world showing thousands of taxis in European capitals clogging the roads. Many European governments and courts have responded vigorously, shutting down Uber in France, Spain, Germany, the Netherlands, Belgium, Denmark and elsewhere. In Spain, a judge's ruling barred telecommunications operators and banks from supporting the company's services, causing Uber to suspend operations.[112] Other countries that have shut them down, levied fines and impounded cars include China, Australia, Thailand, the Philippines, South Africa, South Korea, Taiwan, Brazil and more.[113]

In all of these places, the reason for shutting down the ridesharing companies has been essentially the same: the companies have an unfair advantage over taxis because they circumvent local licensing and tax rules that regular taxi firms must adhere to. That includes using drivers that lack the registration, insurance and safety procedures (including effective background checks) needed to operate commercial vehicles. Neither governments nor judges (when it has gone to court, which has been frequent) have bought the Uber line that it is somehow "different" or "a technology or software company" or "a new kind of service" from traditional taxi or limousine services, and therefore deserving of special treatment.

Uber's response in most of these places, whether in the U.S. or abroad, when it has been ordered shut down, fined and generally excoriated by government officials and court judges, has been to continue operating anyway—and like a misunderstood toddler, berate the bureaucrats. With its "do it now, apologize later" attitude, Uber has offered to pay drivers' fines, banking on the fact that a company valued at $51 billion has enough money to write it off as a business expense. One German critic retorted, "We didn't expect anything else. [Uber] is Wild West capitalism without consumer rights."[114]

Benefiting from Uber's arrogance and clumsiness are the other ridesharing companies, especially Lyft. Despite some of its own questionable tactics, Lyft has positioned itself as the anti-Uber: treating its drivers more pleasantly, being less arrogant and obstructionist toward public officials and establishing a more hospitable public face. Lyft has assigned driver mentors with Lyft experience to new recruits and has organized meet-ups so that drivers can trade stories and information.[115] Many drivers are working for both Uber and Lyft, and driver after driver agrees that Lyft honors and respects their participation more. At the beginning of 2013, Lyft was in just one city, San Francisco. By 2014 it was in 20 U.S. cities, and by mid-2014 it was in 60 cities.[116] It's also heavily funded, with a market valuation of approximately $2.5 billion. Uber has a huge lead, but it's still early in the growth and development of this industry.

Taxi companies, meanwhile, have taken a serious hit. Say what you want about the taxi industry, but Uber, Lyft and the other ridesharing services have not been competing on a level playing field. And the former big kid on the block is feeling the heat. In San Francisco, the number of monthly trips per taxi cab nose-dived from 1,424 to 504 in a year and a half, a decrease that the San Francisco Municipal Transportation Agency attributed largely to the rise of ridesharing. That is consistent with a finding by the San Francisco Cab Drivers Association (SFCDA), an association of registered taxi drivers, that in 2013 one-third of the 8,500 or so taxi drivers in San Francisco—over 2,800—quit driving a registered cab to drive for Uber, Lyft or other ridesharing companies.[117] "For many years, people could make a living driving a cab," says economist Dean Baker. "People drove for 20, 30 years, paid the rent, raised families; it was a real job. Now that is vanishing." Those who have long-despised Big Taxi can celebrate, but be careful what you ask for. Travis Kalanick might one day make people long for the cheerful sight of those bright yellow cabs.

TO UBER OR NOT TO UBER . . . THAT IS THE QUESTION

All of these tell-tales point to a growing cumulative impact on Uber's standing. Headline after headline repeats the familiar litany of controversy, assault, scandal, privacy invasions, protesting drivers, price gouging, all of it overseen by a pompous and juvenile CEO. Passengers of course are generally pleased to see the fares decline, but as Uber continues to rack up one negative headline after another, it has begun to generate a public backlash.

The *New York Times* wrote about the "Uber Shame" of customers fed up with all the "parade of horribles" and who are considering deleting the app from their phone devices. As we saw previously, Sarah Lacy of *PandoDaily* has publicly urged switching to Lyft after being singled out for possible retaliation by Uber executive Emil Michael. Kelly Hoey, a New York–based angel investor, deleted her account out of privacy concerns. "I don't want them to have my information, my credit card or my name," she said. Imran Malek, an engineer at DataXu in Boston who used Uber as much as seven times a week, deleted his Uber app after days "of my finger hovering over the delete button." To him, Uber has come to represent a winner-takes-all culture that "justifies any behavior so long as everyone is getting rich."[118]

Women customers in particular are becoming fed up with Kalanick's sexist "boober-ism." Some have taken to calling Uber's service "rapesharing" instead of "ridesharing."[119] Lisa Abeyta, the founder of a tech company in Albuquerque, New Mexico, was a devoted user of Uber; she said she felt actual pride in being an Uber customer. "We had this feeling we were empowering people," she said. But enough is enough, and finally she deleted the app from her smartphone, sending emails to the company demanding that Uber remove her account completely. "There is a difference between being competitive and being dirty," Abeyta said. "It is bad-boy, jerk culture. And I can't celebrate that."[120]

In Fall 2014, as Uber lurched from one scandal to another, a certain hashtag started to gain popularity on Twitter: #deleteUber.[121] More and more people are concluding that there is something deeply disturbing about Travis's World. Venture capitalist turned author Peter Sims, the Uber customer whose car ride was tracked during a public presentation in Chicago, says, "I've met hundreds of founders and been to thousands of companies. Uber is the most arrogant company I've encountered, and the most unethical. I don't say that lightly. Much as I am impressed with the product design and many aspects of the user experience, I've given up on being able to trust the company, and am no longer using the service."[122]

Andrew Leonard, writing an article for Salon titled "Why Uber Must Be Stopped," agreed with Sims. "There's little doubt that Uber is the closest thing we've got today to the living, breathing essence of unrestrained capitalism. . . . This is how robber barons play. From top to bottom, the company flaunts a street fighter ethos."[123] For more and more people, Uber is becoming the company they love to hate . . . like a political candidate whose "negatives" have climbed the charts. The beneficiaries of this customer flight from Uber have been Lyft, Sidecar and even some reformed taxi companies.

Speaking of political candidates: Uber has responded to its increasing public-relations backlash with . . . more public relations. In August 2014, the company hired David Plouffe, one of the masterminds of Barack Obama's 2008 presidential campaign, as its chief for policy and strategy. It was, to say the least, an über public-relations move. Plouffe is widely seen as the man who put Obama in the White House, and without missing a beat Kalanick said that Plouffe was to be "Uber's campaign manager." Kalanick also has hired at least 161 private lobbyists in at least 50 U.S. cities and states, according to the *Washington Post*.[124] The Plouffe move was met with acclaim by various political leaders within the Democratic Party establishment. Some are hoping that, now with an adult in charge, or at least babysitting Kalanick's worst excesses, Uber might pull up from its nosedive.[125] But others reacted more cynically. Economist and author Juliet Schor, who studies and reports on the sharing economy, said Uber was preparing for the regulatory battles ahead "by hiring Plouffe to bring some old-fashioned political capital to its defense."[126]

Quite a few of Uber's worst media headlines occurred after Plouffe was hired, so the PR wizard has his work cut out for him. He has put his A-list contacts and spin machine into full gear, with moves like hiring an academic such as Princeton's Alan Krueger, an ally from their old Obama administration days, to bring credibility to a favorable report based solely on Uber's otherwise suspect and self-serving internal data. The hiring of Plouffe revealed not only Uber's panic level but also the degree to which Uber and its billion-dollar backers have been able to penetrate into the highest stratospheres of the nation's power chambers and back rooms—despite its questionable business practices, its tirades contemplating threats against journalists and critics, invasions of privacy and mistreatment of drivers.

What Uber continues to have going for it is that, on paper, it looks like an investor's dream. As a global company of a mere 900 employees (estimated—Uber refuses to make its actual numbers public), most based in San Francisco, its expenses and overhead are minimal and its revenue stream has become impressively large, quarter after quarter.[127] Car-rental agency Hertz, with only a quarter of Uber's market valuation, has nearly 30,000 employees worldwide. So for Silicon Valley venture capitalists, they see only a corporation whose numbers are about as ideal as an investor can hope for, poised to make a lot of money.

But investors should be wary. Travis Kalanick has yet to demonstrate that his business model can be successful without depending heavily on what is essentially a government subsidy—not paying the same taxes as your competitors or following the same rules and regulations. In Europe, Hailo is the dominant rideshare company, and it works like Uber and Lyft: tap the Hailo smartphone app to summon a ride, which shows up promptly and at the end of the trip you can rate your driver. The French company BlaBlaCar, which has over 5 million users in Europe and is spreading across the Continent, allows drivers to find passengers to share carpooling costs when driving from city to city. Drivers are not trying to make a living; in fact, they are limited in the amount of money they can charge so that they only offset their costs. Nicolas Brusson, the CEO, thinks this is important, to preserve the "spirit of sharing" and to create a new type of transport network.

The history of the taxi industry going back centuries shows a pattern of alternating periods of deregulation followed by reregulation. At some point, the boot of regulation is going to rearrive, and for good reason—Kalanick, Uber and the ridesharing industry are a train wreck heading into every town they can find. But big numbers (like a $51 billion market valuation) draw a crowd, so investors will continue to hand truckloads of cash to Kalanick, ignoring the warning signs of a company walking a tightrope. Uber may be its own bubble, waiting to burst.

A BETTER FUTURE FOR RIDESHARING

Like Airbnb, Uber and the other ridesharing companies have undeniably created something with potential to do good—it already has helped crack open the taxi monopolies. And if regulated properly, it could provide a little daylight of employment opportunity for people who need a flexible way to make some money. A fair number of Uber and Lyft drivers who I have interviewed say it's been helpful to them, especially part-timers and weekenders who drive for extra money rather than full time. Full-time drivers seem to feel most aggrieved, and that's telling: it's no coincidence, it seems to me, that the drivers who are most content with Uber and Lyft are the ones that drive it the least, and have been with it the shortest.

But at this point it is clear that the ridesharing companies have nothing to do with a "sharing" economy worth its name. Uber and Lyft are just pure naked capitalism, nature red in tooth and claw. Sidecar, conversely, may be evolving a slightly different model that shows promise, and two different studies show that its drivers earn 20 percent more per mile than drivers with the other services, yet Sidecar is less expensive than other ridesharing and taxi services in San Francisco.[128] Sidecar CEO Sunil Paul says he is positioning his company to be the go-to ridesharing service for economically conscious people and characterizes Uber as the service for big spenders who "don't care about six or seven times surge pricing." Sidecar also has launched a same-day package delivery service, which combines the driving of both people and packages together in the same ride. That is supposed to make the ride even less expensive for passengers, and allow drivers to make more money per trip. It's a win-win, says Sidecar.[129] Time will tell if that is the case.

Certainly there are many ways to conduct a ridesharing business with more of an emphasis on the "sharing" part. But to get there will require a widespread recognition that there are very good reasons for regulating this industry. These companies should be required to have proper commercial insurance for their drivers, have the highest standard background checks, meet safety standards for their drivers' cars, limit the size of reserve driver pools and provide a minimum safety net for their drivers (health insurance, retirement, injured workers comp, paid sick days and unemployment insurance) that will allow for a decent standard of living. It's in the companies' best interests, for once the ridesharing software is widely available and fosters a plethora of equally competitive companies—including potentially driver co-ops—why would anyone take a ride from a company that can't be bothered doing proper background checks, paying its taxes, following laws and treating drivers respectfully?

Various companies already provide a sharing alternative and are pointing the way toward a better paradigm. "The biggest capacity we have," says Brusson, "whether in Europe or the U.S., is not planes, trains or buses, it's in cars. There's all these empty seats driving around the country, driving around cities. We are enabling the private car to almost become public transport."[130]

Speaking of public transport, Finland has taken an exciting step. Helsinki's transportation board has launched Kutsuplus, an Uber-like app used for public transportation that, instead of dispatching individual cars, coordinates multiple requests by passengers traveling to nearby destinations. The app pools riders, with each customized route being calculated in real time, so they can share a much cheaper ride on a public mini-bus. Passengers have found that the Kutsuplus trips are comparable to a taxi in speed, only cost about a quarter of the price, and 99 percent of rides arrive on time. The vans also all have free Wi-Fi. This shows great potential for public transportation of the future that is more efficient and cost-effective.[131]

In the U.S., ridesharing companies uRide in the Houston-Austin, Texas, region and CarmaCarpool in Austin provide rides in those cities. (CarmaCarpool also provides a carpool-sharing service among cities in the San Francisco Bay Area.) Riders pay $0.20 per mile, and drivers earn $0.17, deposited straight into their electronic "wallet." No one is getting rich, it's a way of sharing costs (uRide also prioritizes using military veterans who are attending college as its drivers). La'Zooz is a decentralized ridesharing platform that says it "will synchronize empty seats with transportation needs in real time." Cofounder Matan Fields says, "What transportation really needs is real-time ride-sharing," which means that passengers can find noncommercial cars on the go, with no prior planning (unlike BlaBlaCar, which requires prior planning). But like BlaBlaCar, La'Zooz is trying to offer real-time ridesharing in a way that "maximizes the occupancy of cars already on the road," says Field.[132] These and other examples point to a possible future of ride "sharing" in which the venture is not obsessed with profits, market share and IPOs.

The ridesharing app has great potential to usher in a new world of transportation. No one is even sure yet what it will eventually look like—and we'll never get to know, either, if Travis Kalanick is successful in his Ahab-like drive to kill off the competition. As we saw with Airbnb and homesharing, there are "good" ridesharing companies and there are "bad" ones. Uber is a bad one. Like Airbnb, Uber (as well as Lyft) is a rentier capitalist company, taking advantage of a (still) bad economy and the onset of a freelance society to get you to share *your* car with paying guests, while they take their cut from each and every transaction. The ridesharing businesses as presently organized are not ones that will usher in a progressive version of a freelance society, or will greatly help those "regular people" who have no choice but to figure out some way to make the new economy work.

Ridesharing certainly has potential to become something more beneficial—but it comes with some high social and economic costs. Only if it is done the right way, which means with the right regulations, including companies and drivers who pay their taxes, will its potential manifest. Perhaps over time those regulations will slowly emerge, but Uber (like Airbnb) is fighting commonsense reform every step of the way (and for that, Travis Kalanick has won the admiration of other *techno sapiens,* such as those at the *San Francisco Business Times,* which named him "Executive of the Year" for 2014).[133] But if driverless cars ever become a reality then all current bets are off the table. Driverless cars certainly could be a marvelous evolution in human transportation, but like always with new productivity-enhancing technologies, the outstanding question is: Who will benefit? Will it be the general public? Or a handful of venture capitalists and Silicon Valley honchos?

If that technology ends up in the hands of Travis Kalanick, it's pretty clear what the answer to that question will be.

FOUR

RACE TO THE BOTTOM, WITH TASKRABBIT AND ELANCE-UPWORK

IN THE EARLY 1990S, I VOLUNTEERED WITH THE UNITED FARM WORKERS ON its hard-fought campaign to win the first labor contract for farm workers in the history of Washington state. Farm workers are some of the most exploited laborers in America, doing backbreaking work for long hours with few labor protections and the lowest of wages. These largely Latino farm workers were the vineyard laborers and grape pickers for Chateau Ste. Michelle and Columbia Crest wineries, which were owned by U.S. Tobacco. I remember visiting the fields in eastern Washington, and the visceral jolt at watching a gang of day laborers waving their arms and thrusting their uplifted palms toward the stern-faced overseers, who were going to select just a few of them and pay them practically Third World wages. "Take me! Take me!" each of the *braceros* shouted desperately, trying to elbow for position (*brazo* means "arm" in Spanish and *bracero* is a term for a manual worker that literally means "one who works using his or her arms"). The scene showed me what the ghastly face of exploitation looks like, and I have never forgotten it.

I couldn't help but think of that experience when I first heard about job brokerage websites and apps like TaskRabbit, Upwork, Elance and the many others that have sprung up in recent years. Many of these online "sharing economy" businesses have acted as a kind of labor auction, in which any individual or business can rent out a person selected from a lineup of profiles posted on a website. It's like an old-style auction block, but in reverse—instead of the highest bidder winning, workers compete against each other by bidding low—sometimes desperately so—to get hired. "Take me! Take me!" It's as if the workers of the world have united—on the auction block, undercutting each other's prospects.

"A huge precondition for the sharing economy," wrote Kevin Roose in *New York*, "has been a depressed labor market, in which lots of people are trying to fill holes in their income by monetizing their stuff and their labor in creative ways."[1] And these labor brokerage websites and apps are designed to help them do that, in exchange for a percentage of their wages.

Two of the leading companies in this modern day work-mart casino are the businesses/websites Upwork (formerly known as oDesk) and Elance. They function like an eBay for jobs, allowing each worker to hang out her or his shingle to attract buyers of their services. Both companies use what is known as "gamification techniques," in which no matter how highly rated an exemplary worker might be, she or he can always be outbid by another worker willing to work for less money. The buyers of labor can be either other individuals in need of a particular service or businesses looking to ramp up production by contracting with individual gig-preneurs instead of hiring more permanent employees.

That might sound normal enough, until you realize that Upwork and Elance draw from workers located all over the world. Upwork, for example, is a website for freelancing creatives, including website developers, software and mobile app developers, logo designers, article writers, translators, customer service, technical support specialists and more. Elance has a nearly identical business model, though with a focus on other occupations, most of them professional, such as engineering, architecture, legal, finance and management. These are services that in an increasing number of circumstances can be performed by virtually any worker, regardless of location. A logo designer, website developer, architect, lawyer, engineer or translator can receive a work assignment anywhere in the world via the Internet, and email or Dropbox the finished product.

So that pits U.S. workers in direct competition with counterparts in the Philippines, India, Bangladesh, Thailand, Kenya and other locations where cheap, Third World labor can undercut developed-world wages. For example, clicking on the Upwork link that shows the list of logo designers offering their services, one notices that the logo designers from the U.S. or Europe are asking for anywhere from $50 to $150 per hour, while those from South and East Asia and Africa are charging as low as $3 or $4 per hour (with most charging less than $10 per hour).[2] It's the same for "article writers," where those from the U.S. and Europe offer a rate from $15 to $40 per hour while writers from South Asia and East Asia are charging as little as $3 per hour.[3] In every category this pattern holds—those creative workers from developed countries are offering their services at 10 to 30 times the hourly rate of those from the developing world.

Writing articles is something I know a bit about, and this is a formula for reducing the wages of all of these writers in the direction of the lowest common denominator. Freelance writers in the developed world cannot possibly remain economically viable if they must reduce their "ask" to those of Third World wages. The counterargument—that the "creative destruction" of these technologies is allowing customers to purchase the best service for the least cost—will only result in an "arms" race to the bottom among these workers. Certainly in many instances this pricing model is good for the customer, because they can hire cheap labor. But not always. One user observed that, "On oDesk [now known as Upwork], the freelancers bid against each other in a war to the bottom. This drives the perceived costs down for the buyers but it also dramatically drives the quality of the work down as well because the freelancers don't have the time to pay attention to the details, the budget not allowing it."[4]

Regardless of the quality of the work, Upwork and Elance pocket their matchmaker fee of about 10 percent, added on to the workers' hourly rate. And of course it goes without saying that these gig-preneurs do not receive health benefits, retirement, injured worker or unemployment compensation, disability, paid sick leave, holidays or vacations because they are not "employees" of whomever hires them. They are in that quasi-shadow state of employee known as "1099 contractors." They also are not paid while they are looking for their next gig; one contractor complained in an online forum, "I wish Odesk and Elance would compensate me for all the time spent on their site hunting. Especially since we have to compensate them more if we earn more."[5]

Increasingly, these sorts of online job brokerages comprise a bigger chunk of the overall economy. Upwork and Elance have been numbers one and two in this market, and by February 2013, Elance was being used by approximately 500,000 businesses and 2 million registered freelance professionals (according to Elance's internal figures).[6] oDesk/Upwork was even bigger, with 2.7 million freelancers and 540,000 clients worldwide.[7] And then—in a surprise move that jolted the market—the two companies merged into one behemoth in December 2013. An even bigger surprise was that antitrust regulators looked the other way. Today, the two combined companies known as Elance-Upwork (and eventually just Upwork) have 10 million contractors working for them across more than 180 countries (a quarter of them in the U.S.),[8] with combined billings approaching a billion dollars a year.[9] Its nearly 4 million business clients troll all over the globe for bargain wages from contingent labor, which allows them to grow and shrink their workforce as easily as one turns on a water spigot. Elance-Upwork's founding CEO Fabio Rosati waxed enthusiastically about the merged companies' prospects, noting that "independent workers are the fastest-growing segment of the workforce." About a third of the U.S. workforce now operates outside the traditional 9-to-5 job market, he said, and "that number could reach 50 percent in a decade."[10]

Major corporations such as Unilever, Microsoft, NBC, Cisco, Panasonic and Walt Disney have used the platform to hire or manage freelancers, as have millions of small businesses and individuals (in fact, small businesses account for 70 percent of Elance-Upwork's hiring).[11] As an example of one typical use, Facebook subcontracts to Upwork a mammoth ongoing job: screening its 1 billion users' postings, to ensure they comply with its "community standards." Upwork employs roughly 50 people in Turkey, the Philippines, Mexico, India and Morocco to manually screen every piece of content that has been flagged by Facebook users, paying these contractors the princely sum of around $1 an hour (with a potential of $4 on commission).[12] Much of the screened content is extremely disturbing—animal abuse, beheadings, pedophilia, necrophilia, KKK hate, suicides. The Gawker website interviewed some of the screeners, who were disturbed by not only the images but also the low pay. Amine Derkaoui, a 21-year-old Moroccan man, quit, saying, "it's humiliating. They are just exploiting the third world."[13] The other screeners agreed, saying the low pay was typical of the sort of work available on Upwork.

Ironically, their complaints about low pay surfaced publicly just a few weeks after Facebook launched what was then the largest IPO in Wall Street history, raising $16 billion for the company. But it wasn't paying any of that to its 1099 workers. Facebook had "externalized" that ugly side to oDesk/Upwork.

One business client who has frequently used Upwork's service has called it "telecommuting on steroids."[14] Why steroids? One logistical challenge that has plagued these online job brokerages has been the difficulty of monitoring contractors who are scattered all over the world. But Elance-Upwork has a solution for that: it is pioneering the use of new online digital technologies for "employee surveillance" that are nothing short of Orwellian.

Elance-Upwork provides to its clients a suite of tools for online management and supervision to crack down on "cyber slacking"—the notion that poorly paid freelancers should stay focused, hard at work and away from the virtual water cooler. The company has developed software—cheerfully called the "Private Workplace"—that provides minute-by-minute logs of contractors' computer keystrokes, tracks mouse movements and—in the latest innovation in labor surveillance—secretly snaps periodic screenshots, so that the employer can ensure that their potential cyber slacker is on task. The screenshots are taken at random intervals, allowing employers essentially to "look over the worker's shoulder."[15] Stephane Kasriel, who became CEO of Elance-Upwork in April 2015, waxes enthusiastically about the surveillance technology: "The idea behind the screenshots is something similar to the physical office," Kasriel says. "I can see from random screenshots that she seems to be working on the stuff I asked her to."[16]

And Elance-Upwork should know, because the company, based in Mountain View, California, practices what it preaches: its 740-person workforce is composed of a mere 240 full-time employees, along with 500 freelancers, scattered all over the world.[17] Having two-thirds of your workforce filled by contingent labor—none of whom receive any safety-net supports—and only one-third by regular employees is a disturbing snapshot of the preferred future balance for many U.S. businesses. Elance-Upwork is there to show the way. It is the largest player in the digital temp industry that has surged during the economic crisis and continued surging during the recovery. It is expected to grow to somewhere between $16 billion and $46 billion by 2020, according to research firm Staffing Industry Analysts.[18]

As with other sharing economy companies like Uber and Airbnb, big investors and venture capital see hills of gold in the offing. Backers of Elance-Upwork include some of the biggest investor names in Silicon Valley, such as Benchmark, Globespan Capital Partners, Sigma Partners, T. Rowe Price, Kleiner Perkins, Pequot Capital and Citigroup.[19] Investors note, with evident satisfaction, trends like the one identified by German software multinational SAP and Oxford Economics, which surveyed over 2,700 executives and found that 83 percent say they plan to increase use of contingent or intermittent employees in the next several years.[20] So the Elance-Upwork merger is a reflection of a rapidly growing market and an exploding 1099 workforce. Tearing a page out of Travis Kalanick's book, the principals know that "big attracts big," like a gravitational force field, and Elance-Upwork is big and growing toward an eventual IPO, with that Silicon Valley luster of "gold in them thar hills" glowing ever brighter.

But what of the economic consequences for the American workforce? "The hitch in that shiny, gleaming 'isn't it wonderful?' picture," says Stowe Boyd, an analyst at the former Gigaom Research who has studied the Upwork phenomenon, "is the economic arbitrage of outsourcing work," from the United States to cheaper labor in places like the Philippines. The impact on the workforce says Boyd, "is largely a negative."[21] Defenders claim that employers have always tried to get the most highly qualified workers for as little money as possible, which is certainly true. But the reach of the global

Internet- and Web-based job brokerages have infinitely expanded the geographic range and football-stadium-sized pool of job applicants. Businesses large and small (including, as we have seen, those in the sharing economy) are gradually distancing themselves from the workers they hire, making fractured work relationships an increasingly common feature of our outsourced economy. It's how more and more businesses hire today, and it's how more and more Americans are working, whether they want it that way or not.

With the help of Elance-Upwork and other job-brokerage websites, such as TaskRabbit, CrowdFlower, Work Market, Hourly Nerd (for hiring freelance MBAs), Thumbtack, Exec, Freelancer.com and Guru (all of which either currently or in the past have used a similar online auction price structure), it's become an employers' world. Wages are flat, the quality of jobs has declined and a whiff of desperation has crept into the labor force. More and more workers all over the world are lining up online, like so many *bracero* day workers, scrambling for whatever crumbs are tossed their way.

THE TROUBLE WITH RABBITS

While Upwork and Elance pioneered the use of online job auctions so that international freelancers could undercut each other, the type of work those companies specialize in—mostly creative and technical work—has limited its impact on the labor force. Many jobs, particularly service-type jobs, must be performed by someone who is physically present at the job site. Those services can't be outsourced to poorly paid Third World workers. That reality has been a saving grace for millions of domestic jobs in the U.S.

But no more.

TaskRabbit, launched in 2008 in San Francisco, quickly became one of the most popular websites that connected domestic freelancers with customers who needed specific tasks and errands done. CNN called it "one of the biggest up-and-comers in America," *Wired* called it "revolutionary."[22] ABC Nightly News hailed TaskRabbit as a remedy for America's job crisis, because of how it was helping people "take back their lives, be their own boss, help people out, make some money and just feel good again."[23] PayPal billionaire Peter Thiel's Founders Fund and other venture capitalists injected tens of millions of dollars into the company. TaskRabbit was on a roll, in those heady early days.

TaskRabbit began advertising itself, rather slickly, as a friendly and even "neighborly" Web-based service that allows customers to "outsource household errands and skilled tasks" to people "in your neighborhood" who have specific skills and have undergone background checks. The task rabbits—yes, that's what the workers were called, initially—were hired by customers to do any number of specific jobs, such as painting a fence, grocery shopping, raking leaves, delivering restaurant food, assembling a piece of Ikea furniture, driving to a doctor's appointment and other "mini-gigs." Instead of calling it for what it was—a job brokerage for day laborers—the founders wrapped the company in the spin of the sharing economy about "trust" and "peer-to-peer employment," and came up with a name that sounded warm and fuzzy, including a logo with a cute bunny rabbit.

Leah Busque, the founder and CEO of TaskRabbit, who has managed to attract $40 million in venture capital, says all she has done is build a marketplace for doing errands. "Neighbors helping neighbors—it's an old school concept upgraded for today," says the company website.[24] Anne Raimondi, a TaskRabbit executive, was a bit more expansive in her vision: "Really, what we want to do is revolutionize how people work—and also how people find people to do work."[25]

No question, finding work in the middle of a deep economic crisis has been a difficult challenge for many Americans. And even with the recession sort of over, the job market has not recovered for many, many people, with the percent of employed Americans dropping to 57.6 percent in January 2011, its lowest level since 1983 (and still stuck at 58.9 percent in February 2015, significantly lower than before the Great Recession in 2008).[26] Particularly for the millions of unemployed who have been without a job for more than six months, TaskRabbit starts looking attractive. By mid-2013, the service had launched in nine cities with around 11,000 contractors. After the government shutdown in October 2013, TaskRabbit reported that it was swamped with 13,000 applications in a single day.[27] Lately it claims to have 25,000 or so contractors using its website, scattered across 18 U.S. cities, plus London.[28]

Like Elance and Upwork, TaskRabbit also initially created an online auction, but this one for locally based chore labor. As part of its bidding process, it employed all of the now-familiar bells and whistles of the sharing economy, such as "gamification techniques" and "reputation analytics," allowing customers to rate and rank the rabbits and write customer reviews. That in turn allowed TaskRabbit to assess the performance of their day laborers. Often when a person with a ton of experience bid on a job at a fair price, she or he rarely got the job because the experienced person was outbid by another rabbit willing to work for less. Complained one rabbit, "Any self-respecting handyman on Craigslist will charge $18–$25 an hour. Whereas people can bid on TaskRabbit and get some unemployed, desperate person and pay them $8 an hour. With TaskRabbit taking a cut off the top, too."[29] TaskRabbit's cut is a sizable 20 percent taken from each rabbit's earnings (though it used to be 15 percent,[30] and many rabbits complain in online forums that the markup today is considerably higher, sometimes more than 50 percent).[31]

Said one former task rabbit, "All the workers are forced to undercut each other for how much they're willing to be paid or be left with nothing. It's really designed to be a race to the bottom." Cathy, another former rabbit said, "It's basically blind bidding by the task rabbits. We don't get to know what the job poster wants to pay. . . . The job winds up going to the lowest bidder, often up to half of what . . . my supposed 'good bid' was."[32] Like Elance-Upwork, therein lies the problem: in most cases the price charged is getting bid down toward the lowest common denominator, and this acts as a severe downward drag on wages.

Initially, many of the rabbits were positive about their experience, grateful to have any source of income. But after a while, former task rabbits began to speak out about the inequities built into the service and the exploitation inherent in the company's business model.

"Some of the people posting tasks are really wealthy and they want the invisible elves to come in the night and do the dirty work. And they don't want to pay very much," said one former rabbit.[33] Cathy said, "Posters always underestimate the work they need done, and I've done many tasks for less than minimum wage. Why? Because TaskRabbit rates the task rabbit workers and if you don't do it, the poster can complain and you look like the bad guy." That is a common complaint, that oftentimes the job is bigger than what was advertised, or the customer wanted more chores done on top of the original chore without offering any more pay. Yet if the rabbit refuses, she or he could receive a lower ranking from the customer on the TaskRabbit website. Customer complaints over even trivial matters have caused the TaskRabbit masters to suspend or even fire a worker from the service. The ratings system is part of the highly touted "feedback mechanism" of the sharing economy's reputation analytics model, but it lends itself to much abuse and even retaliation. That is combined with an extremely lopsided labor contract that every rabbit has to sign, which states that the "Company may terminate or suspend your right to use the Service at any time for any or no reason."[34] No appeal process, no arbitration, no union representation. There's a lot of stick there, but not much carrot for the rabbits. Cathy compared her life as a rabbit to being "the gum on the bottom of the shoe."

Sarah Kessler, an editor at business and technology magazine *Fast Company,* went undercover in the gigging economy, utilizing TaskRabbit and other job brokerages. For four weeks she hustled for work in New York City, testing, as she put it, "Whether the tech world's solution for the poor job market and income inequality had the answer." She wrote an entertaining yet illuminating testimonial about her experience.

"Setting up a full day of gigs isn't easy," she wrote, in diary fashion. "I get rejected from about five tasks for every one I win. Sometimes I hold spots in my calendar that I could fill with other tasks for jobs I've bid on but haven't heard from. I'm essentially competing for every hour of my employment. Even if I land a gig with a decent hourly wage, it typically looks like nothing once I factor in the time spent looking for jobs and commuting between them." Despite the frequent promise of the sharing economy visionaries—"you can be your own boss, you can be your own microentrepreneur"—she says, "In fact I have no control over when I work, because the only way to get gigs is to be available sporadically and often without much notice."[35]

Kessler also wrote about Stacie, a TaskRabbit success story. While working full time at her regular job, she also made about $6,000 on TaskRabbit in one year, earning her "elite TaskRabbit" status. "If I wasn't working full time, I could do more tasks," she says, "but even if I doubled that, that's still poverty—$12,000 a year. And there are no benefits. You don't know what you're going to wake up to. You could wake up one day, and be like, oh my god, I made $300 today, and then have three days where you're making $12."

Another person, Robyn, commented, somewhat bitterly, "In my two years of nearly unbroken unemployment after the dot com crash, I tried some of these websites and discovered it was like signing up to be slave labor. In most cases, it wasn't worth the effort to apply—or the uncomfortable sensation of smelling desperation in your own body scent."[36]

Kessler adds up her total take for her effort as a Task Rabbit. "My best day suddenly seems like a winner. I made $10 an hour at the dance job, $15 an hour at the Harvard Club, and about $20 an hour wrapping presents: $95 in total. My eight-and-a-half hour day was a best-case scenario. There was no downtime. The only break I had was a 10-minute lunch that I grabbed next to [TaskRabbit user] Mark's apartment before gift wrapping his presents. But when you factor in the time I spend commuting between tasks, I only made $11 an hour." That was after TaskRabbit took its 20 percent cut, and barely higher than the minimum wage in some cities. "Instead of the labor revolution I had been promised," concluded Kessler, "all I found was hard work, low pay, and a system that puts workers at a disadvantage."

Success is hard to come by for most of these task rabbits. And of course none of these "arms for hire" receive any worker benefits or supports. No, this is not "neighbor helping neighbor," this is exploitation by another name.

One unique feature of TaskRabbit, compared to temp agencies and other job brokerages, is that the rabbits are highly educated. Seventy percent of the rabbits hold at least a bachelor's degree, 20 percent have a master's degrees and 5 percent a PhD.[37] Many used to work "good" jobs, but those have withered up and blown away. Certainly for some of the rabbits who, for whatever reason, have no other sources of income or work, TaskRabbit and other labor brokerages provide a marginally helpful service. On the positive side, they can connect the under- and unemployed with potential employers, which allows these workers to have somewhere to turn when they need to make money. It's better than sitting on one's couch surfing television, despondent and flat broke. Advocates rightly argue that these online labor brokerages can also help those who traditionally have been labor market "outsiders" to find paid work. Certainly, if these services weren't taking off in an economy in which, for the last several decades, the productivity gains of the workforce have gone into the pockets of fewer and fewer people, and if these services weren't occurring at a time when the status of the middle class is rapidly eroding, then all of this might have been a welcome add-on to the broader macroeconomy for those people who want to make a little extra money.

Instead, the rabbits are little more than lowly paid day laborers, with declining prospects for better employment. The workers have no bargaining power, not only because they can be dismissed without cause, but also because they are purposefully kept separated from each other by the anonymous technology. They are a dispersed workforce with no means for meeting or strategizing, which prevents them from organizing collectively or trying to coordinate bids to drive up the wage.

One former rabbit was asked if she thought that TaskRabbit was taking advantage of the fact that a lot of people are unemployed. "Absolutely," she said. "They know people are unemployed and underemployed. People desperately need the money. There will always be someone to replace you, and this attitude of, 'Well you should just be grateful that you have this opportunity,' isn't really right."[38]

As mentioned earlier, the media and the visionaries crowned TaskRabbit as "revolutionary," but they did so without ever really talking to the rabbits. One *BusinessWeek* article went so far as to crow "In the Future We'll All Be Task Rabbits."[39] But a former rabbit reacted derisively: "Revolution? Which revolution? The French Revolution? Where Marie Antoinette was beheaded? Because it's very much people wanting peasants."[40]

Leah Busque has defended her company business model, saying—sounding like Travis Kalanick and Brian Chesky—that her company's responsibility to the rabbits is only to provide the best platform possible, nothing more. "We're about empowering these independent contractors to build out their own businesses," she says. "We don't want them to be TaskRabbit employees. It's good for them to have the autonomy and the drive to do what they want, when they want, for the price that they want."[41]

Minus TaskRabbit's 20 percent (or higher) cut, of course. And even if they have to sink to the greyer edges of the labor market to do it, offering themselves like *braceros:* "Take me! Take me!"

FROM PEER-TO-PEER TO TEMP AGENCY

Despite some hiccups and some increasingly vocal disgruntled former workers, TaskRabbit seemed set, slowly establishing its platform as a darling of sharing economy enthusiasts, investors and the media. And then . . . a strange thing happened.

In July 2014, Task Rabbit suddenly announced that it was deep-sixing its online labor auction. The company was doing what in Silicon Valley is graciously called a "pivot"—tech speak for acknowledging that its business model wasn't working, it was losing too much money, and so it had to shake things up. It revamped how its platform worked, particularly how jobs are priced. Instead of an auction model where workers bid on tasks and the lowest bid usually won, workers now had to specify their hourly rates for a greatly limited range of jobs—either housecleaning, running errands, handyman or providing moving help. TaskRabbit had narrowed its core business to those tasks that had been the most requested by customers. In addition, TaskRabbit began using an algorithm to match customers and contractors, suggesting potential workers for each gig. Clients then contacted those candidates to check their availability and skills and—in a major change—the candidates had only 30 minutes to respond to requests. If they didn't respond in that time, the gig moved on to another worker. TaskRabbit would still take a 20 percent cut of each contract.[42]

And that's not all. The company also changed the name of what it called its workers, who would no longer be known as "task rabbits" but as "taskers." The name "rabbit" in a labor context no doubt conjured up memories of the little critters in Michael Moore's film, *Roger and Me,* and what happened to them as General Motors laid off tens of thousands of autoworkers in Flint, Michigan. In a memorable scene, pet rabbits were sold as food by a Flint resident to laid-off workers trying to feed their families.

Despite the changes, many workers were still not happy. While previously they had to submit themselves to an online auction that was a race to the bottom, at least they could pick and choose the jobs they desired. Now, the jobs were being assigned to them. "With the bidding system I could find jobs that interested me," said Stacey Roberts-Ohr, who used to bid on tasks ranging from grant writing to grocery shopping. "Now I have no input on what I'm going to do."[43]

Moreover, with the requirement that each "tasker" had to respond within 30 minutes to accept or lose the offer, TaskRabbit was taking the scourge of "just-in-time scheduling" (which was discussed in chapter 1) to a new and disturbing level. The taskers would remain constantly on call and have little advance notice about when a job might be offered, leaving them in an uncertain limbo that makes it impossible to plan their own lives.

Busque defended the changes as necessary to help TaskRabbit keep up with "explosive demand growth," but published reports said the company was responding to a decline in the number of completed tasks. Too many of the rabbits, it turns out, were not happy campers and did a poor job, despite company rhetoric to the contrary, and an increasing number simply failed to show up for their tasks.[44]

But the real revelation about the "pivot" was that TaskRabbit's new business model had morphed into something more like a traditional temp agency. That transition had begun a year before when TaskRabbit quietly had beefed up that part of its business that helped companies hire ongoing temporary workers for jobs that spanned over multiple days, weeks or months, instead of chore by chore.[45] Many employers already had been using TaskRabbit as a kind of job board from which to recruit temps. Economist Juliet Schor, who studies the sharing economy, said she discovered evidence of ad-hoc temp agencies *within* TaskRabbit; for gigs like copy editing or proofreading, people who rated highly on the site and received a large volume of requests sometimes subcontracted their work to others, taking a bit off the top for themselves. A TaskRabbit within a TaskRabbit.[46]

Supporting businesses and providing temp workers to employers had slowly emerged as TaskRabbit's fastest-growing part of its business. "We realigned the company to support our key business opportunities, namely business services and our marketplace operations," said Busque, in a moment of damage control combined with honesty.[47] The peer-to-peer component of its sharing economy business was being pushed to the sidelines.

Would the new strategy work? In some key ways, it didn't make a lot of sense because it was putting TaskRabbit squarely into competition with a new set of bigger companies—those in the $230-billion-a-year temp hiring industry, dominated by firms like Manpower, Adecco, Kelly Services and others in the U.S. It also was squaring off more directly with similar-sized companies that now closely matched TaskRabbit's specific work platform, such as Handybook, which also offers on-demand housecleaning and home-repair services, and is slightly bigger with $49 million in funding and availability in 26 cities.[48]

But TaskRabbit is gambling that it can provide temp workers who will be less expensive than those provided by Manpower and Kelly Services.

Businesses pay those agencies a minimum of 40 percent of a worker's wage in fees, while TaskRabbit charges only 26 percent for its temping workers.[49] TaskRabbit is fighting back the old-fashioned way—by making its labor cheaper than its competitors. That, and making agreements with companies like Walmart, which has contracted out its deliveries to TaskRabbit because Busque's company can provide labor that is cheaper—and has fewer rights—than even Walmart employees![50]

Perhaps TaskRabbit will succeed in its pivot—though it seems iffy—but whether or not it does, its participation in the peer-to-peer sharing economy is now history for all intents and purposes. You can still hire an individual task rabbit to do odd jobs, but this is no longer the core of its business.

WHY THE SHARING ECONOMY IS SPUTTERING

But TaskRabbit was not the only sharing-economy startup making a "pivot." Suddenly a contagion of pivots—as well as flops—was happening everywhere. In the stronger economy of the mid-2000s (prior to the 2008 crash), there had been a surge in sharing economy companies—"Uber for X" businesses, as they were called, because many of them would specialize and try to dominate in areas such as home cleaning, personal assistants, laundry, fix-it and repair, wine, pet care, gear rental, delivery, moving and dozens more. Within the labor brokerage specialty, a whole host of companies with colorful names—Fiverr, HomeJoy, Campus Bellhops, Hourly Nerd, Wonolo, Freelancer.com, Guru, Fancy Hands, CrowdFlower, Exec, Rev, Thumbtack (belly dancers, anyone?), Postmates, SpoonRocket, Zaarly, Taskhero, Work Market, GoGofers, WeGoLook, Helpouts—had followed TaskRabbit's lead, creating websites that enabled vulnerable workers to hire themselves out as indie contractors and freelancers for ever smaller micro-gigs and amounts of money. Like TaskRabbit, many of them began having difficulties as their business models sputtered.

This of course was not the first time that the froth of Silicon Valley startups had slurped down the drain. When the dot-com boom in the late 1990s eventually went bust, that period's most famous flameouts—Pets.com, Urbanfetch, Kozmo, Webvan, Computer.com—were all gone by 2001.[51] The local lore says that three out of four startups fail, and more than nine out of ten never earn a return.[52]

This time, companies like Cherry (carwashes), Prim (laundry), SnapGoods (gear rental) and Rewinery (wine) all went bust, some of them quietly and some with more clamor. My favorite example is SnapGoods, which is still cited today by many journalists who are pumping up the sharing economy (and haven't done their homework) as a fitting example of a cool, hip company that allows people to rent out their equipment, like that drill you never use, or your backpack or spare bicycle—even though SnapGoods went out of business in August 2012. If one does a search on any of the dozen or so online magazines that write about the tech industry and Silicon Valley, strangely there is not a single article that discusses the collapse of SnapGoods. It just disappeared—poof—without a trace, yet goes on living in the imagination of sharing economy boosters. I conducted a Twitter interview with its former CEO, Ron J. Williams, as well as with whatever wizard currently lurks behind the faux curtain of the SnapGoods Twitter account, and the only comment they would make is that "we pivoted and communicated to our 50,000 users that we had bigger fish to try." Getting even vaguer, they insisted "we decided to build tech to strengthen social relationships and facilitate trust"—classic sharing economy speak for producing vaporware instead of substance from a company that had vanished with barely a trace.

Zaarly in its prime was another sharing economy darling of the venture capital set, with notable investors including Steve Jobs, hotshot venture capital firm Kleiner Perkins and former eBay CEO Meg Whitman on its board. It positioned itself in the marketplace as a competitor to TaskRabbit and similar services, with its brash founder and CEO, Bo Fishback, explaining his company's mission to a conference audience: "If you've ever said, 'I'd pay X amount for Y,' then Zaarly is for you."[53] In Silicon Valley–speak, Zaarly was a "proximity-based, real-time, buyer-powered market," which meant its website and app could instantly connect local customers with local producers for just about anything. This is what's known as the "on-demand" economy, as the *Economist* has favorably lionized it.[54] Fishback once spectacularly showed how different his company was by bringing on stage a cow being towed by a man in a baseball cap and carrying a jug of milk—"If I'm willing to pay $100 for someone to bring me a glass of fresh milk from an Omaha dairy cow right now, there might very well be a guy who would be super happy to do that." Like so many of the sharing economy evangelicals, Fishback saw his company in expansive terms, as growing a "passionate community of buyers and sellers," and beyond that making a connection between "people who had more money than time" and those people who were in the opposite situation. Brandishing his libertarian Ayn Randianism, he saw Zaarly as creating "the ultimate opt-in employment market, where there is no excuse for people who say, 'I don't know how to get a job, I don't know how to get started.'"[55]

But alas, those were the heady, early years, when Zaarly was flush with VC cash. Flash forward to today and Fishback is more humble, as is his company, having gone through several "pivots." The "request anything" model is gone, as are Fishback's lofty ambitions for American workers or his company.

Fishback's cofounder Eric Koester also has bailed. Instead, Zaarly has become more narrowly focused on four comparatively mundane markets: housecleaning, handyman services, lawn care and maid service. Sound familiar? Much like TaskRabbit, its customer base now hires from one of its four categories of "experts," as it calls them—cleaners, maids, gardeners, handymen.

And then there's Exec. Like Zaarly and TaskRabbit, Exec also started with great fanfare as a broader errand-running business, this one focused on hiring a personal assistant for busy, high-powered Masters of the Universe (or at least those who thought they were).[56] Like other sharing companies, initially it had grand ambitions about the peer-to-peer economy and fomenting a revolution over how we work: connecting those with more money than time with those 1099 indies who desperately needed the money. Now, if you go to the company's website, you discover that they too have narrowed their focus: to housekeeping exclusively. And in fact the company was sold to Handybook, mentioned earlier as one of the revamped TaskRabbit's direct competitors.

What happened? A pattern has emerged about the "white dwarf" fate of these once-luminous labor brokerages: after launching with much fanfare and tens of millions of VC capital behind them, vowing to enact a revolution in how people work and how society organizes peer-to-peer economic transactions, in the end many of these companies morphed into the equivalent of old-fashioned temp agencies (and others have simply imploded into black hole nothingness). Market forces have resulted in a convergence of companies on a few services that had been the most used on their platforms. Commenting on TaskRabbit's erratic trajectory, *Fast Company*'s Sarah Kessler wrote, "It's a tacit admission that gig economy platforms may ultimately be an app-powered temporary employment agency rather than a revolutionary new form of work."[57] Indeed, in a real sense, even Uber is merely a temp agency, where workers do only one task: drive cars.

Exec's former CEO, Justin Kan, wrote a self-reflective farewell blog post about what he thought went wrong with his company. His observations are illuminating.

His company had charged customers $25 per hour (which later rose to $30) to hire one of their personal assistants, and the worker received 80 percent, or about $20 per hour. That seemed like a high wage to Kan, but much to his surprise he discovered that, when his errand runners made their own personal calculation, factoring in the unsteadiness of the work, the frequency of downtime, hustling from gig to gig, their own expenses, it wasn't such a great deal. Particularly for the "just-in-time scheduling" nature of this work, in which you were expected to be waiting by your smartphone, constantly on call. Wrote Kan, "It turns out that $20 per hour does not provide enough economic incentive in San Francisco to dictate when our errand runners had to be available, leading to large supply gaps at times of spiky demand . . . it was impossible to ensure that we had consistent availability. Most of our errand workers wanted to work during normal work days, meaning there was an undersupply on weekends"—often when Exec's Masters of the Universe clients wanted someone at their beck and call.[58]

Kan says that the company also acquired a "false sense that the quality of service for our customers was better than it was" because the quality of the "average recruitable errand runner"—at the low pay and just-in-time demands that Exec wanted—did not result in hiring the self-motivated personality types like those that start Silicon Valley companies. (Surprise, surprise.) That in turn led to too many negative experiences for too many customers, especially since, like with TaskRabbit, a too-high percentage of its on-demand workers simply failed to show up to their gigs. (Surprise, surprise.) It turns out, he discovered, that "most competent people are not looking for part-time work." (Surprise, surprise.)

Indeed, the reality that the sharing economy visionaries can't seem to grasp is that not everyone is cut out to be a gig-preneur, or to "build out their own businesses," as Leah Busque likes to say. Being an entrepreneur takes a uniquely wired brand of individual with a distinctive skill, including being "psychotically optimistic," as one business consultant I interviewed put it. Simply being jobless is not a sufficient qualification. In addition, apparently nobody in Silicon Valley ever shared with Kan or Busque the old business secret that "you get what you pay for." That's a lesson that Uber's Travis Kalanick seems determined to learn the hard way as well.

But—and this should be the real take-home lesson for so many of these companies—"When we started focusing only on providing cleaning services," said Kan, "we were able to vet workers against a smaller skill set, provide specific tools, and streamline the interface to make purchasing more intuitive and simpler, resulting in much better growth." That was a lesson that TaskRabbit and Zaarly had learned the hard way as well; by narrowing the scope of their services, these companies would have a better chance of contracting with quality people, and developing real relationships with them, in many cases with professionals who already had their own business as a housekeeper, gardener, maid, handyman, and were simply using these websites as one of several means to market their services.

Kan, like Leah Busque, Bo Fishman and so many of the wide-eyed visionaries of Silicon Valley, had completely underestimated the human factor. To so many of these hyperactive venture entrepreneurs, workers are just another ore to be fed into their machine. They forget that the quality of the ore is crucial to their success, and that quality was dependent on how well the workers were rewarded and treated, which affected whether or not they could attract workers stoked with a positive and entrepreneurial attitude. The low pay and extremely uncertain nature of the work keeps the employees wondering if there isn't a better deal somewhere else. The *Economist* reports that 40 percent of freelancers are paid late, which only contributes to this sense of uncertainty and being underappreciated.[59] No wonder, then, that these on-demand companies that are trying to keep their costs as low as possible have so much difficulty managing, motivating and retaining workers.

Moreover, a degree of tunnel vision has prevented entrepreneurs like Kan, Busque and Fishback from seeing that their business model often is not scalable. Silicon Valley has an expression, "That works on Sand Hill Road"[60]—referring to the upper-crust boulevard in Menlo Park, California, where much of the world's venture capital makes its home. Some things that seem like great ideas—like paying low wages to personal assistants to shuffle around at your every whim and pleasure—only make sense inside the VC bubble that has lost all contact with the realities of life as experienced by everyday Americans.

Consequently, in company after company—TaskRabbit, Zaarly, Exec and more—the original business model morphed into one in which these companies became little more than temp agencies, albeit with more focus on building online capacity via apps. Rebecca Smith, deputy director of the National Employment Law Project, compares the businesses of the gig economy to old-fashioned labor brokers. Companies like Postmates and Uber, she says, talk as if they are different from old-style employers simply because they operate online. "But in fact," she says, "they are operating just like farm labor contractors and garment jobbers and day labor centers of old."[61]

To be sure, the sharing economy apps have proven to be extremely fluid at connecting someone who needs work with someone willing to pay for that work. And many workers have praised the flexibility of the platforms. But at the end of the day, the sharing economy labor brokerages were not about sharing at all, and not very revolutionary. They have failed to thrive because for most people they provide crummy jobs that most people only want to do as a very last resort. These platforms show their 1099 workforce no allegiance or loyalty, and they engender none in return.

THE "SHARE-THE-CRUMBS" ECONOMY

As we have seen, micro-gigging via the various labor platforms in the sharing economy leaves already vulnerable workers no better off, and in some ways worse off. The pay is low, the safety net eviscerated, job security nonexistent. A graphic designer can make $300 in one day, but not have any more work lined up for two weeks and have trouble making rent. A public-relations consultant can count IBM as a client, but still have to choose between squirreling some money away for retirement and affording the smartphone she needs to keep up with clients. A young college graduate goes freelance but can't pay her crippling student loans. A carpenter finds a few weeks of work, but has to choose between paying for health insurance for his family or repairing his truck. If you lose a gig and haven't yet found another, tough luck, you aren't even eligible for unemployment compensation; if your client pays a month late, or stiffs you entirely, tough luck again.[62] And on top of it all, you get paid less than your regularly employed counterparts—on average 25 percent less in hourly wage (with the gap even larger for some occupations).[63]

But here's where the share-the-crumbs economy becomes even more sinister, raising an ongoing labor tragedy into a profound existential crisis. In a regular, full-time job, a worker gets paid "on the clock" for an agreed-upon number of hours per day, week, month, year. Rest and bathroom breaks, staff meetings, time at the water cooler with fellow workers, all of those are paid time in a regular job. A certain amount of on-the-job downtime also is paid time—it is recognized that those moments sometimes give rise to wellsprings of creativity and innovation. Certainly some workers have abused this arrangement, and have taken too many breaks or don't work as hard or as long as they should. But on the whole, this has been a workplace structure that has been successful for American workers and employers alike.

But the freelance society—the gig economy, the 1099 economy—is massively overturning this universal order. In the name of hyper (market) efficiency, suddenly the "extraneous" parts of a worker's day are being eliminated. Micro-gigs with job brokerages like TaskRabbit and Elance-Upwork are reducing workers' value to only those exact minutes someone is raking the leaves, or on the computer, or banging the nails or mopping the floor, or engaged in a specific task, toiling away and producing. The new digital platforms can chop up an array of traditional jobs into discrete tasks, and you will be paid only for those exact productive moments. All of it will be logged on your smartphone, and your performance will be constantly tracked, analyzed and subjected to review by employers and subject to customer-satisfaction ratings.

It's as if New England Patriots quarterback Tom Brady only got paid by the play, or when he threw a completed pass; or members of Congress only got remunerated for the specific times they sat on the floor of Congress, voting on legislation; or if a scientist only got paid for a specific invention, or a chef got paid by the meal or a doctor by the patient or for a surgery performed. It's piecework with no annual salary, no payment for any preparation, or for training or research, only for a specific product or service at the time it is manifest—and all the time and activities that led to that final product have to be done on the individual's own time and dime.

Arun Sundararajan, a professor at New York University's business school, is the sharing economy's favorite academic, trotted out on a regular basis to put a gloss of scholarly respectability over its increasingly questionable practices. He has endorsed Uber's and Airbnb's insistence that "self-policing" via the customer ratings system is sufficient regulation for their companies.[64] He also speaks glowingly of the hyper-efficiency of the new gig economy. In fact, he gives it a rather sinister-sounding name—"monetizing your downtime." These services "are tapping into people's available time more efficiently," he says. We may end up with a future in which some of the workforce will "do a portfolio of things to generate an income—you could be an Uber driver, an Instacart shopper, an Airbnb host and a Taskrabbit," he says.[65]

"Monetizing your downtime." If that sounds like a glorious future to you, then an app called Spare5 is ready for your download. That app, writes Nick Wingfield in the *New York Times,* allows people to monetize "the brief interludes in [their] day when they're waiting for a latte at Starbucks, sitting in a waiting room or riding the bus home." There is no need to relax anymore while you are waiting—what a waste of time!—now you can get paid to perform "nano-gigs," which are even smaller than micro-gigs. "It's the next logical step in the sharing economy," says Wingfield.[66]

One such nano-gig is tagging photos for the Internet retailer Zulily, describing women's shoes with words like "sandal" and "flats." The rate of pay? About a buck thirty per hour. Or you can try your luck on Amazon's service Mechanical Turk. Sarah Kessler did, spending chunks of her time, about two hours every day, labeling photo slideshows at a nickel each. Each slideshow had five photos, and each photo had 11 pages of labels to choose from. "There are slideshows of cats on couches, cats on beds, dogs on beds. Cats in sinks. Dogs with cakes, cats with pizza," says Kessler. "It takes at least 55 clicks to earn five cents. . . . I make $1.94 an hour."[67]

Matt Bencke, the chief executive of Spare5, calls his company's app an "on-demand work platform that breaks large, corporate, operational problems into tiny, bite-sized tasks." It turns out that nanotasks such as providing accurate, detailed tags on photographs—what has been called "metadata"—are becoming increasingly used in e-commerce to help people find the right piece of apparel, a hotel room with the perfect view and more. Getty Images, a big creator and distributor of photographs, wants to make its enormous library of photographs more easily discoverable to people when they are doing Internet searches. So now you don't have to waste your spare time, you can put it to work: Courtney Dale made about $53 per week by using the Spare5 app two to three hours a day.[68] That rate of pay works out to—about three dollars per hour. But hey, it's just spare time, right? Spare time is cheap. Who needs spare time?

Professor Sundararajan helps us understand the value and worth of this brilliant new development. The *New York Times* reports that Sundararajan "says that services like Spare5 can be empowering to people who want more control over when and how they work, even if it is just for peanuts." More likely it will turn everyone into what technology critic Evgeny Morozov calls "psychotic entrepreneurs," always stressed out, anxious and groveling for the next gig, with every interaction recorded, ranked and stored.[69]

This "nano-ization" of work into ever-smaller gigs is what the sharing and peer-to-peer visionaries are demanding of U.S. workers. They want to turn people into, not just micro-preneurs, but nano-preneurs. It's a warped, mad science coming out of Silicon Valley, the logical culmination of a tech-driven, sci-fi doctrine in which the primary allegiance is toward a hyper-efficient allocation of human beings, as if they are machines. Not even temp agencies have had the effrontery to do that. They usually pay a worker a set hourly wage for a specific amount of time, such as a half or full day or a week of labor, with paid rest breaks and lunch breaks, governed by regulations. But that's too inefficient and humane for the new economy gurus. Morozov calls their sharing economy creation "truly neo-liberalism on steroids" because of the way it creates markets everywhere, and out of everything and everybody.[70]

Yet not all labor experts agree with this trend.

"I think it's nonsense, utter nonsense," says Robert Reich, an economist at the University of California, Berkeley, who was the secretary of labor during the Clinton administration. "This on-demand economy means a work life that is unpredictable, doesn't pay very well and is terribly insecure." Can you imagine, he asks, if this turns into an economy "where everyone is doing piecework at all odd hours, and no one knows when the next job will come, and how much it will pay? What kind of private lives can we possibly have, what kind of relationships, what kind of families?"[71]

That's why the share-the-crumbs economy is more than a labor tragedy—it's an existential challenge. In short, the gurus of the sharing economy have been at the vanguard of an audacious attempt to forge an economic system in which individuals and businesses with "more money than time" are able to use faceless interactions via brokerage websites and apps to force an online bidding war among lower-income people to see who will charge the least for their labor, or to rent out their personal property (such as their car or home). It's practically a medieval system in all its modern glory, yet all wrapped under the New Agey mantle of "sharing"—without the employers having to worry about labor protections, minimum wage, safety nets, health care, retirement, enforceable contracts or ongoing relationships of *noblesse oblige* toward those they hire.

In some ways, these trends mark the culmination of an antilabor backlash that began shortly after World War II. That's when the first temp agencies, Manpower and the Russell Kelly Office Service (later known as Kelly Girl Services), were founded in the Midwest.[72] As reported by Erin Hatton in her book *The Temp Economy: From Kelly Girls to Permatemps in Postwar America,* to avoid hostility from unions the agencies portrayed temp work as "women's work," an outlet for homemakers looking to pick up some extra money. They spent millions of dollars and bought thousands of advertisements in the pages of *Newsweek, Businessweek, U.S. News & World Report, Good Housekeeping, Fortune,* and the *New York Times,* showing young, white, middle-class women doing a variety of short-term office jobs. Ad campaigns featuring the Kelly Girls, Manpower's White Glove Girls, Western Girl's Cowgirls and numerous other such "girls" enjoyed remarkable success, with the Kelly Girls becoming cultural icons and the temp agencies expanding nationwide. One of the ads was for the "Never-Never Girl," who the company described in the ad copy as having attractive qualities that sound, rather ominously, like a task rabbit or Uber driver:

> Never takes a vacation or holiday. Never asks for a raise. Never costs you a dime for slack time. (When the workload drops, you drop her.) Never has a cold, slipped disc or loose tooth. (Not on your time anyway!) Never costs you for unemployment taxes and Social Security payments. (None of the paperwork, either!) Never costs you for fringe benefits. (They add up to 30% of every payroll dollar.) Never fails to please. (If your Kelly Girl employee doesn't work out, you don't pay.)[73]

The ad campaigns amounted to a concerted effort to take advantage of the era's gender biases to establish a beachhead of low-wage, irregular work without awaking the ire of powerful labor unions. From selling human "business machines" in the 1970s to "perma-temps" in the 1990s, these campaigns not only legitimized the widespread use of temps, says Hatton, but also began advancing a business model in which permanent employees were portrayed as a "costly burden," a "headache," as a profit-busting affliction that hurt companies' balance sheets. That helped lay the cultural underpinning for a new corporate emphasis on cold-blooded cost cutting and merciless mass layoffs.[74]

That precedent has slowly come to dominate over the last half century. The Kelly Girls paved the way for the "1099 economy" of perma-temps, independent contractors, gig-preneurs, part-timers and freelancers. This is the labor space that TaskRabbit, Zaarly, oDesk/Upwork, Uber and other formerly sharing economy companies have moved into. Like so many "revolutionary" idealisms, over time the original mission has transmogrified into something uglier than was intended, and now must be recognized for what it is. Acknowledging this, Buzzfeed's Charlie Warzel insightfully observed that "any tech reporter who spends their time covering the sharing economy is now, essentially, a labor reporter."[75]

Occasionally TaskRabbit, Airbnb, Uber, Lyft and others have mounted a faint defense by claiming, "Oh, it's not meant to be a *real* job, it's just a way to make a bit of extra money." But that's also what was said about the Kelly Girls and Manpower's White Glove Girls. As Tom Slee, a researcher who tracks the intersection of technology and economics, notes, "Once you say 'extra money,' it's like, 'Oh, we don't need rules and regulations, because it's just extra money.' But this is the same rhetoric that was used back in the 60s around women's jobs. There wasn't equal pay for equal work, because 'it's not a real job, it's just extra money.'" It's a slippery slope toward weakening employment standards, promoting temp jobs and undermining gains that labor unions and progressive politicians have fought for decades to enact.[76]

The "share the crumbs" economy has turned out to be a giant loophole that allows more businesses to dump their regular (W–2) employees and hire a lot more freelancers and independent contractors (1099 workers), cutting their labor costs by 30 percent. No amount of "sharing" rhetoric can wipe away the troubling aspects of the freelance society in which the share-the-crumbs economy is operating. Whatever the merits of its origins, the sharing economy has become a highly capitalized, Silicon Valley–hatched scheme to shift risk from companies to workers and ensure that investors can reap huge profits and lower fixed costs by stripping away worker protections and middle-class wages, ignoring government regulations and avoiding taxes. All done under the mantra of innovation and progress.[77]

It's time that we ask ourselves: What do we want from work, and what do we want the relationship between employer and employee to be? Do we want ours to be a stakeholder society, in which most people experience not only opportunity but also a degree of self-destiny in their immediate and distant employment horizons? Or a freelance society, where the relationship between employer and employee has been severed, and each is an implacable antagonist to the other's ambitions? *What kind of society do we want to live in?*

The answers to these deep questions suddenly are up for grabs, more than they have been in decades. Many of the assumptions and values we have lived by since the New Deal era are slowly eroding. Is the idea of an employer directly hiring an employee, and each of them feeling some degree of obligation toward each other, really that old-fashioned? Is that kind of relationship really becoming an artifact of history? The *Economist* seems to think so, portraying this evolution toward an "on-demand" economy as "a striking new stage in a deeper transformation" of the future of work that "uses the now ubiquitous platform of the smart phone to deliver labor and services in a variety of new ways [that] will challenge many of the fundamental assumptions of 20th-century capitalism."[78] Apparently the forces driving this are regarded as natural and overwhelming, like rainfall, gravity or the tides. And anyone trying to resist must be a hopeless Luddite or a New Deal traditionalist.

But in reality these forces are human-created, a byproduct of certain laws and regulations. If the consequences of this current trajectory are deemed to be undesirable for human advancement, these practices can be outlawed—just like child labor and 60-hour work weeks once were. Or at the very least regulated, like other types of workplace technologies have been. Americans should not allow their moth-to-the-flame fascination with technology, and our fetishizing of hyper-efficiency or love affair with *techno sapien* billionaires, to wrap us inside a straitjacket of our own creation. The *Economist* is certainly one of the more interesting and erudite pro-business media sources, and I personally have long enjoyed its range and sophistication. But we must never forget that the *Economist,* like most economists and so-called "experts," completely missed an $8 trillion housing bubble back in 2006–2008, and was caught blindsided by the most catastrophic economic collapse since the Great Depression. The *Economist* and the other "experts" completely misread the impact that the deregulation of banks, hedge funds, derivatives and credit-default swaps would have on the global economy, not to mention on the rise of inequality. A disaster happened on its watch, even as the *Economist* was entertaining its readers with its sophisticated brand of journalism, based on flawed economic models.

After the collapse in 2008, for a time the *Economist* and many of the other "experts" acknowledged their failings and struck a note of contrition. Now they are back at it again, pounding the drum for deregulation, this time on behalf of the "on-demand" economy. But the evidence is growing overwhelmingly clear that, if we travel too far down this latest deregulatory road, another disaster awaits.

FIVE

UNDERGROUND

THE ROAD TO HELL IS PAVED WITH SILK

BEYOND THE ROAD PAVED WITH RABBITS, TEMPS, INDIES, PERMA-LANCERS and 1099s lies the outer shadows of town where the "greys" reside. The forces compelling people to work off the books are formidable, and an increasing number of workers are drifting into the underground, or "grey" (also known as "informal") economy. Indeed, as the new economy swoops up more and more vulnerable workers, some of them fall further off the edge into ever more precarious territory.

In San Francisco I see signs of this everywhere. Virtually every construction site is composed of Hispanic workers, most of whom appear to be extremely hard working and skilled, and who speak very limited English. At each site, an appointed leader who has sufficient English-speaking capabilities acts as a go-between if necessary with any clients or members of the public. Many of the leaders probably got their first job assignments for day work in the parking lot of a Home Depot or Lowe's, which are spread throughout California.[1] One survey of 300,000 contractors in California found that, incredibly, two out of three responded that they had no direct employees.[2] These off-the-shelf, under-the-table workers are the ones laboring for those contractors, and they are always looking over one shoulder for the immigration authorities.

In virtually every restaurant in San Francisco, the kitchen help is also usually all Hispanic, including the cooks and chefs—even in Italian and other ethnic restaurants. Many of the vendors I meet at flea markets, weekend swap meets and standing on street corners are living on the margins. Walking in my San Francisco neighborhood, it's very common to see Hispanic or Chinese nannies pushing strollers and holding the hands of white, blonde-haired, blue-eyed children; a study by the economist Catherine Haskins found that between 80 and 97 percent of nannies are paid off the books.[3]

When a work crew comes to lay carpet in my house, they are all Chinese—and none of them speaks English except the team leader, who is constantly on his phone talking to his other crews at other job sites. In the evenings, near the garment factories in the South of Market area, the city bus fills up in a matter of minutes with loudly chattering Asian women—mostly Chinese—as they empty out of their workplaces and head home. Some of the San Francisco garment contractors for clothing manufacturer Esprit, which was run by famed Democratic fundraiser and close Hillary Clinton ally Susie Tompkins Buell, was raided by the Department of Labor for failing to pay minimum wage and doctoring payroll records of their immigrant labor.[4]

I still chuckle over the time at a sushi restaurant I congratulated the workers about the Japanese women's soccer team beating the United States for the World Cup in 2011. I figured the gesture would display a congenial sportsmanship and help build a rainbow bridge of cross-ethnic good feeling. But instead the workers looked confused, I felt awkward, and finally one of them blurted out in broken English: "We not Japanese; we Chinese." It turned out all of the workers, including the friendly owner of the sushi shop, are Chinese.

The homeless and destitute street population around Glide Memorial Church in downtown San Francisco traditionally has been mostly African American. Many of the local denizens, their faces looking worn and scarred from too many years of hard living, stand on the street corners trying to sell whatever they can to survive, some of it clearly stolen goods. In the case of the women, what they sell includes themselves. And since the Great Recession, I have noticed a lot more forlorn-looking white men with their hands out, on the dole, showing the grim stare of the substance-addicted, and also hustling to sell.

In my discreet conversations with some of these workers and "life survivors," I have found that most of them are being paid under the table, often for much lower pay than the prevailing wage for that occupation. And because they are not on the books, of course they don't receive any health or other benefits. They also don't benefit from worker protections such as occupational labor, health and safety requirements and rest breaks; if a boss decides to stiff them on their wages, they have little recourse. If they are illegal or quasi-legal immigrants, they are constantly exposed to threats of deportation if they ask for wages that are too high or working conditions that are too demanding. They, in turn, act as a drag on wages for the legal labor force.

Alarmingly, this subterranean dimension of the new economy appears to be the fastest growing, with underground economic activity in 2012 totaling as much as $2 trillion—13 percent of the U.S. gross domestic product, a doubling since 2009.[5]

"You normally see underground economies in places like Brazil or in southern Europe," says Laura Gonzalez, professor of personal finance at Fordham University. "But with the job situation and the uncertainty in the economy, it's not all that surprising to have it growing here in the United States."[6]

In a down economy, one puzzling fact for economists has been that the unemployment rate has declined even as the number of jobs created has disappointed, month after month. Indeed, though the percentage of unemployed people has gone down, the official rate of *employed* Americans has been at its lowest level since 1983. How can that be? In normal times, those two measurements are inversely related—as the number of employed Americans goes up, reflected in a higher employment rate, the number of unemployed Americans, as well as the unemployment rate, goes down. The two countervail each other like opposite ends of a seesaw.

And yet in this strange new world we have entered, *both* the employment rate and the unemployment rate have been declining. How is that possible?

To understand the answer, we first have to recognize that the ways we have tracked and measured unemployment since World War II are now obsolete. The current methodologies are particularly unsuited for today's fragmenting labor force. The Bureau of Labor Statistics utilizes employment surveys that originated in the 1940s in its efforts to measure who is employed full-time, who isn't and who is looking for work. That methodology was adopted at a time when most jobs were permanent and full time, and workers reported to a single employer. Under that paradigm, if you are not looking for work, and you haven't retired, then you are not counted as part of the labor force. You are invisible to the statisticians. Today, sometimes we refer to such people as "discouraged" workers, because they have dropped out of the labor force and are not counted officially as being unemployed.

With the number of discouraged workers increasing, the net effect is that the unemployment rate looks lower than it really is. When the number of discouraged workers reaches a critical mass, suddenly the measurements themselves become distorted. Have we reached that point?

Many experts think so, but it's difficult to track. It's like trying to count ghosts, since many of these discouraged workers have disappeared from official statistics. One recent study by professor Robert Hall at Stanford University and Nicolas Petrosky-Nadeau from the Federal Reserve Bank of San Francisco found that lower middle-income households—those earning about $3,360 a month or $40,032 annually—saw a sizable reduction in labor-force participation of about 5.5 percent. Even lower were those households in the high middle-income quartile (earning up to $5,920 a month or $71,000 a year), in which labor-force participation has fallen by 7.2 percent, the highest of all.[7] These two income brackets form the bulk of the middle class, a broad category that encapsulates the vast majority of Americans. Based on those numbers for labor-force participation, it would appear that 4 to 5 million former middle-class workers have withdrawn into the equivalent of labor purgatory.

On top of that, employment for teenagers has seen huge declines as well, with those living in the poorest households declining by 5 percent, and in the next poorest quartile by 10 percent; young adults aged 20 through 34 also saw declines of nearly 5 percent, with declines in labor-force participation of female workers in both age groups even higher than males.

So it's clear that millions of workers have dropped out of the U.S. labor force, with the official reason being either due to "retirement" or because "they have given up looking for work." Indeed, the Hall-Petrosky-Nadeau study found that among the top 10 percent of high-income households the participation rate also fell, by 3.6 percent; with all their newly gained wealth in this upended Gilded Age, many of them were able to retire early.[8] Yet for most people in all the other income brackets, with the exception of seniors eligible for Social Security, retirement is out of the question. So how can someone simply give up looking for work? People have to feed themselves and their families and keep a roof over their heads, don't they?

The answer seems increasingly obvious: a greater number of workers—millions of them—are drifting into the underground's shadow economy. It is difficult to track the exact number—most people who engage in off-the-books commerce try to hide their unreported and illegal activities, not the least because they want to avoid paying taxes on their under-the-table incomes. Plus, there is a definitional challenge, since the line between the grey and the legal economies can be blurry. Nevertheless, compelling evidence for Americans going "grey" comes from several other indicators beyond the employment rate breakdowns cited above.

For example, economist Edgar Feige at the University of Wisconsin–Madison, who's been researching the underground economy for over 35 years, found that in 2012 working Americans probably earned $2 trillion that did not get reported to the IRS. Just six years earlier, in 2006, the IRS estimated that the government lost $385 billion in income-tax revenue, and in 1992 a mere $80 billion.[9] So these numbers have exploded in recent years, jumping fivefold since the economic collapse. In California alone, over $6.5 billion in taxes may have been lost, thanks to the underground economy.[10] Other statistical anomalies tell a similar story, such as retail sales in 2010–13 being higher than what one would have expected, given the official rate of unemployment.

According to the *New Yorker,* by 2013, "even though household income [was] still well below what it was in 2007, personal consumption [was] higher than it was before the recession, and retail sales were growing briskly." Based on historical patterns, retail sales actually were what you'd expect if the unemployment rate were 1.5 to 2.5 points lower than the official rate.

In addition, we have seen a decrease in the percentage of Americans using banks as they convert to a cash existence. Bernard Baumohl, an economist at the Economic Outlook Group, says, "We suspect the destructive nature of the last downturn and the prolonged weak recovery pushed a record number of people into that murky world of cash transactions."[11] It's typical, he says, "that during recessions people work on the side" while collecting unemployment. "But the severity of the recession and the profound weakness of this recovery may mean that a lot more people have entered the underground economy, and have had to stay there longer."[12]

Shadow economies are often known for illegal activity, such as drug dealing and prostitution, but working under-the-table today also includes domestic workers, such as housekeepers, gardeners, handymen and nannies, as well as restaurant and construction workers, artists, taxi drivers and more. "The jobs are in service industries from small food establishments to landscaping," said David Fiorenza, an economics professor at Villanova University. "Even the arts and culture industry is not immune to working off the books in areas of music and entertainment."

The grey economy also includes firms that hire day-construction laborers, as well as other firms hiring information-technology specialists, Web designers and other new-economy indies paid by the hour. Many have a regular job that pays poorly so they take another job that pays off-the-books, tax free.

"We've always had people who make income without recording it, so it's not really new," said economics professor Peter McHenry. "But the fact that more and more people are doing it shows how bad the job picture is."[13]

As we saw earlier in the chapter, entering the underground economy exposes workers to various risks—no safety net, injured workers compensation, paid sick days or other worker protections. But the impacts of the underground economy are more complex than worker precariousness. As the work of Feige and others have shown, if underground-working Americans aren't paying some $2 trillion in taxes, that means a lot of lost revenue for government, which in turn means fewer services for people—many of whom are people just like the grey economy workers, who badly need a hand. And many of the employers themselves are not reporting all of their business activity and paying their full tax bill to the IRS, in addition to paying a lot less under the table for grey economy workers. That makes it even harder for legitimate businesses to play by the rules, when an increasing number of their competitors aren't paying Social Security payroll taxes, unemployment or workers' comp. It's all done hush-hush in the underground economy.

A DIFFERENT KIND OF "SHARING"

The grey market stretches toward a seedy continuum that at a certain point begins to slide downward into the dark subterranean caves of the freelance society—into nefarious and illegal activities. It's instructive to look at the outer edges of the labor market to understand the tendency of this sharing-type economy—particularly when acting as the motor for a freelance society—to go off the rails if not regulated properly. How deep and sinister can these activities go?

It's no secret that many of the sharing economy visionaries are inspired by an Ayn Rand–type libertarianism that has no use for government, regulation or paying taxes, especially if it gets in the way of their business plans and IPOs. Their mentality is reminiscent of a previous era of robber-baron capitalism, yet it carries a populist aura of being "for the people" going up against "the Man." The sharing economy is called a "peer-to-peer" platform, connecting people to people who are supposedly empowered to be their own entrepreneurs, buying, selling and sharing goods and services. Many of the gurus of the sharing economy don't see themselves as mere businesspeople; they have elevated their rhetoric to that of a philosophy that unquestionably has attracted many followers, particularly among younger people, who have been disappointed by inept politicians and greedy corporations amid rising inequality and decreasing opportunity and feel alienated from "the system." For Millennials and Gen Xers, the faceless purchase of services and goods via Web- and app-based technologies is a core part of their world, what they have always known. Sudhir Venkatesh, a sociologist at Columbia University who researches the underground economy, says, "We have seen the rise of a new generation of people who are much more used to doing things in a freelance way."[14]

One 29-year-old entrepreneur, in writing about the "sharing" economy website and business he had created, and which had become phenomenally successful, was uncommonly blunt: his enterprise, he said, was "at its core . . . a way to get around regulation from the state. If they say we can't buy and sell certain things, we'll do it anyway and suffer no abuse from them."[15] Travis Kalanick couldn't have stated it better—the rules are made to be broken. But this entrepreneur also exhibited occasionally the personal warmth and missionary zeal about trust and sharing of Airbnb's Brian Chesky, writing, "I know this whole market is based on the trust you put in me and I don't take that lightly. It's an honor to serve you. . . . Of all the people in the world, you are the ones who are here, in the early stages of this revolution. You are the ones getting this thing off the ground and driving it forward. Thank you for your trust, faith, camaraderie and love."[16]

Those words were spoken by the sharing economy visionary Ross Ulbricht, founder and creator of the infamous black market website Silk Road.

Where there's a product or service at the right price, there's a customer looking to buy. Silk Road was like a combined TaskRabbit and eBay, a website that allowed customers to purchase goods and services that are not, shall we say, commonly available. They also could hire certain kinds of labor not commonly hired. Silk Road used encryption technology to allow its customers to make their purchases anonymously, and the goods and services the clients bought were illegal. Like eBay, Airbnb or Uber, Silk Road developed a heavily trafficked website to connect entrepreneurs who had things to sell to customers who wanted to buy; like TaskRabbit and Upwork, Silk Road allowed its freelancers to sell their labor and services, offering their "arms for rent."

Except the products and services for sale or hire on Silk Road included drugs, firearms, forgery and fake IDs, gunrunning, computer hacking, anonymous bank accounts, prostitution and—in a twist on "arms for rent"—hit men. Yes, you could hire a Silk Road "rabbit" to murder someone in 10 different countries.[17]

But no worries, in the true spirit of the sharing economy, users got to rate the sellers of products and services, just like you do on TaskRabbit, Airbnb, Amazon or Uber. One satisfied patron wrote on the profile of a seller: "Excellent quality. Packing, and communication. Arrived exactly as described."[18] The customer gave that transaction five points out of five. So the sellers' reputations were verified through customer feedback. And with the kind of trust that exists among thieves, the users of this site were united in their mission, reminiscent of the zeal of the Airbnb community. Wrote Ulbricht: "My primary motivation is not personal wealth, but making a difference. As corny as it sounds, I just want to look back on my life and know that I did something worthwhile that helped people. It's fulfilling to me. . . . It's paradoxical, but the less you focus on your own happiness and focus on others', the happier you'll be."[19]

Sharing, indeed. The Silk Road website looked much like the websites for a lot of sharing economy companies. It displayed its illegal goods in left, right and center columns, like they were choices to be had on Etsy, eBay, Yerdle or Amazon. At its height, the site had over 13,000 products for sale by underground freelancers, 70 percent of those being drug products of one kind or another.[20] It allowed you to buy and sell drugs online just like they were "books or light bulbs," wrote *Gawker*'s Adrian Chen. Chen laid out a small selection of the items available for purchase on Silk Road: "a gram of Afghani hash; 1/8th ounce of 'sour 13' weed; 14 grams of ecstasy; 0.1 grams tar heroin." A listing for "Avatar" LSD included a picture of blotter paper with big blue faces from the James Cameron movie on it. "It's Amazon," wrote Chen. "If Amazon sold mind-altering chemicals." The sellers were located all over the world, a large portion from the U.S. and Canada.[21]

An FBI investigation found that, in the two-and-a-half-year period from February 2011 through July 2013, approximately 1,229,465 transactions were completed on the site, and total revenue generated from these sales amounted to roughly $1.2 billion, which resulted in $79.8 million in commissions, according to the government's sealed criminal complaint. Those are sales figures that even Uber and Airbnb cannot match. This was a seriously lucrative "peer-to-peer" operation, incorporating 146,946 buyers and 3,877 vendors, with 30 percent of users being from the United States.[22] During one 60-day period, 1.2 million messages were sent over Silk Road's private messaging system. This was a major underground operation flying under the radar of officialdom, administered out of a normal-looking home in a normal-looking neighborhood, and occasionally even the public library in San Francisco. Ross Ulbricht was in so many ways a kindred spirit with Travis Kalanick, Brian Chesky and other lawbreaking, tax-avoiding, sharing economy enterprises. He was the biggest "disruptor" of them all.

How did such a huge secret marketplace for illegal goods and services evade law enforcement for so long? Two technological innovations, developed by the hacking culture of Silicon Valley, made it all possible.

The first was that Silk Road was all but rendered invisible to the authorities because its users conducted transactions on their computers using a widely used Internet anonymizing software known as Tor. This tool makes the identification of the physical location of the computers operating the online marketplace, as well as anyone visiting that marketplace, extremely difficult. Tor has been used by activists all over the world to circumvent government censorship of the Internet, including in China, Iran and Syria.[23] Edward Snowden used it to avoid detection during his NSA whistle-blowing. Ironically, according to the *Washington Post*, a significant chunk "of Tor's funding comes indirectly from the U.S. State Department's Internet freedom budget."[24]

The second technological innovation was the use of the encrypted online alternative currency known as Bitcoin. Bitcoin is digital money, the electronic equivalent "of a brown paper bag of cash," says *Gawker*'s Chen, that also made transactions anonymous and even more difficult to track.[25] This crypto-currency is like something out of a William Gibson novel, the weird stuff of science fiction come to life, a decentralized payment system not controlled by any government or company. Adopting the terminology of the sharing economy, Bitcoin has been called a peer-to-peer currency, created and regulated by a network of other Bitcoin holders. Transactions supposedly are "untraceable and have been championed by cyberpunks, libertarians and anarchists who dream of a distributed digital economy outside the law, one where money flows across borders" as easy as electricity particles, says Chen. Silk Road was probably the leading user of the currency, as was an online gambling site known as Satoshi-dice.

Silk Road was an extremely sophisticated operation run by a sharp 29-year-old Millennial using the online code name "Dread Pirate Roberts." Ross Ulbricht, a tall, good-looking boy-next-door type with an uncanny resemblance to the actor Robert Pattinson of *Twilight* vampire fame, lived in San Francisco in a modest apartment on a tight-knit row of single-family walkups in the Portola neighborhood. His neighbors were shocked when they eventually found out that a major crime boss was operating in their midst.

But what is particularly interesting about Ulbricht and Silk Road is that, in a very real way, the libertarian tech culture of Silicon Valley and the sharing economy spawned both of them. San Francisco, writes tech journalist Rachel Swan, is a place "where innovation and the desire for personal freedoms are at once an economic engine, a lifestyle, and a belief system."[26] Like the other sharing economy gurus, Ulbricht saw himself in grandiose terms, as a visionary who was building an alternative to "the system." Like Uber's Travis Kalanick, he saw Silk Road as a revolutionary force countering the status quo. In his online posts, he frequently opined and philosophized; as mulch for his growing ideology, he even started the Dread Pirate Roberts Book Club, an online palaver devoted to discussion of countereconomics, anarchocapitalism and libertarianism.[27] "Silk Road is about something much bigger than thumbing your nose at the man," said Ulbricht. "Silk Road is an ENTERPRISE that is just getting started. It could literally change the world as we know it. It is bigger than any one of us, and it is going to take the dedication and will of MANY talented people, a lot of luck, and RESOURCES to get from here to there."[28]

Ulbricht's philosophy reflects a strain of thought that has been fashionable in Silicon Valley, that of using wealth and power to carve a separatist zone beyond the reach of government. Wrote Ulbricht, "Money is powerful, and it's going to take power to affect the kinds of changes I want to see. Money allows us to expand our infrastructure and manpower to accommodate the growing demands of our market and to pursue paths that will compliment [*sic*] and strengthen what's already been created here." In his own private Technostan, Ulbricht could avoid laws, regulations, taxation and enact his own version of techno-justice. Others in Silicon Valley share Ulbricht's views, if not his methods, and have gone beyond wishful thinking. Some have tried to actualize their own version of a utopian, government-free techno-world.

With the underwriting of billionaire PayPal cofounder and venture capitalist Peter Thiel, Berkeley entrepreneur Patri Friedman (grandson of archconservative economist Milton Friedman) has stockpiled more than $2 million to build a swanky floating libertarian paradise to be anchored off the San Francisco coast and just outside the jurisdiction of the United States.[29] It would be an island-like government-liberated zone and have room for a thousand inhabitants in the live/work cruise ship of their dreams.[30] Stepping closer to the brink, San Francisco entrepreneur Balaji Srinivasan has preached for techno-secession, based on the creation of a separatist society with unregulated digital currency (like Bitcoin), "sharing economy" hotels and unlicensed weapons for all.[31] Others situated along the Silicon Valley continuum, including Travis Kalanick and Brian Chesky, have preached secession from any local laws or tax requirements that are a barrier to their spreading empires. This is "normal" for many in Silicon Valley.

With San Francisco spawning such pirate mentalities, it was inevitable that someone would try to build a new version of a hyper-e-sharing economy, which in the case of Silk Road, was a sprawling black-market bazaar dealing exclusively in the forbidden. "He'd taken all of San Francisco's ideals about tearing down institutions to their extreme," writes Swan perceptively. "Silk Road fulfilled the dark promise of San Francisco's tech culture."

"The pursuit of truth is one of the most noble human endeavors," wrote Ulrich. "Debating these issues is critical for us to construct a world-view that is grounded in reason and can guide us forward."[32] Eventually, in October 2013, the truth in the form of the FBI caught up to Ross Ulbricht and arrested him in a quiet public library in the placid, tree-lined Glen Park neighborhood. He had been logged in to Silk Road under his alias Dread Pirate Roberts, administering his empire that rivaled Uber and Airbnb, and was charged with conspiracy to traffic narcotics, money laundering, computer hacking and paying nearly a million dollars for the murder of six people (none of whom were, as far as anyone can tell, actually murdered). Ulbricht was jailed and held without bail while he awaited trial, and Silk Road was shut down. In May 2015, he was sentenced to life in prison, ending the career of the sharing economy's most successful CEO.[33]

But other websites—with names like Agora, Evolution, Blackbank, Nucleus, Outlaw and even a site called Silk Road 2.0 (shut down a year later in November 2014)—rapidly took Silk Road's place as encrypted black-market trading posts, in what is starting to look like a never-ending game of cyber pirate Whac-A-Mole. With more and more workers feeling like the tossed-off detritus of society, and millions of middle-income Americans becoming "discouraged" dropouts from the labor force, the client base for these kinds of activities has skyrocketed. Ulbricht has many defenders around the world who not only proclaim his innocence but see him as a cult hero. Attorney Tor Ekeland, who represents several high-profile hackers, calls Silk Road "free market capitalism in its purest form." Comparing Silk Road to the sharing economy, he adds that the criminal prosecution of Ulbricht is a more extreme version of attempts to crack down on rideshare companies like Uber, or the New York state attorney general's investigations of Airbnb.[34]

Clearly Attorney Ekeland knows "birds of a feather" when he sees them.

Much of the sharing economy's "brave new world" is a byproduct of the intersection of an increasingly service-sector-based economy and innovations in digital technology that allow the faceless purchase of goods and services. No ongoing relationship is necessary between buyer and seller, you just click your mouse or tap your app, make your online purchase and the product or service shows up at your door. Silk Road, as well as annoyingly ubiquitous online sellers of illegally acquired prescription drugs (like Viagra and Cialis), and the underground economy in general, are only the most extreme examples of this new notoriously acquired capability. The black- and grey-market online brokerages made their exploitation faceless and even anonymous—but beyond their illegal contraband products, are they all that different from other vendors of the "sharing shadow" economy? Airbnb, Uber, Lyft and other companies have hired a phalanx of lawyers and media flaks to ensure they can operate wherever possible without regulations or paying taxes. They are perched along the continuum of the shadowy grey economy, fueled by their 1099 workforce. You can hire an Uber driver, or a task rabbit or temp worker to trim your hedges or build you a website or—sell you illegal drugs. Or worse. Faceless technology meets down-and-out workers desperate to earn money. *By any means necessary.*

What Silk Road shows us is that, left to their own devices, these Web- and app-based commercial platforms have the lethal capacity, with their anonymity and rootlessness, to undermine the values and principles of economic governance that have long fortified the middle-class society. But even more insidious, as we will see in the next section, because those values of economic governance underlie our political values, the commercial facelessness of the sharing economy corrodes that most precious glue that has made the U.S. a special and even indispensable place, both historically and still today—the Tocquevillian virtues of civicness, democratic participation and the social contract.

SYSTEM D AND ITS UNDERGROUND COMPANIES

The U.S. is not the only place where the underground economy and black market are growing. All over the world, the shadow economy workforce is expanding faster than any other sector. In shantytowns, city squares and along roadsides, illegal street vendors and unlicensed hawkers ply their trades and sell their wares. Much of their activity is being enhanced by a global proliferation of digital technologies, including mobile phones as well as Web- and app-based platforms. Remarkably, more and more of these advanced technologies can be found today in the poorest of countries, even in the poorest of regions. We can learn something about how the "sharing shadow" economy in the U.S. might develop by observing how the underground has evolved in these other places, where already it comprises a much greater share of the overall economy.

The sheer scale of the global underground economy is enormous. Robert Neuwirth, in his book *Stealth of Nations: The Global Rise of the Informal Economy,* reports that, for a large part of the world this is simply where the jobs are. The Organisation for Economic Cooperation and Development (OECD), a global think tank funded by 34 of the world's largest governments, concluded in 2009 that *60 percent* of the world's workers—about 1.8 billion people—were working off the books in jobs that were not regulated or registered.[35] In India, the OECD estimates that informal employment is 83 percent of overall (nonagricultural) employment; in Indonesia 78 percent, Kenya 72 percent, Brazil 51 percent.[36] The informal economy has been a major driver of economic growth in these countries and more, and Neuwirth estimates that the value of the billions of underground transactions around the world makes this part of the global economy worth close to an incredible $10 *trillion.*[37] To put that into perspective, if the global shadow economy were united as a single, independent nation—what Neuwirth calls "the United Street Sellers Republic (USSR)—it would be an economic superpower," the third largest economy in the world after the European Union and the United States, and larger than China's economy. Neuwirth has adopted a specific name for this phenomenon—System D, which is an abbreviation for a slang expression borrowed from French-speaking Africa and the Caribbean that essentially translates as "the ingenuity economy, the economy of improvisation and self-reliance."[38]

To Neuwirth, System D is the future of the global economy. It's no longer a handful of market women selling shriveled vegetables, it is multinational in scope and occurring all over the world. Its entrepreneurs and laborers buy and sell a huge variety of products—mobile phones, machinery, computers, textiles, clothes, fake brand-name manufactures and more—around the globe. An army of System D players have created international industries that are opening up opportunities for those who have traditionally been shut out. China in particular has been a major supplier of product for System D vendors, more willing than the U.S., Europe or Japan to cater to this market's special quirks and vices. After the global economic crisis exploded in 2008–9, System D became an important financial coping mechanism, even in developed countries, playing the role of a buffer for families by providing an alternative source of income.[39]

And it is growing at a staggering rate. Despite efforts by developed world powers and leaders like Bill Clinton and his Global Initiative to build economic bridges to the developing world, growth in these countries has been accompanied by *increasing*—not falling—employment in the underground economy.[40] The OECD projects that by 2020 an astonishing *two-thirds* of the world's workers will be employed in the System D underground economy. "There's no multinational, no Daddy Warbucks or Bill Gates, no government that can rival that level of job creation," says Neuwirth. "Given its size, it makes no sense to talk of development, growth, sustainability, or globalization without reckoning with System D."[41]

Whether in the U.S. or around the world, the growth of the System D underground economy presents a number of challenges to governments as well as business, since it exists outside the frameworks of labor laws, trade agreements, taxes, safety nets, copyrights, product safety regulations and environmental policy. The OECD says that pervasive informal employment makes it much more difficult for a government to ensure that workers have fair working conditions, health and safety regulations and adequate pay. According to the OECD report, "Most of those who work informally are insufficiently protected from the various risks to which they are exposed."[42] Women in particular are vulnerable, as they are overrepresented in informal work.

Adding to the challenges, governments in developing countries are all too often corrupt and rife with cronyism and patronage, and so as Neuwirth rightly points out, the shadow economy becomes the easiest path for avoiding crooked officials and circumventing obstructionist and even extortionist bureaucracies. But this in turn further fuels citizen alienation and tax avoidance. Above all then, a growing informal economy is a sign of the lack of trust and faith in public institutions and the role of governments. It is the hallmark of a broken social contract. Many of the people in the shadow economy have given up on government. They have gone "off the grid," having withdrawn that essential "civic glue" that powers effective government—their allegiance, their participation and their tax money.

Thus, the takeaway warning to Americans is that shadow economies can undermine not only the formal economy but political governance as well.

Once the underground reaches a certain critical mass, it robs the government of tax revenue and other tools that make government uniquely capable. It draws citizens away from their government, encouraging them to abandon their own obligations and responsibilities, and in so doing further undermines the civic genius of a robust civil society.

Seen in this light, it's important to recognize that many of the sharing economy companies in the United States are, for all intents and purposes, System D companies. Most of them sometimes operate beyond traditional laws, trying to ignore regulations and tax obligations. No one really knows how many independent contractors are toiling away for them—they don't release their internal numbers, and the sparse data made public appears untrustworthy—but for many of them their own tax avoidance is massive, and their flaunting of existing laws is flagrant and widespread. If the precedent being established by these "sharing shadow" companies becomes a more common business practice, the United States could become increasingly ungovernable. We have seen how the U.S. already has an enormous annual grey economy of around $2 trillion, nearly a seventh of GDP. As Uber, Airbnb and other sharing economy companies reach scale, inevitably they will add to the size of the grey economy in the U.S. At what point does the underground reach such a critical mass that it begins to undermine governance itself?

Sudhir Venkatesh, the sociologist at Columbia, says that when a significant portion of the population avoids taxes and regulations, that has a rebound effect that diminishes confidence in the system. "Too much off-the-books work is not good for the social contract," says Venkatesh. "Economies work best when people have some sense, however abstract, that they are all tied together."[43]

Yet System D entrepreneurism pulls contrary to that democratic need. These businesses engage in many questionable practices, and some even engage in illegal activities, including not paying their taxes, which starves government and public policy of crucially needed revenues. Their grey economy practices encourage workers—the "1099 contractors" and gig-preneurs plying the hand pumps in these companies—to do the same, withdrawing not only from the formal economy but also from their own obligations and responsibilities as citizens. Conservative leaders like Grover Norquist, the most successful antitax activist of our time, who has said he wants to shrink the size of government until he can "drown it in the bathtub," is so impressed with System D companies that he penned an op-ed saying that Uber could help the GOP gain political control of usually Democratic-leaning cities.[44] Norquist evidently applauds the fact that System D companies like Uber, Airbnb and others are depriving governments of both taxes as well as the participation and allegiance of its citizens.

By providing a temptation for anxious workers to make their living outside the legal economy, and promoting a subculture of pirate citizenry, these companies are unraveling centuries of American progress and taking us backward to a mindset that we left behind many years ago, and for good reason. The social contract has a deeper resonance when people perceive that everyone is in the same boat. The essential ingredients that are needed to make political and economic governance work are weakened by citizen withdrawal. Under the leadership of System D businesses, including many sharing economy companies, not to mention Silk Road at the extreme terminus, "We the People" is in danger of degenerating into "I Me Mine." We have to choose from these two conflicting visions.

SIX

ROBOTS AND TECHNO SAPIENS ARE COMING FOR YOUR JOB

WHO CAN FORGET THE BARRELING FIGURE OF THE "B-9, CLASS M-3 GENERAL Utility Non-Theorizing Environmental Control Robot"—otherwise known simply as "Robot," on the popular 1960s TV show *Lost in Space*—shrieking "Warning, Will Robinson!" from inside its glass bubble "head" and washing-machine-like torso. Such cinematic moments have been forever etched into the popular memory and defined the public's understanding of what a robot is.

But today robots look and act much different than Robot from *Lost in Space,* or Hal from *2001: A Space Odyssey.* Meet Bill Pick, a local pharmacist who . . . oops, my mistake, that's PillPick, a robot who is going to make your local pharmacist obsolete. Not far from my house in San Francisco, at the Mission Bay campus of University of California, San Francisco's medical center, a mighty super pharmacist cranks away, 24 hours a day, seven days a week, filling pill prescriptions. PillPick is not ambulatory like Robot and does not converse like Hal. It just does what's it's told, indefatigably, which is to take pill prescriptions written by doctors and fill them, approximately 10,000 times a day.

PillPick, which is manufactured by a Swiss company, is housed in an enormous, tightly secured, sterile room, and it's not very cinematic to look at. It's about as sexy as a giant vending machine, though it towers over its human associates.[1] Inside the room is a labyrinth of rubber conveyor belts, pneumatic pipes and suction-powered, pill-picking arms that, like stumpy mechanical versions of an elephant's trunk, dip into hundreds of stock boxes that hold oral and injectable medications, including toxic chemotherapy drugs. The only human role in this process is filling the stock boxes with the correct medications. It takes a second or two for PillPick's suction-powered arm to push down into a box, grab on to a pill and suck it up. It then bags the pills and slaps a bar code on each prescription, depositing it in a slot from where it is delivered to the right patient. When the pills are administered, a nurse scans the barcode, tracking the path of every drug.[2]

Before installing the indentured robot, UCSF needed about half of its more than 100 on-staff pharmacists to fill prescriptions and check the drugs going to patients. Now most of those pharmacists—pulling down a salary of $111,000 per year[3]—are redundant. For now, UCSF has reassigned most of them to different parts of the hospital to pass the time doing other chores (making IVs, helping adjust patients' drug regimens and other tasks)—few of which require a pharmacist's training. But nearly everyone can see the writing on the wall—the pharma-bot cost $7 million to install, less than one year's salary for all those redundant pharmacists. And it doesn't ask for a raise, or get sick or need health care or a pension, and it doesn't complain about being overworked.

But the UCSF robot, just like the *Lost in Space* robot, in some ways gives a wrong impression of the role that "robots" are predicted to play in the U.S. economy. A better term to use would be "smart machines," which incorporates everything from robotics, software automation, faster computer processing, "big data" (sometimes referred to as "the cloud") and artificial intelligence (known as AI). This is a software-driven revolution, and these technologies can be packed into virtually any object, and used to automate an increasing number of tasks.

For example, it used to be that any company trying to promote its products or services needed to employ an aggressive sales force that would pound the pavement, create brilliant, catchy ads and attract customers and clients. That paradigm is in the process of being completely upended—by a new digital kid on the block. A video on the *Forbes* website called "200 Milliseconds: The Life of a Programmatic Ad Impression," communicates (in the robotic language of the "new advertising") the strange new world we are stepping into: "programmatic ads" that are now aimed at us like heat-seeking missiles by a computer algorithm that thinks it knows us better than we know ourselves. Follow along, as we track the logical illogic of a programmatic ad:

> Jane Doe clicks on a URL and visits a webpage. The publisher's content begins to load in browser. Publisher may find information that is stored on Jane Doe, possibly in its data management platform (DMP). (*My note: all of that happens within 30 milliseconds—0.03 seconds*) Publisher sends available information to its ad server, asking ad server whether an ad campaign is available that would target Jane Doe. If there is a campaign matching Jane

Doe's profile, an ad is served (*within 40 milliseconds*). If no ad campaign targets Jane Doe, the server seeks to match the impression, programmatically requesting response from selected traders, ad networks and supply side platforms (SSPs). If no match is made, the request is sent to an open ad exchange. Open ad exchange sends a bid request containing information on Jane Doe's browser, website URL and ad type to multiple bidders, including traders, ad networks and demand side platforms (DSPs) (*within 75 milliseconds*). Each bidder processes bid request, overlays it with additional user data and marketer's targeting and budget rules (*all within 100 milliseconds—0.1 seconds*). Each bidder's algorithm evaluates the request, selects the creative, and sends it along with optimal bid price to ad exchange. Ad exchange selects winning bid from bidders' responses through second price auction. Ad exchange sends winning ad URL, and price from winning bid, to publisher's ad server (*within 150 milliseconds*). Publisher's ad server tells Jane Doe's browser which ad to display. Jane Doe's browser pulls ad from winning bidder's ad server and sends matching ad to browser. *Browser displays webpage, including matching ad.*[4]

And so an ad is silently delivered to the webpage that Jane Doe is viewing, tailored by a computer algorithm to match instantaneously the "known knowns" and the "known unknowns" of her individual profile, all of this terrible miracle of faux hyper-efficiency occurring within 200 milliseconds—that is, 0.2 seconds, which is literally as fast as an eye can blink. Jane Doe may not want to see this ad, she may not even want to have her interests and desires tracked by anyone, much less a headless computer algorithm in service to corporate advertisers . . . but if she wants to surf the World Wide Web she has little choice in the matter. Paul Baran and Paul Sweezy in their provocative *Monopoly Capital* remarked on the soullessness of advertising in modern capitalism, and the new breed of techno-advertisers seem determined to prove them right with an exclamation point.[5] Programmatic spending on display and video ads, including on mobile devices, tripled in 2014 to $675 million, growing nearly 10 times as fast as the overall display-ad market.[6] AOL laid off nearly its entire ad sales force in January 2015, roughly 150 staffers, as the company attempted to reinvent itself as a "programmatic advertising powerhouse."[7]

Such automated computer algorithms already have replaced many stock traders and brokers—making for some wild rides on Wall Street. Algorithmic trading, also called automated or black-box trading, executes preprogrammed trading instructions based on a range of selected variables, such as timing, price, trade volume and more. The algorithms *automatically* launch trades thousands of times *per second,* trying to gain minute advantages based on lightning-fast oscillations of the market. No humans are sitting at the on-off switch.

And so on May 6, 2010, the ghosts crept into the machine. On that day, a single "high-frequency trade" of $4.1 billion by a mutual fund located in Kansas spooked the rest of the market (for reasons no one quite understands), triggering a massive selloff of stocks.[8] The Dow Jones industrial average plunged nearly a thousand points in only a few minutes, as buy-and-sell contracts inexplicably changed hands 27,000 times in 14 seconds.[9] Then the market recovered in a blink of electrons, leaving all the experts confounded in a swirl of electronic dust over what had happened and why. The "Flash Crash of 2010," as it became known, has acquired legendary status as a kind of "Skynet moment" in which the Terminator machines briefly took over in ways that were never intended. Since then, other mini-flash crashes have occurred, such as the one in April 2013 when a hoax tweet from the Associated Press (which, it turns out, had its Twitter account hacked) reported that the White House had been bombed. The Dow dropped 150 points in a matter of seconds, and currencies, commodities and bond markets around the world gyrated and spasmed, until finally the hoax was debunked, and the markets mostly recovered.[10]

After the 2010 flash crash, the U.S. Securities and Exchange Commission, which oversees the management and functioning of the financial markets, issued an investigatory report that seemed confused and even technologically illiterate. Dr. David Leinweber, director of the Center for Innovative Financial Technology at Lawrence Berkeley National Laboratory, penned an opinion piece openly criticizing the government's level of technological competence and inability to understand, much less oversee, today's markets.[11] Nevertheless, high-frequency trading has continued and apparently is here to stay, in one form or another, for a simple reason: trades involving human participation cost 2.05 cents per share while those done by computer cost 1.08 cents.[12]

Unsurprisingly, tens of thousands of traders and stockbrokers have been axed in recent years, with employees on stocks desks falling by greater than 8.5 percent globally in 2012 alone.[13] With high-frequency trading making up more than half of all stock trading today, many are thinking: bring back the stockbrokers! Europeans, to their credit, have clamped down on speed traders, with France and Italy implementing a trading tax on each transaction as a disincentive for using computers that launch thousands of trades per second.[14] But financial realities clearly point toward a shaky future for the stock trader profession—computers and their algorithms are replacing thousands of traders and brokers.

There's little doubt that we will see more flash crashes, not only on the stock market but in the many industries and occupations in which so-called smart machines have been inserted. Each event is yet another harbinger of the strange new world we are entering. The hope is that, despite those glitches in the machinery, these new technologies will increase productivity, convenience and, ultimately, the quality of life for the vast majority of people. Of course, there will be short-term disruption and dislocation, such as job losses and individual misery, but that's the way Schumpeterian "creative destruction" works, which, we have been assured, will eventually result in many new types of jobs. All will be for the best. Vint Cerf, vice-president of Google who is considered one of "the fathers of the Internet," says, "Historically, technology has created more jobs than it destroys" and "there is no reason to think otherwise" in the case of robots and automation.[15] Kevin Kelly, founding editor of *Wired,* is even more boosterish, saying, "We need to let robots take over. They will do jobs we have been doing, and do them much better. . . . And they will help us discover new jobs for ourselves, new tasks that expand who we are."[16]

Despite those reassurances, the fear is that the hoped-for jobs in the new economy will never materialize. Take, for example, the U.S. company Kodak, which at its height had 145,000 employees in mainly middle-income jobs, and recently declared bankruptcy. Kodak has been replaced by Facebook, or rather by the recent Facebook acquisition Instagram, the Kodak of the digital age. Using Instagram, more than 130 million people have shared some 16 billion photos, a remarkable feat considering that all of Facebook has only about 10,000 employees.[17] In the meantime, the bankrupt Kodak now has only about 8,000 employees—what happened to the other 137,000 former Kodak employees? Where did they find jobs?

Contradicting the optimism of boosters like Cerf and Kelly, many of the new technology companies employ a relatively small number of workers because they use software and smart machines to realize astonishing leaps in labor productivity. Tech expert Martin Ford, author of *Rise of the Robots: How Technology Will Transform the Future Job Market and Economy,* says, "Think of all the high-profile companies we've seen over the past 10 years—Google, Facebook, Netflix, Twitter. None of them have very many employees, because technology is ubiquitous—it gets applied everywhere, to new jobs and old jobs. Whatever appears in the future, whatever pops up, we can be certain that IT (information technology) will get applied right away, and all but the most non-routine-type jobs won't be there anymore."[18] Economist Nouriel Roubini says, "The factory of the future may be 1,000 robots and one worker manning them."[19]

Jerry Michalski, founder of a think tank called the Relationship Economy eXpedition (REX), observes the slow but unrelenting pull toward robotization and says bluntly, "Automation is Voldemort: the terrifying force nobody is willing to name."[20] Economist Paul Krugman says that "smart machines may make higher GDP possible, but they will also reduce the demand for people—including smart people. So we could be looking at a society that grows ever richer, but in which all the gains in wealth accrue to whoever owns the robots."[21]

This worry is not new—people have been agonizing about the invasion of technology and machines since weaver Ned Ludd allegedly smashed his knitting frames in 1779. But the fear is that this time the technologies are so powerful that it will end up differently. As mentioned briefly in the introduction to this book, an Oxford University study of over 700 occupations has estimated that 47 percent of existing U.S. jobs are at risk from computerization over the next twenty years—that's over 60 million jobs threatened by what economist John Maynard Keynes once called "technological unemployment" in his 1930 essay, "Economic Possibilities for Our Grandchildren."[22]

And this is an issue where there are as many viewpoints as there are "experts." The Pew Research Center conducted a study called "AI, Robotics and the Future of Jobs," and they asked nearly 1,900 experts to respond to a question about whether "networked, automated, artificial intelligence applications and robotic devices" will have "displaced more jobs than they have created by 2025." Given that these are experts in their field, who presumably believe in the value and importance of their work, a surprising number of them answered that question in the affirmative. Nearly half (48 percent) foresee a future in which robots and digital machines have "displaced significant numbers of both blue- and white-collar workers"—with many expressing concern that "this will lead to vast increases in income inequality, masses of people who are effectively unemployable and breakdowns in the social order."[23]

The other half of the experts (52 percent) responded that they expect technology "will not displace more jobs than it creates by 2025." While this group anticipates that "many jobs currently performed by humans will be taken over substantially by robots or digital agents," they also have faith that "human ingenuity will create new jobs, industries and ways to make a living, just as it has been doing since the dawn of the Industrial Revolution."

MIT's David Autor stakes out yet a third position: technology won't create unemployment, he says, because "over the long run we find things for people to do. The harder question is, does changing technology always lead to *better* jobs? The answer is no."[24] Watching U.S. workers losing their old jobs and drifting into new 1099 jobs with Uber, TaskRabbit and Elance-Upwork, or with auto companies in Tennessee using armies of temp workers, leaves the experts extremely divided and bickering over this issue.

What is striking to me is that all of these experts have access to the most recent and highest quality information and data, and yet they are near evenly divided. Other contentious science-based issues, such as global climate change, have resulted in a strong consensus in the scientific community, in which 97 percent of scientists agree "that climate-warming trends over the past century are very likely due to human activities," according to NASA.[25] But when it comes to the impact of human technological activities on killing or creating jobs, the technology community has not been able to reach consensus. Everyone has their crystal ball out, and no one knows ultimately what the future holds. Even Erik Brynjolfsson and Andrew McAfee from the Massachusetts Institute of Technology, who celebrate automation in their bestselling book *The Second Machine Age,* nevertheless write that "technological progress is going to leave behind some people, perhaps even a lot of people, as it races ahead."[26] They have faith that technology will create new jobs as it always has in the past, but faith is not a promise, and in the meantime there is a lot of uncertainty over these immense societal changes in which so much is at stake.

Despite such disagreements, what all technologists today can agree on is that a fundamental shift is occurring. Smart machines, artificial intelligence, automation and robotics are being injected into just about everything at home, in the office or in the public domain. Some of the most radical visionaries predict that the human world is on the historical cusp of what they call the "Technological Singularity"—a future era occurring around 2045 in which the current artificial-intelligence explosion will result in machines achieving true intelligence, and even surpassing their human inventors as they design ever smarter versions of themselves. Other technologists scoff at such a notion, but nearly all agree that the human world is in for a profound shakeup. Indeed, famed physicist Stephen Hawking has warned, "We are facing potentially the best or worst thing to happen to humanity in history."[27] The stakes are exceedingly high.

AUTOMATION AND ROBOTS, PROMISE AND PERIL

The new technologies have generated passionate anticipation about what some predict will be a Third Industrial Revolution. Like the previous industrial revolutions, it's a foregone conclusion—and an acceptable price to pay—that many people will lose their jobs, or at least have to change occupations in the short term, while these forces of technology and innovation play themselves out. But who will be most impacted?

It has generally been assumed that automation is primarily a threat to workers who have little education and lower skill levels. Lines of giant robots replacing workers on automobile assembly lines have informed our understanding of what industries and occupations will be shaken up. But experts now predict that many professional jobs—jobs held by college-educated, white-collar workers with advanced degrees—are going to discover that their jobs are also going to be "robotized." Machines directed by increasingly sophisticated software and algorithms have advanced rapidly in capability. Increasingly they are able to perform jobs and tasks utilizing significant intellectual content, including jobs that were once considered exclusively human.

What's known as "middle-skilled" jobs already have been severely impacted due to mechanization and other increases in machine productivity. Since the 1980s, the number of workers in job categories like secretaries, office workers, administrative staff, human resources, tax preparers, repairmen and manufacturing workers has been declining with each recession.[28] Manufacturing has been particularly hard hit. According to the Boston Consulting Group, machines that now perform 10 percent of all manufacturing tasks are likely to account for about 25 percent by 2025. The economics are simple, writes technology forecaster Sue Halpern in the *New York Review of Books:* using a human spot welder costs around $25 an hour, while a robotic one—which is faster and more accurate—costs $8. "The retail giant Amazon 'employs' 15,000 warehouse robots to pull items off the shelf and pack boxes," writes Halpern.[29] Today there are approximately 2 million fewer manufacturing jobs than in 2007, the year before the Great Recession.[30] As the *Financial Times*'s Edward Luce points out, even as manufacturing activity has risen at a fast clip in recent years, the U.S. economy has added few manufacturing jobs. "The difference boils down to robots," says Luce, "which pose an increasingly nagging paradox: the more there are, the better for overall growth (since they boost productivity); yet the worse things become for the middle class."[31]

These trends will only accelerate in the future. Foxconn, a Chinese company that assembles iPhones for Apple and other consumer electronics for companies like Nokia, plans to replace much of its Chinese labor force of over 1.2 million workers with robots.[32] Sascha Meinrath from X-Lab says that 3D printing will change the manufacturing industry yet again, with innovations like 3D printed car parts that can be printed in-house and on demand. "We're going to watch what happens with everything from the Teamsters to shipping to retail," says Meinrath. "We're looking at an entire manufacturing industry facing a crisis like it hasn't since the industrial revolution. We should be paying attention to what that means for the middle class workers who are in jeopardy of being replaced by automation."[33]

But how can this be possible? How can thousands of lines of computer code replace thousands of flesh-and-blood humans? It turns out that many middle-skilled jobs are composed of lots of bite-sized tasks that are not only repetitive but also fairly routine, making it possible to write those tasks into software. Many of those tasks also are not geographically specific and can be done from virtually any location. Given those two criteria, these tasks "can be done faster, and more cheaply, by machines," writes *New York Times* (and formerly *Slate*) technology reporter Farhad Manjoo. "And even when a computer can't completely replace these middle-skilled jobs, it can make them easier to transfer to lower-wage humans—you still need a human being to answer tech support questions, but now you can hire someone in Andra Pradesh, India rather than Alabama."[34]

With middle-skilled jobs already in decline, job growth over the last two decades mostly has occurred at the opposite ends of the employment spectrum, in either high-skill, high-wage professions or in the low-skill, low-wage service sector. Economist David Autor from the Massachusetts Institute of Technology calls it "job polarization," which he blames on a number of factors (including the decreasing power of labor unions), but primarily the rise of automation and information technology.[35] Ironically, low-skilled jobs so far have proven to be less vulnerable to robotization. Jobs like janitors, food service, maids/domestic help, waiters and waitresses, taxi and other types of drivers, gardening, security, home health care and child care are physical jobs that require in situ workers. So they can't be so easily outsourced to another region or country (though, as we have seen, they can be turned over to TaskRabbit, temp agencies and other job-brokerage websites that can use online auctions and gamification techniques to find the cheapest labor possible). According to the National Employment Law Project, low-wage jobs (those that pay between $7.69 and $13.83 an hour) constituted 21 percent of job losses in the Great Recession but 58 percent of new jobs recovered since then—the reverse situation for middle-income jobs, which made up 60 percent of job losses during the recession but only 22 percent of recovery jobs.[36]

So for the moment a certain number of low-skilled jobs have been saved by the fact that they pay too little to bother reorganizing. There's a steady supply of humans willing to do these jobs despite the low wages, so there hasn't been much incentive to invest capital to figure out how to robotize these occupations. At some point, however, experts say that it is likely that robots will be able to do many of these low-skilled, low-wage jobs as well. iRobot Roomba already does an impressive job of vacuuming apartments. If those predicting the eventual widespread use of driverless cars and trucks are correct, it will be the end of taxi and Uber drivers, as well as truck drivers. And guess what: "truck driver" is the number-one occupation for men in the United States, employing 1.7 million people (95 percent male) in 2012.[37] So that would be a big blow to the overall jobs picture. The skills of a truck driver are not easily transferrable to other occupations.

In northern China, a restaurant became the first to be entirely staffed by robot waiters, using three-foot-tall versions of what look like Chinese Fuwa ("good luck") dolls. The robots not only deliver dishes and greet guests but also cook meals. The colorful bots travel along a track inside the restaurant, and reportedly can work for five hours continuously after a two-hour charge. Customer service? No problem, the bots are able to display more than ten expressions on their faces and say basic welcoming sentences to customers—better than some of the waiters I've had in Manhattan or Parisian restaurants.[38]

With most low-skilled jobs not (yet) worth the effort to automate, and many middle-skilled occupations already decimated, what about high-skilled, professional jobs? Surely the professionals are safe?

Not by a long shot. Professional jobs increasingly are in the crosshairs of algorithms and automation. Like many middle-skilled occupations, it turns out that a number of professional jobs—even though they require years of schooling and various degrees—also are fairly routine and geographically portable. They can be reduced by what professor Richard Susskind calls "decomposition," which is "the breaking down of professional work into its component parts."[39] That makes these jobs prime targets for the technologists to deploy their increasingly sophisticated smart machines and software, marking them for redundancy.[40]

For example, the decades-long rise in the number of computer-chip designers has substantially subsided under the pressure from powerful software programs, which are replacing the work previously done by multitudes of draftsmen and logic designers. Ironically, computer programmers also are at risk—apparently they are coding the algorithms that will replace themselves. Software is also impacting occupations that used to be exclusively human domains, such as tax accountants and mortgage and loan officers.[41] Below are several major professions that are being greatly "disrupted" by the application of new technologies and software algorithms.

Medicine and disease diagnosis. Today, a highly skilled radiologist in Bangalore, India, can read the MRI of a patient in Washington, D.C., for a quarter of the price charged by a D.C.–based radiologist (a radiologist is a medical doctor who specializes in the interpretation of medical images like MRIs and X rays). The MRI can be sent digitally over the Internet, and the patient doesn't even have to know.

But now smart machines are being programmed to perform this skill even faster—and cheaper—than the radiologists in Bangalore. Other medical tests also are being robotized in the pursuit of computer-aided diagnosis of disease. A new Pap-screening computer robot, called the BD FocalPoint, uses sophisticated image-searching software to swiftly scan slides to find visual signs of abnormal cells. The FocalPoint has dramatically increased productivity as well as accuracy. A human cytotechnologist normally can examine about 80 to 90 slides a day, but by deploying the FocalPoint, a human analyst can process 170 slides per day. And labs that use the robot catch more instances of cancer and precancerous lesions. This machine is a marvel of medical engineering.[42]

In addition to interpreting Pap tests, MRIs and X rays, smart machines with acute powers to process and analyze images are now regularly used by radiologists to evaluate mammograms and to detect abnormalities on the chest, coronary arteries, colon and prostate biopsies. And that's just the beginning. IBM didn't design its supercomputer Watson just so that it could become the all-time *Jeopardy!* champion. Watson, which on *Jeopardy!* displayed an astonishing capability for speech recognition and responding to questions in a stilted, human-like voice—as well as wiping the decks with the two greatest human *Jeopardy!* champions of all time—has wide application. IBM is using its Watson technology to scour the world's medical textbooks and reference guides for making connections between health and disease symptoms. A doctor inputs symptoms into Watson and receives a ranked list of disease possibilities. Human doctors don't have the time or the capability to keep up with every published journal article, or monitor every potential drug reaction and identify ambiguous symptoms among thousands of patients. But Watson and other supercomputers can do all of that with ease. Computers are going to continue playing an ever-larger role in medicine, and data-intensive technologies will continue to develop. Many experts predict that humanity is on the cusp of a medical revolution.[43]

Like the pharmacists being replaced by UCSF's PillPick robot, should radiologists and other types of doctors and medical specialists be concerned that computers are coming for their jobs? Most experts agree: the answer is yes. While these medical technologies need human supervision (in practice, the humans make the final diagnosis, with the help of the machines), as computers like Watson get better, faster and smarter, fewer humans across a range of specialties will be needed.[44]

"The economic implications here are obvious," says Farhad Manjoo. "As robots help each doctor do more, there'll be less work for everyone, which will push down salaries . . . it's certain that doctors' livelihoods will be affected by these new machines." And the doctors who are the strongest candidates for automation are ones you'd least expect. They are not the general practitioners but the specialists—the most highly paid and highly trained personnel in medicine. That's because the most specialized doctors focus on just one or two types of procedures, and that's what makes them vulnerable to robotization. Because "robots, too, are great specialists," says Manjoo. "They excel at doing one thing repeatedly, and when they focus, they can achieve near perfection."[45]

Robo reporters: When software writes the news. When a small earthquake hit Southern California in March 2014, the *Los Angeles Times* broke the story on its website, a mere three minutes after the tremor struck. The short article was mundane, covering all the obvious details—the time the quake struck, its magnitude and geographic reach. But to the alert reader, the final sentence revealed something unusual: "This post was created by an algorithm written by the author."[46]

Which meant that the article was written by a robot. Given the frequency of earthquakes in Southern California, the earthquake algorithm, nicknamed Quakebot, is kept pretty busy, reporting stories on eight small earthquakes in one week at the end of June 2014. Moreover, Quakebot is not the only robo reporter "employed" by the *Times*. For its Mapping LA project, the newspaper compares neighborhoods with the help of a bot, and for its website called The Homicide Report a bot automates posts about murders in and around Los Angeles.

Or look at this news story, from a site called FriscoFan.com, which posted recaps of San Francisco Giants games:

> **Giants Batter Rockies 3–1**
>
> Ryan Vogelsong worked an impressive seven innings and Mike Fontenot hit a triple to put the Giants ahead in the third as San Francisco slipped past Colorado, 3–1.
>
> With the game scoreless in the bottom of the third, the Giants grabbed the lead when Fontenot drove in Andres Torres and Vogelsong after hitting a triple off starter Jhoulys Chacin.
>
> Vogelsong's record improved to 13–7 on the year after a top-notch outing in which he surrendered no runs on four hits with four strikeouts and no walks. Santiago Casilla worked 2/3 of an inning to pick up the save, his sixth of the season, allowing no runs on no hits while punching out one and walking no one. Chacin got the loss (11–14) and gave up two runs on eight hits with three strikeouts and one walk over seven innings.[47]

A computer wrote that story as well. Automated Insights, a company that analyzes patterns in big data and turns them into readable narratives, created FriscoFan and nearly 400 other sites focused on covering Major League Baseball, NCAA basketball teams, or recapping fantasy football games on Yahoo. Automated Insights built their robo reporters to scour huge amounts of data for interesting trends. In 2013 alone, Automated Insights' busy beaver bots churned out 300 million pieces of content.

ProPublica, the public interest journalism outfit, and *Forbes* magazine also use this algorithm technology, from a company called Narrative

Science; in ProPublica's case, to crank out short, readable narrative descriptions of the more than 52,000 schools in its database,[48] and by *Forbes* magazine to turn quarterly corporate earnings reports of hundreds of companies, including Fortune 500 companies, into short narratives. All of this is being done by robo reporters without the need for human journalists. The bots are driven by big data that exists out there in "the cloud," and they write stories by devouring spreadsheets full of sports scores, stock market oscillations, sales report and other numbers intensive domains. The bots are fast—they beat the human reporters nearly every time. And the human readers can't really tell the difference. A study published in February 2014 in *Journalism Practice* found that readers could not consistently determine whether a sports article was written by a human or a bot. The study found that while the bot content was viewed as bland and not very expressive, it also was perceived as objective and virtually indiscernible from articles penned by the human journalists (perhaps the human sportswriters need to spice up their efforts!).[49]

While the bots are remarkable, no one is suggesting that robo journalism is about to entirely take over the profession, or that bots will be mastering wordplay, wit or writing articles for the *New Yorker* anytime soon. Still, it's another pressure point on a profession that has suffered huge revenue losses in recent years and has been hemorrhaging reporters, due to the economic crisis in 2008 as well as its continued displacement by online digital media. No layoffs of journalists have been attributed to replacement by robo reporters, but there's no question that these bots are another disruption that makes the humans a bit more expendable.

Legal eagle bots: "Kill all the lawyers." "The first thing we do, let's kill all the lawyers," says the character Dick the Butcher in Shakespeare's *Henry VI, Part 2.* And now we may be able to do just that.

Specifically, ultrafast computers and advances in artificial intelligence are rendering some attorney jobs obsolete. For example, new advances in "e-discovery" software allows analysis of millions of documents in a fraction of the time, using a fraction of the personnel for a fraction of the cost. Bill Herr, as a lawyer for a major chemical firm, used to assemble auditoriums of highly paid lawyers to read massive volumes of documents during the discovery process. For several weeks, hundreds of lawyers would pore over every slip of paper, looking for that rare needle in the haystack that could break a case. It is an expensive, labor-intensive process, often costing millions of dollars. Now that mostly can be turned over to computers. And the results are exceptional, says Herr, because "people get bored, people get headaches. Computers don't."

And they are more accurate. Using e-discovery software, Herr reanalyzed work his firm did in the 1980s and 1990s. The human lawyers had an accuracy rate of only 60 percent, he found. "Think about how much money had been spent to be slightly better than a coin toss," he said.[50]

With researchers testing and retesting their algorithms on vast data samples, e-discovery has become increasingly more sophisticated and accurate. Now the techniques go way beyond mere keyword searches. They can extract relevant concepts and figure out patterns of behavior that often will be missed by lawyers examining millions of documents. Cataphora, an information-sifting company based in Silicon Valley, uses its software to comb through documents to find metadata that is startlingly accurate at illuminating the interactions and activities of targeted individuals—who talks to whom, and who did what when. It can discover conversations that have taken place across email, texts, tweets and telephone calls, and spot "digital anomalies" that the targeted individuals might have created in attempting to conceal their activities. A sudden change in an author's email style, for example, from cheery to cautiously formal, can raise a warning about certain activities. Much like the NSA does with its highly controversial phone-call metadata, the Cataphora software attempts to weave that information together in a way that allows a visualization of chains of events and networks of people.[51]

The employment prospects for attorneys have been diminishing for some years, with far more law-school graduates than there are job openings. E-discovery software is part of the reason why.[52] Naturally a certain number of human lawyers are still necessary to administer and manage an e-discovery process, and then to utilize the end product. But Mike Lynch, founder of Autonomy, an e-discovery company, estimated that the shift to e-discovery "would lead to a manpower reduction in which one lawyer would suffice for work that once required 500," according to the *New York Times.* And the upcoming generation of software, he estimated, "could cut that head count by another 50 percent."

No doubt Shakespeare would have been pleased. Lawyering is yet another high-paying profession that is slated for disruption by the new technologies.

"Teach . . . your children well . . ." Education is another field that is slated for technological upheaval, especially the occupation of teaching. Online education is going to fundamentally transform higher education, as at-a-distance students can watch a lecture over the Internet, either live or prerecorded, from virtually anywhere in the world. The possibilities are nearly infinite. A large lecture hall today can hold several hundred students, but an online lecture can be watched by millions. Already students are enrolling in free "massive open online courses" (known popularly as MOOCs). Instead of the best-known professors at Harvard, Yale or Stanford being available to only the most privileged students who attend those campuses, now those professors' lectures can be attended by students in South Africa, Jordan or Indonesia. Economist Nouriel Roubini wonders, "Will we still need so many teachers in the decades to come if the cream of the profession can produce increasingly sophisticated online courses that millions of students can take?" And if not, "how will all of those former teachers earn a living?"[53]

Defenders of the status quo say, quite rightly, that the traditional classroom experience cannot be duplicated online. Few other educational events are as profound and long lasting as a student learning from a skilled teacher and brilliant scholar who cares about imparting knowledge and stimulating thinking. Education also is greatly enhanced by the peer-to-peer contact with fellow students. The friendships and social networking that take place on campus and in dormitories initiate bonds of personal as well as professional relationships that often last a lifetime. It's no coincidence that so many U.S. presidents went to Harvard or Yale.

And yet, the sheer economics of online education make this a truly disruptive enterprise. Colleges and universities have dramatically raised the cost of tuition, far outpacing the growth of an average family's income. Especially in the United States, where a university education is far more expensive than in most other developed nations, students need to borrow substantial amounts of money and parents often have to sacrifice and save for their children's higher education. Many students are piling up $100,000 in college loan debt, only to graduate and discover that they can't find a decent job. The sad fact is, while it's true that immersion on a campus into the middle of a total educational experience is ideal, fewer and fewer young people and their families are able to afford that. Consequently, a great many college students today merely want a credential attesting to some level of occupational competence, and they want it for as little expense as possible.

In the years ahead, as the educational and regulatory standards are worked out, it seems likely that the number of students willing to receive an online university education for reduced costs will keep growing.[54] And that will mean fewer professors and lecturers, plus support staff and infrastructure, will be needed. It seems also likely that a hybrid model will evolve that combines an online education curriculum bundled with quarterly campus visits for meetings, symposiums and face-to-face interactions. Many possibilities exist for ways to weave both types of experiences together.

Beethoven and Bach bot, AI creativity. Surely if there's one safe haven from the onslaught of computers, and the audacious attempts to replace humans with machines, it's in the creative arts and culture, yes? Surely that is the last redoubt of humanity, something uniquely *homo sapien* that will never be modeled or emulated by an algorithm?

Uh-uh, sorry, not looking that way. Computers now are smashing down the door of the creative domain as well. Dr. David Cope, a music scholar and composer from the University of California, Santa Cruz, has built algorithms that compose classical music of such surpassing quality and passion, and mimic the greats like Bach, Mozart and Beethoven, that audiences and critics can't always tell the difference. Call it the Bach-bot.[55]

Beyond music composition, music labels are using an online service called Music X-Ray and its software algorithms to assess the potential of new song hits. In the movie industry, the company Epagogix uses computer algorithms to evaluate screenplays for movie studios that are weighing whether to invest serious money into a project. Nick Meaney, CEO and cofounder of Epagogix, tells how his human analysts evaluate a script by placing a value on all of the major plot points and quantifying thousands of factors—are there love scenes and car chases? And clear villains? How much empathy does the protagonist inspire? The intricate exchange between these factors is then fed into the computer, which compares it to previous films that have done well at the box office. "And they score them according to a directory, in the way a teacher might score a test," says Meaney. The computer algorithm is used to calculate how much money the movie will make. Epagogix will also recommend script changes to make a movie more financially successful, like setting it in a different place or making changes to characters' roles.[56] Epagogix has built a solid reputation in the movie industry for being on the money with its projections and predictions. In 83 percent of cases, its guesstimate has turned out to be within $10 million of the total.[57]

But entertainment analyst Porter Bibb warily compares this method to "screenwriting by numbers." "If you put everything into the meat grinder of big data, you come out with a hugely similar product," says Bibb. "That is taking away a tremendous amount of creativity and it may, in the end, come back to bite the studios." Undoubtedly true, but Richard Furlin, a movie financier with MovieArb, says the proof is in the pudding. He calls Epagogix's methodology "shockingly accurate. It can have a dramatic effect on your portfolio." He only backs a film if it's been vetted by Epagogix and says its recommendations have boosted revenues of movies he's invested in by more than a third.[58]

These are just a few examples of white-collar occupations and advanced-degree professions that already are being dramatically impacted by artificial intelligence, computers and other digital technologies. In so many occupations and industries, the increasing capacity of smart machines and robots to understand speech, to decipher and understand written documents and to automate routine jobs is becoming an increasingly disruptive force. Computers are better than humans at remembering data and factoids, and at finding new connections and relationships. And now they are even making inroads into human creativity. Supercomputers like Watson are improving their ability at understanding speech, imitating human logic and taking over work previously performed by humans in high-paying professions. Innovations will affect many jobs, eliminating ones that were previously secure, as smart machines increasingly take on routine, predictable tasks in profession after profession.

In what areas do robots have a hard time measuring up to humans? At the moment, in two main competencies—manipulating objects in the physical world and in face-to-face conversation. However, as computer power increases, many experts say that the first of these problems can be solved, while others disagree. Junji Tsuda, chairman and president of the Japanese robotics company Yaskawa Electric, one of the world's largest robotics companies, says, "The [computer] brain is developing incredibly fast, both in performance and falling price, but the biggest problem is the hands that do the work. Human hands have incredible precision," he says. "There are more than 10,000 sensors [in human hands]. To put more than 10,000 sensors in a piece of hardware . . . there are many robots under development that are intelligent but can't do anything," says Tsuda.[59]

The second area—face-to-face conversation—might also be within robot capacities in future years, particularly as speech-recognition technology becomes ever more powerful. Yet as we move further into the whirlwind of this Third Industrial Revolution, already the capabilities are so powerful and revolutionary that nearly everyone agrees that workers will face an unprecedented challenge trying to adapt. A lot of people's lives are riding on the outcome.

THE BIRTH OF *TECHNO SAPIENS*

The vision of many technologists and futurists goes well beyond the capacity of robots and automation to kill or create jobs. Many see a positive evolution, indeed even a merger, between humans and smart technology. Erik Brynjolfsson and Andrew McAfee, authors of the best seller *The Second Machine Age,* have been two of the leading intellectual leaders of this perspective. The tech scientists predict that we are in the process of experiencing "two of the most amazing events in human history: the creation of true machine intelligence and the connection of all humans via a common digital network, transforming the planet's economics." Innovators, entrepreneurs, scientists, tinkerers and many other types of geeks, they say, will "take advantage of this cornucopia to build technologies that astonish us, delight us, and work for us."[60]

Noted futurist Jeremy Rifkin goes even further in his most recent book, *The Zero Marginal Cost Society,* describing the emergence of an "Internet of Things" that will precipitate "the meteoric rise of a global Collaborative Commons and the eclipse of capitalism."[61] The Internet of Things (IoT) amounts to a new technology platform that "connects everything and everyone" via billions of sensors scattered all over the world, linked via a super Internet grid. The sensors will be attached to electricity streams, production lines, logistics networks; also implanted into homes, buildings, offices, stores, vehicles and, yes, even into human beings, billions of sensors in constant transmission and communication with each other, a throbbing hive of electronics. I attended a tech conference in San Francisco, and Padmasree Warrior, chief technology officer for Cisco, one of the top tech companies in the world, told the audience, "Technology will become an extension of who we are as human beings. We'll wear a lot more of the technology. We'll probably inject a lot of sensors that will keep track of what's happening in our bodies, so it can be much more predictive."

Inject? Did she say *inject?* I thought, sitting there, in a sea of *techno sapiens* who were dutifully nodding and tapping this out on their laptops. I'm not even sure I can trust my computer and iPhone anymore—every time we turn these devices on, apparently, we are being tracked and metadata-ed by advertisers, corporations, the government. But at least we can turn off our computers and devices and leave them home. *Now they want to inject a nanobot computer into our bodies?* Shouldn't there be, like, a national referendum about this or something?

All of these sensors, both within our bodies and in the external world, will feed a constant stream of Big Data into the IoT global neural network and its algorithms, the "cloud" that will give life to this electronic ant colony. And that will hypothetically provide perfect information about supply and demand, flow of resources, movements of people, waste reduction and more. It will be radically "green," maximizing efficient use of physical resources, energy—as well as humans. What Rifkin describes as a decentralized and deeply networked population of "prosumers"—consumers who have become their own producers of renewable energy, 3D-printed products, online college courses, news, culture/entertainment, and who share cars, homes, clothes and tools on the "collaborative commons"—will bypass the conventional capitalist markets by instead connecting to the commons via the IoT network. On that platform, they can use Big Data to lower the cost to near zero of producing and sharing a wide range of self-manufactured products and services. We are, says Rifkin, entering a "world beyond markets where we are learning how to live together in an increasingly interdependent global Collaborative Commons."

It's a vision that leaves me a bit breathless. Personally—especially if you leave out the human injections part—I find Rifkin's vision, along with similar ones posed by Belgian peer-to-peer theorist Michel Bauwens and digital labor expert Trebor Scholz,[62] to be attractive in certain ways. An interdependent and collaborative commons—who can argue with that? It promises perfection in great and small ways—a milk carton or carton of eggs, for example, will carry sensors and sit on a "smart" refrigerator shelf in your "smart" home, sending signals to the grocery store when it is near empty, automatically requesting immediate delivery—no doubt from a driverless car or drone with automated delivery capability.[63] It taps into many of the right cultural memes about the promise of sustainability, efficiency and creativity via the most beautiful technology, and of producers producing "from each according to his ability, to each according to his need," as Karl Marx once famously wrote.[64] So this is an updated version of that: Marx meets the Jetsons, in the land of the *techno sapiens.*

But Rifkin, Brynjolfsson and McAfee, as well as many new-economy gurus, don't ever really address a looming question: Who would control Rifkin's "collaborative commons," or Brynjolfsson and McAfee's "common digital network"? They seem to assume that the trends they have identified have a power and momentum all their own that will iron out any inequalities. But without a clear blueprint of what kind of public policy needs to be legislated that is capable of solidifying the wobbly ground beneath American workers, there's little reason to assume that these trends will automatically translate into a bright future for the middle class or the poor. The recent track record of our political institutions' failure to reign in the economic institutions is not encouraging: under the watch of the most powerful politicians and the nation's ablest economists, the country went mad with deregulation and suffered the greatest economic collapse since the Great Depression. And even before that, steep levels of inequality had been on the rise and wages had been flat.

This raises reasonable fears over who would benefit from these new technologies. We could well end up with an economy where robots take over all the jobs that the algorithms can model, and most of the profits go to the robots' *techno sapien* owners and managers. The great mass of humans are then left to do the low-skill work that can't be robotized—humdrum tasks and on-demand jobs, like housework, child care, handyman, a patchwork of small, poorly paying gigs—hustling to scrape together enough on which to survive via the "share-the-crumbs" economy.

It's not just some leftist economists or anticapitalist anarchists who are questioning the credibility of the tech booster vision. In January 2015, Microsoft founder Bill Gates, famed theoretical physicist Stephen Hawking and Tesla Motors and SpaceX founder Elon Musk joined dozens of other scientists, entrepreneurs and investors involved in the fields of computers, technology and artificial intelligence to sign an open letter expressing concern over the development of these new technologies. The letter stated that "it is important to research how to reap its benefits while avoiding potential pitfalls," and called for greater focus on safety and social benefits.[65] In a speech at the MIT Aeronautics and Astronautics department's Centennial Symposium, Musk went further, calling artificial intelligence humanity's biggest existential threat and that "with artificial intelligence we are summoning the demon."[66] These are some of the world's top technologists, expressing a growing nervousness about humanity's long-term prospects from machines whose intelligence and capabilities eventually could exceed those of the people who created them.

Some expert technologists are predicting a rather dire future of *Hunger Games*–type dystopia: displacements on a mass scale, leading to ever more vast increases in "income inequality, a continued hollowing out of the middle class, and even riots, social unrest, and the creation of a permanent, unemployable underclass."[67] Back to the future—these are the types of days that many thought the world of developed nations had left behind in the last century, after the devastation of two world wars and the Great Depression. Having learned valuable lessons from that wreckage, we thought we were on a straight-line track toward a brighter future, culminating in the "end of history." But suddenly, nothing is certain anymore. Reinvention is the name of the game.

THE INEFFICIENCY OF EFFICIENCY

With all the anxiety and displacement stemming from the advance of technology, it is easy to regard automation and robots as the enemy. But that would be a mistake. Automation in the past has allowed the replacement of low-end jobs with better jobs. Today, what is taunting us is our national failure to use the advantages of automation to construct an ever more productive economy with decent jobs, and in which the prosperity is broadly shared.[68] The challenge, then, is a political one, not technological.

A lot of the coming battle—and make no mistake, it will be a battle—will be over societal notions of economic efficiency. I remember when I was on a speaking tour in Europe, and one of my lecture stops was in Amsterdam. I was being interviewed by a television show, *Netwerk,* which is like the *60*

Minutes of the Netherlands. A three-person team of producers conducted the interview, one of whom held a rather large boom mic with one of those hairy-looking sweater hoods to record the audio. Discreetly, I said to the middle-aged man holding the boom, "Hey, why don't you give me a lapel mic? That way you won't have to hold that big thing." He looked at me with a bit of a Rembrandt twinkle, and said, "If I do that, I'm out of a job."

Of course! The brilliance of his insight immediately struck me. What good is such mechanical efficiency if it results in more unemployment, or more specifically *his* unemployment? What is efficiency, after all? Is it possible that you can be so efficient that you actually become inefficient?

A famous story illustrates a similar point. In 1955, Walter Reuther, head of the United Auto Workers, told of a visit to a newly automated plant owned by Ford Motor Company. Ford was notorious for its poor wages; its own workers could not afford to buy a car. Pointing to all the robots, the host, Henry Ford II asked the head of one of the largest labor unions: "Walter, how are you going to collect union dues from those guys?" Without skipping a beat, Reuther replied: "Henry, how are you going to get them to buy your cars?"[69]

Efficiency. In its earliest days under the stingy eye of its founder, the first Henry Ford, it seemed efficient to the company to pay as low wages as they could get away with. But eventually even the Nazi sympathizer Ford[70] gave into the economic logic of paying his workers more so that they could afford to buy one of its cars. Ford created more customers for his own company, a virtuous circle, a mutually benevolent—and efficient—feedback loop.

But that logic seems to have eluded the nearsighted designers of the new economy, just as it has not found traction at Walmart and other U.S. companies.

I'm driving to the airport, and the guy who is driving the service car tells me he does this for a living because his last job—he was a cargo agent at a trucking terminal—disappeared as a result of computers and automation. So now he's driving a car for a living—but in a few years apparently driverless cars will displace him yet again. Where does he go then?

Auto companies can use robots to assemble cars that are cheaper for their customers who work in occupations such as checkout clerks. But if grocery stores and department stores replace those clerks with their own robots, then who will buy the cheaper cars? Henry, who's going to buy up all those products and services, if no one has a job?

Indeed, people are being chased from job to job, from obsolescence to redundancy—chased by algorithms and automation, scary and imposing like a Frankenstein monster. The gaps between the haves and have-nots will continue to grow larger. Computer robotics, smart machines, 3D printing and more are threatening to push "Control-Alt-Delete" on workers, and damn the consequences.

It has taken centuries of political agitation, moral outrage and even rebellion to wrest from the owners of the economy some benevolent norms and rules over who can work, for how long and at what wage. The great genius of the New Deal was that, much more than any previous version of the social contract between bosses and workers, it allowed workers to keep a sizable portion of the pie that resulted from mechanization and increased productivity. That resulted in not only higher wages but a measure of job security as well as health care, a decent retirement and other worker protections (sick pay, vacations, injured worker and unemployment compensation and more). That in turn created millions of middle-class consumers to purchase the goods and services produced by the robust U.S. economy, which made for profitable businesses whose goods and services supported families and vibrant communities, amplifying social harmony across demographics and sectors. It was a virtuous circle, finely calibrated.

But the new economy—automated, robotized, freelanced, Uber-ed, contracted, shared, "1099-ed"—threatens to cancel all that in a very heartbreaking way. We are sleepwalking into a tragedy.

Stephen Hawking is the closest scientist we have today to the giants of the past, such as Albert Einstein or Isaac Newton. Beyond the open letter that he signed with other technologists, Hawking has been explicit in his public fears over the future. Writing for the *Independent* newspaper in the UK, Hawking said, "One can imagine such technology outsmarting financial markets, out-inventing human researchers, out-manipulating human leaders, and developing weapons we cannot even understand. Whereas the short-term impact of AI depends on who controls it, the long-term impact depends on whether it can be controlled at all."[71]

Hawking continues: "If a superior alien civilization sent us a message saying, 'We'll arrive in a few decades,' would we just reply, 'OK, call us when you get here—we'll leave the lights on'? Probably not—but this is more or less what is happening. Although we are facing potentially the best or worst thing to happen to humanity in history, little serious research is devoted to these issues. All of us should ask ourselves what we can do now to improve the chances of reaping the benefits and avoiding the risks."

In essence, what Hawking is saying is that technologists need their own version of the medical profession's 2,400-year-old Hippocratic Oath that swears, "*Primum non nocere*"—"first, do no harm." A techno version of the Hippocratic Oath should recognize that sometimes the most efficient arrangement is the one that is inefficient. Because today the human master programmers all too often instruct their robots to do things that end up being quite harmful to other humans, often in the name of progress, innovation and efficiency.

The robots are innocent; the human technologists in the midst of this fall from edenic grace are not. The *robots* aren't the problem; it's the *humans* that are the problem. It's our values and our priorities, just as it has always been throughout history, human against human. Technology does not change our most fundamental drives or divides.

The algorithms are coming, they are slowly encircling us. If we do nothing, there will be no escaping them. "*Primum non nocere.*"

SEVEN

THE SPECTER OF THE ECONOMIC SINGULARITY

ON NOVEMBER 17, 2009, FEDERAL RESERVE CHAIRMAN BEN BERNANKE GAVE testimony to a closed-door session of the Financial Crisis Inquiry Commission, which was investigating the causes of the historical financial collapse that had wrecked the economy in 2008. "As a scholar of the Great Depression," said Bernanke,

> I honestly believe that September and October of 2008 was the worst financial crisis in global history, including the Great Depression. If you look at the firms that came under pressure in that period . . . only one . . . was not at serious risk of failure. . . . So out of maybe the 13, 13 of the most important financial institutions in the United States, 12 were at risk of failure within a period of a week or two.[1]

What has become known as the Great Recession was just the latest upheaval to remind us, with all the stunning force of a violent, barreling tornado, that the working life in capitalist economies can be a precarious one. Any American who began his or her working career in the mid-1960s has been an eyewitness to seven recessions—in 1969, 1973, 1980, 1981, 1990, 2001 and 2008, according to the Economic Policy Institute; and has "lived through inflation, stagflation, oil shocks, oil rationing, the stock market crash of 1987, the savings and loan collapse, the bursting of the dot-com bubble, the bursting of the housing bubble, the stock market crash of 2008," the meltdown of Lehman Brothers, the bailouts of AIG and the financial industry and the auto companies, the issuing of IOUs by the nation's largest state, California, to cover its debts, and a spotty recovery following the worst economic collapse since the Great Depression.[2] She or he has seen the national "unemployment rate climb above 10 percent twice," and all this during a time that has seen virtually no wage growth for the bottom 50 percent of Americans and has witnessed the decline of traditional pensions, which had been one of the pillars of the U.S. retirement system. For all but the most well-off of the 145 million working Americans, navigating the ups and downs of the economy has not been as easy as *Barron's,* Fox News and the Cato Institute make it sound.

Throughout the 20th century, everyday Main Street Americans, when faced with a tough economic situation that threatened them and their families, have found it a life-saver to reach out and grasp the helping hand of government. Since the Great Depression of the 1930s, hundreds of millions of Americans have benefited from the New Deal society that was forged decade by decade, law by law, policy by policy. President Franklin Roosevelt, more than any other previous president, deployed the unique capacity of government to pull people together and bring different sectors to the table to create pools of social insurance that would shield all Americans against the economic risks and insecurities that we all face. Social Security, Medicare, Medicaid, the Federal Housing Administration, the Family and Medical Leave Act, student aid, the Fair Labor Standards Act, the National Labor Relations Act, the Federal Mine Safety and Health Act, Equal Employment Opportunity, the Civil Rights Act, laws against discrimination, consumer protection, the Occupational Safety and Health Act—the list is a long alphabet soup of laws and programs that FDR and successor presidents passed, shaping the world that all Americans alive today grew up in.

Our understanding of who we are as a people is inseparable from these policies—even if we don't always acknowledge it, and even as many Americans today who are dependent on these programs like to bash government. Forty-four percent of Social Security beneficiaries say they haven't ever used a government program; so do 60 percent of recipients of the federal home mortgage interest deduction, 43 percent of unemployment insurance recipients and 40 percent of Medicare recipients.[3] Each of these programs and laws were passed, with painstaking legislative effort, for well-founded reasons. They responded to specific situations and conditions, based on past experiences in which far too many Americans—including the most vulnerable, such as the elderly and children—ended up in tough circumstances through no fault of their own, but because of the roller-coaster swings of the economy.

But it wasn't merely an act of compassion by the wealthy and patrician Roosevelt and the political and business leaders of the time to create the New Deal system. After the devastation of the Great Depression, it also was a way of remaking the broader macroeconomy into one that was more stable and robust, and of using the fiscal stimulus levers of government popularized by British economist John Maynard Keynes to grow the economic pie. That in turn fed a broadly shared prosperity and the middle class, which became the consumer engine that purchased the goods and services produced by America's businesses. It was a virtuous circle, and while the system wasn't perfect, it worked, creating the highest standard of living for more people in American—indeed, in all of human—history. That in turn made the United States the envy of the world, with the middle-class dream becoming an important part of the allure of our national story to countries everywhere. It made the U.S. the most powerful magnet in the post–World War II era, which in turn gave America more clout on the global stage.

But over the last three decades, the American luster has dimmed. Deregulation, deindustrialization, financialization and automation of the economy have shrunk the middle class, resulting in less job security and a reduced standard of living. Since 1979, the U.S. economy has more than doubled in size, yet most of the prosperity from that growth has flowed into the pockets and bank accounts of a fortunate few. In a speech in December 2013, President Barack Obama expressed his grave concern that the top 10 percent now takes in half of the nation's income, compared to one-third previously—a level of inequality not seen since the Great Depression.[4] Three-quarters of Americans have little to no emergency savings to rely on if they lose their jobs; they are living paycheck to paycheck.[5] In terms of living in a society that works for the vast majority of Americans, we are going backward. The fears of many everyday Americans, which Tea Party conservatives have exploited masterfully, are not paranoia. Their quality of life is in fact declining.

Some of the New Deal–type laws and policies that insured Americans against risk have been weakened or overturned. Others have become outdated and no longer fit the society we are becoming. Consequently, the New Deal society is slowly melting into the fog of history, like a once-glorious ship whose time appears to be fading as the ship passes across the sea. Unlike the talented generation of American politicians and business leaders in the 1930s, '40s and '50s, who tackled head-on the challenge of forging a new deal for the country in the face of a paralyzing economic crisis, as well as a second world war, the current crew of politicians and business leaders have watched helplessly or worse, as the recent national collapse accelerated trends that are taking major parts of our economy backward to pre–New Deal conditions.

Consequently, for today's children and grandchildren, the ground looks even shakier than it ever did for their parents and grandparents. Allow me to outline an all-too-possible future for these children and grandchildren, who will soon claim their generational inheritance infused with the hopes and expectations of a still-wealthy New Deal society, but one whose glory and opportunity appear to be fading:

Picture nearly half of American workers—65–70 million people—freelancers, temps, contractors, greys, perma-lancers, part-timers and everything in between—with no steady job, no regular employment to go to, instead all scratching and scrambling for their next gig, micro-gig and nano-gig; being squeezed from multiple sides by a combination of factors that have caused declines in both the quantity as well as the quality of jobs; earning dribbles of money from various sources via the "share-the-crumbs" economy, renting out their labor and what little private property they own via faceless websites and apps and calling that "opportunity for all." Their housing and other basic costs are rising much faster than their gig wages, making the day-to-day an increasing struggle as they watch the robots and other forms of automation perform the jobs that their parents and grandparents used to do, their noses pressed against the window as they see the party going on inside among a small gentry of *techno sapiens;* reading in the history books about the "golden era of the middle class," when people like themselves used to be able to enjoy a decent standard of living and a measure of economic security, now hardly a safety net beneath them, no job protections or security, little in the way of savings or retirement resources, ever smaller numbers of them covered by injured workers' or unemployment compensation, or paid sick leave, vacations or holidays; running exhausted all the time from gig to gig, realizing that they can't get sick or they'll miss out on the five or six McJobs they have arranged with multiple employers; dealing with the faceless insults, frustrations and erratic customer ratings of "1099 companies" like Uber, Lyft, TaskRabbit, Upwork and other app-based job brokerages and temp agencies, who unilaterally can suspend or fire them or chop their contractor's rate of pay with no consultation, much less consideration, and nothing contractually guaranteed; having to skimp every penny because they're not sure where their next gig will come from; hustling to scrape together enough to take care of their families, sometimes they drift back and forth over the increasingly thin line between white, grey and black economies, anguishing over which way lies the "silk road" to economic security for themselves and their families.

This is the topsy-turvy, madcap work life that far too many Americans are inheriting. If current trends continue, it will dead-end in a world that is a far cry from the New Deal world that their parents and grandparents knew. Many of the new-economy visionaries frequently say that Millennials, those 80 million or so Americans who are 18–32 years old, value flexibility and time over having money and a steady job, that they "don't see companies as salary machines," are "changing the very definition of the word 'work,'"[6] "want to have the ability to pursue their passions," "value experiences more than things," "see no reason for a hierarchy"[7] and "expect to make money at what they love"[8]—as if the Millennials comprise some new, post-capitalist generation. The fact that the number of cars purchased by 18- to 34-year-olds declined nearly 30 percent between 2007 and 2011 has been attributed to a change in attitude toward more sharing and more green, anti-car values, rather than the more obvious explanation that in the middle of a near-depression young people have been flat broke.[9]

In the age-old tale of the ant versus the grasshopper, allegedly, young people today are more grasshopper than ant. It's kind of an astounding claim, particularly since it ignores the fact that those same things have been said of every generation of young people since World War II—remember the Beats, the hippies, the Mods, the disco divers, the carefree Boomers, all living for today, without much care for tomorrow. When you're in your 20s, of course you're enjoying a measure of post-parental freedom and rejoice at not being tied down to a 40-hour work week, or anything else for that matter. Particularly with decent jobs for young people extremely hard to find today, who can blame them for living for today and for embracing idealistic values? But when the Millennials reach their mid-30s and 40s, just like every other generation before them, that's when they are going to grow very tired of being broke and living closer to the edge; and that's when they will start thinking more seriously about having steadier income and a more secure livelihood.

Yet, sadly, that's when the Millennials are going to discover something extremely troubling: that the world has fundamentally shifted from the one their parents and grandparents knew. The "good jobs" of the New Deal era will be gone because not enough people bothered to fight the good fight to pass laws and regulations needed to protect those jobs or create new good ones. Instead, the maturing Millennials will find themselves to be little more than "1099 workers" in the gigging economy, subject to the whims and "just-in-time" scheduling of employers and their automated, robotized, freelanced, Uber-ized workplaces. That's when they'll discover that the well-meaning leaders and organizations that told them they were somehow different from all the previous generations—well, they were 180 degrees wrong.

Maybe then, the Millennials will find it within themselves to fight back, like every previous generation has had to do in order to secure its place in an economic world controlled by bosses, CEOs and the latest gang of greedy one-percenters. But will it be too late?

NEW DEAL VS. RAW DEAL

A brief historical tour of labor conditions in previous eras provides some illuminating context. Long before today's 1099 economy arrived, employers and bosses regularly sought to lower labor costs by hiring contractors, freelancers and casual labor instead of regular employees. So the most recent trends moving in the same direction are not new.

In 1902, New York City was the location of a fierce strike of 30,000 Italian immigrant workers hired to build the first subway system. A bankers' syndicate held the primary contract, and it subcontracted the hiring and payment of laborers to the *padroni* labor system, which was used by many companies to hire immigrants. This system, which overlapped with organized crime and the black and grey markets, led to widespread abuses over pay and labor conditions of the type that are returning to haunt U.S. workers today. In the strike, the Italian workers demanded to be paid as employees directly by the syndicate rather than as day workers and contractors by the middlemen.[10] It would take them many years of intense, protracted—and sometimes violent—confrontations to win this fight.

The garment industry also was plagued by underhanded bosses and their henchmen. Employers would regularly undercut industry wages by contracting out work via middlemen known as jobbers. In a situation similar to workers competing via TaskRabbit or Upwork (formerly known as oDesk) today, the subcontractors initiated a race to the bottom by forcing workers to compete against one another over who could offer the lowest piece rates.[11] The 1910 garment workers' strike in Chicago triggered a citywide labor action of 40,000 workers fighting police on horseback, with hundreds of strikers injured and two killed. Only some years later during the peak influence of garment workers' unions was this system rejected in favor of direct payroll employment. It's important to note, says Robert Kuttner, author and coeditor of the *American Prospect*, that these struggles had nothing to do with advances in manufacturing and new technology in the garment and transportation industries, and everything to do with power.[12] Many garment workers recognized the benefits of technology—they were hardly Luddites who wanted to smash the machines—instead the battle was—and still is—over who is going to control and benefit from the technology.

Going further back in U.S. labor history is equally revealing. In the late nineteenth century, workers had few rights, no labor protections and no job security. Conditions were Dickensian; minimum wage and maximum hour laws, which today are common labor standards across most of the world, originally were ruled unconstitutional by the U.S. Supreme Court. It was common for laborers to work 12- to 14-hour days, with child labor widespread, no lunch breaks, no sick days, no unemployment or disability insurance, no safety net for families, and little recourse if an employer reneged on pay. Older workers were particularly vulnerable, with many winding up in the poorhouse when they were too frail to work (as did many orphans).

On-the-job injuries were frequent and devastating, yet when profits declined, as during the depression of the early 1870s, business owners and managers felt no remorse over ramping up production and extending workers' hours, even though it was obvious that would cause more injuries.[13] When workers were killed by such callous "speedups," their spouses and dependents lacked any legal remedies and suddenly were tossed to the lions, with few alternatives for economic support.

(Today Travis Kalanick evidently shows no remorse for unilaterally slicing the rate he pays his Uber drivers, saying the drivers can work longer hours and hustle more fares per hour to make up for it—a dangerous form of speedup for tired, overworked driver-temps, sitting for hours a day behind the wheel of a 3,500-pound death machine. And TaskRabbit unilaterally raises its share of the take from its rabbits' gigs, and suspends a rabbit because of one cranky customer's bad review without any grievance process at all. It's back to the future, in disturbing ways.)

American workers today are standing on some mighty shoulders. Courageous people from bygone decades fought bravely to improve the lot of people everywhere—and for all time, they had hoped. In the 1870s, workers as well as widows in the railroad industry started organizing unions and pushing for the creation of workers' compensation benefits. Progress was not achieved quickly or easily, but a few decades later, success was attained.[14] Other labor unions—United Auto Workers, United Mine Workers, International Workers of the World (Wobblies), American Federation of Labor and hundreds more—fought back against authoritarian capitalism. Today, the designers of the new economy are seeking nothing less than to reverse these gains in worker conditions, accomplished over the past century and a half. Or at the very least, to stand by passively while others unravel these gains.

For several decades now the productivity gains of the workforce have benefited fewer and fewer Americans. Thomas Piketty, Emmanuel Saez and others have shown that the wealth of a small slice of Americans has soared while the wealth of the rest of the population has stagnated or fallen behind. This is not only unfair (and has been called immoral by Pope Francis I), it is also inefficient and counterproductive from the standpoint of stabilizing and expanding the broader macroeconomy (as we will see in the next section).

At this point, in the middle of the second decade of the 21st century, the greatest threats to the workforce and jobs are increasingly clear: a brazen business class, which has forgotten that "believing in capitalism" is not the same as "making money,"[15] and which has plotted, planned and beat back regulations to realize its goal of having the untrammeled right to turn its workforce on and off as needed, like a water spigot; and an increasingly feckless and ineffectual politician class that is letting them get away with it, and in some cases actively supporting this nightmarish vision of American *braceros*-for-hire. The bargaining power of most workers has suffered as a result, even as wages have stagnated and as the costs of housing, health care and education have soared and the safety net has deteriorated. That in turn has driven down consumer purchasing power. And there's no sign that the situation will reverse anytime soon; quite the contrary. As we saw in the previous chapter, the designers of the new economy are planning to bring forward more advanced technology with even greater capabilities for evicting American workers from the jobs that decades of labor activism secured, the consequences be damned.

STARING INTO THE ABYSS OF ECONOMIC SINGULARITY

In a modern capitalist economy, good jobs and high wages have historically provided the primary means for redistributing income and purchasing power from businesses back to workers, in their role as consumers. The success of the postwar development model among developed nations was predicated upon a virtuous feedback loop, in which rising wages led to increased demand for products and services, which in turn helped drive continuous growth. A rising tide floated all boats.

Conversely, as under- and unemployment creep higher, that lowers consumer demand and our aggregate ability to buy up the goods and services that have been produced by the economy. The micro-gigs that are a primary feature of the new economy, in which individuals must continuously cobble together a string of small jobs with low pay to earn a living, contribute toward a type of disruption that the country thought we had left behind in the rear-view mirror. It's practically returning millions of American workers to the scramble of pre–New Deal days.

That retrogression not only impacts individuals and their families but also results in significant consequences that ripple throughout the broader economy. As more and more workers become part time, underemployed or are laid off, they have less money to buy and thus consume less. Businesses have fewer customers and so they must begin cutting back the hours of more workers. It's a spiraling cycle that creates downward pressure on economic growth, spurring the slow creep of deflation and other negative consequences. Past a certain tipping point—and no experts know really where that point is—the positive feedback loop becomes a negative one, a downward cycle that can be difficult to reverse.

Japan has suffered from this fate to some degree for well over a decade; the European Union is in danger of stepping into the same abyss, though in some ways the plight of both of those places is a "known unknown." The United States is possibly even more worrisome, because more than any other place in the world we have embraced this freelanced, contracted, robotized, Uber-ized, automated economy that threatens to leap into the "unknown unknown" without a parachute.

The fact is, the U.S. economy pumps out a nearly unfathomable $16.8 trillion worth of goods and services, and ultimately all of those products must get purchased by someone. My spending is your income, and vice versa. If demand is too low for what any particular business is producing—if there is no spending by customers to provide income to that business—it will have to shut down and stop buying inputs. And then it will have to stop paying wages and lay off its workers.

But a worker is also a consumer—as workers we receive income, and as consumers we spend that income, buying up goods and services from businesses who receive that revenue and pay wages/salaries to their workers (or purchase inputs from other businesses, which then become those businesses' revenue and *their* workers' income). All in all it's a self-perpetuating cycle, a miracle in a way, but a delicate one that is always in a fragile entropic state of falling out of balance. Most importantly, it means that workers are an integral part of the functioning of this cacophonous symphony. When a worker is laid off, or is reduced from full time to part time, or becomes a 1099 worker, gigging from job to job, or is replaced by a machine, that reduction in consumer demand from lower wages has an impact. Certainly if a worker is replaced by a robot, that robot does not go out and consume. If these things happen to too many workers, the aggregate impacts become destabilizing.

Economist Nouriel Roubini, in thinking about the winner-take-all effects of these dynamics, says that "rising inequality becomes a drag on demand and growth, as well as a source of social and political instability, because it distributes income from those who spend more—lower- and middle-income households—to those who save more—high net worth individuals and corporate firms."[16] That can have disastrous consequences. The risk, he says, is that workers will be displaced "before the dust of the Third Industrial Revolution settles. Unless the proper policies to nurture job growth are put in place, it remains uncertain whether demand for labor will continue to grow as technology marches forward." So if there are not enough consumers to buy what the machines or businesses are producing, if the economy becomes even more out of balance, what happens then?

It's frighteningly simple: economic momentum will freeze. Like an engine that seizes up without enough oil, the gears will grind to a halt.

Getting more specific to today's situation: if both the quantity and quality of jobs for millions of 1099 workers is deteriorating, if millions of middle-class *braceros* are forced to turn to TaskRabbit, Upwork, Uber, Airbnb and other "share-the-crumbs" companies, or if we automate most of the jobs, or if we push wages so low that fewer and fewer people have much disposable income, then it will become increasingly tough for a modern mass-market economy to flourish. As jobs and incomes are relentlessly whittled away, at some point we will face the prospect of having too few viable consumers with enough purchasing power and demand to continue driving economic growth in our mass-market economy.

At the end of this perilous sequence lies something truly troubling: as these forces gain momentum, they will unleash a domino effect that ultimately crashes and burns in an Economic Singularity—the tipping point at which our economy implodes from a severe imbalance between overproduction and reduced consumer demand because the wealth has been captured by a handful of powerful economic forces who extract the best of our nation for their own private use. At that point, ongoing recessionary and deflationary pressures become the norm, and the days of the American model projecting an alluring dream of opportunity and prosperity to the world will be over. The Economic Singularity gains traction when, for whatever reasons, too much of society's wealth is extracted by elites who control the economic and political systems, making it impossible for the goods and services to be consumed by everyday people who have too little income, initiating a chronic downward and deflationary cycle.

That dangerous horizon means that fierce debates over the new economy are not just over jobs, fairness and income inequality—ultimately, they are about the sustainability of economic growth, and about the continued viability of America's capitalist development model that has prevailed since World War II and made the U.S. the envy of the world. Economists such as former Clinton administration Treasury secretary Larry Summers have worried about this, saying that unless there is serious government intervention, inequality and a lack of financial resources among those in the bottom half of the income distribution will result in "insufficient aggregate demand—too little spending by consumers and businesses to keep gross domestic product at its capacity."[17] Technology analyst Martin Ford, author of *Rise of the Robots,* says that "a future with a dearth of viable consumers will be a far more zero-sum future."[18] Stowe Boyd, a futurist with the former tech consultancy Gigaom Research, looks into his crystal ball and sees something grim: a kind of Mad Max future in which "an increasing proportion of the world's population will be outside of the world of work—either living on the dole, or benefiting from the dramatically decreased costs of goods to eke out a subsistence lifestyle. The central question of 2025 will be: What are people [useful] for in a world that does not need their labor, and where only a minority are needed to guide the 'bot-based economy?'"[19]

The Economic Singularity is like a black hole toward which no society should approach, lest the gravitational pull accelerates and sucks in all light and goodness. Once the critical mass of singularity has reached fission, it can only be interrupted by either the unstable frothiness of more giant economic bubbles as stimulus (accompanied by sufficient "trickle-down" income), or a massive outright redistribution of existing wealth, as part of a sustained effort to jumpstart consumer demand. But since the political system itself by that point will have been captured by the economic elite, politics and politicians will have ceased to be an instrument for such redistribution. President Barack Obama has undoubtedly been one of the most talented and charismatic politicians of his generation, yet he has been mostly powerless to reign in the mortal spiral that America is spinning around, like a marble rolling around a gravity well. The marble keeps orbiting in a circle but slowly it drops down the inclined plane of the gravity-well funnel, faster and faster in ever tighter circles, finally plunging into the central black hole. During that final kinetic release, the elites themselves mostly will be content to preside over the fissile disruption of a crumbling society, protected behind their residential walls and moats that, in this near-future time, will consist of electronic and digital security apparatuses specially designed for crowd control and, if necessary, intimidation.

We do not want to approach the immense gravitational density of the Singularity. But how close are we to this dangerous moment?

Most likely it's still a ways away, but the trajectory is clear and troubling. And there are degrees of collapse along the singularity spectrum. Already the top 5 percent of households are responsible for around 30 percent of consumer spending, up from 23 percent in 1992. And this shift is accelerating; since 2009, the top 5 percent of income earners saw their household spending climb 12 percent, while spending for all other households fell 1 percent.[20] Over the course of the Great Recession corporate profits climbed by 25–30 percent, while wages as a share of national income fell to their lowest point since World War II.[21] With no relief in sight, according to the Federal Reserve, incomes were flat or falling between 2010 and 2013 for all but the top one-tenth of U.S. income earners, continuing that long-term trend. We are living through a time that has seen one of the greatest wealth shifts in U.S. history.

Prior to the 2008 economic crisis, average people were able to maintain consumption levels despite stagnant wages by loading up on credit; the lack of income growth was an important driver of the housing bubble, because millions of homeowners took out a second loan on their property as a form of ATM machine. But those easy-credit days are over, and we now face a prolonged stasis of diminished consumer demand.

Not surprisingly then, the *Wall Street Journal* reports that a two-tiered economy already has emerged, with wealthy households making gains while middle- and lower-income Americans are struggling. This economic polarization is already transforming the commercial landscape for everything from groceries to clothing to housing to luxury imported beer. "It's a tale of two economies," says Glenn Kelman, chief executive of Redfin, a nationwide real-estate brokerage. "There is a high-end market that is absolutely booming. And then there's everyone in the middle class."[22]

All the telltales indicate that without sensible policy intervention, this trend toward increased wealth concentration at the top is certain to continue. Barry Cynamon of the Federal Reserve Bank of St. Louis and Steven M. Fazzari, economics professor at Washington University, who are the authors of the study showing shifts in consumption patterns among the top 5 percent and bottom 95 percent, concluded, "We fear that the demand drag from rising inequality that was postponed for decades by the bottom 95 percent borrowing is now slowing consumption growth and will continue to do so in coming years."[23] Thomas Piketty's book, *Capital in the Twenty-First Century,* reveals the inclination of modern capitalism to over-reward *rentier*-seeking financial investments and under-reward investment in companies that actually manufacture or otherwise produce something useful for society. Wealth delivers better returns than labor, argues Piketty, and this dynamic will cause wealth to accumulate over time into fewer hands and inequality to rise even more than it has, further undermining aggregate consumer demand.[24]

The trajectory toward Economic Singularity should raise the hairs on the back of everyone's neck. Each new batch of statistics indicating chronic levels of under- and unemployment, greater inequality and reduced consumer spending by the middle class is just another red flag that such a "black-hole" economy may already be closer at hand than we realize. The current trajectory then is a direct threat to the highly successful Keynesian development model that was adopted across the globe over the last 70 years.

U.S. businesses are quick to defend their latest practices by saying that in a highly competitive and volatile global economy, companies are forced to operate more efficiently and productively by cutting back the workforce and squeezing more work out of fewer workers. *Of course* that's what the bosses want—but that doesn't mean the politicians should let them have it. Most of the developed world so far is not rushing to embrace this 1099 economy and freelance society. Certainly some European countries, Japan, Canada and other nations use more temps and freelancers than they used to, but nothing like the level seen in the U.S. And temp workers, freelancers and contractors in these other countries often are provided many of the same job protections and safety-net supports as regular workers.

German autoworkers make a lot more money than U.S. autoworkers, by some estimates twice as much,[25] yet the German auto industry remains globally competitive—it is the world's number-one automobile exporter by far, exporting almost twice as many autos as the U.S.[26]—yet it has not had to resort to antiworker tactics such as replacing huge numbers of permanent workers with independent contractors and temps, like U.S. auto companies have done. It's simply a fallacy that somehow we must turn our economy upside down in order to compete globally. The only country we are competing against by deploying the new economy's antiworkerism is our own. And by degrading the quality of our domestic jobs, it is U.S. companies that are putting pressure on the rest of the world to become more like us in order to compete. *We* are the vortex that is threatening to suck the rest of the world down with us.

China, ironically, is in the position of trying to convert to a more consumer-based economy instead of one that is lopsidedly driven by manufacturing exports. Most experts acknowledge that the key to getting Chinese consumers to start buying more is for China to create a more developed safety net. A safety net is what makes people feel secure enough to spend more, instead of hoarding money under their mattresses. But here in the U.S., we are running in the opposite direction—eviscerating the safety net, reducing workers' ability to spend and wiping out the connective tissue between employers and employees that in the past made U.S. workers feel a degree of security.

Even if the federal government were to launch more fiscal spending to stimulate demand in the economy, as some like Paul Krugman have strongly advocated, its impact would be undermined by the contractionary pressures being experienced by the labor force as a result of the decline in the quality and quantity of jobs, as well as the crumbling of the safety net. These are vital factors in the overall health of the national economy. Widespread reliance on the 1099 economy—TaskRabbited, Uber-ed, automated, robotized and freelanced—over time will undermine crucial mechanisms that keep the economy stable, prosperous and chugging forward. The specter of the Economic Singularity is looming larger on the horizon.

THE "EXTRACTIVE ECONOMY"

As we have seen, the dramatic conditions that would make a society vulnerable to the onset of an Economic Singularity are those in which a powerful elite has commandeered ever-larger amounts of that society's resources. The rest of the population is left to scrap for the middens, via outlets like the sharing economy, temp companies, subcontractors, the underground, the black market and other agencies of the freelance society. These ripe conditions for an Economic Singularity share much in common with what has been called "extractive economies," as detailed by MIT's Daron Acemoglu and Harvard's James Robinson in their insightful book, *Why Nations Fail.*

Why Nations Fail presents the results of 15 years of the author's historical research into the fall and rise of countries and their economies, and "the origins of power, prosperity and poverty." The two authors marshal an impressive amount of historical evidence from the Roman Empire, medieval Venice, ancient Mayan city-states, Europe, England, the Soviet Union, Africa, Latin America and the United States to propose a new theory of why some nations prosper and others fail. They argue, very convincingly, that one of the major factors that differentiates countries is the quality and effectiveness of their economic and political institutions. Author and political economist Will Hutton agrees, saying "Capitalism has to be shaped and governed."[27] In an MIT interview, Professor Acemoglu stated,

> If you want to think about the prosperity or poverty of nations, you have to think about institutions that provide incentives for innovation and investment, and a level playing field, but sadly those institutions are rather rare in history. What we see much more are what we call "extractive institutions," which have been designed by a few people, the elite in society, to extract resources from the rest of society. They don't generally encourage investment or innovation, and they certainly don't provide a level playing field for people to use their talents.[28]

Why Nations Fail makes a strong case that we cannot divorce the economic trajectory of a nation from its political dynamics. Extractive political institutions are going to foster extractive economic institutions, just as inclusive political institutions will create inclusive economic institutions; they are two sides of the same coin. Countries with extractive political and economic systems either fail to develop broadly or begin to fade after fleeting surges of economic expansion. Countries with inclusive political and economic systems allow a more robust engagement in the economy by greater numbers of people, operating on a more equal footing. That in turn allows what Hutton calls "multiple runners and riders," some of whom break out of the pack and foment lots of experimentation and risk-taking, which in turn revitalizes the animal spirits of the economy. "This happens best when economic and political institutions do not fall into the hands of one party or a group of self-interested oligarchs who essentially extract value," says Hutton.[29] Slavery and feudalism are extractive societies; law-governed and democratic market economies tend to be inclusive ones.

The defining characteristics of inclusive institutions, writes the *Financial Times*' Martin Wolf, are the combination of centralization with pluralism: the state must be strong enough to keep private economic power in check, and yet be controlled by widely shared and representative political authority.[30] Not surprisingly, proponents of extractive economies are fundamentally antigovernment; they have no use for regulations or taxes and regard government as something to bend to their will—much like many Silicon Valley new-economy gurus, including Uber's Travis Kalanick and Airbnb's Brian Chesky (and Silk Road's Ross Ulbricht).

Acemoglu and Robinson concluded that countries with inclusive political governments—"those extending political and property rights as broadly as possible," while enforcing the rule of law and providing some public infrastructure—"experienced the greatest growth over the long run." One of the most important takeaways from their exhaustive research is that politics and public policy, and the institutions shaped by policy, have a direct bearing on the overall economic success of a society. The historical patterns they unveiled in their book show that we have important choices to make about how to shape this emerging new economy so that it does *not* lead to an extractive society but instead becomes a contributor to an inclusive stakeholder society, in which inequality is minimized and everyday Americans continue to thrive. There are ways to encourage "good" or "bad" companies, whether "sharing economy" or otherwise, depending on how they are regulated.

Seen in this light, it seems disturbingly clear that the rise of the freelance society and the "share-the-crumbs" economy in the U.S. are the warning signs of a nation that has become corrupted by its own extractive institutions. The elite designers of this new economy are readying the workforce for even greater degrees of extraction, via automation, smart machines, sharing economy and job-brokerage websites and other methods that will vastly expand the size of the 1099 workforce. The onset of the freelance society is also a sign that the political system is failing; this should be greeted with great sorrow, not only in the U.S., but around the world, because it means that one of the world's oldest democracies, which has been an inspiration for so many others, is thrashing about in what may eventually turn out to be its last throes before the crash and burn of an Economic Singularity.[31]

WILL EDUCATION SAVE US?

For many years, economists and education experts have emphasized the importance of education and training in reducing inequality. Now, with a tsunami of job-destroying forces coming closer, some hold out hope that greater education and training will play a key role in keeping the workforce engaged, if not fully employed, and mitigating some of the worst potential outcomes. This perspective views the widening gap as a byproduct of significant shifts in the need for specific skills and occupations, and the failure of America's educational system to provide the right training to keep up with that demand.[32]

Eric Schmidt, executive chairman of Google and author of *The New Digital Age: Transforming Nations, Businesses, and Our Lives* (along with co-author Jared Cohen), has said that the solution not only is more education and training, but education and training specifically in science, technology, engineering and math (what is known as STEM). President Barack Obama also has proposed more STEM, as he and Schmidt see STEM training as a crucial step for preparing the workforce for the future. As a major business leader, Eric Schmidt has proposed that the public and private sectors should partner on this endeavor. Certainly, more training and education always help.

Other experts, such as economist Nouriel Roubini, also favor this idea. Says Roubini, "The gains from technology must be channeled to a broader base of the population than has benefited so far, and that requires a major educational component. In order to create broad-based prosperity, workers need the skills to participate in the brave new world implied by a digital economy."[33]

But other experts are deeply skeptical that education and training will still be the Willie Wonka Golden Ticket to the middle class that they were during the New Deal economy. Robert Kuttner points out that America made its greatest strides toward reducing inequality in the aftermath of World War II, a time when most Americans did not go to college and many factory workers had not completed high school. Since 1980, college graduation rates have soared—yet inequality has increased. Generally, it has widened *among* college graduates with different kinds of degrees, not just between those with college degrees and those with only high-school diplomas or less. So a lot more needs to happen than simply providing more education and training.[34]

Martin Wolf agrees with Kuttner, saying, "Education is not a magic wand. One reason is that we do not know what skills will be demanded three decades hence. Even if the demand for creative, entrepreneurial and high-level knowledge services were to grow on the required scale, which is highly unlikely, turning us all into the happy few is surely a fantasy."[35] That seems particularly so if education classrooms remain unimaginative boxes. Internet sociologist Don Rheingold criticizes the traditional format of students "still sitting in rows and columns, teaching them to keep quiet and memorize what is told to them, preparing them for life in a 20th century factory."[36]

But other experts say that the crisis cannot be fixed even by better educational methods. Martin Ford says the past solutions to technological disruption, especially more training and education, aren't going to work because once robotized and AI companies are dominant, there simply will not be enough jobs left for humans to do, whether those humans are educated and trained or not. "We must decide," says Ford, "whether the future will be one of broad-based prosperity or catastrophic levels of inequality and economic insecurity," and make the necessary adjustments.[37] Silicon Valley insider Jaron Lanier, author of *Who Owns the Future?,* agrees. "It's not easy to accept, but it's true," he says. "Education and hard work will no longer guarantee success for huge numbers of people as technology advances. The time for denial is over. Now it's time to consider solutions."[38]

Despite his optimism, even Google's Schmidt admits that ramped-up STEM education will have only limited impact. He predicts that many jobs ultimately will be eliminated by automation and smart machines, and that there are upper limits to the number of people who will be able to be hired to work advanced STEM jobs. So what happens to those Americans who lose out to this Ahab-like drive in pursuit of the great white whale of technological mastery? Schmidt looks to the government to ameliorate their situation, arguing that society needs a "safety net" for those who lose their jobs so they can "at least live somewhere and have healthcare."

Other well-meaning technologists have settled on a solution of providing a guaranteed living allowance for all the idled workers, ensuring these people at least don't sink beneath a certain minimum level of subexistence (and no doubt relieving their own consciences for having allowed the great American middle class to have gone extinct). But with the current brand of "pick-yourself-up-by-your-bootstraps" conservatism dominating U.S. politics, the passage of such a policy seems unlikely, at least in the near or medium term. And even if it was politically feasible, that policy would result in a rather dismal life for society's castaways, facing a meager subsistence on government dole in a winner-take-all society, with no meaningful work of their own. Its resemblance to the "bread and circuses" life of plebian Romans, in which people were fed and entertained with gladiatorial combat by the emperor to keep them pliant, or the expired Soviet-style system of mass idling of workers—"we pretend to work, and they pretend to pay us"—crippled en masse of boredom and alcoholism, should be a red flag that this is a dead-end antisolution.

Besides, that viewpoint sorely misunderstands how people view work, and its value. Technology analyst Sue Halpern summed it up nicely: work confers identity.[39] She cites the work of Dublin City University professor Michael Doherty, who surveyed Irish workers, including those who drove city buses and stocked grocery shelves, to try and understand if work continues to be "a significant locus of personal identity," even when employment itself is less secure. He concluded that "the findings of this research can be summed up in the succinct phrase: 'work matters.'"[40] That's because people need dignity, and suitable work helps supply that. Another way must be found.

For Kuttner, that other way comes from the revelation that the core of this issue is self-evidently not about education, technology or economic policy—it's about the politics. In fact, he says, "for reasons unrelated to education or technology, a great many jobs can be configured either as casual labor or as normal payroll employment." For example, home health aides in many states are individual contractors—1099 workers with low wages and insecure employment to match. But in states with strong unions, such as California, home health aides have won the right to form bargaining units and are compensated as regular W-2 payroll employees, enjoying a steady paycheck. Warehouse workers for Walmart are 1099 workers, hired and employed by logistics contractors, poorly paid and intimidated by threats of arbitrary dismissal. Elsewhere, many warehouse workers are salaried employees, with permanent jobs and decent compensation.

In cities with strong hotel unions, such as New York and Las Vegas, hotel employees are salaried and receive decent wages and benefits (though an increasing number of those hotel jobs are being threatened by the rise of Airbnb, VRBO and other homesharing websites). The hotel unions in those places have been able to resist management efforts to turn employees into on-call casual labor. In other cities, hotel workers performing the same jobs—even for the same hotel chains—are *bracero* workers, making barely more than minimum wage and often for subcontractors who threaten retaliation if there's a hint of workers organizing.

While I think Kuttner underestimates the good that education can do, his point is well taken. A lot of what we are experiencing as "the economy" is a factor of particular laws and regulations. Change the laws and regulations, and the economy will work differently. Those who overemphasize education, while paying little attention to the politics that have resulted in a "drastically altered social contract," says Kuttner, "are missing much of the story."[41] I couldn't agree more.

Kuttner's perspective is particularly refreshing in light of the alarming political retreat coming from various U.S. leaders and organizations, as well as the public. Far too many Americans seemingly have given up on politics as a way to orchestrate a pivot in the right direction. Even many people that lean progressive, and who traditionally have been more supportive of government's role, seem to have run out of patience with it, especially after the disillusionment with Barack Obama as president. As we will see in the next chapter, certain parts of the "small-is-beautiful" left have always been attracted to an antigovernment, antistatist worldview, and that perspective is powerfully present among certain leaders and groups of the sharing economy.

Instead of any updating or renewal of a New Deal–type world, they propose what they regard as a more modern vision: a world composed of individual gig-preneurs who "monetize" their personal assets, freelancers clustered with their Facebook and social network friends and associates, collaboratively consuming and "sharing" via the Internet of Things, renting out their property, their labor, their "arms" in order to survive. They have seemingly given up on struggle or challenging the extraction economy that is overtaking American workers. Instead, these "sharing economy progressives" have decided that the best strategy is to make lemonade from the lemons by carving out a new private sphere that they will manage.

But this vision is shortsighted, tragically flawed, as well as ahistorical. Not only will it fail to prevent the wholesale flushing of the middle-class society that made America a world leader, but it robs people of any hope that mass resistance or collective power can make a difference. Yet historically speaking, that has been the only strategy that has *ever* been successful for average people trying to turn an extractive economy into an inclusive one.

Americans are standing at a major crossroad about the type of society we want to live in. Responding to the impact that the new economy is having on people's jobs will be one of the defining challenges of the next two generations. Long-existing efforts by pro-business groups like the Chamber of Commerce, the Koch brothers' Americans for Prosperity, the American Legislative Exchange Council (ALEC), the Cato Institute and others to vanquish labor unions and corral the workforce ultimately will backfire—because they lead toward the Singularity onset, when the economy implodes from too little demand and too much elite capture, leaving the rest of us to scramble for the crumbs.

It is crucial that we figure out how to set the economy on a different course, or the great American nation will pay a bitter price.

EIGHT

THE NEW ECONOMY VISIONARIES

LEADERS LEADING US . . . WHERE?

DESPITE THE MANY ALARMING TRENDS AND DOWNSIDES DOCUMENTED IN THE previous chapters, the new economy has been hyped and celebrated as something that gives more freedom and opportunity to U.S. workers. It has been treated as if it is a genuine herald of the future. The popular media, which ought to be asking hard questions and exposing the many contradictions and inconsistencies, instead has fallen victim to a gold-rush mentality. Americans are usually infatuated with winners, and nothing seems to inoculate a company against investigative diligence more than a multi-billion-dollar valuation.

Silicon Valley is especially treated with extreme deference. Ironically, just as the media missed other major stories in recent years because of its failure to probe and investigate, such as the absence of weapons of mass destruction in Iraq, and an enormous $8 trillion housing bubble that eventually burst and collapsed the economy, and until recently the overheating of the planet (coverage of global climate change seems to have improved some), so too the media mostly has been lackadaisical when it comes to scrutinizing the techno-visionaries.

If the media were to scratch a bit deeper beneath the golden surface and probe more resolutely into the dealings and practices of the companies and leaders of this venture-capital-stoked movement, it would discover that beneath the shiny luster it's not all that alluring. Mostly it's "business as usual" along the Silicon Valley–Wall Street axis, which hates regulations, taxes, government oversight and democracy, and instead worships authoritarian management, extractive monopolies, a cult of "disruption" and high-flying IPOs.[1]

One of the curious aspects of the sharing economy, for instance, that has not really been explored, is that wide-eyed visionaries and evangelists on both the left *and* the right champion it, and its conjoined twin the freelance society. Historically, usually the left and the right come together only in the middle of a "populist moment." Populism usually is an upwelling phenomenon that taps into people's hopes and fears, oftentimes beyond rationality. Initially populism is directed against what is viewed as elite interest, but lacking rationality, eventually the elites (or some faction of elites) are able to get out in front of the wave and use the various means at their disposal to divert it in a direction that reestablishes elite control. The dialectical clash of thesis/antithesis results in a "new normal," but history is filled with examples of such "change" that turned out to be false positives. This is what has been happening with the sharing economy.

The sharing economy philosophy is comprised of an oddball brew of progressive utopianism, free-market libertarianism, environmental aspiration and antigovernment mistrust that has appeal for both conservatives and many liberals/progressives. Particularly for those from the left side of the political aisle, antigovernment passions strain aggressively against a deeply valued progressive pillar favoring government intervention, which has had a significant impact in a whole range of vital areas including civil rights, the environment, labor rights, reducing inequality, indeed the whole range of New Deal programs that have fostered a more broadly shared prosperity. That contradiction has created splits within the left, even as it has fostered strange bedfellows with conservatives within the sharing economy camp.

In assessing the sharing economy, economist Doug Henwood notes that "the sales pitch that accompanies this revolution is an update of what Richard Barbrook and Andy Cameron, writing almost twenty years ago, called the 'Californian Ideology.'"[2] What Barbrook and Cameron saw as an "amalgamation of opposites" was rooted in a "new faith [that] emerged from a bizarre fusion of the cultural bohemianism of San Francisco with the hi-tech industries of Silicon Valley." Wrote the two authors, "The Californian Ideology promiscuously combines the free-wheeling spirit of the hippies and the entrepreneurial zeal of the yuppies"—a marriage sealed by a common antigovernment mistrust.[3]

The New Left of Abbie Hoffman, Tom Hayden and Students for a Democratic Society (SDS), which included the yippie and student protest movements of the 1960s, battled the government over the Vietnam War, while the right wing in the 1960s led by Barry Goldwater was rabidly suspicious of "big government."[4] So by stitching together the New Left and New Right's "antistatism," the Californian Ideology provided "the means to reconcile radical and reactionary ideas about technological progress," wrote Barbrook and Cameron. "While the New Left dislikes the government for funding the military-industrial complex"—an aversion now exacerbated mightily by the Edward Snowden revelations about the monstrous intrusions of the national surveillance state—"the New Right attacks the state for interfering with the spontaneous dissemination of new technologies by market competition."[5] Writes Henwood, "For Barbrook and Cameron, individualism and techno-utopianism were merged into a single, seductive package."[6]

So there are some long-standing roots that enable the left and the right to find common cause in today's sharing economy. Pro-business *Forbes* cheers the sharing economy as "an economic revolution that is quietly turning millions of people into part-time entrepreneurs." The far right sees it as a way to roll back government even further, spur more privatization and kill entitlements and the safety net, such as Social Security and Medicare. The Ayn Rand, libertarian right of computer geeks and *techno sapiens* hope to make gobs of money from their disruption and unleash themselves upon the world as the next corps of Masters of the Universe. And the centrist to center-right, like *New York Times* columnist Thomas Friedman, has signed aboard for the sharing economy ship, Friedman writing a column headlined "How to Monetize Your Closet" that celebrates this "budding new economic activity" that "offers a new avenue for the middle class to create wealth and savings." A lot of people, he continued in another column, "can still earn a good living by building their own branded reputations, whether it is to rent their kids' rooms, their cars or their power tools."[7]

On the left, the sharing economy invokes many traditionally progressive values: decentralization, sustainability, grassroots empowerment and opposition to hierarchy. Among many liberals and progressives today, there is a palpable sense that government—and most recently President Barack Obama—has failed them, and a new ethos of self-reliance has taken root that eschews big government. This self-reliance especially runs rampant through the philosophy of many social entrepreneurs and sharing economy visionaries. Its intellectual precursors on the left include political theorists like anarchist intellectual Murray Bookchin and his concept of "radical municipalization," and E. F. Schumacher's deep green philosophy based on "small is beautiful."

The liberal-progressive's sharing economy bible, *What's Mine Is Yours: The Rise of Collaborative Consumption* by Rachel Botsman and Roo Rogers, is a polite manifesto written for a hip, networked demographic, a tract of revolutionary fervor that stretches toward utopianism. The authors make breathless claims about the power of what they call "a quiet yet powerful revolution of collaboration," and lasso into their new sharing taxonomy everything from Airbnb to Zipcar to swap meets to Netflix—and then pronounce it HUGE.[8] While overly broad, the book performed a valuable service by connecting the dots of various nascent phenomena to show the shape of their "sharing economy" constellation, set like the Big Dipper against the sky. The book has been a major success and made Botsman an international movement leader because it tapped the rich vein of its readers' ecological urgency and anticonsumerism, mixed with a techno gadget optimism that promised a near-effortless fix, requiring virtually no personal sacrifice, to some seemingly intractable crises. "We believe we are in an optimistic and momentous time of change . . . the transition away from consumption for consumption's sake," wrote the authors.[9] The fact that these crises have only gotten worse since the book's publication in 2010 has not diminished its appeal or its authors' enthusiasm.

Yet I find something terribly sad about Botsman's vision for a new economy. Even at its best, if this is how we "share"—via faceless and impersonal interactions over the Web and apps—it's just more evidence that we've lost something basic and essential. If there's any quality that has always been synonymous with "sharing," it's human contact—face-to-face, hand-to-hand, person-to-person. But not anymore—apparently even our language deceives us now. We no longer know our neighbors, and now we share with strangers who have been rated by other strangers over the Internet. Also in its boosterish zeal, Botsman's book only superficially grapples with the plight of workers and labor. Yet as *Buzzfeed*'s Charlie Warzel insightfully observed, the sharing economy is now essentially a labor platform. It has real-world impacts on people trying to make a living, that most basic of human endeavors.[10]

To the extent that Botsman and other "sharing economy progressives" entertain anything having to do with labor and work, it is in the context of their vision of a decentralized economy in which everyone is liberated to be her or his own entrepreneur. This is a vision they very much share with conservatives. On the right, Jeremiah Owyang, founder of Silicon Valley–based Crowd Companies, writes in the *Wall Street Journal* that "conservatives love the entrepreneurial spirit and innovation surrounding the sharing economy." He says that "the sharing economy is actually a form of tech-based capitalism, not the app-powered, hippie communes some perceived it would be."[11] He suggests that it delivers a platform for individuals to build their own businesses. And of course President George W. Bush promoted the "ownership society," which had overlapping planks with the sharing economy in his move toward decentralization of the safety net and federal devolution of certain powers to the states. His also was a philosophy of more self-reliance and less "big" (though W's "small government" had a gargantuan military and an over-expanding surveillance state, a drastic difference from the small government of sharing economy progressives).

Meanwhile, on the left, various proponents have said that the sharing economy offers a viable alternative to slaving away for corporate America. Instead of just being pawns on the ladder, with set hours and wages working to make the Man rich, the little guys or gals are empowered to work for themselves as their own microentrepreneurs. Despite so much evidence to the contrary, supposedly you can now work at what you want, when you want, and besides that you can "monetize"—rent out—not only your labor but also (for those of modest means) the little bit of property that you call your own. You can downsize, consume less stuff, avoid the rat race. Yes indeed, "small is beautiful," for both the left and the right—yet each embraces its own priorities of what should be "small."

But how can the left and the right really share this same ground if their basic principles are so divergent? That's what has been rather remarkable about the sharing economy—its ability to promise a lot of things to many different audiences, and speak several languages at once to different ears. Its multilingualism has crossover appeal, reflected in the upbeat titles of the many "booster books" that effuse about the wonders of the sharing and peer-to-peer economies and collaborative consumption:

> *How to Get Rich Using Airbnb;*
> *Getting Paid for Everything You Do: Work as Much as You Want Whenever You Want;*
> *How to Make Money without Having a Job;*
> *Sharing Is Good: How to Save Money, Time and Resources through Collaborative Consumption;*
> *The Lateral Freelancer: How to Make a Living in the Share Economy;*
> *Airbnb: Make Money While You Sleep;*
> *What's Mine Is Yours: The Rise of Collaborative Consumption;*
> *Network Society and Future Scenarios for a Collaborative Economy;*
> *The Mesh: Why the Future of Business Is Sharing;*
> *Big Bang Disruption: Strategy in the Age of Devastating Innovation;*
> and *Peers Inc: How People and Platforms Are Inventing the Collaborative Economy and Reinventing Capitalism.*

Many of these books read like how-to, self-help, get-rich-quick guides, with a smarmy tone extolling the reader that "you too can have it all." But can we? Technology expert Sascha Meinrath, founder of X-Lab and the Open Technology Institute, is blunt in his rebuttal of the portrayal of the sharing economy as either "small," "beautiful" or helping the little guy and gal.

"Now that we have a few years of watching how the sharing economy operates, as well as its impacts, there are great causes for concern," he says. In my interview with him, he said that the upsides of the on-demand technologies are obvious, but the "devil part of the Faustian bargain is being ignored." In particular, he worries about the inequality gap increasing as a result of the on-demand technologies being applied to a vast and growing army of 1099 workers.

"While everyone is enamored by the shiny potential of these systems—and, to be clear, their liberatory potential is substantial—their current operationalization, as well as future trajectory, are bleak," says Meinrath. "I would go so far as to say that they may be driving an extreme wealth divide" that allows for little mobility. Like so many other people I interviewed for this book, Meinrath says there is a dire need for "updated social norms, consumer and worker protections—a new social contract for a 21st-century economy. Otherwise, we'll be looking at an ever-increasingly bimodal distribution of wealth by 2050."

The sharing economy "promise" recalls a different era, one that is not so encouraging. As mentioned in the introduction, economist Juliet Schor calls the combination of the sharing economy with the freelance society the "post-industrial peasant model." Schor elaborates: "This is very much the way peasant households operated: labor demands were variable across the year. They had a varied set of activities and streams of income, and different forms of access to goods and services, such as bartering. That's where we're headed."[12]

A return to the peasantry sounds delightful if you are going to the Renaissance Faire for the weekend, but sounds bleak if that encapsulates your future economic prospects. For many of the most exuberant proponents of the sharing economy, as well as the CEOs and leaders of the various companies, those kinds of words from Meinrath and Schor are viewed as raining on their parade. Sharing economy leaders on both the left and the right have resisted regulation, saying "let's not rush, let's see how it plays out, let's wait and see," even as a few companies, especially Uber and Airbnb, have become the 800-pound gorillas dominating the landscape. The evangelists and the faithful have exhibited a tendency to circle the wagons and become defensive rather than directly address such critiques, even when the criticisms are coming from fellow technologists like Meinrath and thought leaders like Schor who recognize the potential of the sharing economy and share many of its goals and ambitions.

The fact that the sharing economy has become a Rorschach test in which many viewers see what she or he wishes to is no doubt fueled by the difficult economic times that so many Americans have been experiencing. People are desperate for answers to the riddles of their increasingly insecure lives and grasping at populist straws. Airbnb CEO Brian Chesky and Rachel Botsman both wax effusively like silver-tongued crusaders about the primary currency of the sharing economy being "trust" and "belonging"[13]—but in reality *New*

York's Kevin Roose is closer to the bull's-eye when he writes that the sharing economy "isn't about trust, it's about desperation." He chides proponents for leaving out an important part of the story, "namely, the sharing economy has succeeded in large part because the real economy has been struggling." What compels people "to open up their homes and cars to complete strangers is money, not trust," he says.[14]

You know, the green stuff, and the constant daily scramble to earn enough of it. It's a fairly obvious point, yet that realization seems to escape so many of the sharing economy proponents, as well as so many in the media that report on this sharing phenomenon. Everyday people and their strive-to-survive activities are mostly invisible, and I can't help but wonder why. What is it about the sharing economy worldview that is so invested in ignoring the earthquake crack that is opening beneath everyone's feet? Americans have always liked to see themselves as a classless society, but reality has a way of engulfing you if you ignore it.

Unfortunately, too many of the sharing economy visionaries seem to be in denial about the seismic wave that is overtaking the nation. Regardless of which side of the political aisle it's coming from, the vision of a sharing economy acting as an economic engine for a freelance society is tragically flawed. When you add in the oncoming wave of robots, automation and AI, the combination may prove to be deadly.

IS THE SHARING ECONOMY GREEN?

The left's conception of the sharing economy also is deeply infused with the "green" values of environmentalism and sustainability. Some of the proponents from the right also value this angle, or at least are not too annoyed by it. But here again, hype is racing ahead of reality.

The green advocates say that the sharing economy is a smart way of using fewer resources by sharing what we have and producing and consuming less new stuff, so the cumulative impact will be good for the planet. Van Jones, former Obama administration official and author of *The Green Collar Economy* (which praises the sharing economy, particularly what is called collaborative consumption), says, "If you supplement a formal economy with an economy based on sharing and bartering you will have a lighter footprint."[15] Jones talks passionately about a future economy where more people are sharing their cars, homes and personal property. He told the Shareable conference in San Francisco that we can "do it in a way that doesn't require all this consumerism and destruction" because "all these technologies and new companies exist that can help people earn and save money and have an economy that works and doesn't undermine the planet."[16]

Annie Leonard of the "Story of Stuff" project, in a short video on how to turn society toward a more environmentally sustainable direction, also considers the sharing economy/collaborative consumption a key "game changer" that has the potential to redirect the basic trajectory of the economy.[17] In this endeavor, Leonard and Jones have an odd enviro soulmate—none other than Travis Kalanick, who has sung the praises of the environmental benefits of Uber. Kalanick claims that Uber is "reducing congestion in the city," and boasts about "how many cars are off the road because of this, how good this is for the environment."[18] His claim that Uber drivers will be so ubiquitous that car-loving Americans will give up their own automobiles seems like more brash marketing hype, yet it's finding traction among many sharing economy progressives.

But the *Washington Post*'s Catherine Rampell dismisses Kalanick and his green ridesharing claims. "Thus far there is no evidence that ridesharing passengers are getting rid of their own cars," she says, citing a recent University of California Transportation Center study based on ridesharing customers in the San Francisco area.[19] Even more troubling, that same study also found that ridesharing companies in fact are taking away business, not just from traditional taxis but also from more environmentally friendly transit modes. Nearly half of respondents said that if they had not had the option of using a ridesharing service, they would have instead used a bus, bike, train or simply walked. Rampell observes that what keeps cars off the road are regulations (like the often-derided medallion system) capping the number of livery cars available. If ridesharing is not implemented correctly, it could well lead to *more* cars on the road as drivers troll for passengers, congesting traffic and fouling the air (which, as we saw in chapter 3, is Kalanick's strategy—to flood the streets with Uber cars).

Indeed, journalist Bob Sullivan says that ridesharing could very well lead to the "end of mass transit as we know it." The economics of public transit systems are built around the busiest bus lines which are profitable, and subsidize the other routes which are often nearly empty. That equation is crucial in allowing a public transit system to be citywide and extended to less-populated parts of the city, for late-night service, and more. If a ridesharing company like Uber begins offering vans that sprint up and down the busiest and most profitable routes, such cherry picking would destroy revenue for public transit.[20] In San Francisco that threat already has left the station: a startup called Leap has been launched (without required approval from regulators), offering a private, plush, $6-a-ride shuttle service with Wi-Fi, USB ports and snacks along preferred routes.[21] In Spain, the National Federation of Bus Transportation (Fenebús) has called for the closure of a ridesharing company because its operations were impacting the ridership of the mass transit companies.[22]

So the environmental benefits of ridesharing are mixed at best, and with automobiles playing such a huge role in carbon emissions and environmental degradation, that alone is a significant blow to the much-hyped claim that this type of sharing industry will have salutary impacts.

Beyond ridesharing, it's not clear at all that homesharing, property sharing or many types of goods and services sharing are going to dramatically benefit the environment. Juliet Schor, who has been supportive of the sharing economy and has been researching its impacts, calls into question this environmental benefit claim. "It is a truism among 'sharers' that sharing is less resource intensive than the dominant ways of accessing goods and services," she says. "The actual environmental impacts of the [sharing] sites are far more complicated, however."[23]

The sharing companies, for example, are trying to open new markets that swell the volume of commerce and boost consumption. "To assess overall ecological impacts," says Schor, "we have to consider ripple effects. My students and I have found that Airbnb users are taking more trips now and that the availability of cheap ride services is diverting some people from public transportation. That means the platforms result in higher carbon emissions."

The idea that the sharing economy will automatically allow society to use less "stuff" also shows little understanding of what I call the "economics of depreciation." If more people are sharing the same device, it just means that device will wear out more quickly and you will have to replace it sooner. For example, let's look again at ridesharing. A typical person drives approximately 12,500 miles per year, going back and forth to work, the grocery store, the movies and other trips. So that means their car will last them approximately 12 years (assuming around 150,000 miles for the life of the auto). But if a driver starts using their car for Uber's ridesharing, to transport other people around the city, she or he will use their car a lot more. They could very well drive 45,000 miles per year or more, driving around and around, looking for passengers (just as taxis have always done). So that means the same car, instead of lasting 12 years, will now last fewer than four years. And so the owner will have to buy a new car a lot sooner.

The "economics of depreciation" would also apply when "sharing" your bicycle, your electric drill, your washing machine or just about any other type of personal property (though not so much one's home, which is built to last for many years, regardless of the number of occupants). Instead of your power drill or bicycle lasting 20 years, with more people sharing that device it will wear out faster and need to be replaced sooner. Crucially, it's not only the number of devices produced that is important, but the number of "usage hours" put on each device. If you put on more "usage hours" for your shared items, it just means those items will wear out more quickly and have to be replaced sooner.

Certainly if you never use your television set and barter or sell it to someone who doesn't own one, then one less new television will be produced. It seems reasonable that with more people bartering and sharing devices, a bit less stuff might be consumed. But when multiple people are sharing the same devices, the impact probably will be less dramatic than is assumed by sharing economy proponents. In fact, says Schor, "despite the widespread belief that the sector helps to reduce carbon emissions, there are almost no comprehensive studies of its impact." Right now the claims of environmental sustainability for the sharing economy are more theoretical than actual, as far as anyone can tell.

Beyond the uncertainty over the environmental sustainability claims, there is another factor to consider. As we have seen in previous chapters, declines in consumer spending have a depressive impact on the overall economy, including on job creation. No greater proof of this is needed than what happened during the Great Recession, when consumer spending plummeted and the unemployment rate zoomed to over 10 percent—even as carbon emissions in the developed world saw a sizable decline. From an economic standpoint, any amount of consumption, whether personal or business or government related, is good—it creates jobs. During the Great Depression, the unofficial slogan of FDR's Works Progress Administration was "You dig a ditch, you fill it in"—because that aimless action still provided a job, which put money in some person's pocket that allowed her or him to buy goods and services from American businesses who had employees to pay. As Paul Krugman has been fond of saying, "My spending is your income," yet another virtuous circle that has real-world implications.

That's not to say that the United States as a society should not look for ways to reduce consumption and make our modern lifestyle environmentally sustainable. But we have to realize that, particularly with the pressures that are being exerted on jobs and the workforce by the new economy, we have to work harder to find the "sweet spot" between consumption and job creation on the one hand and environmental sustainability on the other.

Bottom line, so far there is little in the way of solid evidence or data that shows that the sharing economy results in a more green economy. The "green promise" has turned out to be more faith-based than actual.

SHARING, RATHER THAN OWNING, THE SHARING ECONOMY

Certainly there are some "truly sharing" companies out there trying to balance the conflicting demands of growing their business or organization while at the same time maintaining their core beliefs and values. Finding the sweet spot is never easy. Juliet Schor, one of the few researchers to develop a systematic methodology for assessing the sharing economy, says "there's a class of platforms, typically non-profits"—that is, *not* Uber, Lyft, Airbnb, TaskRabbit, Elance-Upwork—that qualify as comprising a truly sharing economy. "Couchsurfers stay at each others' homes without payment. Gifting sites such as Freecycle and Yerdle enable people to offer free stuff to each other."[24] Online consignment and thrift stores like thredUP (which has attracted $50 million in venture capital) and Threadflip ($21 million) facilitate the swapping of clothes and apparel, while Swapstyle.com is good for bartering fashionable clothes and other items. Time banks (through which members trade services like babysitting, carpentry or tutoring), landsharing (people with land allow its use by gardeners), seed and tool libraries, as well as "shop local" forms of consumption and production (such as food swaps and pop-up repair collectives) have emerged, also adding to the richness and diversity of a truly sharing economy.

What most of these companies and organizations have in common, besides their Web- and app-based user interfaces, is that the vast majority of the items being exchanged are fairly inexpensive, so not a lot of money trades hands. Besides these commercial companies, on the civil society side there are organizations like GrowNYC, an innovative, grassroots organization that has organized free community events called Stop 'N' Swap. The public is invited to bring in clean, reusable, portable items they no longer want (such as clothing, housewares, games, books and toys), and to take what they want in exchange. The events are open to anyone, and any items left over at the end of the day are recycled or donated—truly a sharing-based community. Collectives like Growing Power in the Midwest and Co-op Power in the Northeast operate similarly, providing participants with income, food and energy.

Yerdle was created by Adam Werbach, former national president of the Sierra Club, and Andy Ruben. They were tired of seeing landfills getting choked up with usable items and wanted a way to help reduce waste. When I interviewed Werbach at his San Francisco office, he spoke about his company trying to be a force to rally people's "better angels"—not only consumers, but also other sharing economy executives. With a motto of "we all have things we barely use" and a mission to "reduce the number of new items purchased by 25%," Yerdle has created a massive online flea market that lets shoppers post, search and bid on items that people are willing to swap. Bids are done via an app and website with credits instead of dollars. If you offer something for swapping, you receive a certain number of credits, which you can then spend on another item. In effect, Yerdle has created its own currency that can only be spent on the website. It has grown from its initial launch to a reported 325,000 members and has raised some $10 million in venture capital.

Other companies/websites are working hard to maintain a truly sharing ethos, such as Neal Gorenflo's Shareable, which maintains a valuable clearinghouse of news, information and networking; Peers, originally co-founded by an Airbnb executive, often has been little more than a PR flak for Airbnb, but has also acted as a catalyst to build the sharing economy movement;[25] Lisa Gansky's Mesh, which is another website acting as a hub of sharing economy information and resources; Etsy, which provides an online sales platform connecting craftspeople to customers looking to buy "unique goods" (with Etsy taking 3.5 percent of each transaction); and Loconomics, a San Francisco–based freelancer-owned co-op for tasks and short-term jobs, but unlike TaskRabbit its freelancers are members with voting rights equal to the administrators who run it.

Internationally, a truly sharing economy is small but growing. Peerby, which is based in the Netherlands but has a global reach, is a website and mobile app with the nifty idea of enabling consumers to borrow products from other people located in their neighborhood; it took me a minute to sign up, and immediately I saw a map showing dozens of users in my San Francisco neighborhood with whom I could swap and borrow. The People Who Share website, headquartered in London, tries to spread awareness about the sharing/collaborative economy, including mounting large campaigns such as Global Sharing Day, which reaches 70 million people. Enspiral, based in New Zealand, fosters collaborative networks of social entrepreneurs, trying to act as a beehive of innovation for business, technology and social change.

The *Guardian* newspaper reports on a "borrowing shop" in Berlin, Germany, in which participants share and swap various items of personal property. Very little money changes hands. Borrowing shops and other collaborative projects that focus on sharing resources are popping up all over the German capital, with similar projects in other cities like Kiel, Würzburg and Vienna.[26] In addition, a true form of car-sharing is flourishing in Germany—the *Guardian* reports 760,000 Germans are registered with companies like Tamyca, DriveNow and Car2Go, enterprises in which little money actually changes hands.

Says Schor, "Innovative practices of this type, based on social solidarity, ecological consciousness and open access, are proliferating."[27] They are pioneering a path for how these new Web-based technologies can be used to create a true sharing economy. These and other examples show that you can "share" and do something useful when no one has a primary motivation of making gobs of profit.

But since the term "sharing economy" has been so tainted by its association with the likes of Airbnb, Uber, TaskRabbit and Lyft, perhaps a better name would be the "solidarity economy." Already there is an organization in New York City using that name (Solidarity NYC) and term, saying that the solidarity economy "meets human needs through economic activities—like the production and exchange of goods and services—that reinforce values of justice, ecological sustainability, cooperation, and democracy."[28] That strikes the right tone and posture, it seems to me, and clearly states what this movement ought to be about. Such a movement would not include Uber, Airbnb or TaskRabbit.

While all of that is well and good, the main drawback that prevents these "truly sharing" or "solidarity-economy" companies, organizations and websites from having a significant impact is that all of them are quite small and undercapitalized. Few of them are making enough money to expand in any dramatic way, and none of them are producing the bang of the billion-dollar babies, Airbnb, Uber and Lyft. Juliet Schor says, "Their Achilles Heel is that most haven't figured out the economic models that will yield robust and growing volumes of trades and reciprocal relations."[29] Which is a nice way of saying that, in truth, the "truly sharing" solidarity companies are still only boutique operations that cater to a relatively small number of customers. It's rather like the co-op movement in the U.S. in that way—the companies are to be admired for their values and their vision, but an honest assessment can't help but recognize the obvious limits of their reach and influence.

The solidarity/truly sharing proponents have a significant challenge, because in truth most people like owning their own stuff. It goes way beyond convenience—it has to do with an innate human drive to secure one's own place in the world, and nothing represents that more than ownership over certain material possessions. This typical human response is in some ways fear based, and very powerfully ingrained. The leaders of this movement have taken on the task of rewiring a very basic human drive. Nevertheless, there are some good economic (and to a lesser extent environmental) arguments to be made in favor of "truly sharing" services, and we humans have demonstrated a capacity to learn and to overcome other fear-based attitudes, such as the tribalism that leads to prejudice and discrimination. So there's hope. These companies and organizations are seeding a new idea of how a Web- and app-based interface can be deployed for truly sharing purposes that, if some of them ever caught on and scaled up, might one day be a game changer.

Schor, who was an early admirer of the sharing economy, has become considerably more cautious in her assessment. "The meteoric rise of the sharing economy has raised a compelling set of questions," she says. "Is it really about sharing? Is there anything new here? Does it represent a better model for organizing work and consumption? After three plus years of studying these initiatives, I can definitively say that the answers to these questions are maybe, maybe and maybe." Somewhat wistfully, she admits that "the platforms that are growing are . . . the large, well-funded for-profits that are getting most of the attention—Uber, Lyft, and Airbnb. But none of them are in the sharing business." Increasingly, she says, they are "more about earning money (for providers) and managing labor and other costs cheaply (for the platforms) than the feel-good values of sociability, carbon footprint reduction, and efficiency that were emphasized when they started." These sites, she says, are mainly "taking advantage of collapsing labor markets rather than creating shared risk and reward."[30] The moment is reminiscent of the early days of the Internet, "when many believed that digital connection would become a force for empowerment. The tendency of platforms to scale and dominate (think Google, Facebook, and Amazon) offers a cautionary tale."[31]

Schor still believes in the potential of the peer-to-peer platforms, calling them "potentially powerful tools for building a social movement centered on genuine practices of sharing and cooperation" in production and consumption. But achieving that potential will require democratizing the ownership and governance of the platforms. Democratic governance, she says, is vitally necessary to "mitigate against race to the bottom dynamics and preserve value for consumers." But, she cautions, "Whether we can get there before Uber, Airbnb and other for-profits have achieved durable domination is now the question. If we do, we'll have a shot at a true sharing economy."[32]

If there is any shot at all, it seems obvious that the truly sharing companies must act to publicly distance themselves from the bad—meaning faux-sharing economy—companies, which are profiting greatly off the sharing brand. Many of these solidarity-economy companies and leaders regularly appear with Uber, Airbnb, Lyft and TaskRabbit representatives at various conferences, as if they are all under one big happy tent. But increasingly the 800-pound gorillas are squashing not only the name "sharing economy" but also the public's perception of what that concept even means. It's hard to see how that can be helpful to the truly sharing/solidarity companies. A very public and quarrelsome divorce is in order. Perhaps the slogan of truly sharing economy advocates should be: "Share. Don't Own. The Sharing Economy."

WHAT A DIFFERENCE FOURTEEN YEARS CAN MAKE

Like Juliet Schor, other early proponents of the new economy have had a change of mind. Daniel Pink, who wrote the seminal book *Free Agent Nation* in 2001 that launched much of the freelancer hoopla, has made a substantial about-face. Pink, a former speechwriter for Al Gore, in his book rapturously described the new economy as one in which freelancers can be "free from the bonds of a large institution, and agents of their own futures. They are the new archetypes of work in America."[33] In Daniel Pink's world of 2001, the typical free agents were latte-sipping, cell-phone chatting, solo-preneurs working out of their homes to create their own microbusinesses. They were networked and tech savvy, using the Internet in clever ways. At the time, freelancing appeared to Pink to be the wave of the future, where the right kind of person could be an independent operator and win most of the time. Pink's portrayal of a freelancer, which he himself embodied as he became a best-selling author, contributed greatly to a stereotype that was endlessly repeated and mythologized in the media.

Pink was writing while the dot-com, new-economy bubble of the late 1990s was still exuberant, but that exuberance turned out to be "irrational." When the bubble burst, a lot of those free agents, gig-preneurs and independent contractors ended up flat on their backs. But that didn't matter, the exuberance about the wonders of the freelancing life had second and third lives, following Pink's book. Indeed, it spawned a flood of imitators. Bookstore shelves and Amazon have been groaning under the weight of bubbly titles like *The Wealthy Freelancer: 12 Secrets to a Great Income and an Enviable Lifestyle; Six-Figure Freelancing: The Writer's Guide to Making More Money; Secrets of a Freelance Writer: How to Make $100,000 a Year or More; Creative, Inc.: The Ultimate Guide to Running a Successful Freelance Business; The Ultimate Freelance Success Guide: How to Start an Online Business Freelancing and Go from $0 to $4200 per Month; The Freelancer's Bible; The Art of Freelance Blogging: How to Earn Thousands of Dollars Every Month as a Professional Blogger; My So-Called Freelance Life: How to Survive and Thrive as a Creative Professional for Hire; Freelance Success: Write Your Way to a Dream Lifestyle;* and many others. More self-help, get-rich-quick guides, encouraging the unsuspecting to take a leap into the abyss. "You have nothing to lose but your chains."

Sara Horowitz, founder of the Freelancers Union, wrote one of these books, called *The Freelancer's Bible,* with a subtitle that claims it will show you "everything you need to know to have the career of your dreams—on your terms." Sara Sutton Fell, CEO of professional job service FlexJobs, has been a bubbly cheerleader of the new economy, saying it is "especially exciting for people who want to have work fit into their lives—instead of trying to find time for life outside of work." Self-starting and the ability to choose projects gives freelancers "more ownership over their careers, rather than working on someone else's terms," she says, sounding like Leah Busque and Travis Kalanick.[34]

Other new-economy evangelists have gushed exuberantly about the wonders and joys of having no steady job, dwindling pay and no workplace that provides a safety net. The New Deal social contract has been pronounced obsolete and so "last century," as the new economy has been credited by *Forbes* with "blowing up the industrial model of companies owning and people consuming" and allowing "everyone to be *both* consumer and producer."[35]

But by 2015, Daniel Pink had taken a sharp U-turn. In an interview I did with him, Pink greatly qualified his previous views.

"Remember, I wrote *Free Agent Nation* in 2001, before smartphones or widespread broadband; it was also before Facebook, Twitter, before the cloud, before fears of robots taking all our jobs, and before Uber, Airbnb, TaskRabbit, etc. etc." In short, he says, he did not take into account the explosiveness of technological change that would occur in the ensuing decade and a half. "In a way, the conditions I described back then now almost seem quaint."

Pink then went on to make some prescient points. He noted that one of the biggest changes in recent years is in Corporate America, and the increasingly blurred boundary between who's a contractor, temp or free agent and who's an employee (the labor force transition I delineated in chapter 1). "More and more risk is shifting to individuals, even for individuals who get W-2s. They've got 401(k)s rather than traditional pensions. They're paying a much larger share of their health insurance and medical costs. They don't expect to be with employers forever. They're in charge of their own professional development."[36] As this risk shift from organizations to individuals deepens, fueled in part by technology, we are seeing a corresponding decline "of companies acting as a *de facto* quasi-welfare state," says Pink, the disappearance of what he calls the "invisible New Deal" in which companies provided health insurance, retirement, and many other safety-net benefits. In addition, he sees more and more people moving back and forth across the thinning borders that separate Free Agent Nation and Corporate America. "It's almost as if people have become dual citizens," he says now.

But even with his updated perspective, Pink fails to grasp the depths of the abyss that so many working Americans are staring into. He went on to say in our interview that the big difference is not over whether or not people are freelancers or independent contractors, but "who has skills that are in demand and who doesn't." He used an example of two hypothetical workers, Maria and Fred, to illustrate his point.

"If Maria has skills that are valuable, she can go out on her own [as a freelancer] if she wants and likely do fine. Or she can take a 'job,' but she'll likely accept a job only at places that treat her with sufficient respect and autonomy. On the other hand, suppose Fred doesn't have skills that are in demand. He's in big trouble. And his actual form of employment isn't the most urgent issue."

It's going to be tough for Fred to sell his services on an open market as a freelancer because "the talent market doesn't value what he's selling very highly—although TaskRabbit and Uber might offer him a chance to make some extra cash." He might have to settle for low wages, limited hours and meager-to-nonexistent benefits, "akin to the life of a struggling, underpaid, beleaguered freelancer." Not a pretty picture, painted by the former champion of freelancers. In sum, says Pink, "Whatever side of the blurred boundary they land on, Maria will probably be OK and Fred probably won't. I'm optimistic about Maria and concerned about Fred—but for reasons that have little to do with free agency and everything to do with skills."

Daniel Pink's distinction between Maria and Fred is helpful to some extent, but the reality is that the new economy that is taking shape will provide a daunting challenge even for many of the skilled Marias. For example, the lack of a safety net that used to come from Maria's employer—the former "*de facto* quasi-welfare state," as Pink called it—is going to be an ongoing challenge. Sure, if she makes enough money, she will be able to purchase some of that safety net on her own—but as an individual, she will pay inflated prices because she will not benefit from any economies of scale that come from being part of a larger pool of insured people (for health care, Obamacare mitigates that somewhat, but mostly for the poorest people who receive a federal subsidy). Also, if Maria makes enough income, she will be able to afford to take some days off when she's injured or sick, or go on a vacation. But Maria will have to be fairly high income indeed to feel secure enough to enjoy the peace of mind that would allow her to do that. Most likely we will see many more skilled Marias working while they are sick and injured, and taking fewer and shorter vacations.

Some have argued that these 1099 workers may not have paid vacations but they will have more flex time in their day-to-day schedule, including while they are looking for their next gig (which is unpaid time). But in reality a flexible schedule is more likely to have stressful downtimes of uncertain length, not calm vacations or any prolonged time spent relaxing. What will happen to our psychologies, as well as to our families, as tens of millions of stressed-out workers suddenly are faced with these sorts of details, having to figure them out on their own?

And let's face it, not all individuals will have it together enough to figure out all of these details. As much as we wish all U.S. workers were deeply networked and tech savvy, and able to use the Internet in all sorts of clever ways, and capable of figuring out how to invest their own money in the stock market or save for their retirement, or savvy enough to compare and contrast health-care plans, or unemployment or injured compensation plans (if such plans ever materialize for individual workers), and more, it's not very realistic to assume they automatically will be, or that they will easily learn how on their own. It is going to be tough for a lot of people to figure out these sorts of details. Heck, that's what companies hire entire human-resources departments for. Now suddenly workers are supposed to be their own HR department, as well as figure out how to make a decent living? Perhaps at some point a new service will spring up in the private sector to help people connect to these missing safety-net components via various insurance products that might be created (see chapter 10 for details on that). But even then, a lot of skilled workers may not be able to afford much of a safety net for themselves and their families, depending on their income level, particularly if they are not part of a larger insurance pool.

In addition, there are many skilled Marias out there—very sharp and competent people—who do not possess the entrepreneurial or hustler mindset. These people will not be very good at juggling multiple gigs, micro-gigs and nano-gigs with a range of employers, billing them all, making sure they all pay (and legally pursuing those employers who drag their feet over paying). I fear that Daniel Pink and others with a similar viewpoint are overestimating the number of people who have the type of personality that is able to undertake that kind of "I don't know where my next job is coming from" existence and make it work. Perhaps if they know they have no choice, some of them can learn these skills. But that learning curve will not come automatically or easily.

So I see problems ahead, and fairly significant ones, even for the skilled Marias.

And for Fred—poor Fred—yes, it's going to be even tougher for the lesser skilled. Perhaps more than most people realize, or want to think about. For Pink and others, the obvious solution for Fred is more education and training (and of course allocating the funds for that). As we saw in chapter 7, President Obama, Google's Eric Schmidt and others have pushed the education theme, particularly in STEM. Certainly, more education and training can't help but be useful.

But the real question is, with automation, smart machines, AI and robotized companies becoming even more dominant, will there even be enough jobs left for humans to do, even many of the skilled ones? Erik Brynjolfsson, Andrew McAfee, Kevin Kelly and other technology optimists say that new jobs will be created just as they always have been. But Martin Ford, Nouriel Roubini, Paul Krugman and others counter that the scale of jobs being replaced by automation and robotization is mind boggling—much greater than in previous eras (remember, the Oxford University study found that 47 percent of existing U.S. jobs are at risk of being eliminated due to computerization over the next 20 years). A heck of a lot is at stake in getting this right.

The signature genius of the New Deal era was the deployment of government's unique ability to pull people and various interests together and create "safety-net" pools of social insurance that helped to insure all of us against the risks that we all face. In many ways it was a very efficient system (though of course it had its bureaucratic problems and inefficiencies, but what large bureaucracy doesn't?). If that's crumbling away, and individuals are more and more on their own, frankly I fear for not only the Freds but also for many of the Marias. A reimagining of the safety net and social contract for the new economy is going to be one of the great challenges of our times.

NINE
LABOR'S DILEMMA

IT WAS VALENTINE'S DAY, 2014, AND THE LABOR MOVEMENT WAS HOPING TO receive a big, wet love kiss of good news. Organized labor had been taking body shots for years, with union membership across the country dropping faster than a pugilist with a glass chin. Now the United Auto Workers was in a battle to organize a union at the Volkswagen assembly plant in Chattanooga, Tennessee, and it seemingly had found the right formula: an employer, the German company Volkswagen, which had been pushed by its own powerful union back in Germany to support the bid of the UAW to represent the Chattanooga workers. Volkswagen, used to coexisting with the German unions in cooperative tension, responded affirmatively and signaled to its workers that affiliation with the UAW would be a good thing.

However, this was red-ribbed conservative country, Tennessee is a "right-to-work" state, and the entire Republican establishment, including the former mayor of Chattanooga, now U.S. senator Bob Corker, pulled out the stops to try and swing the autoworkers against the union.[1] They told Tennesseans that the union wanted to take away their guns, that a win for the union meant their dues would go to support the Democratic Party and abortion baby killers, and many other scare stories. Still, unions had a history of winning 60 percent of votes in which the employer was unopposed. The chances looked good.

When retired Circuit Court judge Samuel Payne, a neutral observer to the counting of the ballots, walked into the Volkswagen training facility to announce the election results that Valentine's night, no one uttered a word. Judge Payne's face looked hard and dark like an obsidian mask. Everyone knew that much more than the unionized fate of the 1,500 or so workers at the Chattanooga plant was riding on this vote. This was about whether the labor movement could plant a small flag in Confederate soil and reverse its decades of decline and woe . . . or whether the antiunion "right-to-work" forces could maintain their fortressed Southern wall. In a brief, terse statement, Judge Payne announced to a roomful of reporters the results: 626 workers voting for the union, 712 voting against. The UAW had lost. It was jaw-dropping news that flashed like lightning across the country. How could a union, especially the once-powerful autoworkers union with 400,000 members, lose an unopposed campaign?[2]

The loss was viewed by the media and labor watchers as yet another step down in the long descent of labor. As sociologist Jake Rosenfeld points out in his book *What Unions No Longer Do,* labor unions once wielded enormous clout in American life, from workers' wages to occupational health and safety to retirement security to presidential elections. At its peak during the mid-1950s, the unionization rate was greater than one in three workers;[3] now it's closer to one in nine (11.3 percent), and just one in 16 (6.7 percent) in the private sector—the lowest levels in a century.[4] During the "golden age" of U.S. capitalism in the middle of the 20th century, the labor movement was the leading institution fighting for economic equality. Unions may have only negotiated legally on behalf of 35 percent of the workforce through collective bargaining, but they were setting standards for the nation. Organized labor was a key reason for the Democratic Party's 40-year lock on the U.S. House of Representatives that lasted until 1994, and because it so clearly represented the working class, it received a degree of bipartisan support.

Not only did Democrat president Franklin Roosevelt famously say that, "If I were a worker in a factory, the first thing I would do is join a union," but Republican president Dwight Eisenhower said, "Only a handful of unreconstructed reactionaries harbor the ugly thought of breaking unions. Only a fool would try to deprive working men and working women of their right to join the union of their choice."[5] Writes Rosenfeld, "Unions leveraged their bargaining power to deliver tangible benefits to workers while shaping cultural understandings of fairness in the workplace. The labor movement also helped sustain an unprecedented period of prosperity" across America.[6]

The current moribund state of the labor movement must be considered carefully in any discussion about the impact of the new/sharing economy on jobs and the workforce. Any historical graphs that chart the stagnation of U.S. workers' wages, the decline of the middle class, the rise of inequality and the extreme tilt in favor of the wealthy, exactly match the decline of labor unions.[7] Nearly half of all states are now "right to work," meaning workers don't have to pay dues to a union that bargains collectively on their behalf, robbing those unions of important revenue. At the same time, organized labor's capacity to deliver the working-class vote to the Democratic Party also has diminished, with the Republican Party increasingly sweeping up that constituency. The consequences of this downfall already have been severe, including curtailed advocacy for better working conditions and reduced pressure on bosses and business owners to negotiate with their workforces. The Great Recession further exacerbated labor's decline, as well as the continued decline in the outlook of American workers and their families. Prospects today are alarming—if U.S. workers lost so much ground over the last few decades while unions still retained some clout, how much more will workers lose now that labor is on the ropes, buckling at the knees.

The situation has reached a critical point, where the loss of good jobs, the increase in bad jobs and the looming threats from automation and robotization are combining into a perfect storm threatening to flood the very foundation of the American dream. Now, at this gravest hour of need, where is labor? Given the heroic role that the labor movement has played in the lives of U.S. workers, it's like looking into the sky and wondering: Is Superman going to come? Or has he been critically harmed by some kind of kryptonite?

LEARNING FROM HISTORY

Many within the labor movement, including at the highest levels of leadership, are trying to figure out what happened to their Superman. For the last 15 years, the uneasy consensus seemed to hold that labor was going through a difficult historical patch, but with renewed focus, determination and organizing, led by unions such as the Services Employees International Union (SEIU), which actually saw some increases in its union membership in occupations like janitors and home-care workers, the decline in union membership would at least stabilize, and possibly, maybe, eventually turn around. But the Chattanooga loss was the equivalent of a St. Valentine's Day Massacre. Superman is on life support. Suddenly some labor leaders are coming to a different, darker, conclusion.

David Rolf, head of Services Employees International Union Local 775 in Seattle and a vice president of SEIU International, is one such union leader. A hugely successful organizer who has led storied unionizing drives in Los Angeles and Seattle, and whose credentials as a labor leader are second to none, Rolf says that the labor movement is in its death throes. In most parts of the country, he says, unions are nearly buried and gone. The biggest remaining local unions are clustered in a handful of urban regions, particularly on the liberal coasts, declining but not yet disappeared. "If you're a union leader in Seattle or New York or L.A., you can think things are OK," Rolf says. "But there goes Wisconsin; there goes Indiana. If right-to-work passing in Michigan"—where the UAW once reigned supreme—"isn't Lenin's statue coming down in Red Square, I don't know what is."[8]

Most labor leaders and activists concur that the union movement is in something close to mortal peril, writes Harold Meyerson in the *American Prospect.* The inadequacies of the 1935 National Labor Relations Act (also known as the Wagner Act), which union-busting employers ignore without suffering any consequences, when combined with the changing conditions of the workforce and technology, have made organizing private-sector workers extremely difficult. Labor has been largely unsuccessful in expanding its ranks into many new industries and occupations. On top of that, the decline in manufacturing and the offshoring of millions of jobs has resulted in further union member reductions. More recently, the rise of independent contractors, freelancers, temps, the self-employed and all the other categories of 1099 workers has further thinned the ranks.

Superman's vital signs are approaching a flat line.

Rolf believes, controversially within the labor movement, that it won't be possible to revive Superman. The industrial trade union model, based for the past 80 years on collective bargaining and union contracts, is not coming back, he says, quite publicly, much to the chagrin of many labor colleagues. In a thoughtful and compelling essay he distributed to his colleagues within the labor movement in 2012, titled "The Death of Trade Unionism, and toward the Birth of a Labor 3.0," Rolf argued that unions should acknowledge their inevitable, and even imminent, demise and focus their energies and resources on bequeathing what little is left to a new form of organizing, which would involve incubating new institutions that can better address workers' concerns. "The once powerful industrial labor unions that built the mid-century American middle class are in a deep crisis and are no longer able to protect the interests of American workers with the scale and power necessary to reverse contemporary economic trends," he wrote in his paper. "The strategy and tactics that we've pursued since the 1947 Taft-Hartley Amendments"—which narrowed the ground rules under which unions may operate—"are out of date and have demonstrably failed to produce lasting economic power for workers."[9]

Beginning in the 1980s, Rolf told me when I interviewed him, strikes and job actions ceased being effective, and middle-class people learned that if they went on strike, not only would they probably not win but they could lose their jobs. "That was the lesson of PATCO," he says, referring to the strike in 1981 of 13,000 air traffic controllers, which led to President Ronald Reagan firing all of those who did not return to work. Joseph McCartin, a history professor who wrote a book about the conflict, says that "more than any other labor dispute of the past three decades, Reagan's confrontation with the Professional Air Traffic Controllers Organization, PATCO, undermined the bargaining power of American workers and their labor unions. It also polarized our politics in ways that prevent us from addressing the root of our economic troubles: the continuing stagnation of incomes despite rising corporate profits and worker productivity."[10]

McCartin's book, published in 2011, captured the very real drama of this seminal labor history moment. "No strike in American history unfolded more visibly before the eyes of the American people," he wrote, "or impressed itself more quickly and more deeply into the public consciousness of its time than the PATCO strike."

Between 1962 and 1981, there had been 39 illegal work stoppages against the federal government. But once Reagan fired the PATCO strikers, no significant federal job actions followed. By 2010, the number of workers involved in walkouts was less than 2 percent of what it was during the days when Reagan himself led an actors' strike in 1952.

Although Reagan was a conservative, McCartin says, he often argued that the right of workers in the private sector to organize was fundamental in a democracy. This was part of the philosophical basis for Reagan's support for Lech Walesa's anti-Communist Solidarity movement in Poland. While he opposed public sector *strikes* like PATCO's, Reagan supported government workers' efforts to *unionize* and bargain collectively. As governor of California, he had extended such rights in the Golden State and was prepared to do the same as president, according to McCartin.

But the PATCO strike left an impression on future Republicans that over time has become divorced from Reagan's own avowed beliefs regarding public-sector unions. As the Republican Party has shifted to the right, conservatives have come to regard the PATCO firings not as a limited blow to prevent one union from breaking the law—which is how Reagan portrayed it—but instead as an important crackdown against unionism itself. In hindsight, writes labor history professor Jefferson Cowie, it's clear that the PATCO strike was "the pivotal event—both symbolically and substantively—in . . . the massive realignment of class power" between U.S. employers and employees.[11] Over three decades later, still suffering from the aftermath of the largest economic collapse since the Great Depression, and with the GOP moving further to the right than where Reagan himself ever stood, the long-term costs of his action are incalculable.

"It is clear now," says McCartin, "that the fallout from the strike has hurt workers and distorted our politics in ways Reagan himself did not advocate. No strike since the advent of the New Deal damaged the U.S. labor movement more."[12]

David Rolf is acutely aware of this history. Without the clout that unions once wielded as a result of their ability to mount strikes (and other types of job actions), organized labor has been unable to muscle employers into increasing wages or preserving jobs and safety-net provisions, even as productivity and corporate profits have risen. Consequently, says McCartin, inequality has surged to heights not seen since, ironically, Reagan was a boy in the 1920s.

So what to do? How can labor reverse these trends? There are seemingly an endless number of forks in the road, and for every one of them the destination is extremely uncertain. But the one destination that's clear, says Rolf, is where the labor movement will end up if it keeps going the same direction that has led to this dire juncture.

What Rolf is proposing, essentially, is that labor go back—back—back to its pre–New Deal roots. He is an avid student of labor history, and its stories and lessons inform his controversial opinions and recommendations. When I interviewed him, he recounted some of that history and its relevance for today.

"In the early 20th century, the American labor movement was more decentralized and had lots of different and competing strategies," he says. "Essentially those were competing experiments, with a range of origins, goals and structures, to see which ones would be most successful." Some of those strategies were less than savory. In Seattle, unions were led by mobs of white workers, some of them thugs who had a tendency to rough up Asians. In Detroit, gangsters got heavily involved. In other places the local labor movements were led by communists, anarchists, immigrants and activists for specific reforms, such as the eight-hour-day. "The sum total of all this wasn't just unions but a range of very different movements. The Yiddish-speaking socialists had very little in common with the iron workers who blew up the *L.A. Times*," says Rolf.[13]

But then, with the passage of the National Labor Relations Act (NLRA) in 1935, all the different labor strategies were consolidated and brought under one big umbrella. President Franklin Roosevelt wanted to give workers greater rights to form trade unions, but he also wanted some regularity and uniformity brought to the labor movement chaos. That had its pluses and its minuses. It created larger unions that could exert more leverage and power on behalf of their members, but it abolished the previous creative craziness. "The NLRA was enacted amidst a national landscape of massive industrial strikes, a great depression, fears of a growing Communist movement abroad (though a comparatively small one here). The government had to figure out a strategy to calm the situation down," Rolf told me. "Big business was willing to come to the table, to compromise and give something away, in order to have a more orderly situation."

The passage of the NLRA gave birth to the labor movement of the 20th century and enshrined collective bargaining as the dominant mode of worker organizing. "But in some ways the imposition of laws such as the National Labor Relations Act, and later the Taft-Hartley amendments, curbed the power of the workers," says Rolf.

The agreements and compromises made seemed like the right thing to do at the time. But flash forward 80 years, and conditions have changed dramatically. Rolf thinks it's time to revive that creative craziness, to break out of the standardized labor organizing mold, and unleash new strategies, led by new organizations, even if they aren't labor unions. It's time for new tactics, says Rolf. "We must look to the future and invest our resources in new organizational models that respond to our contemporary economy and the needs of today's workers"—not those of yesterday, Rolf told journalist Harold Meyerson.

"I don't have a single strategy for reviving labor, or for what will build worker power. I want to see competing models again," he says, including ones where workers are opposed to their employers, those where they sometimes work with them, and those where workers have no single employer (increasingly the situation of more and more workers). He says that labor is only beginning to grapple with the huge increase in the number of 1099 workers, and the sharing economy and such. But he as well as other labor leaders recognize that these new categories of workers, and the new labor platforms like Uber, Task Rabbit, Upwork and others, challenge the very essence of the employer-employee relationship.

In some ways Rolf's vision, what he has called Labor 3.0, already is occurring, but on a small scale. An expanding amount of organizing around labor issues is taking place outside the traditional structures of labor unions. The National Domestic Workers Alliance, led by its founder and director Ai-jen Poo (a recipient of a MacArthur Foundation Genius award in 2014), has organized domestic workers to demonstrate and hold public events that help to educate the public and raise consciousness about their plight. Domestic workers are some of the most exploited workers in the United States. As most of them are contractors, freelancers or temps, they are denied many of the basic rights that most American workers traditionally have benefited from. Poo and the NDWA have shown a level of lobbying sophistication that has been inspiring. In 2010, they and their allies passed a law in New York state for a domestic workers Bill of Rights which is attempting to protect them from discrimination and harassment and grants full-time workers (working for a single employer) the protection of injured workers' compensation and other labor rights (one day of rest per week and three paid sick days per year). Since that passage, California, Massachusetts and Hawaii have passed similar legislation. The NDWA also has acted as a resource for domestic workers, informing them about their rights. The alliance has expanded to chapters in

42 cities and has set its sights on raising domestic workers' minimum wage to $15 per hour.[14]

Other third-wave labor organizations include the New York Taxi Drivers Association and the National Taxi Workers Alliance, whose members also are self-employed, independent contractors with few labor rights. Like the domestic workers alliance, the Taxi Alliance advocates for its labor and largely immigrant constituency, including trying to grapple with the law-breaking and tax-avoiding onslaught of Uber, Lyft and the ridesharing companies. Like many immigrant workers centers, the Taxi Alliance provides a range of services, including English classes, counseling over immigration and legal issues (including assistance in filing for citizenship), and even assistance with their children's schools.

Other examples of Labor 3.0 organizations include the Freelancers Union, National Writers Union, Restaurant Opportunities Center (known as ROC), Asian Immigrant Women's Advocates, Coalition of Immokalee Workers, CoWorker.org, WASHTech and numerous workers centers all across the country. Workers centers fight for worker justice among nonunion workers, often those excluded legally or in practice from formal labor markets and labor laws. While not yet sufficiently powerful, Rolf sees them as a promising hub of activity.[15]

Rolf has taken a bold step toward trying to incubate even more of this kind of groundswell labor activity. In 2014, with funding from his union SEIU and some pro-labor foundations, Rolf launched what he calls the Workers Lab. Drawing from the venture capital and startup model of Silicon Valley, the Workers Lab describes itself as "an accelerator" that invests in "community organizers, economic justice organizations, issue campaigns, and businesses to create scalable and self-sustaining solutions that improve conditions for low-wage workers." The Workers Lab is a research and resource center, but also seeds and invests in organizations that, in Rolf's words, "have the potential to build economic power for workers, at scale, and to sustain themselves financially."[16]

This Johnny Appleseed approach also extends to some of the tactics and campaigns being tried. Rolf and his union led a major campaign in 2013 to pass a voter initiative in SeaTac, located in the suburbs of Seattle where the region's airport resides, to increase the minimum wage to $15 per hour. All the naysaying experts said it would never win, but the campaign won by a 77 vote sliver after multiple recounts and attempts at electoral sabotage by local businesses who opposed the increase. SeaTac's minimum wage became the highest in the country, more than twice the federal minimum wage. A year later, none of the scare stories that opponents predicted would happen to the local economy had come true.[17]

At the same time, Rolf took his campaign for a $15 minimum wage into the heart of the 2013 mayoral race in Seattle, and the eventual winner ended up pledging to increase the local minimum to that level. In the summer of 2014, Seattle enacted the $15 minimum wage, becoming the first major city to do so.

Seattle's example has fed into a domino effect, with New York, Los Angeles, Chicago, San Francisco, Oakland, even conservative San Diego, all significantly increasing their city's minimum wage to anywhere from $12 to $15 per hour. New York state passed a $15 minimum wage that will be phased in by 2021. In all these different cities, union members and oftentimes labor unions have been at the forefront of these campaigns. Nevertheless, critics say that this won't do much to revive the labor movement because the pay increase goes to members of the general public, most of whom are not union members. Most union members make at least two to three times the minimum wage. Even though few actual union members directly benefit from these initiatives, union members' dues are being spent to win these campaigns. Why should unions care about a $15 wage for non-union workers?

In response, Rolf says, "We can't be the movement that's just about us. We have to be the movement that's about justice for all."[18] This kind of "legislating by ballot box" is part of a long-term strategy, not only to protect the interests of union members, but also to raise the public profile of the good that unions do, after years of falling membership. "The labor movement that people flocked to by the tens of millions in the 1930s wasn't known for fighting for 500-page contracts," says Rolf. "They were known for fighting for the eight-hour day, fighting to end child labor."

With labor's resources engaged in the electoral game via ballot initiatives, lots of different pieces of legislation suddenly could be in play that potentially benefit union members as well as workers in general. As someone who has run ballot initiative campaigns myself, I know that there is no better way to build up your membership lists, to mobilize supporters and give them hope and inspiration, as well as to create a flywheel that cranks out new organizers. Also, by mounting initiative campaigns and putting legislation before the voters, you drive the public debate and galvanize the public's attention in a way that negotiating a union contract can never do. So this is a promising vehicle for labor unions that they should have thought of decades ago.

Other new and creative ideas for reorienting labor's direction are coming from other quarters. Chicago labor attorney Thomas Geoghegan wrote a seminal book back in 1991 about the challenges of labor, *Which Side Are You On? Trying to Be for Labor When It's Flat on Its Back*. That book became a classic, inspiring many young labor activists, including a friend of mine who told me "*Which Side Are You On* is why I became a labor lawyer." In 2014, Geoghegan published another book, *Only One Thing Can Save Us: Why America Needs a New Kind of Labor Movement,* which, like his previous book, is chock full of both criticisms and new ideas for the labor movement.

I interviewed Geoghegan about some of those ideas, one of which is that organized labor should make a bargain with the right, accepting the right's demand for a national right-to-work law in exchange for passing a statute that defines the right to organize as a civil right under the 1964 Civil Rights Act. Doing so would amount to tacit acceptance that labor laws under the Taft-Hartley regime now function mainly as tools of corporations to *block* unionization. This idea also was proposed by Richard Kahlenberg and Moshe Marvit in their 2012 book, *Why Labor Organizing Should Be a Civil Right: Rebuilding a Middle-Class Democracy by Enhancing Worker Voice.* Letting this go in some ways would further undermine attempts to get collective-bargaining agreements, but in return it would create civil-rights remedies for violations of federal labor laws. Just like racial minorities can sue employers for discrimination, if a worker was fired or harassed by her or his bosses for trying to organize a union at their workplace—now a commonplace occurrence—that worker could file a lawsuit against the violation of their right to organize.

Labor attorneys I have spoken to say this would be a giant improvement over the legal status quo, providing private causes of action. Currently any labor disputes or grievances are adjudicated, not by the court system, but by the National Labor Relations Board, which is a slow and tedious process due to chronic underfunding and understaffing as a result of frequent partisan interference. But if a complainant could file a civil-rights case, that would empower a worker to rush into federal court, where it is possible to win a restraining order against the employer, use discovery proceedings to plow through embarrassing corporate records and get a jury trial that might force a company to pay compensatory and punitive damages for labor-law violations.[19] The right to discovery would in itself be invaluable, says Geoghegan. "The plaintiff can discover all the relevant company records relating to union-busting, or any corporate matter that might relate to the case, or possibly lead to relevant evidence. Then he or she can put the boss under oath and ask up to seven hours of questions." Nothing like that is available under current labor law, but it is available for those seeking racial or gender discrimination remedies.[20]

A second related idea in Tom Geoghegan's book is for what might be called "proportional unionism." This would mean that unions would not represent an entire workplace, but only represent that percentage of employees in a bargaining unit that indicates they want a union. If this rule had been in place in the Chattanooga fight, the UAW would have ended up representing 47 percent of the workers instead of none of them. Conversely, if they had won a majority of the workers' votes, they would have ended up representing only those workers, instead of all of them. It gets rid of the "all or nothing" nature of union elections and would allow unions to spread into more places, even where they don't command majority support, which would allow labor to gain a foothold in even anti-union regions. It does create the problem of what is known as "free riders"—the members who pay dues are subsidizing all of the coworkers who benefit from the improvements that the union brings. But Geoghegan sees that as an acceptable price to pay. And this rule is something that the Obama appointees on the National Labor Relations Board could impose without the need to pass legislation.

"In European countries, where unions don't even have to pretend to represent the majority, but just a militant minority, there isn't 'agency' shop," says Geoghegan. Agency shop refers to the legal requirement that workers who choose not to join a union that bargains collectively on their behalf nonetheless contribute union dues. "In that sense, Sweden is a right-to-work state. If labor had a broader ability to represent not just 7 percent but have agreements covering 25 percent or more of the U.S. private sector workforce, yes, I suggest we at least should consider such a deal."

Beyond his creative innovations in labor law, Geoghegan also is willing to grapple with what he calls "a growing caste system of temps" more than most mainstream labor leaders. "Yes, we're becoming a nation of temps," he says. "We're back in this situation because labor is now as weak as it was back [in the 1930s]." The solution, he insists, is to bring back a real labor movement. "That's exactly what a labor movement is supposed to challenge. If it's not there to keep us all from becoming a nation of temps and independent contractors, then there is no point to it."[21]

I asked David Rolf about Geoghegan's proposals, and he said they are worth trying. The labor movement is grasping for the way forward. Despite its weaknesses and shortcomings, it still has more clout and resources than nearly every other organization identified with left progressivism. Which is itself a comment on the state of left progressivism. Labor leaders like David Rolf and Tom Geoghegan are controversial, both within the labor movement and outside it, particularly within the Democratic Party, which they also have criticized for its fecklessness and lack of principle in support of working Americans. Rolf has invested a lot of hope in the new type of Labor 3.0 organizations, but others are not so optimistic. "Rolf says we need to become Labor 3.0," moaned one union official.[22] "Christ." Another labor leader told me, "Right . . . Freelancers Union, National Domestic Workers . . . two of about eight examples of alleged Labor 3.0 that we all keep talking about."

But Rolf is not deterred. "What's now required of us in labor is *not* a sentimental longing or attempt to turn back the clock to a different economy in a different era, or a return to the collective bargaining that worked well in an era of mass industrial production. Rather, we need to figure out what's on the *other side* of our Valley of Death. What new activities we should reallocate resources to, and what new organizational model could work. . . . We need to find the right ideas and then fund the right ideas . . . for replacing the legacy union movement with new forms of worker organization, worker power and worker advocacy."[23]

Will any of the new types of third-wave labor organizations that Workers Lab is trying to seed be able to step up and lead U.S. workers into this new and precarious era?

THE CURIOUS CASE OF SARA HOROWITZ AND THE FREELANCERS UNION

One of the more successful of the Labor 3.0 organizations is the Freelancers Union, based in New York City. With so many workers drifting into the 1099 economy, it is the foremost national organization representing freelancers and looking out for their interests.[24] The founder, president and CEO of the Freelancers Union, Sara Horowitz, is an enormously talented and successful social entrepreneur. She is a labor attorney by trade; her father was a union lawyer and her grandfather was a vice president of the International Ladies' Garment Workers' Union. Burned by her own personal experience, in which she was hired as a young attorney by a labor-law firm only to discover that she was not a regular employee but a contractor, with no retirement or health insurance, she channeled her outrage into starting the FU in 1995 to advocate for freelancers and independent workers.[25]

Since its launch, the Freelancers Union has grown and expanded (according to its internal numbers) to nearly 250,000 members (it's free to be a member, with most members in New York). It has achieved some impressive gains on behalf of freelancers, not the least of which is recognition of freelancers as a distinct—and growing—classification of workers. But does it have the right strategy that will allow it to fulfill Rolf's mission of becoming powerful enough to change people's lives? Is it scalable enough to reach millions, and is it financially sustainable?

Horowitz has been at the forefront of the effort to try and enact affordable health insurance for freelancers, audaciously creating her own insurance company (which eventually closed down in 2014, due to complications arising from the launch of the Affordable Care Act). She also inaugurated two health clinics, one in Manhattan and another in Brooklyn, which double as networking locations for freelancers, offering education and professional development classes, free yoga, meditation and other member events (part of her vision of an "integrated health care and wellness model" for FU members). The Freelancers Union has ambitious plans to expand by opening clinics in 15 more facilities in New York, Los Angeles, Philadelphia, Jersey City, Portland, Austin and San Francisco.

In addition to trying to create health care for freelancers, the Freelancers Union has launched a National Benefits Platform, which provides an easy, searchable Web interface that helps freelancers in any ZIP Code find local providers of benefits like health insurance, 401(k) retirement and life, liability, dental, and disability insurance (though the individual freelancer is still on her/his own in signing up for these safety-net features). The FU also played an important role in getting New York City's municipal government to abolish a business tax for independent workers earning less than $100,000 per year, which had resulted in freelancers being doubly taxed. It also developed an online "contract creator" that helps freelancers to draft legal contracts for their clients, and a client scorecard so the freelancers can rate those clients. Horowitz also has plans to develop a plan for unemployment insurance for 1099 workers, since currently they are not eligible for state-run unemployment compensation. The Freelancers Union has been trying as much as anyone to assist freelancers and to legitimize freelancing as a career path.

As the Freelancers Union has increased media and public awareness about the plight of this rapidly growing demographic, Sara Horowitz's national profile has rocketed into the stratosphere. She has been featured on numerous major media outlets and business shows, including the *New York Times,* Wall Street Journal Report, CNN Money, Fox Business News, the *Economist*, NBC, *Wired, Fast Company,* PBS, NPR and others. Like Ai-jen Poo, she also has been awarded a prestigious MacArthur Foundation Genius fellowship. She has been named to the New York Federal Reserve Bank board of directors, a rarely bestowed honor. She also was named one of *Businessweek*'s Top 25 Most Promising Social Entrepreneurs and one of the World Economic Forum's 100 Global Leaders for Tomorrow. Horowitz presents herself as a rare and valued species—a leaning-lefty who sounds like a businesswoman and who smartly uses a market-based venture not only to try and provide affordable health care to freelancers but also to bring in revenue that could fund her organization's other goals.

And yet, despite her many solid accomplishments, there is something about Horowitz's vision for the new economy—and for freelancers—that is troubling. That's because her vision, taken to its logical conclusion, would amount to an even greater undoing of the New Deal structures, and of the historical role of the federal government, than many right-wing ideologues could ever hope to get away with. Sara Horowitz may end up being the lefty that helps make a core part of the far right's agenda palatable to many unsuspecting people.

For starters, like many of the antistatist left, which as we saw in chapter 8 has roots in the anti–Vietnam War protests of the 1960s, often her statements are tinged with antigovernment rhetoric. Like in some of her writings, when I interviewed her she accused both government and the private sector of "stumbling into the 21st century," saying that "neither has proven up to the task" of being "entrusted as guardians of the social good."[26] She says, "We must reinvent the role of government . . . government is increasingly hamstrung by debt and a lack of public confidence . . . we can't rely on them as we traditionally have."[27] Consequently, "we need a complete reorientation of . . . government's relationship to workers." While antigovernment postures are fairly common among social entrepreneurs, even progressive ones, it seems unfortunate—and unnecessary to her mission—that Sara Horowitz has added this theme to her verbal arsenal.

But for Horowitz, it's not just rhetoric. Instead of relying on government for safety-net-type support policies, she has put forward a different notion, rooted in self-reliance and the private sector. She says, "I believe there is another strategy where civil society—such as nonprofits, social-purpose businesses and other institutions—create a new support system to get their basic needs met."[28] For example, she wants individuals to be able to buy health insurance through groups like the Freelancers Union, or labor unions, church groups or other private organizations, for all the usual reasons such as that would allow individuals to be part of a larger pool and realize some bargaining power with the large insurance companies. But she has another goal as well: it also would allow smaller groups like hers to act as an agent for their individual members, binding those members to the organization over something tangible (like health care). That would naturally catalyze a membership base that would make her organization more influential.

Horowitz calls this her "new mutualism," and it is based on a simple premise: that not only freelancers but workers in other occupations and industries should band together to set up their own institutions to serve their mutual needs. In my interview with her, she said, "We have to stop thinking that 'advocacy' means 'government.'" Government would continue to play a role in supporting the development of these institutions—she points to France's health-care system, which allows occupation-based *mutuelles* to contract with the larger Sickness Insurance Funds that are overseen by the national government—but Horowitz is not a proponent of anything like a single-payer health-care system. Instead, she boils it down to the simple maxim of "New mutualism demands a new role for government."[29]

So Horowitz, who comes from a strong labor family background, has turned 180 degrees from her long and deep roots in the New Deal world, and instead has based her organization in the private sector, with a relationship toward government that is ambivalent at best. Interestingly, she has adopted—and appears to think she has co-opted, for her own "better angels" purposes—the language of the U.S. business community, which has dominated American discourse since Ronald Reagan stood at the podium and said, "Government *is* the problem." Horowitz is certainly aware of the important role that government has played in the past in enabling labor unions to advocate on behalf of average American workers, and the subsequent rise of the middle-class society. But more than most other people who are identified as progressive, she is deeply skeptical about government's role in the future, particularly when it comes to guaranteeing the safety net and worker protections. She believes that in the new economy, that role can be better accomplished by private organizations like hers.

Even more interesting, Horowitz roots her antigovernment, pro-private-sector strategy in the work of her hero, labor leader Sidney Hillman and his philosophy of "social unionism." On the wall in front of her desk at the FU office is a decades-old photo of Hillman, who was the head of the Amalgamated Clothing Workers of America (ACWA) from 1914 to 1946.[30] The ACWA's social unionism in the 1920s included not only fighting for workers' rights, higher wages and union contracts, but the union also offered low-cost cooperative housing and unemployment insurance to union members. Hillman also founded an insurance company and a bank that would serve his members' interests, even making loans to garment businesses that employed ACWA members. Hillman had strong alliances with many progressive reformers of the time, including Jane Addams and Clarence Darrow, who assisted the Amalgamated in its early strikes in Chicago in 1910 and New York in 1913. Hillman's ACWA was a full-service union, and this inspires Horowitz.

"The social unionism of the 1920s had it right," she says. "They said: 'We serve workers 360 degrees. It's not just about their work. It's about their whole life.' We view things the same way."[31] With the shifting economy, the crumbling of the employer-based safety net, the decline of organized labor and the diminishing role of government, she believes the conditions are right for a strategy based around private organizations—she calls them "mutual aid societies"—that assume the role of mini New Deal–type agencies for their members. "Whether you like it or don't like it, it's unlikely we're going to see growth in government over the next few years," she told the *New York Times*. "But we're not going to see any reduction in social needs for workers. And we need these social-purpose institutions in place to serve their growing social needs."

There is a sensible logic to her position, and her citation of the work of Hillman as her philosophical basis puts a stamp of labor progressivism on her strategy. In many ways, I admire the work of Horowitz and the Freelancers Union, and the innovative (though very limited) safety-net programs they are trying to set up for 1099 workers. But there is a major blind spot in her rationale. While Hillman and other labor leaders were pioneers in their time with their fashioning of social unionism, they were happy to hand off many of the multifunctions of their union to the government. They recognized that if the federal government was in the hands of the right president and Congress, it would have far more scale, reach and capacity to make a significant difference in the lives of tens of millions of American workers. In fact, Hillman was a key figure in corralling labor's support for Franklin Roosevelt and the Democratic Party. Once FDR was elected, Hillman became an influential advisor to Roosevelt's administration as they crafted the New Deal.

So in a very real sense, Horowitz's strategy is unwinding the work of Hillman and taking it backward. She is attempting to reestablish what Hillman created in the pre–New Deal era, before Hillman happily handed it off to FDR's programs. In Hillman's time, there was little tradition or track record of government playing much of a role in establishing a safety net for workers, or in regulating the relationship between employers and employees. So the work of Hillman and other labor leaders to create a "360-degree" union was farsighted and the right thing to do at that time. But today, we have a long history of government playing this role. It's a hard-fought history, achieved by people like Hillman and all the workers who stood up for themselves, in some cases fighting bloodied battles against business owners and their hired goons. It makes no sense to me to simply give up on this tradition just because the performance of government in recent years has been disappointing, or because Barack Obama failed to live up to expectations. Yet that seems to be exactly what Horowitz—as well as many other progressives and social entrepreneurs, so enamored with the sharing economy—are advocating.

Horowitz seems to actually believe that hundreds or thousands of private organizations can spring up and substantially fill the gap being left by government retrenchment in this extremely conservative era. Yet it is hard to imagine that private organizations could ever be numerous or comprehensive enough to form the backbone of an effective safety net without introducing glaring inefficiencies. To cite just one example, that of health care. Already one of the major problems with the U.S. health-care system is that there are too many different insurance players, each replicating their own layers of administrative bureaucracy. It drives up the complexity as well as the cost of health care unnecessarily, as comparisons to more efficient and lower-priced health-care systems around the world show. Micah Weinberg, a health-care economist and president of the Bay Area Council Economic Institute, says that under plans like Horowitz's, in which private organizations would organize their own insurance systems, it could add an infinitely more complex layer of hundreds of administrative bureaucracies, making the overall system less efficient and cost-effective. The number of health-insurance companies, he says, should "adhere to the Goldilocks rule: not too few but not too many. Enough to create competition, but not so many that the system becomes overly complex." So Horowitz's plan would amount to a step backward.

Of course she has a point when she says that the laws and regulations have not evolved to accommodate the changes in the workforce, specifically the large and growing army of independent workers. If the New Deal had kept pace with the needs of the workforce, then 1099 workers already would have access to an individualized safety net that provides some level of affordable health insurance, retirement, unemployment insurance, injured workers' and disability compensation and paid sick days and vacation that is not tied to an individual's specific workplace. Horowitz says, quite rightly, "the New Deal protections are stuck in the last century . . . the New Deal must be updated to reflect this new reality," and that will require creating a completely new paradigm for worker supports and building completely new systems. "The 'new' New Deal," she says, "must be rooted in portability and mobility. The protections and rights must be centered on the individual, not the job, and must move with the individual from gig to gig."[32]

Horowitz is one of the few national leaders who has gone beyond merely thinking about this problem and is actively trying to do something about it. But there is an outstanding strategic question here: Who should be empowered to be the agent of this change? Should it be primarily private organizations like the Freelancers Union? Or should it be foundationally the government? Why shouldn't activists and organizations pressure government to evolve today's out-of-date laws and social contract, so that existing employers have to contribute to the safety net of any person who works for them, whether that person is a regular employee or a contractor, freelancer or 1099 worker? That's how it works in many countries in Europe—temp workers and contractors for the most part receive the same types of benefits and supports as regular full-time workers. Why not push for an evolution of laws and regulations designed to achieve the same goals in the United States?

I asked Horowitz that question in my interview with her. She deflected the question, simply saying that we have to stop thinking that government is the answer to everything. But isn't that what President George W. Bush said, in pushing for his "ownership society" that ultimately was rejected by most Americans? "I've already identified a thousand leaders across the country" who are going to lead this, she said. All I could think of was President Papa Bush's extolling of a "thousand points of light."

Besides her strategic blueprint that seems to have given up on lobbying or pressuring government, other parts of Sara Horowitz's vision seem too improbable for the task at hand. For example, she fully embraces the notion that the sharing economy, or collaborative consumption as it is sometimes called, can play a viable, catalytic role in freelancers taking back their lives and creating a "new" New Deal. Horowitz has called the sharing economy the new "Industrial Revolution," as large a shift in the workforce as when society evolved from an agricultural to an industrial economy.[33] She has written, "For the workers of the Gig Economy, social media, collaborative consumption, and crowdsourcing are tools of the trade."[34] Employees are "leaving the traditional workplace and opting to piece together a professional life on their own" via the sharing economy. Waxing hyperbolic, she proclaimed in the *Los Angeles Times* in August 2014 that "the Era of Big Work is indeed over, and good riddance." Freelancers, she said, "are thriving in this new marketplace, creating powerful new platforms for working and living—co-ops, credit unions, community health and wellness centers—tailor-made for millennial technology and the 21st-century economy. . . . Millions of freelancers are working when they want and how they want. They're building gratifying careers but also happy lives. And they're helping build a support system so they can live the lives they want . . . welcome to the Era of Meaningful Independence."[35]

But as we have seen in previous chapters, the sharing economy as currently practiced, particularly by its major companies, has little to do with "sharing" and everything to do with "taking," or using Web- and app-based technologies to rake in gobs of profit and steamroll laws, tax obligations and anyone in the path—including their own workers. Consequently, workers in the sharing economy—whether freelancers, contractors, indies, task rabbits, temps, part-timers, self-employed, micro-giggers, solo-preneurs and the like—are hardly thriving. More often than not, they are barely hanging on. They lack job security, decent wages and a sufficient safety net for the individual worker and her or his family.

Indeed, that reality was confirmed by one of the Freelancers Union's own studies, in which it surveyed 3,000 of its members and found that over 80 percent had been jobless or underemployed during the previous year without having access to unemployment insurance. More than 60 percent had resorted to using their credit cards or borrowed money from friends and family to "make ends meet," and 12 percent had to turn to government assistance. The survey also found that 58 percent of the group's members earned less than $50,000 a year from freelancing and that 29 percent earned less than $25,000. Finally, the study found that a whopping 77 percent of FU members had been cheated by a client during their careers, and 40 percent had trouble getting paid during the previous year, with the average wage loss being a sizable $6,000 (and a cumulative total of over $3 million uncollected).[36]

In short, the Freelancers Union's own study found that the life of most freelancers and 1099 workers is a precarious existence, where you are always hustling to find the next paying gig and can't be sure you will have sufficient support if something unlucky happens. The vast majority of these workers are discovering, in quite dramatic ways, that they are merely an input into the company machine, scrambling like modern day *braceros* to eke out whatever they can from what is more accurately a "share-the-crumbs" economy. They are in no way enjoying "Meaningful Independence" or having the "career of their dreams," much less "on their own terms," as the subtitle of Horowitz's book *The Freelancer's Bible* says.

Despite that reality, Horowitz's vision leaps toward being expansive, even utopian. "What I really see developing," she says, "is an entirely new economic model, one that weaves together companies, entrepreneurs, workers, and other organizations favoring long-term sustainability over short-term profit, and shared power over top-down control."[37] Horowitz has caught the Brian Chesky/Rachel Botsman "trust-and-share" bug, writing about the necessity to "rebuild the trust we need for a more mutualist society."[38] Like many of the sharing economy gurus, she lays claim to being a revolutionary leader of a movement that sees itself as transforming our "owning culture" into a "sharing culture" that is more than a mere means for commercial transactions. The sharing economy is not an app, she says, "it's a mindset based on trust and cooperation. And freelancers are leading the way."[39]

It all sounds so egalitarian, even Jeffersonian. Writes Horowitz, "We're no longer simply lawyers, or photographers, or writers. Instead, we're part-time lawyers-cum-amateur photographers who write on the side."[40] Going forward, she says, more and more "careers" will "consist of piecing together various types of work, juggling multiple clients, learning to be marketing and accounting experts, and creating offices in bedrooms/coffee shops/coworking spaces." Not only that, but in between all that juggling of our different income streams, as our wages are being squeezed and the safety net is being shredded, we are to be encouraged by being able to "monetize" the little bit of property that we own.

Incredibly, for someone who has the labor pedigree that she has, Horowitz (as well as other visionaries of the sharing economy) extols the virtues of this broken-up work day. Horowitz writes glowingly that "today a freelancer could have a couple of graphic design clients, but she also could have a portfolio of other jobs, like renting her spare room on Airbnb and driving a car for Lyft and working in her local food co-op and scoring some singing gigs on the weekends."[41] Try juggling all that during a breathless work week—the concept of "downtime" and "time off" from work is being shoveled into the ashcan of history, along with workers' wages and the safety net.

Karl Marx once famously imagined a communist society in which "nobody has one exclusive sphere of activity," making it "possible for me to do one thing today and another tomorrow, to hunt in the morning, fish in the afternoon, rear cattle in the evening, criticize after dinner, just as I have a mind, without ever becoming hunter, fisherman, herdsman or critic."[42] Risibly, the wild-eyed visionaries of the sharing economy have adopted a neo-Marxian credo, but this is Marx turned upside down. Marx envisioned his new society *after* vast inequality and ownership had been tamed. But the freelance visionaries like Sara Horowitz plan for it even as inequality and disparity are rampant and increasing.

Workers of the sharing economy, unite! We have nothing to lose but . . . owning our own stuff. Oh, and decent jobs.

This kind of magical thinking is overly simplistic and ahistorical, to think we could succeed by bashing government and carving out private enclaves of sharing and freelancing amid the immense forces of wealth and power that for decades have been slowly turning our economic and political institutions into an extractive system. To its credit, the Freelancers Union has been sponsoring local workshops for freelancers around the country to facilitate networking and skill-building, and it maintains a helpful website. The local workshops are a lifeline, though the number of workshop participants is not large (an average of 35–40), nor are the number of participants in its online discussion forums—of its claimed 250,000 (nonpaying) members, fewer than a thousand participate online in around 200 "conversations" in the 16 or so "spark" cities which are their most active locations. Their online community is not vibrantly active.[43] But at least Horowitz is trying to raise the freelancer flag and have it recognized. She is one of the few leaders who is. And under her tutelage the freelancers are learning some important skills and forming relationships that hopefully will be helpful.

But what these freelancers are *not* learning from this "union" is about how to wage a political struggle, or of how to be engaged citizens. The FU shows little interest in focusing on how to make government work. Rather than empowering or valuing government, Horowitz projects a narrow vision of helping people to gather within their own private networks, "sharing" and learning among each other, renting out their property and labor to live—and seemingly giving up on the big picture. Giving up on politics, on struggle, on challenging the extraction economy that is overtaking American workers—especially younger workers—like a tsunami gaining force and speed. In her writings, Horowitz reflects an awareness of labor history and class struggle going back to the 19th century, but in no way does her Freelancers Union resemble the Farmers Union, the Grange or the Farmers Mutual Benefit Association, its clear Populist-era predecessors. Farmers were independent contractors and freelancers in their day, standing up for their collective interest by opposing the monopolistic practices of the Robber Barons. In the 1870s, the Grangers won control of 11 Midwestern state legislatures, and the Populist movement was a prime catalyst behind the Interstate Commerce Act of 1887 and the Sherman Antitrust Act of 1890. Yet Horowitz's is a movement that is not interested in cultivating such political muscle, nor even in emphasizing this buried history.

Also to its credit, the Freelancers Union has been especially focused on pulling together young freelancers around the country. More and more people are becoming part of the internationally disposable labor pool, and young people should be up in arms over how the older generations have done so little to preserve the world they benefited from. But as we saw in chapter 7, many of the sharing economy leaders seem to view Millennials as some new, postcapitalist generation that have less materialistic values and that seem to be particularly well-suited, attitude-wise, toward plugging into this freelance and sharing economy. Horowitz fully subscribes to this outlook.

Yet in my interview with Sarah Kessler, a 27-year-old reporter and editor for the business tech magazine *Fast Company,* Kessler took issue with that view of her generation. "I don't think Millennials are like aliens, or somehow have different needs. It's not that easy to patch it all together [from various gigs and micro-gigs]," says Kessler. "Not everyone can do without a safety net." At the several Freelancers Union events I have attended in San Francisco, the young freelancers seem no less anxious and confused about their future, and no more savvy about their prospects, than previous younger generations. The ones I have met seem fairly unprepared for the life of a freelancer in the middle of a new economy heading toward ever greater amounts of automation, robotization and AI. These young people are inheriting a world that will be a far cry from the New Deal world that their parents and grandparents knew, yet they are learning few of the skills that might help them to organize politically.

This is the real tragedy of Sara Horowitz and her Freelancers Union: she believes she can make headway on her advocacy for freelancers by going private and mostly avoiding the politics (even though, as previously mentioned, her organization successfully lobbied in New York City to abolish a law that was doubly taxing freelancers). History shows that's impossible. A government with the right priorities, as Sidney Hillman well knew, is needed now more than ever. With the rights of workers and the safety of the New Deal support system under attack from so many powerful forces, local, state and federal governments have important work to do. If people like Sara Horowitz, with all her labor background, aren't going to defend the role of government and help figure out a way to modernize government's role for the new workforce, who will?

Author Michael Lind has said, "Would-be progressive populists who find they get applause by denouncing both big government and big business may be populist, but they're not progressive."[44] While I admire the part of Sara Horowitz's work that has educated the public and policy makers about the plight of freelancers and brought attention to the need for a newly designed safety net and social contract for the workers of the new economy, her overall vision and strategies raise important tactical questions: Do we keep pushing government to do what it ought to do, and build upon the most relevant parts of a decades-old legacy? Do we keep trying to win in the political arena, to ensure that our politics corral our economics, and not the other way around? Or do we retreat into our own private spheres, interconnected over an impersonal Internet and digital technology network that is controlled by the *techno sapiens* and Masters of the Universe who are saying, quite clearly, that they have a vision for the future that looks, sounds and smells like something truly horrific? This is a fundamental question, an important fork in the road—and leaders like Sara Horowitz want us to take the wrong fork.

The fork we must take, the path forward, is clear: Americans must organize, whether within labor unions, churches, the workplace, NGOs, third way labor orgs, the Grange, League of Women Voters or Kiwanis clubs, on the Internet and off, in the streets, in the boardrooms and in state capitals and city halls, to direct and refocus the unique powers of government toward the crucial task of forging a new safety net for a new economy. Only representative government has the constitutionally bestowed power to bring together the different sectors of society, including business leaders, labor leaders, community leaders, neighborhood activists and everyday Americans, and seek consensus on such an important matter. Government, with all of its obvious shortcomings and challenges, is still where all Americans meet. Sitting around the Big Roundtable, we must negotiate a new relationship, and a new social contract, between workers and employers, between companies and communities and between fellow Americans.

It's to that crucial fulcrum task that I turn in the next chapter.

TEN

SOLUTIONS I

A NEW SOCIAL CONTRACT FOR THE NEW ECONOMY

IN MAY 2014, A CONFERENCE TOOK PLACE IN THE HEART OF LONDON, YET another of the hundreds of "what went wrong" variety that have been organized since the collapse of 2008. The theme of the conference was "Inclusive Capitalism," with a preamble of, "How can we act to make our economic system more equitable, more sustainable and more inclusive?"[1] Despite its radical-sounding theme, this event was not organized by left-of-center establishments like the Fabian Society, the Greens or *Prospect* magazine. It took place in historic Guildhall and Mansion House, the official residence of the Lord Mayor of London, and its speaker list and invite-only attendees looked like a mini Davos: Bill Clinton, Prince Charles, the International Monetary Fund's Christine Lagarde, governor of the Bank of England Mark Carney, Google's Eric Schmidt, *Financial Times* economist Martin Wolf, Lynn Forester de Rothschild and a host of CEOs and executives from leading companies and commercial banks like Honeywell, UBS, Alcatel-Lucent, Unilever, GlaxoSmithKline, China International Capital Corporation, Dow Chemical and more.

Even at Davos, the World Economic Forum's annual confab of the world's fabulously wealthy and powerful, the theme of inequality has had top billing for the last several years. It's a bit jarring to hear speeches from plutocrats that contain echoes of Occupy Wall Street, but perhaps theirs reflect a personal recognition that, as Voltaire once said, every man is guilty of all the good he did not do. All told, gathered inside the venerable, gilded medieval hall were over 220 leaders from the worlds of politics, business and finance, from 27 countries representing over $30 trillion—one-third—of the world's financial assets. They discussed the future of capitalism, or more precisely, as Unilever's CEO Paul Polman put it, "The capitalist threat to capitalism."[2]

The conference participants and keynotes did not exactly burst forth from that ancient manor with a bridge plan for the future—like so many previous confabs, mostly it was a lot of, to paraphrase Winston Churchill, "jaw-jaw." Yet there was one hopeful seed of an idea introduced by the unlikeliest of characters: Bill Clinton's former Treasury secretary, Lawrence Summers. I say "unlikeliest" because numerous economists consider Summers to be one of the American architects of the disastrous financial deregulation that led to the global collapse in 2008. Economist Dean Baker has written, "There is a multi-count indictment [against Summers] that includes his support for the repeal of Glass-Steagall, his opposition to regulating derivatives, and his protection of the big banks in his years as President Obama's national economic adviser."[3] Another economist I know compares Summers to a celebrity chef who "not only burned the meal but burned down the entire restaurant—yet somehow he never gets fired, he just keeps on cooking."

Indeed, in his address at Guildhall, Summers showed no hint of humility or atonement for his prior economic sins. But the kernel of an idea that he introduced, and which he has continued to develop via another initiative called the Commission on Inclusive Prosperity, which he co-chairs, provides a clue as to the way forward for we Americans.

What Summers has proposed, which speaks directly to the challenges of the new economy, is the notion of the "portability" of the social contract. The United States, says Summers, is unique compared to other nations "in providing significant aspects of basic economic security" through the employer-employee contract. As we have seen, the safety net in the United States has depended on employers acting as mini agents of the New Deal for their own employees, where most of the supports for workers and families accrue to an individual based on her or his employment in a specific workplace, and often with a single employer for a considerable length of time. As businesses have shed employees in favor of subcontracting or hiring independent contractors, says Summers, "the unraveling of the traditional employer-employee relationship has made it more difficult to provide basic economic security," which has resulted in "leaving families to face risks on their own."[4]

In today's new economy, many workers are no longer employed for very long by a single employer. More and more have multiple employers; indeed, in the gig economy some rabbits, taskers and 1099 workers have multiple employers *in a single day.* As we have seen, none of these employers are legally or contractually obligated to provide a safety net for their 1099 workers (indeed, these workers now are liable for paying not only their half of the Social Security and Medicare payroll deductions, but the employer's half as well, an extra 7.65 percent deduction from their wages). So with the New Deal social contract fraying, and more and more Americans being shoved into jobs not covered by the laws and regulations of the existing social contract, it's time for a new approach.

In Summers's report for the Commission on Inclusive Prosperity, he cited the example of health-care insurance to illustrate his point. "In the United States, the prototypical manner in which a middle-class family receives health care insurance is through an employer. In Europe and much of the developed world, health care is delivered" either directly through the government or indirectly via nonprofits that are closely regulated by the government. "As a consequence, this means that as employment changes and the employer-employee relationship unravels, American families are left far more vulnerable than their counterparts in other countries." That was one of the major selling points for passing the Affordable Care Act: it has liberated workers to move more easily from job to job. No longer are their employment prospects hurt by "job lock" in which they do not dare leave a job for fear of losing their health care. That change alone gives slightly more bargaining power to workers with their employers.

But as the Summers report goes on to say, "other elements—including pensions, workers' compensation, and unemployment compensation—are all still tied to employment." And that increasingly has become a major problem as more Americans become unmoored from any particular job or company. They are losing their access to important components of the safety net.

That erosion has accelerated as more employers abuse the "independent contractor loophole." As we saw in chapter 1, companies can evade paying approximately 30 percent more per employee, which is the average cost for various safety-net features, by hiring an independent contractor, temp or freelancer. Under the current system, employers actually have an incentive to fire their entire workforce if they can, and go 100 percent with 1099 workers, or as high a percentage of them as possible. Sounds extreme? We saw in chapter 1 how the large pharmaceutical company Merck sold its factory in Philadelphia and the new owner fired all 400 Merck employees and rehired them as independent contractors—Merck then contracted with the company to continue making the same antibiotics for them.[5] Once enough businesses engage in that kind of practice, it unleashes a race to the bottom, putting pressure on all businesses to adopt that strategy to compete. These perverse incentives are destroying the U.S. labor force and turning tens of millions of workers into *bracero* day laborers. It's also greatly destabilizing the broader macroeconomy.

So the problem to be solved is not merely one of inequality, which is typically thought of as *income* inequality—who makes how much money, what the gap is between the highest and lowest paid, and what proportion of the population is in the middle. The challenge really needs to be reimagined as one over how to provide the support structures that individuals and families need in order to prosper and feel a measure of security, *and that is not dependent on any single employer.* I call this "personal infrastructure"—just as we understand the importance of investing in physical infrastructure like bridges, roads, ports and airports, or for energy efficiency in order to maintain society, we have to invest in the support structures that maintain individuals and families. Sometimes that will mean paying higher wages—but not always. In today's increasingly insecure age, a middle-class standard of living is not only about income levels or economic growth rates but also about adequate support structures for people that can be carried over from job to job. These also should be necessary parts of our nation's infrastructure investment.

So the question becomes, how do we replace any single employer or business as the central point for delivery of the New Deal benefits basket and spread the load and risk? How do we allow the increasingly sizable army of millions of Americans who are becoming 1099 workers to retain access? That is the big challenge today that every generation has a stake in.

I believe it's possible to evolve our system to retain the best parts of the New Deal safety net while still fostering a vigorous entrepreneurial climate. The key word, as Summers said, is "portability": we have to figure out how to make the personal support infrastructure for workers and families portable, so that the safety net follows the worker from job to gig and employer to employer. The net needs to protect the worker, regardless of her or his employment situation. Here's how we can do that.

A SAFETY NET FOR A MULTIEMPLOYER WORLD

Fortunately, we already have a working model that can be adapted. It's called a "multiemployer plan," which is an employee benefit plan to which more than one employer contributes. Multiemployer plans operate like insurance plans; they provide benefits for participants through pooling of risk and economies of scale for the employees covered by the plan. Crucially, multiemployer plans allow mobile workers to earn and retain their benefits even as they transfer from employer to employer or job to job, a portability which helps to avoid interruptions in coverage.[6]

Such multiemployer plans are often found in industries like construction and mining and, increasingly, among some Silicon Valley companies as well. Most construction workers, for example, are independent contractors and temp workers. They contract with an employer to do a specific job, and once that job is finished, their relationship with that employer ends. Then the construction worker has to look for a new job with a new employer. In any given year, that worker may end up working for numerous employers at various jobs and projects. These are the types of conditions that more and more American workers in many different occupations and industries are being subjected to, as they become independent contractors, freelancers and other categories of 1099 workers. These are also the conditions for many regularly employed part-time W-2 workers, and even an increasing number of full-time W-2 workers.

Despite the fact that these construction workers are hired on a contingency basis, the types of benefits offered by a multiemployer plan are often fairly comprehensive and substantial. The benefits are on a par with those provided by large corporations to their regular employees, including:

- Health-care benefits
- Pension benefits
- Unemployment benefits
- Occupational illness/injury benefits
- Vacation, holiday and severance benefits
- Disability/sickness insurance
- Training and education (including apprenticeships and educational scholarships)
- Financial assistance for housing
- Child-care centers
- Life insurance
- Accident insurance
- Legal services[7]

So how are such plans funded? That's a key question, since someone has to pay for all the different pools of social insurance established to support each worker and her or his family. Typically the employer pays a set amount per worker, which is set aside in a fund. The specific amount paid by the employer is written into an agreement (say, $3 or $4 per hour worked by each employee, above the baseline wage). That amount paid by the multiple employers is a kind of "personal infrastructure" levy for each worker; it pays for each worker's safety net. The fund is governed by a board of trustees, with equal numbers of employer and employee representatives appointed. The trust agreement generally provides how the benefits are to be determined, with the board of trustees given the authority to determine the level of benefits.

It all sounds perfect for part-time and 1099 workers, just like what's needed—but there is a catch. In most cases, these multiemployer plans are the products of collective-bargaining agreements that typically involve one or more local labor unions. The unions often are guild unions, that is unions representing a particular craft or occupation that have enough collective muscle to persuade multiple employers to sign on the dotted line. For example, the International Union of Operating Engineers (IUOE) is a 100-year-old union with a membership of 400,000 nationwide. Operating engineers operate, maintain and repair heavy construction equipment to build the nation's highways, power plants, dams and buildings.[8] Through a multiemployer plan for its members, the IUOE has been able to attain a middle-class level of benefits, wages, conditions and even training and apprenticeships for its members.

The multiemployer plan administered by IUOE Local 9 in Colorado has an hour-bank system, in which hours worked by an employee for a contributing employer are accumulated in much the same way funds accumulate in a savings account, or in one's personal Social Security accounts. A participant can accumulate four months (500 hours) of unemployment coverage for use when the member is having difficulty finding the next job, a constant worry in the construction and trades industry. Local 9 also maintains a defined-benefit pension fund with $8 billion in assets, funded predominantly by employers; it is the fifth largest labor-management pension plan in the country, with no unfunded liabilities and benefits guaranteed by the U.S. Pension Benefits Guaranty Corporation.[9]

Another labor union, the International Brotherhood of Teamsters, maintains the largest multiemployer defined-benefit pension plan in the U.S., the Western Conference of Teamsters Pension Trust. The WCTPT has 583,000 worker-participants, and it is a $35 billion fund that receives "personal infrastructure" contributions from more than 1,400 employers, ranging from small companies with fewer than 50 employees to major corporations like Coca-Cola, Safeway and United Parcel Service. It was founded in 1955 and designed to allow union workers—truck drivers, vegetable packers, floor sweepers, construction workers—to benefit from the security of a pension safety net, despite frequent job changes and multiple employers.[10]

These multiemployer vehicles have been operating semi-quietly, beneath the radar, despite the fact that they are in widespread use, providing a safety net for millions of Americans. Some of the plans provide only pensions; others provide other safety-net components, such as health care, unemployment benefits and such, and are called "welfare plans." As of 2012, there were 2,740 multiemployer pension plans in existence with $624 billion in assets and over 15 million workers participating. And there were approximately 1,800 multiemployer welfare, or nonpension plans, providing health care and other kinds of personal infrastructure, with nearly 6 million workers participating.[11] So these are not obscure, never-been-tried vehicles. These are duly constructed legal entities, overseen by the National Labor Relations Act (NLRA) and the Employee Retirement Income Security Act (ERISA), which permits multiple employers to contribute money into a joint trust on behalf of a specific individual employee, based on the number of hours the employee works for each employer.

But what if I'm not a member of a union, and as an independent contractor or freelancer have no hope of joining a union anytime soon? For those workers, there is another model, known as a multiple employer welfare arrangement (MEWA). Primarily used for health care, a MEWA is an arrangement to provide medical benefits to an employee who has two or more employers, even if there is no collective-bargaining agreement reached with those employers. Typically, a MEWA will involve employers who are members of a profession, trade or business association that offers medical coverage to association members.[12]

In Silicon Valley, where a constant churn of thousands of contractors, temps and freelancers are hired and let go every week, a similar model is emerging. Agencies like MBO Partners act as the "employer of record" for contingent tech workers, providing a bridge between contracted employees and their multiple employers. The services of MBO Partners and similar agencies include providing "centralized benefit administration" for the worker's access to safety-net provisions such as health benefits, injured workers compensation, disability, 401(k), as well as payroll administration, tax deductions, overtime and more.

All of these different types of multiemployer plans show potential for creating an effective safety net for contingent 1099 workers. It's all a matter of whether the laws and regulations have been structured in the right way. Here's how we can adapt these models for the current challenges.

INDIVIDUAL SECURITY ACCOUNTS

What it comes down to is this: there's absolutely no reason why, just because a business decides to outsource a job to a temp worker, freelancer, independent contractor or a franchise, instead of hiring regular employees who are covered by standard labor laws and contracts, that the employer should be able to evade paying a few dollars more per hour for each worker to provide a safety net. Similarly, regardless of how many employers a person works for, a worker should not be denied the civilized and modern-day necessity of access to a support system for herself and her family. We either go forward and evolve as a society, or we go backward.

So when Uber, TaskRabbit, Elance-Upwork, Facebook, Manpower, Kelly Services or any other business is hiring their 1099 workers, in addition to the wages that they pay, they should also pay on top of that a small levy of a few dollars per hour that is invested in an "Individual Security Account" for each worker's safety net. This is an elegant way to address this, because then it's not necessary to argue over whether the worker is actually an employee of that company or an independent contractor. That point becomes irrelevant. Either way, the employer allocates the necessary financial resources that are set aside for each employee's safety net. This method also would be structured to take advantage of existing safety-net infrastructure and programs. Here's how it could work in a simple, straightforward way.

First, any employer hiring a freelancer, independent contractor, temp or any other type of non-regular 1099 worker would pay a few dollars more per hour in addition to wages, to be invested in an Individual Security Account (ISA) for each worker's safety net. The amount any business paid into the ISA would be prorated according to the number of hours the worker was employed by that business (if wages were not based per hour but on completion of a job, such as for an Uber driver, the company would chip in a percentage of the gross wages for that job into the worker's ISA). These accounts would be prearranged so that the employer (as well as the employee) would pay via payroll deductions into existing state and federal safety-net programs—Social Security, Medicare, unemployment insurance and injured workers' compensation. For workers with multiple employers, that worker would earn a contribution from each employer based on the number of hours worked, or a percentage of gross wages, accumulated in their ISA, as in an hour-bank system. The worker's account in each of these existing programs would be identified and tracked with a personal ID number (such as a Social Security number).

Second, for those employers that do not currently provide health care to their employees, each employer would pay into the worker's ISA a prorated amount (based on the number of hours worked or a percentage of gross wages) that would go toward the worker's purchasing health insurance through one of the Obamacare exchanges or co-ops. In addition, for paid sick days, vacations and holidays, since there are no existing legally mandated social insurance programs for those in most states, the employer also would deposit funds into the worker's ISA, prorated by the number of hours worked or a percentage of gross wages, needed for providing those supports.[13]

So, for example, suppose Donna is employed 20 hours a week by a hairdresser, contracts for 10 hours a week with TaskRabbit, and drives 10 shifts for Uber. She would earn 50 percent of her benefits from the hairdresser, 25 percent from TaskRabbit, and another percentage based on her wages driving for Uber. That would amount to earning over three-fourths of her full benefits (based on a 40-hour work week). Or suppose George contracts for

14 hours a week with Upwork, drives 10 shifts for Lyft, makes 15 deliveries for Postmates and does seven gigs cleaning houses for Handy. He would earn a percentage of his benefits from each company, prorated to the number of hours worked or a percentage of his wages.

The Individual Security Accounts could be overseen by the government (much as it does for an individual's Social Security account today, tracked with a personalized number) or private entities (regulated by the government), much as insurance companies or agencies like MBO Partners do today for various safety-net features, or labor unions like IUOE, Teamsters, SEIU and others do for millions of workers. These ISAs would be collected into a larger insurance pool and professionally managed. This would form the basis for a safety net that the worker would draw upon as needed, just as any regular employee would.

So that means when a 1099 worker loses her or his job (which happens many times a year for these types of workers), she or he would have some unemployment compensation to fall back on; the same if she or he was injured on the job, or became too disabled to work, or fell ill and could not work a shift. It also could be structured to provide some paid vacation days per year, just as regular employees have. In many ways, this would work in a similar fashion to the way Social Security and Obamacare work now, in which a retirement account or a health-care account is established for individuals who work for multiple employers. Each employer who hires that worker would chip in to the Individual Security Account to cover the various components of that worker's safety net. The principle of this system is simple: the employer contributes (as does the employee), no matter what the employee's classification as a worker. The 1099/independent contractor loophole would be closed.

How much would all of this cost? Surprisingly, it's not that expensive. We can make pretty decent estimates as to what the costs would be, and the amount of employers' contributions for each 1099 worker, by looking at how much employers currently pay for their regular employees. The U.S. Bureau of Labor Statistics calculates such things on a regular basis. Using data from September 2014, we can see that the wages and salaries for all civilian workers (government and private sector) in the United States averaged $22.13 per hour. U.S. employers also paid an additional $7.44 per hour—about a third more—to make sure all of those workers had access to a safety net composed of Social Security, Medicare, federal and state unemployment insurance and state injured workers' compensation (all legally required for regularly employed W-2 workers), as well as health insurance, long- and short-term disability insurance and paid sick days, vacation and holidays.

But if we focus just on private-sector workers, which is where most 1099 and part-time employees are working today, and within that, just on service-sector workers and sales and office workers—which are the majority of 1099 workers—it's much less expensive. For sales and office employees, it cost their employers only about $5.37 per hour, and for service-sector workers, even less, about $2.91 per hour to give them the security of a comprehensive safety net.[14]

But those numbers based on BLS tables are actually the upper limit of what this will cost. By carefully designing the safety net, we could make this even less expensive. The example above assumes about two weeks/10 paid vacation days (since that's what the BLS figures are based on), which could be scaled back initially to four or five days (and would still provide far more than tens of millions of working Americans currently receive). The same with paid holidays, which could be scaled back, or even not included initially. The number of sick leave days could be limited initially to cut that cost. Scaling back the safety-net basket in various ways would reduce the overall cost, so that employers would pay only an extra $2.27 per hour for private-sector workers in the services industries, and $4.19 per hour for sales and office workers.[15] That's a small amount of money to provide millions of 1099 workers health insurance, Social Security, Medicare, unemployment, injured workers' compensation, disability, paid sick leave and vacations (but no paid holidays, in this example)—regardless of their employment situation.

And it would likely cost even less. Low-income wage-earners are eligible for Obamacare subsidies for health care, reducing that cost even more for the employer. Health care is by far the greatest expense of this proposed safety-net basket, consuming 34 percent of the overall basket. The breakdown of the other expenses is: Social Security (21 percent), vacations (16 percent), holidays (9 percent), injured workers' compensation (6 percent), Medicare (5 percent), sick leave (4 percent), unemployment (4 percent), long- and short-term disability (1 percent). With these numbers as our guide, we could propose different mixes to make it even more affordable, phasing in certain benefits over time to get a program like this up and running, and then build on it over the years. (This model reflects the history of Social Security, which initially in the 1930s had modest benefits. But over the years, as it proved itself to be economically useful, practical, as well as popular, it was expanded.)

For example, simply providing a minimum basket composed of worker supports that are already legally required for regular W–2 employees (in other words, Social Security, Medicare, federal and state unemployment insurance and injured workers compensation) would cost a mere $1.50 per hour for service workers and $1.87 per hour for sales and office workers in the private sector. That's less than two dollars per hour to provide a basic safety net to millions of workers who currently have nothing. The world's lone remaining superpower can't afford that?

Also, once the vast insurance pools of previously uncovered workers are formed, with billions of dollars in play, and insurance companies bid to supply these parts of the safety basket, the impact of "economies of scale" is likely to reduce costs even further. Indeed, one can envision a whole new business springing up of "central administrator companies" that do nothing but administer "safety-net plans" for 1099 workers, offering in a competitive market a package of benefits that is purchased by individual workers, with each employer of that worker kicking in a certain percentage of salary into the worker's Individual Security Account. A minimum level of coverage would be mandated by law, with more expensive plans providing more benefits and coverage also being available, such as gold, silver and bronze plans (much like the way the Affordable Care Act works now for health care). Each worker would shop for the safety-net package she or he can afford. Of course, the rules, products and services would have to be regulated and closely monitored by the government to ensure quality, fairness, cost-effectiveness and no fraud. But economies of scale resulting from a competitive market of insurance-type companies offering more than health or life insurance, and acting as central administrators offering an entire package of safety-net features, would further reduce costs.

And of course, if the U.S. could ever reduce the terribly expensive price we pay for health care (especially when compared to other developed nations, which deliver far better health-care metrics to a greater proportion of their populations for half the cost), that also would be a great help in bringing down the expense of this safety-net basket. (In the next chapter, I provide a plan for dramatically reducing the high health-care costs in the U.S. that politicians and experts from both the right and the left agree are threatening to bankrupt the country.)

So Travis Kalanick (Uber), Leah Busque (TaskRabbit) and all the other CEOs of companies involved in the hiring of armies of 1099 workers and part-timers would be legally required to bank the allotted amount of money into each worker's Individual Security Account, based on the number of hours each worker labored, or, for those paid by the job, a percentage of gross wages. The excuse that these workers are independent contractors or freelancers who are not actually employed by them would be moot; if you contract with them, *the employer pays.* Over time, employers even might want to attract more high-quality workers by sweetening the pot a bit, adding a few more vacation or sick days, or a small amount toward ongoing training and education, or paid parental leave (after the birth of a child, or due to sickness in the family), housing assistance, and other possibilities.

In short, what we are talking about is extending legal parity to 1099 workers and part-timers so that they are on the same safety-net footing as regular and full-time workers. That's a better proactive strategy than mounting lawsuits over misclassification of workers, which is the current method used for redress. The goal of such litigation is to win a court ruling that says the workers have been misclassified as contractors when in fact they really are W-2 employees. These are tough lawsuits to win, and also hugely expensive, time consuming, a drain on national resources and ultimately a forum in which there are few winners. It creates a hodgepodge legal landscape in which no one is quite sure of the rules. "Worker misclassification is going to become weaker and weaker" as more workers migrate from regular jobs into the 1099 category, says Denise Cheng, a researcher at MIT and an expert on the sharing economy. "It doesn't make sense to hinge everything on that. What we should think through is, 'What should the protections be for an independent contractor?'"[16]

That's exactly what this proposal does. And fortunately, it turns out this is not exactly rocket science, as it is already being done elsewhere. The European Union, for example, has passed legislation that makes it illegal to treat part-time or temporary employees differently than regular, full-time employees.[17] The EU guarantees that those working through temporary employment agencies receive equal pay and conditions as regular employees in the same business who do the same work, starting on Day 1. The principle of equal treatment applies not only to pay but also to the basic working and employment conditions, including the duration of working time, overtime, breaks, rest periods, night work, vacations and holidays.[18]

But my proposal would do even more than create legal parity—it would create universality. Even during the height of the New Deal era, a certain number of workers were always left out of the support system. Farm workers, for example, were excluded from the National Labor Relations Act (though California years later included them via state law). The American labor force has always had insiders and outsiders. So this structure of universal Individual Security Accounts would bring everyone into the fold to a much greater degree than they are now.

An important consequence of this proposal is that, by putting nearly all employees on a similar footing, we would greatly reduce the incentives for employers to resort to temps, freelancers, part-timers and individual contractors as a way of avoiding paying for benefits and worker supports. Employers would still have the freedom to use a 1099 worker, and might have good reason to do so because that would still allow the flexibility to ramp up their workforce, depending on customer demand. Flexibility is a recognized good in the labor markets, to some extent, and this proposal would not prevent that. But by enacting laws and regulations that extend the concept of multi-employer plans and legal parity between different categories of workers, we will go a long way toward removing the corrosive antagonism and perverse incentives created by these vastly unequal categories of workers.

It also liberates workers to seek their own creative space in the labor market, driven by their passions and individual genius instead of being in "job lock" at a particular company because it happens to be one of the remaining few that provide a level of worker support that they and their families need. Liberating employees like this would unleash the innate genius and talent of the American workforce. This would be the basis for a "truly sharing" economy worth sharing.

Many business leaders and lobbyists like the Chamber of Commerce, of course, will complain that such a requirement will be a "job killer," that it will be expensive and hurt businesses and put them at a competitive disadvantage. But especially if the policies become national and universal, like Social Security is, then all employers will be affected equally and no one will be impacted more than another. For many service-sector businesses, their competition usually is local, so especially within a certain industry (like restaurants, for example) or occupation (like computer programmers), all local employers will be affected equally. And most of the costs can be passed on to the consumer, but since the millions of workers benefiting also are consumers, it will create a virtuous circle in which a rising tide will lift all boats.

Other businesses will complain that it will hurt them against their international competitors. But most businesses in the U.S. compete only domestically, in the huge U.S. internal market. For those that compete internationally, they can rest easy knowing that most of their international competitors are located in nations that already have policies like this in place, and have had them for years. Are American businesses somehow less vital and competent than those in Europe, Japan, Korea, Israel, Brazil and elsewhere?[19]

Or look at it this way: Sure, an employer might say that this will be expensive to take on. But policy makers need to recognize that it's going to be increasingly expensive for society *not* to do it. We've already seen how, because Walmart pays so poorly and provides such a sparse safety net, the rest of society—read, taxpayers—have to foot the bill for things like food stamps, Medicaid, subsidized housing and expensive hospital emergency room visits (instead of doctor's office visits) for Walmart employees (*Forbes* reports that Walmart costs U.S. taxpayers an estimated $6.2 billion annually in public assistance for its workers).[20] *Either way, we pay.*

So increasingly the numbers are on the side of modernizing the social contract in this way. Rebecca Smith, deputy director for the National Employment Law Project, asks, "Why shouldn't Uber, Lyft, and their kin be required, just like other labor brokers are . . . to pay the payroll taxes that ensure workers have access to basic benefits like workers' compensation when they are injured and Social Security when they retire? Given the kind of huge revenue being generated in some of these companies, it's not a lot to ask."[21]

In the past, business hostility and deep-pocketed donor influence over politicians have prevented much headway in enacting these kinds of Individual Security Accounts. The last time a bill to offer some benefits for private-sector temp workers got even so much as a committee hearing in Congress was in 1971.[22] A federal bill to give employees seven days of paid sick leave a year has been introduced into the U.S. Senate every session since 2004 but has never made it to the Senate floor.[23]

"There's a very strong strain of economic thought in the United States that one of the reasons why we are as productive and successful economically as we are is that there's so much flexibility in the labor markets," says Seth Harris, former U.S. deputy labor secretary. But economies also suffer when employers don't invest in training or pay living wages, he says, and "there's a need to find a balance." One of the "tragedies of the temp workers' situation" is that it treats "workers as disposable inputs rather than valuable assets for their companies," says Harris.[24]

That's the attitude on the part of so many U.S. businesses that has to change—workers must be valued again, and a sense of shared partnership has to be rediscovered. Sixty years ago, most CEOs assumed some level of responsibility for all their stakeholders, including their employees. "The job of management," proclaimed Frank Abrams, chairman in 1951 of Standard Oil of New Jersey, which was one of the largest oil producers in the world (and eventually became Exxon), "is to maintain an equitable and working balance among the claims of the various directly interested groups . . . stockholders, employees, customers, and the public at large."[25] Abrams's predecessor, Walter Teagle, initiated worker representation at Standard Oil of New Jersey in 1918, which was emulated by Germany after World War II when they designed their system of economic democracy within corporations, known as "codetermination" (more on that in the next chapter).[26]

So American business leaders used to think differently about these matters. Current attitudes among this group have only resulted in unleashing a race to the bottom for all. Increasingly, it is damaging not only to workers and families but to the very fabric of American society. The major point here, which is a philosophical one about the type of society we want to live in, bears repeating: Just because a business decides to outsource a job to a temp worker, freelancer, independent contractor or a franchise, instead of directly hiring a regular employee, or just because a person works for multiple employers, there's no sound reason, economic or otherwise, that those employers should be able to wiggle out of paying a couple more dollars per hour so that each of their workers can know the civilized security of a basket of supports for herself and her family. As we saw in chapter 1, businesses today are using all sorts of tricks—hiring third-party operations like temp agencies, private contractor businesses and franchises—to turn their employees into freelancers, temps, perma-temps and individual contractors. It's all part of a strategy by parent companies to evade responsibility for providing a decent, middle-class wage and a safety net for their employees. If they have their way, apparently every American worker will be turned into a 1099 employee with minimal personal infrastructure supports, just because it's cheaper for their bottom line. But is that really what's best for the nation?

With legal parity between different categories of workers and the proposed multiemployer Individual Security Account as the basis for the new economy's safety net and social contract, every worker would have access to the following: health insurance, Social Security, Medicare, unemployment insurance, injured workers' compensation, disability and a few days of paid sick days and vacations. Basing a new social contract for the new economy on such a system holds great potential. Besides benefiting individuals, this "new New Deal" would act as an automatic stabilizer and ongoing stimulus for the macroeconomy, helping to maintain the consumer spending that drives the economy and creates jobs.[27] It would form the basis for keeping the U.S. economy plowing forward into the 21st century, enriched by technology and innovation instead of being disrupted and impoverished by it. That would amount to a giant step in the right direction.

In this insecure age, with the threat of ongoing job loss and debility hanging like a sword over our heads, as well as declining prospects for an army of 1099 workers and a looming Economic Singularity, the personal safety net based on extending greater legal parity between 1099 workers, part-timers and regular full-time workers will be increasingly necessary to ensure productive and satisfied workers, healthy families, vibrant communities, prosperous businesses and a more stable macroeconomy. We can move forward, confident with the knowledge that many other developed countries have already taken this fork, and for the most part it's worked out well. The United States is the clear outlier here (well, OK, there is one class of Americans lucky enough to enjoy a generous level of safety-net support—members of Congress, as well as many state legislators and city councilors, who spare themselves nothing and provide European-level support for themselves and their families).

In the next chapter, we'll look at other solutions and reforms that need to be enacted if we truly want to transform our 20th-century industrial-based economy into one that is a better fit for the 21st century's "Information and Innovation Age."

ELEVEN

SOLUTIONS II

MAKING THE NEW ECONOMY WORK IN THE INFORMATION AND INNOVATION AGE

WE AMERICANS HAVE OUR WORK CUT OUT FOR US. THE *ECONOMIST* SAYS making the necessary adjustments to prepare for the new economy "will be more of a problem for America, which ties many benefits to [specific] jobs, than Europe, which has a more universal approach" based on portability of benefits attached to the individual.[1] Compared to many other countries, the United States has the wrong institutions and regulations—ones that are ill suited to the enormous challenges presented by the onset of the new economy.

Besides figuring out how to adapt the safety net for all workers—especially 1099 and part-time workers—in this post–New Deal era, we also have to figure out what to do about the possibility of runaway "technological unemployment." As we have seen, automation and robots, job-brokerage websites and apps in the not-so-sharing economy and new-economy companies like Facebook that are replacing old-economy companies like Kodak, yet hiring a lot fewer employees, are already greatly impacting the jobs picture. Individual Security Accounts funded by multiple employers won't be very useful if there are not enough jobs and gigs for people to do. Perhaps it is true that new types of employment will be created to replace the old, as the technological boosters have promised. But what if they are wrong? Nearly all experts are in agreement that the quality of jobs is going to continue to decline, and quite possibly the quantity of jobs as well. Either way, the U.S. needs to prepare for a job-constrained future and evolve our system in ways that make it better suited to the turbulent era we are heading into. As we reconfigure the new economy for the 21st century, here are other important changes that would make a crucial difference:

Job sharing. Sometimes known as "short work," this is a strategy that has been deployed extensively in Germany (where it's called *Kurzarbeit*), the Netherlands, Sweden and other places. The way it works is that current employees reduce their working hours by 5 to 10 percent so that other employees can be hired. In Germany, they even managed to reduce some employees' hours without significantly reducing their pay. Some workers are quite willing, even happy, to cut back their hours for a period of time, as it allows more leisure and family time. If we are going to have a "sharing" economy, then why not share our jobs?

From a macroeconomic standpoint, there is little difference between creating a new job or better sharing existing jobs, as long as aggregate wage levels are not significantly reduced. Job sharing can result in millions of people staying employed during an economic downturn, as it did quite effectively in Germany following the crash in 2008. Even when the economy is running smoothly, job sharing can result in employment for those that don't have it, as well as greater flexibility for work-family balance for those who do have it. In the U.S., 28 states plus the District of Columbia already have passed laws that permit job sharing, yet even in those places this strategy has not been used that much, certainly not as widely or effectively as in Europe.[2]

Especially if it turns out to be true that there is going to be a sizable future increase in "technological unemployment" due to more automation and robotization, then it makes sense to better utilize job sharing.

Vocational training, apprenticeships and job placement. In a potentially job-constrained future, it becomes all the more important to develop and expand the skills of workers and target that training to the jobs that are available. Apprenticeships, which are jobs in which inexperienced workers are paid to learn a set of skills through on-the-job training, have worked extremely well in many advanced economies to prepare workers and to help businesses meet their need for skilled workers. Unfortunately, the U.S. has really neglected this strategy.

Americans could learn a lot from places like Germany, Switzerland, Austria and Denmark, which have ambitious vocational training and job-placement programs. Truly impressive, these programs foster a highly trained workforce geared for the global economy. In Germany, 65 to 70 percent of teenagers enter "dual track" apprenticeship programs in which on-the-job training is combined with classroom time. Half as many young Germans go to college as in the United States; instead, companies pay for apprenticeships to educate a workforce with the skills that pay off on the job.[3] Germany has job training for older workers as well, and Sweden, Austria, Switzerland, Finland and other nations also have well-funded vocational and educational training for workers of all ages. Meanwhile in the U.S., we have nothing comparable to such a comprehensive and efficient training system. We spend a lower percentage of our national wealth on job retraining for the unemployed than any of the Western European nations, and the system of vocational training and apprenticeships is fragmentary at best.

In Denmark, not only do they have well-funded job-training centers but also impressive job-placement services that are used to match retrained workers' new skills with suitable employment. The Danish system, which is called "flexicurity" (short for "flexible security"), permits relatively easy hiring and firing of workers in exchange for job training and retraining, and generous unemployment support for those who lose their jobs. In addition, Denmark has a robust "personal infrastructure" system for all its workers, and laid-off workers are provided the support to maintain themselves during their displacement and retraining period.

But what really sets the Danish system apart is that they have job placement down to a quasi-science. Experts prepare what is known as a "bottleneck analysis," using pollsters to survey employers on what jobs they expect they will need in coming years, and using that feedback to identify the next labor shortages and to pick the correct training courses for retrainees. The Danes have discovered that a proactive government can help a flexible labor market to flow better.[4]

In a job-constrained future, effective vocational and job training in the U.S. could make the difference in whether millions of underskilled workers find suitable employment, and whether businesses find the skilled workers they need. The U.S. has a small apprenticeship system of only 375,000 apprentices, heavily concentrated in the building and construction trades,[5] usually for older males (average age 29),[6] and apprenticeship standards vary widely across the country. Ironically, over 3,500 German companies operate in the U.S., and they have had to become vocal advocates for more job training because they complain that it's hard to find qualified American workers, especially in high-quality industrial production.[7] More of these firms are taking matters into their own hands, working with local education providers to train their workers.[8] The German automaker Volkswagen opened the "Volkswagen Academy" in Chattanooga, Tennessee, prior to opening its newest auto plant there to ensure that their new employees would be well trained.[9] At their U.S. subsidiaries, large German companies have actively implemented dual-apprenticeship programs for young Americans, combining vocational/

technical training with in-school instruction, often in collaboration with local community colleges.[10]

What makes the U.S. neglect so puzzling is that numerous studies show that training programs pay off. A Swiss study found that employers in Switzerland spend around $3.4 billion annually training apprentices, yet see a return of approximately $3.7 billion each year from apprentices' work during training.[11] In the U.S., the state of Washington realized a return on investment for apprenticeships of $23 for every public dollar invested—substantially higher than for any other workforce-training program, including community colleges (which are also very valuable, with an investment return of $3 for every public dollar invested).[12] These programs benefit businesses and also workers: researchers have found that U.S. workers who complete an apprenticeship make about $300,000 more than comparable job seekers in their lifetimes.[13] So our neglect of this important component has poorly served our workforce and our nation's future.

The Obama administration has tried to reverse this pitiful track record by moving forward with its TechHire initiative. TechHire is a public-private effort involving 21 cities and regions, 300 private-sector employers and universities and community colleges to expand training programs, "coding boot camps" and online courses. With an estimated 500,000 job vacancies nationwide for technology jobs, the goal is to rapidly train workers for a well-paying job, often in just a few months.[14] Other fledgling job-training efforts are underway, often utilizing the public-private partnership model, including the Tennessee Tech Program, LearnUp in San Francisco, the Nanodegree program at AT&T and Western Governors University, a nonprofit online institution.[15] Job-training and apprenticeship programs are a win-win, so the best of these programs should be scaled up as part of a significantly greater national investment. It has been especially odd that conservatives and Republicans, who tend to see themselves as the pro-business party, have not been actively supporting these sorts of efforts. Now is the time to step forward, before the full impact of job losses resulting from automation and job-brokerage websites strikes.

Profit sharing. With wage and productivity growth diverging so widely, an increasing share of business profits has gone to shareholders and CEOs and little of it to workers, since wages are stagnant and most workers don't own much stock. If Travis Kalanick really believes his drivers are his "partners," why not turn Uber into a more inclusive capitalist company with profit sharing for his driver-partners? That could be in the form of an employee stock-ownership plan (ESOP), or profit-and-gain sharing programs, which pay employees a percentage of company profits without granting ownership. Inclusive capitalism would truly be a "sharing" thing to do, spreading the wealth beyond top executives to a wider segment of workers, and emphasizing the significance of group, rather than individual, performance.

Studies show that companies that adopt profit sharing often benefit from a higher degree of worker loyalty and greater effort, as well as lower turnover rates (something Kalanick desperately needs help with).[16] It fosters more of a "we're all in this together" mentality and would allow workers to reap some of the benefits of the productivity gains resulting from technology and automation. Even workers who lose their job could still retain stock in the company. And for those startup mentalities so fond of disruption, doing this also would be a "disruptive" thing to do to the typical Silicon Valley ethos. Paging Mr. Kalanick?

Codetermination and works councils—economic democracy. In a job-constrained era, many company decisions will have to be made about which technologies to deploy, who to lay off, whether to use job sharing and profit sharing and other decisions that affect the number and quality of jobs. So it makes sense now to think about decision-making structures within a company, especially who in the company should have input into these crucial decisions.

U.S. corporate leaders have grappled with these sorts of questions before. In 1918, Standard Oil of New Jersey, the inheritor of the legacy of oil baron John D. Rockefeller and one of the largest oil companies in the world, made a dramatic shift in its model of corporate governance. Led by its then-president, Walter Teagle, it announced that its employees would be given "a voice in the fixing of their compensation, hours of labor, conditions under which they work and live, and everything affecting the welfare of themselves and their families." The plan was for "representatives to be chosen by the workmen to represent them at the company's councils and every man employed will have a vote."[17]

Labor historian Robert Zieger writes that this design of economic democracy within a corporation was to shortly become part of a wave of corporate governance. Besides Standard Oil, other large corporations such as Goodyear, United States Rubber, International Harvester and others had come to the conclusion that "it was essential for corporations to gain the active loyalty of their employees." To the business leaders of these corporations, "concern for employee welfare" (expressed via efforts for worker representation) "made good sense." Employers had come to an understanding, writes Zieger, that "the long working day, the fear of arbitrary dismissal, and the subsistence wage were vestiges of the industrial past. Workers who had economic, social and psychological ties to the corporation, they felt, performed their tasks more efficiently, were less critical of management's policies, and were less prone to absenteeism and frequent job changing."[18] Indeed, Walter Teagle and Standard Oil issued a press release stating its rationale for this change: "It is felt that the establishment of such a relationship will give the company a better understanding of the wants and ambitions of the workmen, and at the same time give the workmen a better understanding of the aims and plans of the management."[19]

Compare that attitude among business leaders of the largest corporations in the 1920s to the attitudes espoused by leading CEOs today, who want to hire 1099 workers with low wages, no job security or safety net, and with no voice or input into crucial decisions that affect workers and their families. Business owners today want a workforce they can turn on and off like a light bulb. The conditions of the workers in the 1910s and '20s—"the long working day, the fear of arbitrary dismissal, and the subsistence wage"—are increasingly becoming the conditions that tens of millions of workers are coping with once again today.

Sadly, the legacy of worker representation and empowerment within big companies did not survive in the United States. But it did take root and flourish elsewhere. Germany, Sweden and other European countries have been able to implant into their "social capitalism" soil a substantial degree of worker representation, as well as job sharing and job training (as explored above). And they have found that doing so has allowed them to maintain their competitiveness, labor productivity and the flexibility needed to adapt to the global economy. Ironically, by adapting some of the strategies from Standard Oil and the largest U.S. corporations from the 1920s, these countries have been able to foster more economic democracy than we have in our own country. That includes what I call a "culture of consultation," which has led to greater cooperation between employers and employees, making it possible to implement many other progressive directives.

In Germany and Sweden, for example, this culture of consultation has been advanced by specific institutions, one of which is called codetermination. Just like in Standard Oil, codetermination in Germany allows workers at major corporations and businesses to elect up to half of the representatives on corporate boards of directors that sit side by side with stockholder representatives. From the current American standpoint, this is like requiring Walmart to allow its workers to elect up to 50 percent of its board of directors, a concept unimaginable for most Americans today. Yet many European nations deploy some version of this as standard procedure.

Codetermination in Germany, Sweden and elsewhere also includes employee "works councils" in most workplaces, which provide worker representation at the job-site level (that's in addition to their representation by more traditional labor unions, which are quite influential). Works councils allow employees a great deal of input and consultation within the workplace. Europe in effect has borrowed from the Standard Oil playbook to reinvent the modern corporation and make these private entities more accountable to the labor force, as well as to public and democratic values. Yet U.S. policymakers, political analysts, economists as well as the media and general public have barely noticed.[20]

The impact of codetermination has been immensely significant. Not only has it provided a level of economic democracy at both the corporate board level and in the workplace, but these practices have helped the businesses that use them by fostering information sharing and consensus building between business managers and workers. Research has shown that works councils are associated with lower rates of absenteeism, more worker training, better handling of worker grievances and smoother implementation of health and safety standards.[21]

Fortune 500 companies in Germany use codetermination and remain extremely profitable. Germany exports as much trade as does the U.S., even though it has only a quarter of our population. At the same time, German autoworkers earn an hourly wage that is twice as high as U.S. autoworkers.[22] With a strong autoworkers union reinforced by codetermination laws and works councils, companies like Volkswagen and Daimler are pushed to invest in a skilled, participative workforce, which has benefited both the workers and the companies.[23]

So if we want to craft an inclusive business model in the United States, one that allows the various stakeholders in a company to have some input into decisions over technology deployment, automation and potential job losses, all we have to do is go back to our corporate governance roots—the "Standard Oil" benchmark. American labor attorney Thomas Geoghegan has proposed that states should offer tax breaks to companies that try out codetermination by allowing their rank-and-file employees to elect a third to a half of their corporate boards of directors. Doing so, says Geoghegan, would allow U.S. companies to test drive an alternative model to the current dysfunctional stockholder model.

For nonprofits, Geoghegan would go even further. He proposes a mandate that universities and medical centers must allow their employees to elect one-third of their boards of directors. Nonprofits are not driven by the same for-profit calculations, and usually they are rooted in their home states, "so they can't go off to Delaware," says Geoghegan. "A blue state or two might try mandating this limited kind of codetermination," he says. "Having employees elect at least a third [of the board of directors] may bring a bit more accountability to not-for-profits and make them hew closer to their charitable missions."[24]

Besides solutions for the jobs crisis, the United States also needs to rethink ways to improve and make more cost effective our existing safety-net supports. Here are important changes that would make a difference:

Health care—reduce costs. With the implementation of the Affordable Care Act, about 8 to 11 million Americans who did not previously have health insurance now do.[25] That is a considerable improvement, but with originally 45 to 50 million Americans without health care prior to Obamacare, it means we still have a long way to go. So there is a great need for state and local governments to partner with nonprofit and nongovernmental organizations to conduct a vigorous campaign of targeted outreach to 1099 workers and even grey-economy workers to ensure high rates of participation. Legally, every individual is required to sign up for health care, and low-income and many moderate-income people are eligible for federal assistance and, in some states, additional assistance (prorated based on income level) to help them afford health care for themselves and their families. So the public and private sectors should team up to assist all workers, regardless of their employment situation, to gain access to health care. Doing so will make the overall workforce more healthy and therefore more productive.

Beyond that, looking at the bigger picture it's important to further evolve the health-care system in the U.S., with an eye on reducing costs. Health care in the U.S. is hideously expensive, consuming a massive 17 percent of the nation's gross domestic product to cover only 84 percent of the population—that's *twice* as expensive as in most other developed countries, where 100 percent of their populations are covered, and puts the U.S. at a competitive disadvantage. Obamacare, even if more fully implemented, will do little to dramatically affect that. The only proven method for reducing the high cost of health care is to move away from the "for-profit" medical model used in the U.S. and adopt a "nonprofit" model, used by most countries in the world. Nonprofit health care has been especially successful in Germany, France, Japan, Australia and elsewhere. This model is different from Canada's or the United Kingdom's single-payer system (also known as government-run "socialized" medicine), as it still relies on *private insurance companies* as the backbone of the system. But unlike in the U.S., where private insurance companies are for-profits, with CEOs and other executives pulling down enormous salaries and beholden to stockholders, these insurance companies are *nonprofits.* It turns out that when you remove the profit motive from health care, you can drastically reduce costs; it also turns out that making high rates of profit off of people's health is a pretty backward idea.

By reducing national health-care costs to a figure closer to that of other advanced economies—anywhere from 8 percent to 12 percent of GDP for

100 percent coverage of their populations—we would free up billions of dollars that can be used for other important needs, such as funding Individual Security Accounts for U.S. workers, as well as investment in the nation's physical infrastructure (which creates jobs), education and job training.

Retirement and Social Security—expand it. As we have seen, 1099 workers currently are required to pay not only their half of the Social Security payroll deduction, but the employer's half as well, an extra 6.2 percent deduction from their wages. That needs to be fixed by creating multiemployer Individual Security Accounts. But in the bigger picture, the overall U.S. retirement system is in rickety shape and needs to be overhauled.

The problem is that it is composed of a public-private hybrid, with Social Security as the public portion and the private portion composed of private pensions and personal savings. Many Americans' personal savings withered during the economic collapse in 2008 and still have not recovered, while private pensions are disappearing and not usually portable—in 1980 about 40 percent of private-sector workers had a guaranteed pension but by 2006 that had fallen to 15 percent, and today it's lower still.[26] Workers who have a pension with a particular employer are afraid to change jobs because they will lose their ability to keep paying into it and further expand their retirement income.

The best way to make retirement fully portable is for the U.S. to do what many other developed nations have already done, which is to greatly expand Social Security and increase its retirement payout for each retired worker. Social Security is fully portable—you pay into it no matter where you work, even if you are a freelancer—and it has been the most effective antipoverty program ever enacted in the U.S. Almost half of elderly Americans would be poor (incomes below the federal poverty line) without Social Security; for nearly two-thirds of elderly beneficiaries, Social Security provides the majority of their cash income, and for one-quarter of beneficiaries Social Security is the sole source of retirement income.[27] It is particularly crucial for elderly women and racial/ethnic minorities.[28] Contrary to what critics say, Social Security is a financially stable program, and with a few minor tweaks will remain so well into the future.

But the real problem with Social Security is that its payout is so meager. By design, Social Security is only supposed to replace about one-third of your wages at retirement. That is really quite stingy, and only about half the amount of retirement income that is paid out by other nations' retirement systems. By reconfiguring how Social Security is funded, it would be possible to double the Social Security payout for every working American—a plan I call Social Security Plus.[29]

One easy step toward expanding the payout to create Social Security Plus would be to remove what is known as the "payroll cap," which results in an individual who makes more than $118,500 a year not paying any more Social Security tax on income above that level. Unlike other taxes, such as the income tax, which is a progressive tax in which the more income you make the more tax you pay, with the Social Security tax, the higher your income the lower the percentage of your income that you pay. Millionaire bankers pay less than 1 percent of their income into the Social Security fund, while an average worker is paying 6.2 percent of her or his wages (with employers matching another 6.2 percent). That's due to this payroll cap that only taxes Social Security up to $118,500.

So removing this cap not only would be far more fair, it also would take us a giant step toward finding the revenue to make Social Security Plus a truly portable national retirement system that provides an adequate level of elderly security. With this in place, private pensions would be much less important; in fact, they might become unnecessary (and the $130 billion annual tax subsidy that companies receive for providing private pensions could be added to funding for Social Security Plus).[30] Combined with other ways to pay for its expansion, Social Security Plus would allow any worker, regardless of her or his employment situation or how many employers she or he works for, to be able to save more for retirement. And doing so would cost no more of our nation's wealth than the current hybrid private-public retirement system, but it would be far more efficient and fair. Social Security, which is one of the most popular government programs ever enacted—even a majority of Republicans say they don't want to see benefits cut—already is structured like an Individual Security Account, in which the employer and worker both pay into the worker's personal account. We can enhance its stability and value with only a few tweaks to the current system.

(I authored and coauthored two different plans for the New America Foundation that explain how to fully pay for a Social Security Plus expansion; see the endnote for citations.[31])

Sick leave—it makes good sense. Now that we've seen that it's possible to design a safety net with Individual Security Accounts that allow for paid sick leave for any category of worker, allow me to make a case for why paid sick leave for all U.S. workers is long overdue. Not only is it good for the worker, it's also good for consumers as well as for the American economy.

The United States is still one of only a handful of nations that has no national law guaranteeing paid sick leave. More than 160 nations around the world ensure paid sick days, with 127 allowing a week or more annually.[32] But as President Obama highlighted in a speech, current U.S. policy leaves

43 million workers—38 percent of the private labor force—without a single paid sick day.[33]

Certain demographics are particularly hard hit. Low-income workers are especially vulnerable, since they are less likely to have access to paid sick days. Ninety percent of private-sector workers with earnings in the top 10 percent of their occupation receive paid sick days compared to only 23 percent of workers in the bottom 25 percent.[34] Workers who have a college degree are more than twice as likely to have paid leave than those with less than a high-school education.[35] And women are less likely than men to have paid sick days, which is a particularly dumb policy since 80 percent of mothers have responsibility for their children's doctor visits.[36] Yet that can cost them their job: 23 percent of adults say they've been threatened with termination or fired for taking time off from work when they or a family member were ill.[37]

In the 160 nations with paid sick leave, if you are sick they want you to stay home and take care of yourself; and if your child is sick, they want you to stay home and not worry about losing the wages you need for food or rent. But in the good ol' USA, if you are sick, we want you to report to work and infect your coworkers and customers; if your child is sick, we force you to choose between being a good parent or being the breadwinner.

During the swine flu outbreak in the spring of 2009, at one point President Barack Obama urged workers with flu symptoms to "stay home." But far too many American workers, especially many service-sector and low-income employees, couldn't afford to. So there is a much greater chance that employees handling food in a restaurant or handing out change in a grocery store are "working sick." "Excuse me sir, would you like some swine flu with your french fries?"

An illness should not be something that can disrupt your working life or even impoverish you. Instead, you should be able to heal, go back to work, and get on with your life.

Child care—supporting families. Among the major advanced democracies, the United States is one of the few that has no coherent child-care policy. Consequently, child care is hard to find, of mediocre quality and prohibitively expensive. This especially jeopardizes women's place in the workforce, as well as the health of families.

A 2014 report from Child Care Aware found that the cost of child care in the United States can easily run over $10,000 annually, whether for an infant or four-year-old, and does not always guarantee quality care.[38] Lynette Fraga, executive director of Child Care Aware, says, "Child care is one of the most significant expenses in a family budget, often exceeding the cost of housing, college tuition, transportation or food."[39]

Meanwhile, across the pond in most European countries, child care is widespread and much less expensive than in the U.S., often a sixth or less of the price. Sweden, France, Belgium and Denmark are considered to be child-care leaders in Europe, offering universal, high-quality, and publicly funded child care. In Denmark, full-time professional child care costs parents around $360 per month (which includes lunch) for a professional state-run nursery,[40] and in Sweden, working parents pay a small percentage of their income which amounts to a ridiculously low $13 per month (including breakfast and lunch) for professional care.[41] One British chap who moved for work with his family to Sweden observed, "[In Sweden] childcare is seen as a basic service. It is as much a part of the infrastructure of going out to work as decent transport."[42]

In short, child care is personal infrastructure for families, especially for women who bear the heaviest load in taking care of children. But in the United States it is woefully lacking, both in supply and quality. Having decent and affordable child care available would be a great help to the entire labor force, especially many 1099 workers.

In addition to the "job solutions" and ways to make the safety net more efficient and cost effective, here are two other proposals that would greatly help 1099 workers. These personal infrastructure supports are precisely geared to their unique employment needs.

Tax deductions for freelancers and independents. Most U.S. businesses benefit from all sorts of business-related tax deductions. As Travis Kalanick and Leah Busque frequently remind everyone, independent contractors and freelancers essentially are in business for themselves, eligible to deduct legitimate business expenses. Those include a home office deduction, deductions for office equipment and supplies, business-related travel, health-care expenses and more. Yet many of these workers are poorly informed about these provisions and cannot afford a tax accountant to figure them out. Many don't even realize that as an independent entrepreneur they are eligible for these deductions. Local and state governments, partnering with nongovernmental organizations like the Freelancers Union, could distribute information and educate these 1099 workers about how to take advantage of self-employment provisions in the federal tax code. These workers are leaving a lot of money on the table by not taking all the tax deductions for which they are eligible. And much of that realized potential would come from federal tax deductions, so that would be money received from the feds and spent in the local economy. That would result in a win-win for the workers as well as the local and state economies.

Internet access and speed. Many 1099ers increasingly rely on the Internet to make their living, yet Internet access in the U.S. remains expensive and the speeds are slow (especially compared to international competitors). Government could partner with the private sector to ensure an affordable, high-speed Internet connection in every community, and this would greatly benefit those indie and freelancing workers who depend on the Internet for their occupations, enhancing their income opportunities and increasing their potential for more sales of services and products.

Political reform. Finally, anyone watching the three-ring circus in Washington, D.C., is painfully aware that politics in the United States—especially at the federal level—is working poorly. It will be difficult to enact the right policy responses if the political system has been "captured" by elite economic forces. Sadly, that "postdemocratic" outcome appears to be occurring, as the U.S. becomes more and more an extractive system. The United States badly needs political reforms that will allow the needs of American workers and the middle class to have a more solid seat at the table of political power.

Here are six important political changes that would vastly improve U.S. representative democracy: public financing of campaigns, free media time for qualified candidates, automatic (universal) voter registration of all eligible Americans, national direct election of the president, abolition of the filibuster in the U.S. Senate and proportional representation electoral systems for electing all legislative chambers. These reforms together, enacted at federal, state and local levels, would provide a powerful and badly needed jolt to the American republic. They would foster a multiparty democracy in which new political parties and leaders could emerge, capable of articulating a pro-worker and "stakeholder society" agenda, and pushing for changes such as a new safety net/social contract via Individual Security Accounts, job sharing, codetermination as well as nonprofit health care, expanded Social Security and more. Such a renewed democracy would advance a more participatory and engaged citizenry, which in turn would produce policy that better reflects the priorities of everyday Americans, and create an inclusive nation that works for the many instead of the few.

All of my proposed changes would help evolve the United States in a direction that better prepares it for the new economy and for the Information and Innovation Age. Many other proposals have been put forward by smart, credible thought leaders seeking to find ways to modernize the U.S. economy, and quite a few have merit. I'm thinking of proposals such as more physical infrastructure spending as a way of updating our roads, bridges, airports, seaports, schools and buildings, which would also create more jobs; creating an infrastructure bank for that purpose; increasing the minimum wage; investing more in clean energies; taxing capital gains at the same rate as any other form of income; eliminating tax benefits that encourage offshoring; expanding AmeriCorps, which would directly create jobs for out-of-work young Americans; strengthening and better enforcing labor laws; and numerous other proposals.[43]

While there are many good ideas worthy of consideration, not all of them deal with the fundamental crisis of figuring out how to redesign our safety net for the army of 1099 and part-time employees who work for multiple employers. Also many meritorious proposals don't focus on what to do about the looming era of "technological unemployment" and Economic Singularity, or on the crisis created by increasing numbers of U.S. workers becoming untethered like helium balloons from good and secure jobs offered by conscientious employers who have acted as mini New Deal hosts for their workers. Many laudable reforms also don't directly deal with workers' loss of political power. I have focused most of my recommendations on those specific dilemmas.

While ideally these changes would be implemented on the national level, so that all businesses and employers are subjected to the same rules, it's not necessary. These changes can be implemented at the local or state level as well. Three states (California, Connecticut and Massachusetts) and 18 cities (including Washington, D.C., New York City, Philadelphia and Seattle) have passed paid sick leave policies.[44] San Francisco, where I live, has a paid sick leave policy, as well as a requirement that city contractors must provide to their covered employees twelve paid days off per year.[45] Also in San Francisco the city government passed a law for universal health-care coverage before Obamacare was passed, which created health-care accounts for uncovered workers employed by certain businesses that were notorious for not providing health care for their employees (especially restaurants and other service-sector jobs). The employers either had to provide insurance or pay into each worker's health-care account a certain amount of money, which could be used by the worker to purchase health insurance. The businesses were allowed to pass that cost on to their customers (San Francisco restaurants patrons saw a new charge on their bill of 4 percent, dedicated to providing health care for these workers).

A similar strategy could be used for requiring employers in a particular city or state to pay into existing safety-net systems for each of their 1099 workers, or to establish Individual Security Accounts. It's not necessary to wait for Washington to get its act together (which could be a very long wait indeed). Passing the right laws and regulations at the local and state levels could start the transition toward the right kind of new economy. In some cases, "angel employers" could implement these policies within their own companies and push for it within their industries. In March 2015, Microsoft took a step in that direction, announcing that its 2,000 vendors and contractors would have to provide 15 paid days off (for sick days and/or vacation time) to their employees who do work for Microsoft. Microsoft's representative Bradford Smith explained the company's rationale, saying, "The research shows that employees who do get these kinds of benefits are far likelier to be happier, have higher morale and are far more likely to be productive."[46]

And then there are some bad ideas . . .

Alongside the many good ideas out there are also some bad ones. Already in chapter 7 we saw that some well-meaning business and economic leaders have proposed a guaranteed living allowance to ensure that demobilized workers who can't find employment in a job-constrained environment don't sink below an inhumane existence. But this "toss 'em a bone" solution will only create a permanent underclass reminiscent of life in Imperial Rome. Too much idle time and a lack of meaningful work will breed the wrong kind of mischief. Rather than throwing a few coins to those on the lowest rungs, it would be far better to put that money toward creating large and cost-effective pools of social insurance for personal needs like health care, unemployment, injured worker compensation, paid sick leave, vocational training and more. The resulting economies of scale would produce an affordable safety basket for everyone.

Also in the category of bad ideas: it is time to admit that certain past policies have failed. Some of these include too-low income taxes on the wealthy and restrictive labor laws that have severely curtailed the level of union membership. Both of these stand out, like a person in a bathing suit at the North Pole, because they have coincided so contemporaneously with rising levels of inequality, middle-class insecurity, flattened wages and decreased prospects for so many. With the wealthy hoovering up more and more of the nation's wealth, and passing less of it on to American workers, that has left insufficient financial resources for other badly needed priorities. Historically, progressive taxation has limited the concentration of income and wealth and also provided crucially needed revenue for social spending, research and development, physical infrastructure spending and other important national needs that today are being short-shrifted due to lack of funding. As economist Thomas Piketty has emphasized, progressive taxation of income and wealth has a strong influence on the structure of inequality in market economies. If the tax rates on the affluent become too low, over time that results in a strong tendency to accumulate ever greater amounts of wealth (which is passed on to their heirs), further distorting not only aggregate consumer demand (and creeping toward an Economic Singularity) but also corrupting politics, resulting in an extractive system.

It's useful to remind ourselves that under two previous Republican presidents, the highest income tax bracket was as high as 90 percent (under Dwight Eisenhower, in the 1950s) and 50 percent (under Ronald Reagan in the 1980s), and yet the national economy still chugged ahead with great power and steam.[47] Today the highest income tax bracket is less than 40 percent—and unsurprisingly the wealthy own and control a lot more of everything than they used to. Beyond the actual tax rate, upper income Americans benefit from numerous loopholes and tax-deferred subsidies for things like home mortgage interest deductions, 401(k)-type savings accounts, inheritance tax loopholes and more that Americans with less income do not benefit much from, if at all (for example, federal subsidies for the home mortgage interest deduction amount to around $70 billion per year, yet 86 percent of this deduction goes to the top 10 percent income bracket; meanwhile, the federal government's largest affordable housing program spent barely half that amount).[48]

Wealthy corporations and hedge funds also profit immensely from the low effective taxation rate on capital gains, and tax avoidance schemes like offshoring of profits (the latter alone costs the U.S. Treasury $100 billion to $200 billion yearly). Eliminating these tax rules that shelter high-income households and corporations would raise their effective tax rates and make the tax code more fair and better aligned with crucial national priorities. Adding a financial transactions tax would raise $200 billion and reduce purely speculative stock market trading, as well as erratic algorithmic trading on Wall Street.[49]

Also, as we have seen, with labor laws being so weak and undermining the organization of unions, average workers have lost much of their bargaining power with employers. The balance between employers and employees, between business and labor, is a delicate one, like the wings of an aircraft in which you need both right and left to fly. Today, that delicate balance has tilted too far in one direction, producing an aircraft that is badly careening off course and is threatening to crash.

Bosses and CEOs, of course, want minimal regulation and maximum unilateral power to decide matters for their businesses. But as the financial collapse of 2008 showed, what they want is not always good for the broader macroeconomy. There are a number of examples of advanced economies, such as Germany's and Sweden's, in which they have struck a different balance between the various economic sectors without compromising competitiveness or commercial success. Thomas Geoghegan's proposals from chapter

9, such as making the right to organize a labor union a civil right, and also resetting the rules to allow "proportional unionism," seem like good places to start in a bid to revive labor unions, as well as David Rolf's ideas for incubating and encouraging a new breed of Labor 3.0 organizations.

There are many potential ways to use the tax code to better distribute the aggregate wealth to benefit society, as well as to rectify the defects in labor law with a goal of fostering a new and healthy power balance between employers and employees. We have nothing to lose by trying new approaches and directions.

TWELVE
CONCLUSION
MARIA'S LIFE MATTERS! LONG LIVE MARIA FERNANDES!

IF I COULD BUNDLE ALL THE SOLUTIONS AND REFORMS I HAVE PROPOSED IN the previous two chapters into one omnibus piece of legislation, I would call it the Maria Fernandes Matters Act, to honor the deceased Dunkin' Donuts worker we met in chapter 1 so that her short, 32-year life would not have ended in vain. According to the official coroner's report, Maria died in her Dunkin' Donuts uniform from asphyxiation while she slept in her automobile between shifts, done in by a deadly dose of carbon monoxide fumes from a gas can she kept in her car; in reality, she died from her exhaustion over working three part-time jobs, as she scrambled to make ends meet. Her bleak options left her living too close to the edge, unmoored from any semblance of a caring society, with not enough of a safety net to catch her as she began to fall. Many people who heard about Maria's tragedy were shocked—no doubt because quite a few of them thought: "There, but for the grace of God, go I."

For far too many Americans, it is becoming agonizingly clear that their own situation increasingly shares some uncomfortable realities with Maria's. More Americans, as they venture further out on the limb alone, are faced with conflicting choices that make their working lives feel like a gamble. *New York Times* columnist Paul Krugman reported about a recent household survey conducted by the U.S. Federal Reserve, which found that "47 percent said that they do not have the resources to meet an unexpected expense of $400" and "would have to sell something or borrow to meet that need." Only $400! More than 3 in 10 Americans reported going without some kind of medical care in the past year because they couldn't afford it, and the same number have no retirement savings or pension.[1] Americans are entering a new era of anxious de-humanity that most of us have not known in the post–World War II period.

This shift manifests in numerous ways, little and grand. As we have seen in previous chapters, a shuttle driver for Facebook or Google must choose between working split shifts that result in a 16-hour day, or being home for his children's bedtime and breakfast; an autoworker for one of the Big Three labors as a perma-temp for a subcontractor, for years denied the higher wages, benefits and job protections accorded to the permanent employees he works alongside; a task rabbit hustles from gig to gig, trying to please her multiple employers in a single day, earning $250 one day but nothing for the next eight days and now she can't pay her utility bill; an Uber driver chases what's left of the American Dream in his car, driving for a company that chops his wages without warning and disrespects him (and everyone else) with impunity; an elderly Airbnb host feels remorse over operating an illegal hotel, and seeing neighbors evicted by greedy professional landlords, but she's in survival mode so she turns her decades-old home into an inn for trendy tourists, for as many nights as she can tolerate; a laid-off newspaper reporter tries to become a freelance journalist and has to choose between new school clothes for her kids or outfitting her home office with new equipment.

Faced with tough choices, some Americans have tried to put on a brave face and make it work by going solo. The *New York Times* published interviews with some "solo-preneurs" who tried to turn their own personal lemons into lemonade. Rona Economou worked as a lawyer at a large Manhattan law firm until she was laid off. She decided to pursue her dream of opening a Greek food stall at a local street market. This was supposed to be her "chance to indulge a passion, lead a healthier life." Instead she found herself working seven days a week, sunup to sundown. "The second I feel a cold coming on, I'm taking Cold-Eeze, eating raw garlic," she told the *Times*. "I can't afford to shut the shop down," especially since no employer now pays for her sick leave or health care. A healthier life is not on the menu, it seems.[2]

Rona is not alone. It's not that easy to make it on your own, yet in the first two years after the economic collapse, with unemployment soaring across the country, more Americans started businesses—565,000 of them a month in 2010—than at any period in the previous decade and a half.[3] Despite that plucky can-do American spirit, most of those new entrepreneurs did not succeed (though Rona Economou's food stall has hung in there). According to Paul Bernard, who advises professionals on how to start a small business, "The reality is that, even during boom times, most new businesses fail." He decried the media for making heroes out of former lawyers and investment bankers who relaunched themselves as profitable cupcake kings and dog-jewelry designers, since it gives a false impression of the hardships of going it alone.[4]

Unquestionably for more and more Americans, the working life has become a greater gamble. Some of these freelancers, contractors, temps and solo-preneurs will make it in their new careers, but, statistically speaking, more will fail. Others will end up somewhere in between, holding on to a precarious existence. But nearly all of them will end up with a less secure life, wondering month after month if they will be able to find enough new clients or customers to pay for their lives. Many of them will have to cope with the physical exhaustion, lack of certainty and sleep and loss of free time and the emotional roller coaster that comes with suddenly being thrust into the precarious life of being a 1099 worker or self-employed. And naturally they will have none of the safety-net supports that come with a traditional job, unless they can afford to purchase them on their own. They also don't qualify for any compensation when they are unemployed, sick or injured on the job, and they don't get paid while they continually look for their next job. Even an increasing number of regularly employed, full-time workers are feeling the squeeze, with less job security, declining wages and a shredding safety net to catch them if they fall off the path. In so many ways, the reality of the indie worker's life is the exact opposite of what the evangelists of the new economy have been promoting.

The origins of this crisis-in-progress are clear: businesses are using all sorts of legal loopholes and tricks to "1099" their employees as a way of dodging responsibility for providing good, decent, middle-class jobs. Employers are taking advantage of ruinous labor and economic policies that allow them to turn their workforces on and off at will, like one switches off a water faucet. The labor movement, once the guardian of American workers, has been whittled back to a remnant of its former self. Increasingly, intrusive robots, automation and AI are creating ever more opportunities for businesses to function with fewer workers and to deep-six the social contract between employers and employees. And in the latest troubling trend, Web- and app-based technologies of the so-called "sharing" economy have made it astonishingly easy to hire indie contractors, freelancers, temps and part-timers. Why wouldn't every employer eventually replace all of their regularly employed W–2 workers with as many robots and 1099 workers as possible? A business owner would be crazy not to, watching as competitors go this route and dramatically slash their labor costs by a third or more. These strategies are the new performance steroids of the economy—once the competing businesses in your industry or occupation are doing it, you don't dare not do it.

With the world rushing toward a convergence between the developed and developing worlds, and inequality mounting around the globe, more and more people—even those used to a middle-class existence—are becoming "contingent." Whether you are a task rabbit, perma-temp, gig-preneur, casual labor, self-employed, solo-preneur or some other name, it all pretty much adds up to the same thing: more and more workers are facing a work world in which they are treated like just another input for employers to feed into their business machines. Consequently, millions of U.S. workers are on increasingly shaky ground in this new economy.

The solutions and reforms that I have proposed are designed to update the social contract, renew the sense of economic security and rekindle the mutually beneficial relationship between employers and employees and the different stakeholders of the American dream. In the post–World War II era, the United States has been the wealthiest, most productive and most alluring nation because it created a middle class society that was the envy of the world. In our nation's 225-year history, the United States often has achieved greatness, arising from the ability of our political system and democratic culture to usher Americans past our national hatreds, ignorances and internal contradictions that have periodically laid us low.

But today, our national aspirations for greatness are faltering once again. In the 21st century, a nation as wealthy as the United States should not be a place where hardworking people like Maria Fernandes die alone in the parking lot of a convenience store as a result of poor working and living conditions; or where everyday Americans can't find the supportive safety net they need for themselves and their families; or where companies act like the robber barons of old, looking to "hire one half of the working class" to undercut the other half, to paraphrase Gilded Age railroad magnate Jay Gould.

No question, we are an affluent, technologically advanced country—but are we a humane, civilized society? Are we indeed "the Rulers *and* the Ruled," as it says on a painted ceiling fresco outside the chamber of the United States Senate? Or are we increasingly just "the Ruled"? Those are the daunting questions facing us today. If we don't alter the current trajectory, we will see many more Maria Fernandeses.

THE DIRECTION OF HISTORY'S ARROW

The evangelists of the new economy, including many technological and economic experts, often sound deterministic about the profound changes occurring in our society. We are told that the forces of modernization are inevitable, that they are being driven by the natural and immutable economic laws of "creative destruction" and the drive for technological innovation. We are told that technology is "special," and companies that conduct their business over the Internet and apps deserve an entitled place where the rules are different, and the usual laws and policies shouldn't apply. It's as if there is no driver to this self-steering machine, and any attempt to change the course is not only hopelessly doomed to fail but also standing in the way of "progress." Even worse, skeptical or critical voices are written off as those of New Deal revanchists or antitechnology Luddites. We are told this by many of the same experts who missed an $8 trillion housing bubble and were caught napping while the worst economic collapse since the Great Depression happened on their watch.

But in fact these changes are not natural or inevitable at all, they are very much "path dependent"—that is, the result of certain laws and regulations that have defined the present-day as well as historical relationships between business, workers, private property, government, technology and the larger society. Child labor once was allowed, as was the 60-hour work week; women and minorities were excluded from certain occupations, both by custom and law; workers' right to organize was suppressed and hindered, even more than it is today. But over time, those and other exploitative practices were banned, barred and abolished, viewed as not in keeping with American values or aspirations. We have a long history of shaping the national economy through government policy, as well as expanding popular participation and pluralism.

Thomas Jefferson, James Madison, Alexander Hamilton and others of that remarkable generation of "founding brothers" believed in an active citizenry engaged with their government; Hamilton in particular believed in a strong federal government that could forge a national economy out of a motley baker's dozen of states. Abraham Lincoln extolled government "of the people, by the people and for the people," and flexed the federal muscle bestowed upon him by Hamilton and others to end the horror of slavery, as well as to launch the construction of a transcontinental railroad (completed four years after his death, in 1869), which gave a major boost to the national infrastructure and economy.

Later presidents battled against oligarchic forces of immense power, which had been unleashed by the "creative destruction" of the Industrial Revolution in the late 19th and early 20th centuries (including the robber barons that Lincoln's railroad had spawned). President Teddy Roosevelt, in his first address to Congress in 1901, attacked corporate monopolies that were wrapping their tentacles around the nation's throat like a giant octopus (that was how contemporary cartoonists depicted the robber baron conglomerates). He attacked big-business practices that he called "real and grave evils," "hurtful to the general welfare" and "crimes of cunning," saying "great corporations exist only because they are created and safeguarded by our institutions; and it is therefore our right and our duty to see that they work in harmony with these institutions."[5] But the Trust Buster didn't just talk, like some presidents do; he used the "visible hand" of government to take action: he broke up the Northern Securities Company (which impacted the interests of powerful banking magnate J. P. Morgan), and he reined in other powerful companies like DuPont, American Tobacco Company and John D. Rockefeller's Standard Oil.

Roosevelt's successor, William Howard Taft, prosecuted monopolies even more vigorously, including breaking up the Standard Oil Company in 1911, which was one of the largest and most powerful companies of all time (a comparable act today, in terms of market value, would be like breaking up Goldman Sachs, ExxonMobil and Apple *combined*). Taft's moves were bold and gutsy, and his successor, Woodrow Wilson, marked the high point of Progressive reforms on the economy. Wilson said, "If there are men in this country big enough to own the government of the United States, they are going to own it." And so Wilson worked to pass the Clayton Antitrust Act in 1914 and created the Federal Trade Commission and the Federal Reserve Board to increase regulation of the financial sector and the national economy.[6]

The point is, every generation—and each presidential administration—must remain vigilant. Despite all the federal activity during the Progressive era to corral powerful and corrupt commercial interests, less than 20 years later there was Teddy's cousin, Franklin Roosevelt, in the midst of a Great Depression, railing against the practices of "the unscrupulous money changers,"[7] and articulating the greatness of a nation that had "come to a clear realization" that "true individual freedom cannot exist without economic security and independence."[8] The passage of the New Deal was both the result of a desire to better the living and working conditions of everyday Americans and a recognition that the national economy, when left to its own devices, tended to skid off the rails and crash over the cliff, after being driven there by the one-percenters of that time period.

The threat back then was from monopolies and dangerous concentrations of wealth that treated the economy like their own personal fiefdoms. Yet out of that decades-long battle came the social contract and a middle-class society, crystallized finally in the form of the New Deal and built upon over subsequent decades. The threat today not only is from the latest gang of robber barons who crashed the economy in 2008, but also because those elite interests are at the cusp of winning what they previously had lost: the reindenturing of American workers, and the unraveling of the social contract.

All of those presidents and leaders, and their uplifting oratory and ideals that undergirded bold policies, amounted to a grander, more generous vision for the world compared to the small, grubbing, libertarianism put forth by the likes of Travis Kalanick, Brian Chesky, Ross Ulbricht, Leah Busque, Stephane Kasriel and other Ayn Rand fundamentalists, *techno sapiens* and Silicon Valley apparatchiks. This current bunch of "unscrupulous money changers" has been 3D-printed from the same mold as Cornelius Vanderbilt, the 19th-century railroad and shipping magnate who famously said, "Law? What do I care about the law? H'ain't I got the power?"[9]

The democratic visions of Jefferson, Hamilton, Lincoln, Taft, Wilson, the Roosevelts and others were steeled in the struggles against kingly tyranny, slavery, civil war, greedy wealth and power, and finally a Great Depression that caused vast inequality. Responding to each era's challenges, these great American leaders proposed a renewed vision of representative government and responsible citizenry, both advancing as well as bound by laws and regulations; their proposed world was composed of multiple stakeholders participating in the arduous process of self-governance, and constructing a civil society so that we can build a world that works for the vast majority of all Americans. Making government work is a hard, hard business, requiring patience and a measure of fortitude, yet that—even more than technological innovation or creative destruction—is the golden contribution of our nation's legacy.

Don't get me wrong, I am not a knee-jerk foe of technology and innovation. I enjoy my iPhone and iPad as much as the next person. But how important are those trinkets, as well as all the other techno-flash jewelry being consumed today, in facing the most important challenges of the 21st century? We must develop the "precautionary principle" to say no, especially to any technology or innovation that poses a threat we don't understand. We should deploy appropriate levels of regulation to ensure that "creative destruction" remains as creative as it is destructive. And we should remain the master of technology, and not let it master us, by ensuring that our efforts to "transcend the human" don't result in our "forsaking humanism."[10]

Just as the New Deal social contract was created by a series of laws and institutions, so too will the downward spiral into a freelance society be defined by what should be called the Raw Deal social contract, and its related laws and institutions. Add to the looming Singularity crisis the challenges of global climate change and the government's intrusive, hyper-spying on all Americans, and that unholy trinity portends a dystopian future of alarming proportions.

Tragically, if our society continues to take the wrong fork in the road—if we make the wrong policy choices over the next generation—it will undermine our national future, perhaps irretrievably. The American republic may very well go the way of the Roman republic, which eventually transmogrified into a postdemocratic empire that was dominated by a small class of aristocratic elites who took advantage of numerous layers of informal and grey economies to extract for themselves the best of society's resources. I shudder at the prospect of a robotized, high-tech infested, surveillance-saturated and weaponized modern-day version of Imperial Rome on steroids. It would make for a great movie, no doubt—but only if the movie ends and viewers have the option of exiting the theater. How sad and tragic if it turns out that even the American republic, which has been the inspiration for so much good in the world, is fated to fulfill the prophecy of the early 20th-century German sociologist Robert Michel and his "iron law of oligarchy," which said that at the end of the day, even in a democracy, rule by an elite is inevitable.[11]

But I don't believe there is anything inevitable about this. We can take a different fork in the road. This process can be shaped and guided in a different way, along a different path—by smart government policy as well as by popular demand, as more and more people realize that, as workers, they are being rendered expendable and disposable, and as a society we are heading in a direction that will take us over yet another cliff.

Despite America's great wealth and power, at the current time we cannot match many of our international competitors when it comes to transitioning to a stakeholder society because we have the wrong institutions and regulations. But by passing the right laws and regulations at local, state and federal levels, and by providing incentives for the private sector, we can begin a transition to a more hopeful version of the new economy. This will not mean a "big-government" takeover, but rather a "smart-government" intercession using government's unique power to regulate and to bring various sectors of society to the negotiating table as a step toward achieving consensus over a new social contract and a new economy. A stakeholder society recognizes the legitimate interests of all its various stakeholders and uses the least level of government regulation necessary so as to prevent choking off entrepreneurship; but it also harnesses and steers the economy in a way that creates a vibrant climate for workers and consumers, in addition to businesses and entrepreneurs, each contributing their unique role to a virtuous circle in which "my spending is your income," and vice versa. These integral players do not have to be forever fated to be pitted against one another.

The wise words of President John F. Kennedy, which I invoked to open this book and which I now use to close it, eloquently combine the right mix of idealism and pragmatism and call forth the guiding spirit for the challenges that we face:

> How do we eradicate the barriers which separate substantial minorities of our citizens from access to education and employment on equal terms with the rest? How, in sum, can we make our free economy work at full capacity—that is, provide adequate profits for enterprise, adequate wages for labor, and opportunity for all?[12]

That was Kennedy in 1962, and since then and before, America has always been at its best when it stood for both the vibrancy of business and entrepreneurship ("profits for enterprise") as well as a square deal, a fair deal, a new deal for everyday working people ("adequate wages for labor . . . opportunity . . . access to education and employment"). All of it balanced by the "visible hand" of government, bringing the stakeholders to the table as partners. In the annals of the human trajectory, *that* tripartite balance, *that* audacious bid, is what has made us an indispensible nation and an inspiration to the world. We are only at the outset of what is bound to be a decades-long journey—"the end of the beginning"—to relaunch our nation in the right direction of History's Arrow. During that time, our way forward should be guided by our constantly asking and re-asking ourselves: Do we want a *new* New Deal—or a Raw Deal?

That is the choice we Americans face. Are we up to the task? The future Maria Fernandeses want to know. I pray that, once again, we are.

ACKNOWLEDGMENTS

IN WRITING A BOOK LIKE *RAW DEAL*, WHICH IS TRYING TO LOOK AT CURRENT trends and extrapolate to uncover their future impacts, I felt compelled to seek out numerous viewpoints as a cross-reference and reality check. In that regard, I am grateful to the following people, including colleagues, mentors and strangers, who provided helpful information, insight, feedback, perspective and wisdom.

Thanks to my colleagues at the New America Foundation, Sherle Schwenninger, Michael Lind, Anne-Marie Slaughter, Parag Khanna, Phil Longman and Barry Lynn; among former New America colleagues, Micah Weinberg, Mark Paul and Leif Hasse. A special thanks to Sascha Meinrath of X-Lab and Open Technology Institute, and Lenny Mendonca from McKinsey & Company and Peter Sims from Silicon Guild and BLK SHP. Thanks also to Daniel Pink, Adam Werbach, Tim O'Reilly, Dean Baker, David Rolf, Dmitri Iglitzin, Tom Geoghegan, Mark Breslin, Harold Meyerson, Bob Kuttner, Sarah Kessler, Peter Ginna, Martin Thunert, Philip Oltermann, Chris Jerdonek, Rob Richie, Jacob Hacker, Peter Richardson, Juliet Schor, the Freelancers Union's Sara Horowitz and Dan Lavoie, Jakob Köllhofer, and Tom Slee.

One of the central "characters" of this book is actually a place—my hometown of San Francisco. I have learned so much about its past, present and future as a result of talking to many, many people who have a stake in the "disruption" that is occurring in this land of earthquakes (technological, seismic and otherwise). I can't thank enough Steve Jones and Tim Redmond, formerly with the *Bay Guardian,* not only for their support for this project, but also their intrepid journalism over the years; also dear, sweet Ted Gullicksen, head of the Tenants Union, who has always been supportive of my work and who left us way too soon, but not before sharing his deep insights; the people's attorney, Joe Tobener, plus Randy Shaw, Matt Gonzalez, David Owen, Gray Brechin, Brant Arthur, Woody Hastings, June Brashares, Kelly

Dessaint and others for sharing their insights and experiences as knowledgeable denizens of the City of St. Francis.

A very special thank you to Theresa Flandrich, another star of this book, who opened my eyes to the "sharing face" of exploitation in her North Beach neighborhood. And to Frederic Larson and Catherine "Catbird" Blum for sharing their stories.

Plus thank you to the various 1099 workers, Uber and Lyft drivers, task rabbits, Google bus drivers and many other people whose voices have not been heard enough. I hope I have credibly represented their anonymous stories. They are unsung heroes.

Thank you to my agent, Don Fehr from Trident Media Group, and his assistant Brittany Lloyd, for ably steering this project into a good port. And also to my editor at St. Martin's Press, Karen Wolny, and her assistant Laura Apperson as well as Gabrielle Gantz and Christine Catarino, for assisting me every step of the way toward launching the boat from the safe harbor into unknown but adventurous waters. Thanks for their patience and guidance. Thanks also to the production crew, led by Alan Bradshaw, and copyeditors Ryan Masteller and Joshua Evans, and countless others who moved this project along.

And once again, I must express my deepest gratitude to my life partner, Lucy Colvin, for her invaluable feedback on the manuscript and spirited discussions, and also for her love, patience and encouragement during the many months while I was grinding out this book. Thanks for peeling me off my chair and taking me out into the sun every now and then. I guess it's my turn to cook, eh?

Thanks to everyone for your support and encouragement. I couldn't have done this without you.

Steven Hill
San Francisco

NOTES

INTRODUCTION

1. John F. Kennedy, "Yale University Commencement," Miller Center, University of Virginia, June 11, 1962, http://millercenter.org/president/speeches/speech-3370 (accessed April 2, 2015).
2. Marc Andreessen, "Why Software Is Eating the World," *Wall Street Journal,* August 20, 2011, http://www.wsj.com/articles/SB10001424053111903480904576512250915629460 (accessed June 11, 2015).
3. Steven T. Jones and Parker Yesko, "Into Thin Air: 'Shareable Housing' Is Causing Apartments to Vanish from SF's Rental Market—Yet Popular, Profitable Sites Like Airbnb Violate Local Laws," *San Francisco Bay Guardian,* August 6, 2013, http://www.sfbg.com/2013/08/06/thin-air (accessed March 20, 2015).
4. Evelyn M. Rusli, "Uber CEO Travis Kalanick: We're Doubling Revenue Every Six Months," *Wall Street Journal,* July 6, 2014, http://blogs.wsj.com/digits/2014/06/06/uber-ceo-travis-kalanick-were-doubling-revenue-every-six-months/ (accessed March 20, 2015).
5. Casey Newton, "Temping Fate: Can TaskRabbit Go from Side Gigs to Real Jobs?" *The Verge,* May 23, 2013, http://www.theverge.com/2013/5/23/4352116/taskrabbit-temp-agency-gig-economy (accessed March 20, 2015).
6. See, for example, "The Future of Work: There's an App for That," *The Economist,* January 3, 2015, http://www.economist.com/news/briefing/21637355-freelance-workers-available-moments-notice-will-reshape-nature-companies-and (accessed March 20, 2015).
7. Darwin Bond Graham, "Uber's Tax-Avoidance Strategy Costs Government Millions. How's That for 'Sharing'?" *48 Hills,* July 1, 2014, http://48hills.org/2014/07/10/ubers-tax-avoidance-strategy-costs-government-millions/ (accessed March 30, 2015).
8. Drew DeSilver, "U.S. Income Inequality, on Rise for Decades, Is Now Highest since 1928," *Fact Tank: News in the Numbers,* December 5, 2013, http://www.pewresearch.org/fact-tank/2013/12/05/u-s-income-inequality-on-rise-for-decades-is-now-highest-since-1928/ (accessed March 20, 2015).
9. Emmanuel Saez and Gabriel Zucman, "Wealth Inequality in the United States since 2013: Evidence from Capitalized Income Tax Data," NBER Working Paper Series: Working Paper 20625, October 2014, http://www.gabriel-zucman.eu/files/SaezZucman2014.pdf (accessed March 20, 2015).
10. Jesse Bricker, Lisa J. Dettling, Alice Henriques, Joanne W. Hsu, Kevin B. Moore, John Sabelhaus, Jeffrey Thompson, and Richard A. Windle, "Changes in U.S.

Family Finances from 2010 to 2013: Evidence from the Survey of Consumer Finances," *Federal Reserve Bulletin* 100, no. 4 (September 2014), http://www.federalreserve.gov/pubs/bulletin/2014/pdf/scf14.pdf (accessed March 29, 2015); cited in Matt Bruenig, "The Top 10% of White Families Own Almost Everything," *Demos,* September 5, 2014, http://www.demos.org/blog/9/5/14/top-10-white-families-own-almost-everything (accessed March 29, 2015).

11. Tim Fernholz, "The Bottom Ninety Percent of US Families Are No Wealthier Than in 1986," *Quartz,* October 18, 2014, http://qz.com/283059/ninety-percent-of-us-families-are-no-wealthier-than-they-were-in-1986/ (accessed March 20, 2015).
12. Floyd Norris, "Corporate Profits Grow and Wages Slide," *New York Times,* April 4, 2014, http://www.nytimes.com/2014/04/05/business/economy/corporate-profits-grow-ever-larger-as-slice-of-economy-as-wages-slide.html (accessed May 13, 2015).
13. David Wessel, "Big U.S. Firms Shift Hiring Abroad: Work Forces Shrink at Home, Sharpening Debate on Economic Impact of Globalization," *Wall Street Journal,* April 19, 2011, http://www.wsj.com/articles/SB10001424052748704821704576270783611823972 (accessed March 20, 2015).
14. Scott Thurm, "U.S. Firms Add Jobs, but Mostly Overseas," *Wall Street Journal,* April 27, 2012, http://www.wsj.com/articles/SB10001424052702303990604577367881972648906 (accessed May 13, 2015).
15. Rana Foroohar, "The Artful Dodgers: Companies That Flee the U.S. to Avoid Taxes Have Forgotten How They Got So Big in the First Place," *Time,* September 11, 2014, http://time.com/3326573/the-artful-dodgers/ (accessed March 15, 2015).
16. Floyd Norris, "Corporate Profits Grow and Wages Slide," *New York Times,* April 4, 2014, http://www.nytimes.com/2014/04/05/business/economy/corporate-profits-grow-ever-larger-as-slice-of-economy-as-wages-slide.html (accessed May 13, 2015).
17. Joel Friedman, "The Decline of Corporate Income Tax Revenues," Center on Budget and Policy Priorities, October 24, 2003, page 3, http://www.cbpp.org/files/10-16-03tax.pdf (accessed on March 29, 2015).
18. See "Policy Basics: Where Do Federal Tax Revenues Come From?" Center on Budget and Policy Priorities, March 11, 2015, www.cbpp.org/cms/?fa=view&id=3822; and Friedman, "The Decline of Corporate Income Tax Revenues," pages 4–5.
19. Barbara Garson, "Freelance Nation: When Good Jobs Turn to Bad," Salon, August 20, 2013, http://www.salon.com/2013/08/20/freelance_nation_when_good_jobs_turn_to_bad_partner (accessed March 30, 2015).
20. United States Census Bureau, "Income, Poverty and Health Insurance Coverage in the United States: 2013," United States Census Bureau Newsroom, September 16, 2014, http://www.census.gov/newsroom/press-releases/2014/cb14-169.html (accessed March 21, 2015).
21. "The Low-Wage Recovery: Industry Employment and Wages Four Years into the Recovery," National Employment Law Project, April 2014, http://www.nelp.org/content/uploads/2015/03/Low-Wage-Recovery-Industry-Employment-Wages-2014-Report.pdf (accessed April 28, 2015), page 2.
22. United States Conference of Mayors, press release, August 11, 2014, http://www.usmayors.org/pressreleases/uploads/2014/0811-release-metroeconwagegap.pdf (accessed March 20, 2015); Bernice Napach, "Why Wages Will Stagnate for Another 14 Years," interview with Tyler Cowan, *Yahoo!,* August 14, 2014, http://finance.yahoo.com/news/in-this-job-market-the-trend-is-not-your-friend-144022484.html (accessed March 20, 2015).
23. Kevin Roose, "Does Silicon Valley Have a Contract-Worker Problem?" *New York,* September 18, 2014, http://nymag.com/daily/intelligencer/2014/09/silicon

-valleys-contract-worker-problem.html; see also Edward Walker, "Beyond the Rhetoric of the 'Sharing Economy,'" *Contexts* 14 (Winter 2015): 12–19, doi: 10.1177/1536504214567860, http://ctx.sagepub.com/content/14/1/12.full.pdf+html, page 16.

24. Mike Berg, *Invisible to Remarkable: In Today's Job Market, You Need to Sell Yourself as "Talent," Not Just Someone Looking for Work* (Bloomington, IN: iUniverse, 2012), 13.
25. Sara Horowitz and Fabio Rosati, "53 Million Americans Are Freelancing, New Survey Finds," *Freelancers Union,* September 4, 2014, https://www.freelancersunion.org/blog/dispatches/2014/09/04/53million (accessed March 29, 2015).
26. MBO Partners, "2014 State of Independence in America Report," http://info.mbopartners.com/rs/mbo/images/2014-MBO_Partners_State_of_Independence_Report.pdf (accessed March 20, 2015); see also Susan Adams, "More Than a Third of U.S. Workers Are Freelancers Now, but Is That Good for Them?" *Forbes,* September 5, 2014, http://www.forbes.com/sites/susanadams/2014/09/05/more-than-a-third-of-u-s-workers-are-freelancers-now-but-is-that-good-for-them/ (accessed March 20, 2015).
27. Eric Morath, "Broadest Unemployment Measure 'Less Rosy,'" *Wall Street Journal,* March 15, 2015, http://www.wsj.com/articles/broadest-unemployment-measure-less-rosy-1426461694 (accessed April 6, 2015).
28. Oxford Martin School, "NEWS RELEASE: Oxford Martin School Study Shows Nearly Half of US Jobs Could Be at Risk of Computerisation," September 18, 2013, http://www.futuretech.ox.ac.uk/news-release-oxford-martin-school-study-shows-nearly-half-us-jobs-could-be-risk-computerisation (accessed March 20, 2015).
29. Andy Mukherjee, "Robots May Spell 'Control-Alt-Delete' for Workers," *Reuters,* October 23, 2014, http://blogs.reuters.com/breakingviews/2014/10/23/robots-may-spell-control-alt-delete-for-workers/ (accessed March 20, 2015).
30. Erik Brynjolfsson and Andrew McAfee, *The Second Machine Age: Work, Progress, and Prosperity in a Time of Brilliant Technologies* (New York: W. W. Norton, 2014).
31. Aaron Smith and Janna Anderson, "AI, Robotics, and the Future of Jobs," Pew Research Center Report, August 6, 2014, http://www.pewinternet.org/2014/08/06/future-of-jobs/ (accessed March 20, 2015).
32. Farhad Manjoo, "Will Robots Steal Your Job? You're Highly Educated. You Make a Lot of Money. You Should Still Be Afraid," *Slate,* September 26, 2011, http://www.slate.com/articles/technology/robot_invasion/2011/09/will_robots_steal_your_job.html (accessed March 20, 2015).
33. Neil Irwin, "Aughts Were a Lost Decade for U.S. Economy, Workers," *Washington Post,* January 2, 2010, http://www.washingtonpost.com/wp-dyn/content/article/2010/01/01/AR2010010101196.html (accessed March 20, 2015).
34. Tomio Geron, "Airbnb and the Unstoppable Rise of the Share Economy," *Forbes,* February 11, 2013, http://www.forbes.com/sites/tomiogeron/2013/01/23/airbnb-and-the-unstoppable-rise-of-the-share-economy/ (accessed March 20, 2015).
35. Ibid.
36. Charlie Pye, reader's comment in Sarah Kessler, "Pixel & Dimed: On (Not) Getting By in the Gig Economy," *Fast Company,* May 2014, http://www.fastcompany.com/3027355/pixel-and-dimed-on-not-getting-by-in-the-gig-economy (accessed March 20, 2015).
37. Kessler, "Pixel & Dimed."
38. Bambi Francisco Roizen, "Crowdflower Helps You Earn Extra Bucks," *Vator.tv,* March 30, 2010, interview with Lukas Biewald, http://vator.tv/news/2010

-03-30-crowdflower-helps-you-earn-extra-bucks. His comment is made at the 5:09 mark on the video.

39. Caille Millner, "Cheap Labor Is Part of American Life," *San Francisco Examiner,* December 13, 2013, http://www.sfgate.com/living/article/Cheap-labor-is-part-of-American-life-5063133.php (accessed March 20, 2015).
40. Newton, "Temping Fate: Can TaskRabbit Go from Side Gigs to Real Jobs?"
41. Nick Timiraos and Kris Hudson, "How a Two-Tier Economy Is Reshaping the U.S. Marketplace: The Advance of Wealthy Households, While Middle- and Lower-Income Americans Struggle, Is Reshaping Markets for Everything from Housing to Clothing to Beer," *Wall Street Journal,* January 28, 2015, http://www.wsj.com/articles/how-a-two-tier-economy-is-reshaping-the-u-s-marketplace-1422502201 (accessed March 20, 2015).
42. All capitalisms are not the same. For example, in my book *Europe's Promise: Why the European Way Is the Best Hope in an Insecure Age* (Berkeley: University of California Press, 2010), I made a distinction between the Wall Street capitalism practiced in the United States and the "social capitalism" practiced in Europe.
43. Sara Horowitz, "How Do We Define True Wealth? (And How Do We Get There?)," *Freelancers Union,* Freelancers Broadcasters Network, January 11, 2014, https://www.freelancersunion.org/blog/dispatches/2014/01/09/q-juliet-schor/ (accessed March 20, 2015).
44. Dani Rodrik, "From Welfare State to Innovation State," *Project Syndicate,* January 24, 2015, http://www.project-syndicate.org/commentary/labor-saving-technology-by-dani-rodrik-2015-01 (accessed March 20, 2015).
45. Laura Shin, "The 85 Richest People in the World Have as Much Wealth as the 3.5 Billion Poorest," *Forbes,* January 23, 2014, http://www.forbes.com/sites/laurashin/2014/01/23/the-85-richest-people-in-the-world-have-as-much-wealth-as-the-3-5-billion-poorest/ (accessed March 20, 2015).

CHAPTER 1

1. Alexandra Goldman, "Curbing the Google Bus," *Al Jazeera America,* February 5, 2014, http://america.aljazeera.com/opinions/2014/2/google-bus-san-franciscopublictransitrentgentrification.html (accessed March 20, 2015).
2. Alexandra Goldman, "The 'Google Shuttle Effect': Gentrification and San Francisco's Dot Com Boom 2.0," Professional Report, University California at Berkeley, Spring 2013, http://svenworld.com/wp-content/uploads/2014/01/Goldman_PRFinal.pdf (accessed March 20, 2015).
3. Joe Fitzgerald Rodriguez, "Activists, Union Challenge Google Bus Pilot Program," *Bay Guardian,* February 19, 2014, http://www.sfbg.com/politics/2014/02/19/activists-union-challenge-google-bus-pilot-program (accessed April 29, 2015).
4. John Coté and Marisa Lagos, "Google Says $6.8 Million for Youth Muni Passes Just a Start," *San Francisco Chronicle,* February 28, 2014, http://www.sfgate.com/news/article/Google-says-6-8-million-for-youth-Muni-passes-5273937.php (accessed March 20, 2015).
5. Rebecca Solnit, "Diary," *London Review of Books,* February 7, 2013, http://www.lrb.co.uk/v35/n03/rebecca-solnit/diary (accessed March 20, 2015).
6. Jeff Elder, "Google to Make Security Guards Employees, Rather Than Contractors," *Wall Street Journal,* October 3, 2014, http://blogs.wsj.com/digits/2014/10/03/google-to-make-security-guards-as-employees-rather-than-contractors/ (accessed March 20, 2015).
7. Aaron Taube, "Facebook Shuttle Bus Driver Explains Why He's Furious about His Job," *Business Insider,* November 18, 2014, http://www.businessinsider

.com/facebook-bus-driver-explains-why-hes-furious-2014-11 (accessed April 29, 2015).

8. Kristen V. Brown, "Facebook's Bus Drivers Push to Unionize," *San Francisco Chronicle,* November 19, 2014, http://www.sfgate.com/news/article/Facebook-bus-drivers-push-to-unionize-5804445.php (accessed March 20, 2015).
9. Teamsters, "Long Days, Low Pay for Facebook Drivers," *Teamsters News,* October 3, 2014, http://teamster.org/news/2014/10/long-days-low-pay-facebook-drivers (accessed March 20, 2015).
10. Jessica Guynn, "It's a Long, Tiring Haul for Silicon Valley Bus Drivers," *USA Today,* August 14, 2014, http://www.usatoday.com/story/tech/2014/08/13/facebook-shuttle-bus-drivers/13478347/ (accessed March 20, 2015).
11. Steven Greenhouse, "Facebook's Shuttle Bus Drivers Seek to Unionize," *New York Times,* October 5, 2014, http://www.nytimes.com/2014/10/06/business/facebooks-bus-drivers-seek-union.html (accessed March 30, 2015).
12. Teamsters, "Facebook Drivers Vote to Join Teamsters," *Teamsters News,* November 19, 2014, http://teamster.org/news/2014/11/facebook-drivers-vote-join-teamsters (accessed March 20, 2015).
13. Darwin Bond Graham, "The Flipside of San Francisco's Displacement Crisis: The Influx of the Very Rich," *48 Hills,* May 5, 2014, http://48hills.org/2014/05/05/flipside-san-franciscos-displacement-crisis-influx-rich-darwin-bond-graham-yahoo-began-running-hulking-purple-buses-san-francisco-2005-google-followed-two-years-lat/#permanently-moved (accessed March 20, 2015).
14. Jessica Guynn, "San Francisco Split by Silicon Valley's Wealth," *Phys.org,* August 22, 2013, http://phys.org/news/2013-08-san-francisco-silicon-valley-wealth.html (accessed March 20, 2015).
15. Brown, "Facebook's Bus Drivers Push to Unionize."
16. Clifford Coonan, "Workers Threaten Mass Suicide at Company That Supplies Apple," *The Independent,* January 12, 2012, http://www.independent.co.uk/news/world/asia/workers-threaten-mass-suicide-at-company-that-supplies-apple-6288160.html (accessed March 20, 2015).
17. Lydia DePillis, "This Is What a Job in the U.S.'s New Manufacturing Industry Looks Like," *Washington Post,* March 9, 2014, http://www.washingtonpost.com/blogs/wonkblog/wp/2014/03/09/this-is-what-a-job-in-the-u-s-new-manufacturing-industry-looks-like/ (accessed March 20, 2015).
18. Rebecca Smith and Claire Mckenna, "How the Domestic Outsourcing of Blue-Collar Jobs Harms America's Workers," National Employment Law Project and National Staffing Workers Alliance, March 2015, http://www.nelp.org/content/uploads/2015/03/Temped-Out.pdf (accessed April 29, 2015), page 1.
19. Michael Grabell, "The Expendables: How the Temps Who Power Corporate Giants Are Getting Crushed," *ProPublica,* June 27, 2013, http://www.propublica.org/article/the-expendables-how-the-temps-who-power-corporate-giants-are-getting-crushed (accessed March 20, 2015).
20. Ibid.
21. Rebecca Smith, "The Permanent Temp Economy," *US News and World Report,* September 8, 2014, http://www.usnews.com/opinion/articles/2014/09/08/nations-growing-numbers-of-temp-workers-need-labor-protections-unions (accessed March 20, 2015).
22. Michael Grabell, "Temporary Work, Lasting Harm," *ProPublica,* December 18, 2013, http://www.propublica.org/article/temporary-work-lasting-harm (accessed March 20, 2015).
23. Michael Grabell, "Taken for a Ride: Temp Agencies and 'Raiteros' in Immigrant Chicago," *ProPublica,* April 29, 2013, http://www.propublica.org/article/taken

-for-a-ride-temp-agencies-and-raiteros-in-immigrant-chicago (accessed March 20, 2015).

24. Steven Greenhouse, "U.S. Cracks Down on 'Contractors' as a Tax Dodge," *New York Times,* February 17, 2010, http://www.nytimes.com/2010/02/18/business/18workers.html?_r=1 (accessed March 21, 2015).
25. Cari Tuna, "Employers and Workers Clash in Court Over 'Contractor' Label," *Wall Street Journal,* October 20, 2009, http://www.wsj.com/news/articles/SB10001424052748704112904574477991168814928 (accessed May 5, 2015); also see Donna Goodison, "Ex-Cable Installer Sues Comcast," *Boston Herald,* October 2, 2009, http://www.bostonherald.com/business/business_markets/2009/10/ex_cable_installer_sues_comcast (accessed May 5, 2015), page 27.
26. Greenhouse, "U.S. Cracks Down on 'Contractors' as a Tax Dodge."
27. Lauren Weber, "Wage-Law Enforcer Favors Proactive Approach," *Wall Street Journal,* http://www.wsj.com/articles/boss-talk-wage-law-enforcer-favors-proactive-approach-1419972132 (accessed March 21, 2015).
28. Greenhouse, "U.S. Cracks Down on 'Contractors' as a Tax Dodge."
29. James Surowiecki, "The Underground Recovery," *New Yorker,* April 29, 2013, http://www.newyorker.com/magazine/2013/04/29/the-underground-recovery (accessed March 21, 2015).
30. Greenhouse, "U.S. Cracks Down on 'Contractors' as a Tax Dodge."
31. Claire Gordon, "How Employers Can Legally Strip Your Job of Benefits," *AOL Jobs,* April 27, 2012, http://jobs.aol.com/articles/2012/04/27/how-employers-can-legally-strip-your-job-of-benefits (accessed May 5, 2015).
32. Brian Pedersen, "Employees Turned into Contract Workers at Tucson PR Firm," *Arizona Daily Star,* March 18, 2009, http://tucson.com/news/employees-turned-into-contract-workers-at-tucson-pr-firm/article_1b109902-c538-55b5-9c8b-e6c91c51d13b.html (accessed March 30, 2015).
33. Tuna, "Employers and Workers Clash in Court over 'Contractor' Label."
34. National Employment Law Project, "Independent Contractor Misclassification Imposes Huge Costs on Workers and Federal and State Treasuries: A Survey of Research," *National Employment Law Project,* August 2014, http://www.nelp.org/page/-/Justice/IndependentContractorCosts.pdf?nocdn=1 (accessed March 21, 2015).
35. Robert Kuttner, "Why Work Is More and More Debased," *New York Review of Books,* October 23, 2014, http://www.nybooks.com/articles/archives/2014/oct/23/why-work-more-and-more-debased (accessed March 21, 2015). Even in the sensitive realm of foreign policy, private contractor firms like Blackwater are increasingly present in countries all over the world, providing frontline national security services and support for the U.S. government and military, often with an appalling lack of accountability.
36. Ibid.
37. Bob Egelko, "Court Rules FedEx Drivers in State Are Employees, Not Contractors," *San Francisco Chronicle,* August 28, 2014, http://www.sfgate.com/bayarea/article/Court-to-FedEx-Your-drivers-are-full-time-5717048.php (accessed March 21, 2015).
38. David Weil, *The Fissured Workplace: Why Work Became So Bad for So Many and What Can Be Done to Improve It* (Cambridge, MA: Harvard University Press, 2014).
39. Kuttner, "Why Work Is More and More Debased."
40. Katherine V. W. Stone, *From Widgets to Digits: Employment Regulation for the Changing Workplace* (New York: Cambridge University Press, 2004), cited in Kuttner, "Why Work Is More and More Debased."

41. Weil, *The Fissured Workplace,* page 183.
42. http://nymag.com/daily/intelligencer/2014/09/silicon-valleys-contract-worker-problem.html.
43. SherpaVentures, "SherpaVentures On-Demand Economy Report," *Scribd,* 2014 ODE Report, http://www.scribd.com/doc/235776320/SherpaVentures-On-Demand-Economy-report (accessed March 21, 2015).
44. Michael Grabell, "U.S. Lags behind World in Temp Worker Protections," *ProPublica,* February 24, 2014, http://www.propublica.org/article/us-lags-behind-world-in-temp-worker-protections (accessed March 21, 2015); see also Organization for Economic Cooperation and Development (OECD), "Detailed Description of Employment Protection Legislation, 2012–2013," OECD EPL Database, update 2013, http://www.oecd.org/els/emp/All.pdf (accessed March 21, 2015).
45. Organization for Economic Cooperation and Development, "OECD Indicators of Employment Protection," *OECD.org,* http://www.oecd.org/employment/emp/oecdindicatorsofemploymentprotection.htm (accessed March 21, 2015).
46. Rachel L. Swarns, "For a Worker with Little Time between 3 Jobs, a Nap Has Fatal Consequences," *New York Times,* September 28, 2014, http://www.nytimes.com/2014/09/29/nyregion/3-jobs-plenty-of-dreams-and-the-fatal-consequences-of-one-dangerous-decision.html (accessed March 21, 2015).
47. Tania Branigan, "Toddler Left Dying after Hit and Run Prompts Soul Searching in China," *Guardian,* October 17, 2011, http://www.theguardian.com/world/2011/oct/17/toddler-hit-and-run-china (accessed March 21, 2015).
48. Tom Hayden, "Woman Who Worked in Four Jobs, Overcome by Fumes, Dies as She Naps in Car," *NJ.com True Jersey,* August 26, 2014, http://www.nj.com/union/index.ssf/2014/08/deceased_woman_in_elizabeth_worked_four_jobs_napped_in_car_overcome_by_fumes_police_say.html (accessed March 21, 2015).
49. Dunkin' Donuts, "Dunkin' Donuts Press Kit," *Dunkin' Donuts Newsroom,* October 28, 2014, http://news.dunkindonuts.com/presskits/dunkin-donuts-press-kit (accessed March 21, 2015).
50. Gary Strauss, "Dunkin' Brands CEO Got Plenty of Dough in 2013," *USA Today,* March 26, 2014, http://www.usatoday.com/story/money/business/2014/03/26/dunkin-brands-ceo-got—plenty-of-dough-in-2013/6923985/ (accessed March 21, 2015).
51. Deal Book, "Dunkin' Donuts Parent Files for an I.P.O.," *New York Times,* May 4, 2011, http://dealbook.nytimes.com/2011/05/04/dunkin-donuts-parent-files-for-an-i-p-o/ (accessed March 21, 2015).
52. Amy B. Dean, "Workers Are Constantly on the Edge of the Knife," *Truthout,* September 12, 2014, http://www.truth-out.org/news/item/26120-workers-are-constantly-on-the-edge-of-the-knife (Accessed March 21, 2015).
53. Nancy K. Cauthen, "Scheduling Hourly Workers: How Last Minute, Just-in-Time Scheduling Practices Are Bad for Workers, Families and Business," *Demos,* March 14, 2011, http://www.demos.org/publication/scheduling-hourly-workers-how-last-minute-just-time-scheduling-practices-are-bad-workers (accessed March 21, 2015).
54. Steven Greenhouse, "A Push to Give Steadier Shifts to Part-Timers," *New York Times,* July 15, 2014, http://www.nytimes.com/2014/07/16/business/a-push-to-give-steadier-shifts-to-part-timers.html?_r=0 (accessed March 21, 2015).
55. Greenhouse, "A Push to Give Steadier Shifts to Part-Timers."
56. Maria E. Canon, Marianna Kudlyak, and Marisa Reed, "Is Involuntary Part-Time Employment Different after the Great Recession?" Federal Reserve Bank of St. Louis, July 2014, available at https://www.stlouisfed.org/publications/re/articles/?id=2536.

57. "Employee Benefits in the United States—March 2014," Bureau of Labor Statistics, News Release, USDL-14-1348, July 25, 2014, available at www.bls.gov/news.release/pdf/ebs2.pdf.
58. Sarah Jane Glynn and Joanna Venator, "Workplace Flexibility," Center for American Progress, Washington, D.C., 2012, available at https://cdn.americanprogress.org/wp-content/uploads/issues/2012/08/pdf/flexibility_factsheet.pdf.
59. Greenhouse, "A Push to Give Steadier Shifts to Part-Timers."
60. Cauthen, "Scheduling Hourly Workers."
61. Glynn and Venator, "Workplace Flexibility."
62. National Employment Law Project, "Going Nowhere Fast: Limited Occupational Mobility in the Fast Food Industry," *National Employment Law Project Data Brief,* July 2013, http://nelp.3cdn.net/84a67b124db45841d4_o0m6bq42h.pdf (accessed March 21, 2015).
63. Susan Berfield, "Fast-Food Wages Come with a $7 Billion Side of Public Assistance," *Bloomberg Business,* October 15, 2013, http://www.bloomberg.com/bw/articles/2013-10-15/mcdonalds-low-wages-come-with-a-7-billion-side-of-welfare (accessed March 21, 2013).
64. Tiffany Hsu, "Nearly 90% of Fast-Food Workers Allege Wage Theft, Survey Finds," *Los Angeles Times,* April 1, 2014, http://articles.latimes.com/2014/apr/01/business/la-fi-mo-wage-theft-survey-fast-food-20140331 (accessed March 21, 2015).
65. Susan Berfield, "Fast-Food CEOs Make 1,000 Times the Pay of the Average Fast-Food Worker," *Bloomberg Business,* April 22, 2014, http://www.bloomberg.com/bw/articles/2014-04-22/fast-food-ceos-make-1-000-times-the-average-fast-food-worker (accessed March 21, 2015).
66. Clare O'Connor, "Report: Walmart Workers Cost Taxpayers $6.2 Billion in Public Assistance," *Forbes,* April 15, 2014, http://www.forbes.com/sites/clareoconnor/2014/04/15/report-walmart-workers-cost-taxpayers-6-2-billion-in-public-assistance/ (accessed March 21, 2015).
67. Christine Owens, "Trying to Raise a Family on a Fast-Food Salary," *Reuters,* August 29, 2013, http://www.reuters.com/article/2013/08/29/us-family-fast-food-idUSBRE97S0ZT20130829 (accessed March 21, 2015).
68. Melanie Trottman and Julie Jargon, "NLRB Names McDonald's as 'Joint-Employer' at Its Franchisees," *Wall Street Journal,* December 19, 2014, http://www.wsj.com/articles/nlrb-names-mcdonalds-as-joint-employer-of-workers-at-its-franchisees-1419018664 (accessed March 21, 2015).
69. O'Connor, "Report: Walmart Workers Cost Taxpayers $6.2 Billion in Public Assistance."
70. Esther Kaplan, "Americans Are Working So Hard, It's Actually Killing People," *Nation,* November 17, 2014, http://www.thenation.com/article/186425/work-speedups-have-consequences-boss-never-imagined (accessed March 20, 2015).
71. Kerry A. Dolan, "Inside the 2014 Forbes 400: Facts and Figures about America's Wealthiest," *Forbes,* September 29, 2014, http://www.forbes.com/sites/kerryadolan/2014/09/29/inside-the-2014-forbes-400-facts-and-figures-about-americas-wealthiest/ (accessed March 21, 2015).
72. Dean, "Workers Are Constantly on the Edge of the Knife."
73. Rosa DeLauro, "Miller, Harkin, Warren, DeLauro Introduce Legislation to Establish Fair Work Scheduling Practices," *Rosa DeLauro,* July 22, 2014, http://delauro.house.gov/index.php?option=com_content&view=article&id=1657:miller-harkin-warren-delauro-introduce-legislation-to-establish-fair-work-scheduling-practices&catid=2&Itemid=21 (accessed March 21, 2015).

74. Cherri Delisline, "I've Worked at McDonald's for 10 Years and Still Make $7.35 an Hour," *Quartz,* July 26, 2014, http://qz.com/240827/ive-worked-at-mcdonalds-for-10-years-and-still-make-7-35-an-hour/ (accessed March 21, 2015).
75. Leslie Patton, "McDonald's Workers Arrested at Protest near Headquarters," *Bloomberg Business,* May 22, 2014, http://www.bloomberg.com/news/articles/2014-05-21/mcdonald-s-tells-employees-to-stay-home-as-protests-loom (accessed March 21, 2015).
76. Delisline, "I've Worked at McDonald's for 10 Years and Still Make $7.35 an Hour."
77. Trottman and Jargon, "NLRB Names McDonald's as 'Joint-Employer' at Its Franchisees."
78. Weber, "Wage-Law Enforcer Favors Proactive Approach."
79. Gregory Wallace, "Facebook's Bus Drivers Set for Raises after Union Vote," *CNN Money,* February 22, 2015, http://money.cnn.com/2015/02/22/technology/facebook-bus-drivers-union/ (accessed April 29, 2015).
80. Franklin Roosevelt, "Second Inaugural Address," *American Presidency Project,* January 20, 1937, http://www.presidency.ucsb.edu/ws/?pid=15349 (accessed March 21, 2015).
81. David Bacon, "Teaching Today: Leleua Loupe's Journey as a Freeway Flyer," *Capital and Main,* February 11, 2015, http://capitalandmain.com/inequality/teaching-today-leleua-loupes-journey-freeway-flyer/ (accessed March 21, 2015).
82. Motoko Rich, "Publishers Announce Staff Cuts," *New York Times,* December 3, 2008, http://www.nytimes.com/2008/12/04/business/04publish.html?_r=0 (accessed March 21, 2015).
83. Henry Blodget, "Capt. Sullenberger: Stop Cutting Pilot Pay or Next Plane Will Crash in River," *Business Insider,* February 24, 2009, http://www.businessinsider.com/capt-sullenberger-stop-cutting-pilot-pay-or-next-time-plane-will-crash-in-river-2009-2#ixzz3V4zrVyzI (accessed March 21, 2015).
84. Joan Lowy and Michael Sniffen, "Pilot Who Landed Plane in Hudson River Slams Pay Cuts by Airlines," *Seattle Times,* February 25, 2009, http://www.seattletimes.com/politics/pilot-who-landed-plane-in-hudson-river-slams-pay-cuts-by-airlines/ (accessed March 21, 2015).
85. Joshua Rhett Miller, "Low Pay One of Many Difficulties Facing Regional Pilots," *Fox News,* May 13, 2009, http://www.foxnews.com/story/2009/05/13/low-pay-one-many-difficulties-facing-regional-pilots/ (accessed March 21, 2015).
86. Matthew L. Wald, "Pilots Set Up for Fatigue, Officials Say," *New York Times,* May 13, 2009, http://www.nytimes.com/2009/05/14/nyregion/14pilot.html?_r=0 (accessed March 21, 2015).
87. David Saltonstall, "Continental Connection Flight 3407 Co-Pilot Rebecca Shaw's Husband, Mother Come to Her Defense," *Daily News,* May 15, 2009, http://www.nydailynews.com/news/continental-connection-flight-3407-co-pilot-rebecca-shaw-husband-mother-defense-article-1.411059 (accessed March 21, 2015).
88. Tina Brown, "The Gig Economy," *Daily Beast,* January 12, 2009, http://www.thedailybeast.com/articles/2009/01/12/the-gig-economy.html (accessed March 21, 2015).
89. CNN Money, "76% of Americans Are Living Paycheck-to-Paycheck," *CNN,* June 24, 2013, http://money.cnn.com/2013/06/24/pf/emergency-savings/ (accessed March 21, 2015).
90. Marion Crain and Michael Sherraden, *Working and Living in the Shadow of Economic Fragility* (Oxford: Oxford University Press, 2014), page xiii.
91. Valentina Pop, "Unemployment on Slow Downward Trend, Report Says," EUObserver, September 4, 2014, https://euobserver.com/social/125465 (accessed March

30, 2015). In Europe, less than half of temporary workers in a given year had managed to land a full-time permanent contract three years later, one report notes. In Germany, one-fifth of workers are considered "low wage," which exceeds the OECD average (though that is still much lower than in the U.S., where a quarter of workers are "low wage"). Temporary work, a pillar of the German "flexicurity" model, has become overused and not proven to be a sure pathway to a permanent job, as was originally promised by the Social Democratic government of Gerhard Schröder. Many of Schröder's labor market reforms benefited Germany initially but later, under the administration of Chancellor Angela Merkel, became the basis for the self-defeating austerity policies that bedeviled the eurozone and the European Union.

CHAPTER 2

1. Juliet Schor, "Debating the Sharing Economy," *Great Transition Initiative,* October 2014, http://www.greattransition.org/publication/debating-the-sharing-economy (accessed March 21, 2015).
2. Evgeny Morozov, "The 'Sharing Economy' Undermines Workers' Rights," *Financial Times,* October 14, 2013, http://www.ft.com/intl/cms/s/0/92c3021c-34c2-11e3-8148-00144feab7de.html?siteedition=uk#axzz3VvyB8F2U (accessed March 30, 2015).
3. Steven T. Jones, "Renting Isn't Sharing," *San Francisco Bay Guardian,* May 20, 2014, http://www.sfbg.com/2014/05/20/renting-isnt-sharing (accessed March 21, 2015).
4. Brian Chesky, "Introduction," *Airbnb,* July 16, 2014, http://blog.airbnb.com/belong-anywhere (accessed March 21, 2015).
5. "About Us," Airbnb website, https://www.airbnb.com/about/about-us (accessed May 30, 2015).
6. Between 1900 and 1915, more than 15 million immigrants arrived in the United States. That was about equal to the number of immigrants who had arrived in the previous 40 years. In 1910, three-fourths of New York City's population was comprised either of immigrants or first-generation Americans (the sons and daughters of immigrants). Not only were the numbers of immigrants swelling, the countries from which they came had changed dramatically as well. Unlike earlier immigrants, the majority of the newcomers after 1900 came from non-English-speaking European countries, especially from countries in the south and east like Italy, Poland and Russia. These were countries quite different in culture and language from the United States at the time. See "Immigrants in the Progressive Era," Library of Congress, retrieved on March 17, 2015, http://www.loc.gov/teachers/classroommaterials/presentationsandactivities/presentations/timeline/progress/immigrnt/.
7. "Peter Iskandar," Anti-Eviction Mapping Project: Documenting the Dispossession of SF Bay Area Residents, http://www.antievictionmap.com/peter-iskandar-1/ (accessed March 30, 2015).
8. C. W. Nevius, "Developer Peter Iskander's Tactics against Tenants," *San Francisco Chronicle,* April 15, 2011, http://www.sfgate.com/bayarea/nevius/article/Developer-Peter-Iskander-s-tactics-against-tenants-2374970.php (accessed March 21, 2015).
9. J. K. Dineen, "Chinatown Hotel Next Up in S.F. Gentrification Wars," *San Francisco Chronicle,* March 27, 2015, http://www.sfgate.com/bayarea/article/Chinatown-hotel-next-up-in-S-F-gentrification-6161916.php (accessed March 30, 2015). Tina Cheung at Chinatown Community Development Center, who

counsels tenants, says, "Agreements and notices written only in English are not fully understood yet become the basis for 'breach' evictions. Some evictions are attempted without any legitimate basis just to scare tenants into moving," she says. See http://48hillsonline.org/2015/01/05/facing-evictions-tenant-agenda-2015/.

10. Melanie Young, "Ellis Act Evictions: Diego Deleo," *KALW Radio,* December 18, 2013, http://kalw.org/post/ellis-act-evictions-diego-deleo (accessed March 21, 2015).
11. Melanie Young, "Ellis Act Evictions: Theresa Flandrich," *KALW Radio,* December 18, 2013, http://kalw.org/post/ellis-act-evictions-theresa-flandrich (accessed March 21, 2015).
12. Delene Wolf, "Rent Board Annual Report on Eviction Notices," *Residential Rent Stabilization and Arbitration Board,* March 11, 2014, http://www.sfrb.org/modules/showdocument.aspx?documentid=2700 (accessed March 21, 2015).
13. Jessica Kwong, "Former Tenants Sue after SRO Housing Made into Group Apartments," *San Francisco Examiner,* November 13, 2014, http://www.sfexaminer.com/sanfrancisco/former-tenants-sue-after-sro-housing-made-into-group-apartments/Content?oid=2911878 (accessed March 21, 2015).
14. "San Francisco's Eviction Crisis, 2015," San Francisco Anti-Displacement Coalition, April 2015, https://sfadc.files.wordpress.com/2015/04/final-draft-4-20-sm.pdf (accessed May 4, 2015).
15. Devin O'Brien, "Zumper National Rent Report: April 2015," *Zumper,* May 7, 2015, https://www.zumper.com/blog/2015/05/zumper-national-rent-report-april-2015 (accessed May 28, 2015).
16. Tim Redmond, "SF Lost 1,017 Rent-Controlled Apartments in 2013," *48 Hills,* January 31, 2014, http://48hills.org/2014/01/31/sf-lost-1017-rent-controlled-apartments-in-2013/2/ (accessed March 21, 2015).
17. Sara Shortt, "Numbers Don't Tell the Real Tale of San Francisco Evictions," *San Francisco Chronicle,* October 14, 2104, http://www.sfgate.com/opinion/openforum/article/Numbers-don-t-tell-the-real-tale-of-San-5822840.php#photo-6999661 (accessed March 30, 2015).
18. Steven T. Jones, "Tobener Law Center," *San Francisco Bay Guardian,* May 13, 2014, http://www.sfbg.com/2014/05/13/guardian-small-business-awards-2014-tobener-law-center (accessed March 21, 2015).
19. Carolyn Said, "Window into Airbnb's Hidden Impact on S.F.," *San Francisco Chronicle,* http://www.sfgate.com/business/item/Window-into-Airbnb-s-hidden-impact-on-S-F-30110.php, (accessed March 21, 2015).
20. CARTODB, "Airbnb's Neighborhood Presence," *CARTODB,* http://ampitup.cartodb.com/viz/49562818-96a3-11e4-a463-0e853d047bba/public_map (accessed March 21, 2015).
21. Tim Redmond, "The Missing Story—and the Missing People—at the Airbnb Hearing," *48 Hills,* August 7, 2014, http://48hills.org/2014/08/07/big-lies-missing-points-airbnb-hearing/#permanently-moved (accessed March 21, 2015).
22. Randy Shaw, "Mayor, Supervisor Kim Give Teeth to Airbnb Law," *Beyond Chron,* October 8, 2014, http://www.beyondchron.org/mayor-lee-supe-kim-win-enforceable-airbnb-law/ (accessed March 21, 2015).
23. Aaron Glantz, "Conversion of Apartments to Rentals for Tourists Is Surging," *New York Times,* July 21, 2011, http://www.nytimes.com/2011/07/22/us/22bchomes.html?_r=0 (accessed March 21, 2015).
24. Carolyn Said, "Airbnb Foes Want Tougher New Law," *San Francisco Chronicle,* November 25, 2014, http://www.sfgate.com/business/article/Airbnb-foes-want-toughernew-law-5915094.php (accessed March 21, 2015).

25. Darwin Bond Graham, "The Flipside of San Francisco's Displacement Crisis: The Influx of the Very Rich," *48 Hills*, May 5, 2014, http://48hills.org/2014/05/05/flipside-san-franciscos-displacement-crisis-influx-rich-darwin-bond-graham-yahoo-began-running-hulking-purple-buses-san-francisco-2005-google-followed-two-years-lat/#permanently-moved (accessed March 21, 2015).
26. Steven T. Jones, "The Problem with the Sharing Economy," *San Francisco Bay Guardian*, May 1, 2012, http://www.sfbg.com/2012/05/01/problem-sharing-economy (accessed March 21, 2015).
27. Steven T. Jones, "Residents vs. Tourists," *San Francisco Bay Guardian*, February 4, 2014, http://www.sfbg.com/2014/02/04/residents-vs-tourists (accessed March 21, 2015); Airbnb, "Airbnb Economic Impact," *Airbnb blog*, http://blog.airbnb.com/economic-impact-airbnb/ (accessed March 21, 2015).
28. Jones, "The Problem with the Sharing Economy."
29. Matt Phillips, "Most Germans Don't Buy Their Homes, They Rent. Here's Why," *Quartz*, January 23, 2014, http://qz.com/167887/germany-has-one-of-the-worlds-lowest-homeownership-rates/ (accessed March 21, 2015).
30. "Virtual Tour of San Francisco City Hall," Slideshow, "Ornate Wooden Paneling" and "Four Demons," http://sfch.budryerson.com/#(24) and http://sfch.budryerson.com/#(28) (accessed March 30, 2015).
31. Said, "Window into Airbnb's Hidden Impact on S.F."
32. Tom Slee, "The Shape of Airbnb's Business," *Whimsley*, May 26, 2014, http://tomslee.net/2014/05/the-shape-of-airbnbs-business.html (accessed March 21, 2015).
33. Both the *San Francisco Chronicle* study and the Slee study used a similar methodology. They created automated scripts that "scraped" information on San Francisco listings from the Airbnb website over the course of several hours in May 2014. Data included hosts, properties, neighborhoods, rates and ratings and other factors. Duplicates were removed and other quality assurance measures were taken.
34. Conor Dougherty, "Apartment Rents Climb as Vacancies Drop," *Wall Street Journal*, April 2, 2014, http://www.wsj.com/articles/SB10001424052702304157204579475751782514742 (accessed March 20, 2015).
35. Said, "Window into Airbnb's Hidden Impact on S.F."
36. Steven T. Jones, "Into Thin Air," *San Francisco Bay Guardian*, August 6, 2013, http://www.sfbg.com/2013/08/06/thin-air (accessed March 22, 2015).
37. Said, "Window into Airbnb's Hidden Impact on S.F."
38. Jones, "Into Thin Air."
39. Joe Eskenazi, "2014: The Year in Housing," *San Francisco Weekly*, December 30, 2014, http://www.sfweekly.com/sanfrancisco/2014-the-year-in-housing/Content?oid=3317161 (accessed March 22, 2015).
40. Darwin Bond Graham and Tim Redmond, "Investigation: New Condos Aren't Owned by San Francisco Residents," *48 Hills*, September 29, 2014, http://48hills.org/2014/09/29/investigation-new-condos-arent-owned-san-francisco-residents/#permanently-moved (accessed March 22, 2015).
41. Jonah Owen Lamb, "Middle-Class Housing in SF Lags behind Homes for Rich or Poor," *San Francisco Examiner*, December 20, 2014, http://www.sfexaminer.com/sanfrancisco/middle-class-housing-in-sf-lags-behind-homes-for-rich-or-poor/Content?oid=2913582 (accessed March 22, 2015).
42. Tim Redmond, "Why Has City Planning Gotten a Free Pass on Airbnb?" *48 Hills*, May 7, 2014, http://48hills.org/2014/05/07/why-has-city-planning-gotten-a-free-pass-on-airbnb/#permanently-moved (accessed March 22, 2015).
43. Tim Redmond, "The Airbnb Files—How a Friend of the Mayor Avoids Law-Enforcement," *48 Hills*, June 16, 2014, http://48hills.org/2014/06/16/airbnb-files

-friend-mayor-avoids-law-enforcement/#permanently-moved (accessed March 22, 2015).

44. Bob Egelko, "S.F. City Attorney Sues 2 Landlords over Short-Term Rentals," *San Francisco Chronicle,* April 24, 2014, http://www.sfgate.com/bayarea/article/S-F-city-attorney-sues-2-landlords-over-5425826.php (accessed March 22, 2015).
45. As just one example of the change in wealth demographics, the number of "super-rich" San Franciscans who are worth $30 million or more increased by nearly 30 percent in three years, from 4,230 to 5,460. Heather Knight, "Psychology Studies Suggest Rising Wealth Means More Jerks in S.F.," *SFGate,* January 26, 2015, http://www.sfgate.com/bayarea/article/Psychology-studies-suggest-rising-wealth-means-6039481.php (accessed April 30, 2015).
46. Redmond, "The Missing Story—and the Missing People—at the Airbnb Hearing."
47. Dan Raile, "Unicorn v. Leviathan: The Battle between Airbnb and San Francisco Rages On," *PandoDaily,* April 20, 2015, http://pando.com/2015/04/20/unicorn-v-leviathan-the-battle-between-airbnb-and-san-francisco-rages-on (accessed May 12, 2015); Tim Redmond, "Almost Nobody Has Registered under the Airbnb Law," *48 Hills,* February 18, 2015, http://48hills.org/2015/02/17/almost-nobody-registered-airbnb-law/ (accessed March 22, 2015).
48. Ed Lee, "Mayor Lee's 2015 State of the City Address," *SFMAYOR,* January 15, 2015, http://sfmayor.org/index.aspx?page=1029 (accessed March 22, 2015).
49. Jessica Plautz, "Portland Could Soon Be the Most Airbnb-Friendly City in the U.S.," *Mashable,* July 23, 2014, http://mashable.com/2014/07/23/portland-airbnb/ (accessed March 22, 2015). For Berlin, see Jeevan Vasagar, "Berlin Housing Law Threatens Sharing Economy by Restricting Rents," *Financial Times,* April 30, 2014, http://www.ft.com/intl/cms/s/0/1e8299a0-d065-11e3-af2b-00144feabdc0.html (accessed March 30, 2015).
50. Eric T. Schneiderman, "Airbnb in the City," *New York State Office of the Attorney General,* October 2014, http://www.ag.ny.gov/pdfs/Airbnb%20report.pdf (accessed March 22, 2015).
51. William Alden, "The Business Tycoons of Airbnb," *New York Times Magazine,* November 25, 2014, http://www.nytimes.com/2014/11/30/magazine/the-business-tycoons-of-airbnb.html (accessed March 22, 2015).
52. David Streitfeld, "Airbnb Listings Mostly Illegal, New York State Contends," *New York Times,* October 14, 2014, http://www.nytimes.com/2014/10/16/business/airbnb-listings-mostly-illegal-state-contends.html (accessed March 22, 2015).
53. Josh Dzeiza, "Airbnb Comes under Fire in New York City," *The Verge,* January 21, 2015, http://www.theverge.com/2015/1/21/7865959/airbnb-under-fire-new-york-city-city-council (accessed March 22, 2015).
54. Drew Grant, "Oh Noshi, It's Toshi! Airbnb Opportunist Goes Legit with New Hotels," *Observer,* September 25, 2012, http://observer.com/2012/09/oh-noshi-its-toshi-airbnb-opportunist-goes-legit-with-new-hotels/ (accessed March 22, 2015).
55. Ibid.
56. Anti-Eviction Mapping Project, "The Commodification of Everyday Life: This Bed's for Sale," *Anti-Eviction Mapping Project Report,* http://www.antievictionmappingproject.net/airbnb.pdf (accessed March 22, 2015).
57. Streitfeld, "Airbnb Listings Mostly Illegal, New York State Contends."
58. Tom Slee, "Airbnb in New York: Economical with the Truth," *Tomslee.net,* November 2013, http://tomslee.net/wordpress/wp-content/uploads/2013/11/airbnbny_handout.pdf (accessed March 22, 2015).
59. Leonard Greene, "Airbnb Nets $40M in Illegal NY Listings: AG," *New York Post,* October 16, 2014, http://nypost.com/2014/10/16/airbnb-nets-40m-in-illegal-ny-listings-schneiderman/ (accessed March 22, 2015).

60. Katie Couric, "World 3.0: Airbnb CEO Brian Chesky," *Yahoo! News,* http://news.yahoo.com/katie-couric-airbnb-ceo-brian-chesky-213147409.html (accessed March 22, 2015).
61. Streitfeld, "Airbnb Listings Mostly Illegal, New York State Contends."
62. Dzeiza, "Airbnb Comes under Fire in New York City."
63. Susan Stellin, "Co-op vs. Condo: The Differences Are Narrowing," *New York Times,* October 25, 2012, http://www.nytimes.com/2012/10/07/realestate/getting-started-choosing-between-a-co-op-and-a-condo.html (accessed March 22, 2015).
64. Tim F., "My Co-op's Luddite Response to Airbnb and My Solution," *Startup Harbor,* July 30, 2014, http://startupharbor.me/2014/07/30/my-co-ops-luddite-response-to-airbnb-and-my-solution/ (accessed March 22, 2015).
65. Rhonda Kayson, "What's Up in New York?" *New York Times,* December 26, 2014, http://www.nytimes.com/2014/12/28/realestate/new-york-airbnb-and-rent-regulation-will-be-hot-topics.html (accessed March 22, 2015).
66. Streitfeld, "Airbnb Listings Mostly Illegal, New York State Contends."
67. Bruce Golding, "Lawmakers Want to Triple Taskforce for Airbnb Crackdown," *New York Post,* March 12, 2015, http://nypost.com/2015/03/12/lawmakers-want-to-triple-task-force-for-airbnb-crackdown/ (accessed March 22, 2015).
68. Roy Samaan, "Airbnb, Rising Rent, and the Housing Crisis in Los Angeles," Los Angeles Alliance for a New Economy (LAANE), March 2015, http://www.laane.org/wp-content/uploads/2015/03/AirBnB-Final.pdf (accessed April 30, 2015), page 9.
69. Airbnb, "Hey, I'm Ghc!" *Airbnb,* https://www.airbnb.com/users/show/1463129 (accessed March 22, 2015).
70. Tim Logan, Emily Alpert Reyes, and Ben Poston, "Airbnb and Other Short-Term Rentals Worsen Housing Shortage, Critics Say," *Los Angeles Times,* March 11, 2015, http://www.latimes.com/business/realestate/la-fi-airbnb-housing-market-20150311-story.html#page=1 (accessed March 22, 2015).
71. Samaan, "Airbnb, Rising Rent, and the Housing Crisis in Los Angeles," 18.
72. Tim Logan, "Can Santa Monica—Or Anyplace Else—Enforce a Ban on Short-Term Rentals?," *Los Angeles Times,* May 13, 2015, http://www.latimes.com/business/la-fi-0514-airbnb-santa-monica-20150514-story.html (accessed May 25, 2015).
73. Inside Airbnb, "How Is Airbnb Really Being Used in and Affecting Your Neighborhood?," *Inside Airbnb,* http://insideairbnb.com/portland/ (accessed March 22, 2015); Anna Walters, "Air Invasion," *Wilamette Week,* March 11, 2015, http://www.wweek.com/portland/article-24210-air_invasion.html (accessed March 22, 2015).
74. Slee, "The Shape of Airbnb's Business."
75. The 18 cities are San Francisco, New York, Paris, London, Barcelona, Berlin, Edinburgh, Rome, Amsterdam, Toronto, Vancouver, Chicago, Los Angeles, San Diego, Rio de Janeiro, Mexico City, Bangkok and Tokyo.
76. Slee, "The Shape of Airbnb's Business."
77. Jones, "Residents vs. Tourists."
78. "Beds, Breakfasts and Billions," Katie Couric, "World 3.0: Airbnb CEO Brian Chesky," *Yahoo! News,* June 2, 2014, interview with Brian Chesky, specific comments made beginning at the 6:27 mark of the video, http://news.yahoo.com/video/beds-breakfasts-billions-025613897.html (accessed April 30, 2015).
79. Airbnb, "Helping Hosts Make Their Home Safer," *Airbnb,* https://www.airbnb.com/home-safety (accessed March 22, 2015).
80. Airbnb, "Home Safety Terms and Conditions," *Airbnb,* https://www.airbnb.com/home-safety/terms-and-conditions (accessed March 22, 2015).

81. Jones, "Into Thin Air."
82. Couric, "World 3.0: Airbnb CEO Brian Chesky."
83. Airbnb, "350,000 Hosts. 15 Million Guests. 190 Countries.," *Airbnb,* https://www.airbnb.com/trust (accessed March 22, 2015).
84. George Hobica, "10 Incredible Airbnb Horror Stories," *Fox News,* May 8, 2014, http://www.foxnews.com/travel/2014/05/08/10-incredible-airbnb-horror-stories/ (accessed March 22, 2015); Ryan Tate, "More Airbnb Horrors Emerge," *Gawker,* August 1, 2011, http://gawker.com/5826607/more-airbnb-horrors-emerge (accessed March 22, 2015).
85. EJ, "Violated: A Traveler's Lost Faith, a Difficult Lesson Learned," *Around the World and Back Again,* June 29, 2011, http://ejroundtheworld.blogspot.com/2011/06/violated-travelers-lost-faith-difficult.html (accessed March 22, 2015); Ryan Tate, "Woman Utterly Pillaged Via Airbnb," *Gawker,* July 27, 2011, http://gawker.com/5825262/woman-utterly-pillaged-via-airbnb (accessed March 22, 2015).
86. Adrian Chen, "Airbnb Pillage Victim Says Company Tried to Keep Her Quiet," *Gawker,* July 29, 2011, http://gawker.com/5825996/airbnb-pillage-victim-says-company-tried-to-keep-her-quiet (accessed March 22, 2015).
87. Jones, "Into Thin Air."
88. Ron Lieber, "Questions about Airbnb's Responsibility after Attack by Dog," *New York Times,* April 10, 2015, http://www.nytimes.com/2015/04/11/your-money/questions-about-airbnbs-responsibility-after-vicious-attack-by-dog.html (accessed April 11, 2015).
89. Austin Carr, "Watch Airbnb CEO Brian Chesky Salute RISD, Whip Off His Robe, Dance Like Michael Jackson," *Fastcompany,* February 17, 2012, http://www.fastcompany.com/1816858/watch-airbnb-ceo-brian-chesky-salute-risd-whip-his-robe-dance-michael-jackson (accessed March 22, 2015).
90. Jones, "Into Thin Air."
91. Brian Chesky, "Belong Anywhere," *Airbnb,* July 16, 2014, http://blog.airbnb.com/belong-anywhere/ (accessed March 31, 2015).
92. Tim Redmond, "Who's Going to Enforce the New Airbnb Law? Because Nobody Is Doing It Now," *48 Hills,* August 5, 2014, http://48hills.org/2014/08/05/whos-going-enforce-airbnb-law-nobody-now/#permanently-moved (accessed March 22, 2015).
93. For example, in New York City, Airbnb has 25,724 listings compared to Roomorama's 2,688 listings; in San Francisco, Airbnb has nearly 5,000 listings throughout the city while VRBO has 1,200 and Roomorama 303 properties.
94. Jones, "Into Thin Air."
95. Jones, "The Problem with the Sharing Economy."
96. Chenda Ngak, "Sandy Volunteers Connect with Victims Using Amazon, Airbnb, Crowdmap," *CBS News,* November 16, 2012, http://www.cbsnews.com/news/sandy-volunteers-connect-with-victims-using-amazon-airbnb-crowdmap/ (accessed March 22, 2015).
97. Airbnb, "Airbnb Disaster Response," *Airbnb,* https://www.airbnb.com/disaster-response (accessed March 22, 2015).
98. Yahoo! Finance, "Industry Center Lodging, *Yahoo!,* http://biz.yahoo.com/ic/40/40231.html (accessed March 22, 2015).

CHAPTER 3

1. Alyson Shontell, "All Hail the Uber Man! How Sharp-Elbowed Salesman Travis Kalanick Became Silicon Valley's Newest Star," *Business Insider,* January 11,

2013, http://www.businessinsider.com/uber-travis-kalanick-bio-2014-1#ixzz3VEBLNRgE (accessed March 23, 2015).

2. Evelyn M. Rusli and Douglas MacMillan, "Uber Gets an Uber-Valuation," *Wall Street Journal,* June 6, 2014, http://www.wsj.com/articles/uber-gets-uber-valuation-of-18-2-billion-1402073876 (accessed March 23, 2015).
3. Kelly Dessaint, "My Uber Breaking Point," *disinformation,* February 4, 2015, http://disinfo.com/2015/02/uber-breaking-point (accessed May 27, 2015).
4. See, for example, La'Zooz, a decentralized ridesharing platform that says it "will synchronize empty seats with transportation needs in real time" and match like-minded people to create a great ridesharing experience for a "fair fare" (http://lazooz.org/).
5. Joshua Barrie, "South Korea Just Charged Uber CEO Travis Kalanick with Operating an 'Illegal' Taxi Service," *Business Insider,* March 18, 2015, http://www.businessinsider.com/south-korea-charges-uber-ceo-travis-kalanick-2015-3 (accessed March 23, 2015); Duncan Robinson, "Boost for Uber as Brussels Considers Regulation of Ride Sharing," *Financial Times,* April 5, 2015 (accessed April 6, 2015). http://www.ft.com/intl/cms/s/0/6464d39e-d932-11e4-b907-00144feab7de.html.
6. Michael B. Farrell, "Cab Drivers Irate as Ban against Livery App Reversed," *Boston Globe,* August 17, 2012, http://www.bostonglobe.com/business/2012/08/16/smartphone-car-service-uber-stirs-cab-industry/svU8D77Z9J5orUEQRz8o3M/story.html?camp=pm (accessed March 23, 2015).
7. Paul Carr, "Travis Shrugged: The Creepy, Dangerous Ideology behind Silicon Valley's Cult of Disruption," *PandoDaily,* October 24, 2012, http://pando.com/2012/10/24/travis-shrugged/ (accessed March 23, 2015).
8. Tim Bradshaw, "Lunch with the FT: Travis Kalanick," *Financial Times,* May 9, 2014, http://www.ft.com/intl/cms/s/2/9b83cbe8-d5da-11e3-83b2-00144feabdc0.html#axzz3VEGjs4PF (accessed March 23, 2015).
9. Mickey Rapkin, "Uber Cab Confessions," *GQ,* March 2014, http://www.gq.com/news-politics/newsmakers/201403/uber-cab-confessions (accessed March 23, 2015).
10. For an estimated comparison of costs between Uber and taxis, see note 81.
11. Uber, "Safest Rides on the Road," *Uber,* https://www.uber.com/safety (accessed March 23, 2015); "Uber Background Checks," *Uber Blog,* April 25, 2014, http://blog.uber.com/driverscreening (accessed March 23, 2015).
12. Tracey Lien and Russ Mitchell, "Uber Sued over Unlawful Business Practices; Lyft Settles," *Los Angeles Times,* December 9, 2014, http://www.latimes.com/business/technology/la-fi-tn-uber-lyft-20141209-story.html (accessed March 23, 2015).
13. Uber contracts with Hirease to carry out background checks, which uses publicly available data to screen applicants. The data comes from sources such as federal and county courts, national sex-offender registries, and a Multi-State Criminal Database search, which includes information from state authorities (http://www.washingtonpost.com/posteverything/wp/2014/12/19/stop-attacking-uber-for-lax-safety-standards/).
14. Carmel Deamicis, "Passenger Sues Uber over Alleged Sexual Assault," *PandoDaily,* March 24, 2014, http://pando.com/2014/03/24/passenger-sues-uber-over-alleged-sexual-assault/ (accessed March 23, 2015).
15. Joe Fitzgerald Rodriguez, "Leaving Room for Error," *San Francisco Examiner,* May 29, 2015, http://www.sfexaminer.com/sanfrancisco/lax-background-checks-compromise-safety-of-ride-hail-apps-study-says/Content?oid=2931669 (accessed June 2, 2015).
16. Suhasini Raj, "Women Accuses Uber Driver of Rape in India," *New York Times,* December 7, 2014, http://www.nytimes.com/2014/12/08/world/asia/woman-ac

cuses-uber-driver-in-india-of-rape.html?_r=1&gwh=6B505FEE9EB4098B7248A9735168CBE3&gwt=pay&assetType=nyt_now (accessed March 23, 2015).

17. Nida Najar and Suhasini Raj, "Uber Driver in India Accused of Rape Faces Other Charges," *New York Times,* December 9, 2014, http://www.nytimes.com/2014/12/10/world/asia/new-delhi-uber-driver-accused-of-rape-faces-other-charges.html?gwh=42113D8A56941DB8270D176FB9900439&gwt=pay (accessed March 23, 2015).
18. Rachel Riley, "Women in Two Sexual Assaults Used Uber," *Boston Globe,* December 17, 2014, http://www.bostonglobe.com/metro/2014/12/16/least-two-women-who-reported-sexual-assaults-boston-sunday-were-using-uber-police-say/cFHpgzcfIoBYiTfWgOqYOK/story.html# (accessed March 23, 2015).
19. Kevin Montgomery, "Uber Driver Arrested for Allegedly Kidnapping a Drunk Woman," *ValleyWag,* June 3, 2014, http://valleywag.gawker.com/uber-driver-arrested-for-kidnapping-a-drunk-woman-1585725711 (accessed April 2, 2015).
20. Chelsia Rose Marcius, "Uber Driver Nabbed for Stealing $5K Worth of Jewelry from Orthodox Jewish Couple: Cops," *New York Daily News,* http://www.nydailynews.com/new-york/nyc-crime/uber-driver-nabbed-stealing-5k-worth-jewelry-cops-article-1.2184052 (accessed May 7, 2015).
21. Julie Zauzmer and Lori Aratani, "Man Visiting D.C. Says Uber Driver Took Him on Wild Ride," *Washington Post,* July 9, 2014, http://www.washingtonpost.com/blogs/dr-gridlock/wp/2014/07/09/man-visiting-d-c-says-uber-driver-took-him-on-wild-ride/ (accessed March 23, 2015); Francis Whittaker, "Uber Driver in Massachusetts Accused of Kidnapping and Raping Rider," *BuzzFeed,* December 18, 2014, http://www.buzzfeed.com/franciswhittaker/uber-driver-in-massachusetts-accused-of-kidnapping-and-rapin#.eb2rbbN8y (accessed April 2, 2015).
22. Ellen Huet, "Uber Driver with Felony Conviction Charged with Battery for Allegedly Hitting Passenger," *Forbes,* June 3, 2014, http://www.forbes.com/sites/ellenhuet/2014/06/03/uber-driver-with-felony-conviction-charged-with-battery-for-allegedly-hitting-passenger/ (accessed March 23, 2015).
23. Vivian Ho, "Uber Driver Accused of Hammer Attack on S.F. Rider," *San Francisco Chronicle,* September 27, 2014, http://www.sfgate.com/crime/article/Uber-driver-accused-of-hammer-attack-on-San-5783495.php (accessed March 23, 2015).
24. Olivia Nuzzi, "Uber's Biggest Problem Isn't Surge Pricing. What If It's Sexual Harassment by Drivers?" *Daily Beast,* March 28, 2014, http://www.thedailybeast.com/articles/2014/03/28/uber-s-biggest-problem-isn-t-surge-pricing-what-if-it-s-sexual-harassment-by-drivers.html (accessed March 23, 2015).
25. Brian Slodysko, "Uber Adds Safety Checklist to App after Drivers Charged with Sex Assault," *Chicago Sun Times,* December 31, 2014, http://chicago.suntimes.com/news-chicago/7/71/251756/uber-adds-safety-checklist-app-drivers-charged-sex-assault (accessed March 23, 2015).
26. Sam Biddle, "Uber Driver, Here's How We Get around Background Checks," *Gawker,* June 27, 2014, http://valleywag.gawker.com/uber-driver-heres-how-we-get-around-background-checks-1596982249 (accessed March 23, 2015).
27. Guardian Staff, "Uber Driver Accused of Sex Assault Used Wife's Name for Account, Company Says," *Guardian,* December 31, 2014, http://www.theguardian.com/us-news/2014/dec/31/uber-driver-accused-of-sex-assault-used-wifes-name-for-account-company-says (accessed March 23, 2015).
28. Nitasha Tiku, "Uber CEO on Driver Assault, 'It's Not Real and We're Not Responsible,'" *Gawker,* September 16, 2013, http://valleywag.gawker.com/uber-ceo-on-driver-assault-its-not-real-and-were-n-1323533057 (accessed March 23, 2015).
29. Rodriguez, "Leaving Room for Error."
30. Biddle, "Uber Driver, Here's How We Get Around Background Checks."

31. Kale Williams, "Uber Denies Fault in SF Crash That Killed Girl," *San Francisco Chronicle,* May 7, 2014, http://www.sfgate.com/bayarea/article/Uber-denies-fault-in-S-F-crash-that-killed-girl-5458290.php (accessed March 23, 2015).
32. Henry K. Lee, "Former Uber Driver Charged with Girl's Crosswalk Death in SF," *San Francisco Chronicle,* December 9, 2014, http://www.sfgate.com/crime/article/Former-Uber-driver-charged-in-girl-s-crosswalk-5944049.php (accessed March 23, 2015).
33. Carolyn Said, "Uber to Vet Drivers More Thoroughly," *San Francisco Chronicle,* February 12, 2014, http://blog.sfgate.com/techchron/2014/02/12/uber-to-vet-drivers-more-thoroughly/ (accessed March 23, 2015); Olivia Nuzzi, "The Ten Worst Uber Horror Stories," *Daily Beast,* November 19, 2014, http://www.thedailybeast.com/articles/2014/11/19/the-ten-worst-uber-horror-stories.html (accessed March 23, 2015).
34. California Public Utilities Commission, "CPUC Strengthens Insurance Requirements for Transportation Network Companies," *California Public Utilities Commission,* November 20, 2014, http://docs.cpuc.ca.gov/PublishedDocs/Published/G000/M143/K291/143291941.PDF (accessed March 23, 2015).
35. Quote at the 2:50 mark from video "Four Things about Uber You Wish You Never Knew," http://www.whosdrivingyou.org/.
36. Carolyn Said, "Uber Extends Insurance to Working Drivers without Passengers," *San Francisco Chronicle,* March 14, 2014, http://www.sfgate.com/technology/article/Uber-extends-insurance-to-working-drivers-without-5316981.php (accessed March 24, 2015).
37. Lydia DePillis, "Über Mensch: What Happens When Travis Kalanick Has Nothing Left to Fight?" *New Republic,* April 29, 2013, http://www.newrepublic.com/article/113059/ubers-travis-kalanick-fights-startups-playing-his-own-game (accessed March 24, 2015); Nitasha Tiku, "Taxi and Limousine Commission Tells Uber It Can't Legally Operate a Taxi App in NYC, Uber CEO Disagrees," *Observer,* September 6, 2012, http://observer.com/2012/09/taxi-and-limousine-commission-tells-uber-they-cant-legally-operate-in-new-york-city-uber-ceo-disagrees/#ixzz3VNRt4DtS (accessed March 24, 2015).
38. Ben Smith, "Uber Executive Suggests Digging Up Dirt on Journalists," *BuzzFeed,* November 17, 2014, http://www.buzzfeed.com/bensmith/uber-executive-suggests-digging-up-dirt-on-journalists#.fiPb221B7 (accessed May 2, 2015).
39. Sarah Lacy, "The Horrific Trickle Down of Asshole Culture: Why I've Just Deleted Uber from My Phone," *PandoDaily,* October 22, 2014, http://pando.com/2014/10/22/the-horrific-trickle-down-of-asshole-culture-at-a-company-like-uber/ (accessed March 24, 2015).
40. Johana Bhuiyan and Charlie Warzel, "'God View': Uber Investigates Its Top New York Executive for Privacy Violations," *BuzzFeed,* November 18, 2014, http://www.buzzfeed.com/johanabhuiyan/uber-is-investigating-its-top-new-york-executive-for-privacy#.lido00AZp (accessed April 2, 2015).
41. Ellen Cushing, "Uber Employees Warned a San Francisco Magazine Writer That Executives Might Snoop on Her," *San Francisco Magazine,* November 29, 2014, http://www.modernluxury.com/san-francisco/story/uber-employees-warned-san-francisco-magazine-writer-executives-might-snoop-her#sthash.48UtPblf.dpuf (accessed March 24, 2015).
42. Peter Sims, "Can We Trust Uber?" *Medium,* September 26, 2014, https://medium.com/@petersimsie/can-we-trust-uber-c0e793deda36 (accessed March 24, 2015).
43. Kashmir Hill, "'God View': Uber Allegedly Stalked Users for Party-Goers' Viewing Pleasure (Updated)," *Forbes,* October 3, 2014, http://www.forbes.com/sites

/kashmirhill/2014/10/03/god-view-uber-allegedly-stalked-users-for-party-goers-viewing-pleasure/ (accessed March 24, 2015).

44. Sam Biddle, "Uber Used Private Location Data for Party Amusement," *Gawker,* September 30, 2014, http://valleywag.gawker.com/uber-used-private-location-data-for-party-amusement-1640820384 (accessed March 28, 2015).
45. Bhuiyan and Warzel, "'God View': Uber Investigates Its Top New York Executive for Privacy Violations."
46. Jason Mick, "Uber Exec Threatens to 'Spend Millions' to Stalk Female Reporter and Her Family," *Daily Tech,* November 19, 2014, http://www.dailytech.com/Uber+Exec+Threatens+to+Spend+Millions+to+Stalk+Female+Reporter+and+Her+Family/article36907.htm (accessed March 28, 2015).
47. Andy Kessler, "Travis Kalanick: The Transportation Trustbuster," *Wall Street Journal,* January 25, 2013, http://www.wsj.com/articles/SB10001424127887324235104578244231122376480 (accessed March 28, 2015).
48. Darwin Bond Graham, "Uber's Tax-Avoidance Strategy Costs Government Millions. How's That for 'Sharing?'" *48 Hills,* July 10, 2014, http://48hills.org/2014/07/10/ubers-tax-avoidance-strategy-costs-government-millions/#permanently-moved; Darwin Bond Graham, "Uber Ireland 2 of 4," *Scribd.,* July 2, 2014, http://www.scribd.com/doc/232316744/Uber-Ireland-2-of-4 (accessed March 28, 2015).
49. Andrew Yeager, "The City of Birmingham Is Preparing for Uber," *WBHM,* June 24, 2014, https://www.wbhm.org/News/2014/raffertyuber (accessed March 28, 2015).
50. Alan Alexander, "Yellow Cab of Birmingham President Shaky about Uber's Entrance," *Birmingham Business Journal,* June 24, 2014, http://www.bizjournals.com/birmingham/morning_call/2014/06/yellow-cab-of-birmingham-president-shaky-about.html (accessed March 28, 2015).
51. Yeager, "The City of Birmingham Is Preparing for Uber."
52. Quote at the 8:08 mark from video "Four Things about Uber You Wish You Never Knew," http://www.whosdrivingyou.org/.
53. Marissa Mitchell, "Uber Blasts Birmingham Councilwoman over Transportation Code," *ABC,* July 29, 2014, http://www.abc3340.com/story/26144790/uber-blasts-birmingham-councilwoman-over-transportation-code (accessed March 28, 2015).
54. Cameron Smith, "Dealing with Uber, Birmingham City Council Must Understand That Common Sense Regulation Is Not the Same as Deregulation: Opinion," *AL.com,* September 25, 2014, http://www.al.com/opinion/index.ssf/2014/09/dealing_with_uber_birmingham_c.html (accessed March 28, 2015).
55. ABC News, "Tuscaloosa Police Arrest 2 in Undercover Uber Sting," *ABC,* September 17, 2014, http://www.abc3340.com/story/26558198/tuscaloosa-police-arrest-2-in-undercover-uber-sting (accessed March 28, 2015).
56. "Taxi Driver Salaries," Salary.com, http://www1.salary.com/Taxi-Driver-Salary.html (accessed March 28, 2015); "Occupational Employment and Wages, May 2014: 53-3041 Taxi Drivers and Chauffeurs," U.S. Bureau of Labor Statistics, March 25, 2015, http://www.bls.gov/oes/current/oes533041.htm (accessed April 2, 2015).
57. Shontell, "All Hail the Uber Man! How Sharp-Elbowed Salesman Travis Kalanick Became Silicon Valley's Newest Star." Read more: http://www.businessinsider.com/uber-travis-kalanick-bio-2014-1#ixzz3VknURoE0.
58. Ellen Cushing, "The Smartest Bro in the Room," *San Francisco Magazine,* November 21, 2014, http://www.modernluxury.com/san-francisco/story/the-smartest-bro-the-room (accessed March 28, 2015).

59. Kara Swisher, "Man and Uber Man," *Vanity Fair,* December 2014, http://www.vanityfair.com/news/2014/12/uber-travis-kalanick-controversy (accessed March 28, 2015).
60. Aaron Sankin, "Why New York Taxis Are Powerless against Uber's Price War," *Daily Dot,* July 18, 2014, http://www.dailydot.com/technology/uber-nyc-taxi-cheaper-price-war/ (accessed March 28, 2015).
61. Ibid.
62. Carr, "Travis Shrugged."
63. Catherine Rampell, "Who Will Win the Ridesharing War? Probably Not Consumers," *Washington Post,* October 2, 2014, http://www.washingtonpost.com/opinions/catherine-rampell-consumers-likely-to-lose-the-uber-lyft-ride-share-war/2014/10/02/f4810f74-4a6c-11e4-a046-120a8a855cca_story.html (accessed March 28, 2015).
64. Dean Baker, "Don't Buy the 'Sharing Economy' Hype: Airbnb and Uber are Facilitating Rip-Offs," *Guardian,* May 27, 2014, http://www.theguardian.com/commentisfree/2014/may/27/airbnb-uber-taxes-regulation (accessed March 30, 2015).
65. Adrianne Jeffries, "Uber the Outlaw: A Rogue Startup Fights the Taxi Power," *Verge,* September 7, 2012, http://www.theverge.com/2012/9/7/3300244/uber-taxi-new-york-travis-kalanick-rogue (accessed March 30, 2015).
66. Cushing, "The Smartest Bro in the Room."
67. Rampell, "Who Will Win the Ridesharing War?"
68. Uber, "What Is Longest You Have Gone without a Ping When Online?" *Uberpeople.net,* September 30, 2014, http://uberpeople.net/threads/what-is-longest-you-have-gone-without-a-ping-when-online.4359/ (accessed March 30, 2015). See photo of driver congestion at http://uberpeople.net/threads/driving-in-la-since-the-latest-pay-cut.2388/#post-22656 (accessed April 2, 2015).
69. Emily Badger, "Now We Know How Many Drivers Uber Has—and Have a Better Idea of What They're Making," *Washington Post,* January 22, 2015, http://uberpeople.net/threads/what-is-longest-you-have-gone-without-a-ping-when-online.4359/ (accessed March 30, 2015).
70. Alison Griswold, "How to Speak Uber," *Slate,* April 16, 2015, http://www.slate.com/articles/business/moneybox/2015/04/uber_says_it_ll_generate_1_million_jobs_this_year_depends_how_you_define.single.html (accessed May 4, 2015).
71. Douglas MacMillan, "Uber Cuts Deals to Lower Car Costs," *Wall Street Journal,* November 25, 2013, http://blogs.wsj.com/digits/2013/11/25/uber-cuts-deals-to-lower-car-costs/ (accessed March 30, 2015).
72. Matt McFarland, "Uber's Remarkable Growth Could End the Era of Poorly Paid Cab Drivers," *Washington Post,* www.washingtonpost.com/blogs/innovations/wp/2014/05/27/ubers-remarkable-growth-could-end-the-era-of-poorly-paid-cab-drivers (accessed March 19, 2015).
73. Jonathan Hall and Alan Krueger, "An Analysis of the Labor Market for Uber's Driver-Partners in the United States," posted at Emily Badger, "Read: Uber's New Study of the Demographics, Earnings and Employment Decisions of Its Workers," *Washington Post,* January 22, 2015, http://www.washingtonpost.com/blogs/wonkblog/wp/2015/01/22/read-ubers-new-study-of-the-demographics-earnings-and-employment-decisions-of-its-workers/ (accessed March 19, 2015).
74. Maya Kosoff, "Uber Drivers Speak Out: We're Making a Lot Less Money Than Uber Is Telling People," *Business Insider,* October 29, 2014, http://www.businessinsider.com/uber-drivers-say-theyre-making-less-than-minimum-wage-2014-10#ixzz3VwcvFdBq (accessed March 30, 2015).
75. Johana Bhuiyan, "What Uber Drivers Really Make (According to Their Pay Stubs)," *Buzzfeed,* November 19, 2014, http://www.buzzfeed.com/johanabhui

yan/what-uber-drivers-really-make-according-to-their-pay-stubs#.yhrWxKxvB2 (accessed March 30, 2015).

76. Luz Lazo, "Some Uber Drivers Say Company's Promise of Big Pay Day Doesn't Match Reality," *Washington Post,* September 6, 2014 (accessed March 30, 2015).
77. Comments by FuzzyElvis, CyberTec69 and Chilcabby, "Uber Study: UberX Drivers Grossed $16.50/Hr (B4 Expenses) during Oct. in 20 Biggest Markets," *UberPeople.net,* January 22–28, 2015, http://uberpeople.net/threads/edited-uber-study-uberx-drivers-grossed-16-50-hr-b4-expenses-during-oct-in-20-biggest-markets.12156 (accessed March 31, 2015).
78. Bianca Barigan, "Why Los Angeles Uber Drivers Say It Sucks to Be Them," *Curbed,* October 24, 2014, http://la.curbed.com/archives/2014/10/why_it_sucks_to_be_an_uber_driver_in_los_angeles_right_now.php (accessed March 31, 2015).
79. Nick Aster, "Sharing Economy Revolution Turns Violent in Paris: What Can We Learn?" *TriplePundit,* January 20, 2014, http://www.triplepundit.com/special/sharing-economy-paris-uber/ (accessed March 31, 2015). The comment comes from the online forum at the end of the article.
80. Zara, "Beating the Winter Slump—Price Cuts for Riders with Guaranteed Earnings for Drivers," *Uber News,* January 8, 2015, http://blog.uber.com/PriceCut2015 (accessed March 31, 2015).
81. One study of 21 cities found that Uber was less expensive in all of those cities except for New York and Philadelphia. And when a tip is added in, which Uber drivers are not allowed to accept, New York and Philadelphia taxis are more expensive than an Uber ride as well. A taxi in Los Angeles was nearly twice as expensive as an Uber ride; in other cities taxis were more like 10-20 percent higher than Uber. Sara Silverstein, "These Animated Charts Tell You Everything about Uber Prices in 21 Cities," *Business Insider,* October 16, 2014, www.businessinsider.com/uber-vs-taxi-pricing-by-city-2014-10.
82. Kosoff, "Uber Drivers Speak Out"; Maya Kosoff, "Uber Drivers across the Country Are Protesting Today—Here's Why," *Business Insider,* October 22, 2014, http://www.businessinsider.com/uber-drivers-across-the-country-are-protesting-tomorrow—heres-why-2014-10#ixzz3W1lg8lPW (accessed March 31, 2015).
83. Lazo, "Some Uber Drivers Say Company's Promise of Big Pay Day Doesn't Match Reality."
84. Goober, "$5 Donation Button for No Kid Hungry," *UberPeople,* December 9, 2014, http://uberpeople.net/threads/5-donation-button-for-no-kid-hungry.8637/ (accessed March 31, 2015); Maya Kosoff, "Uber Drivers Protest: 'You Can't Make a Living Working Only for Uber,'" *Business Insider,* September 15, 2014, http://www.businessinsider.com/uber-new-york-city-office-protests-2014-9#ixzz3W1oJTGH7 (accessed March 31, 2015).
85. Washington, Colorado and New York states, plus San Francisco and Chicago, among others. See Ellen Huet, "What Happens to Uber Drivers and Other Sharing Economy Workers Injured on the Job?," *Forbes,* January 6, 2015, http://www.forbes.com/sites/ellenhuet/2015/01/06/workers-compensation-uber-drivers-sharing-economy/ (accessed May 4, 2015).
86. OSHA, "Preventing Violence against Taxi and For-Hire Drivers," Osha.gov, https://www.osha.gov/Publications/taxi-driver-violence-factsheet.pdf (accessed March 31, 2015).
87. Keven Montgomery, "Lyft Guts Luxury Service, Sticking Drivers with $34,000 SUVs," *Gawker,* September 22, 2014, http://valleywag.gawker.com/lyft-guts-luxury-service-sticking-drivers-with-34-000-1637828788 (accessed March 31, 2015); Jay Barmann, "Lyft Kills Their Lyft Plus Program, Drivers Stuck with SUVs They

Don't Want," *sfist,* September 22, 2014, http://sfist.com/2014/09/22/lyft_kills_their_lyft_plus_program.php (accessed March 31, 2015).

88. Doug Henwood, "What the Sharing Economy Takes," *Nation,* February 16, 2015, http://www.thenation.com/article/196241/what-sharing-economy-takes (accessed March 20, 2015).
89. Adam Lashinsky, "Uber Banks on World Domination," *Fortune,* September 18, 2014, http://fortune.com/2014/09/18/uber-banks-on-world-domination/ (accessed March 31, 2015).
90. Huet, "What Happens to Uber Drivers and Other Sharing Economy Workers Injured on the Job?"
91. Harry Campbell, "Do Uber Drivers Even Want to Be Employees?" *Forbes,* April 22, 2015, http://www.forbes.com/sites/harrycampbell/2015/04/22/do-uber-drivers-even-want-to-be-employees/2/ (accessed May 28, 2015); Harry Campbell, "Could Every Driver on the Road One Day Work for Lyft or Uber?," *Forbes,* May 19, 2015, http://www.forbes.com/sites/harrycampbell/2015/05/19/could-every-driver-on-the-road-one-day-work-for-lyft-or-uber (accessed May 28, 2015).
92. Kosoff, "Uber Drivers Speak Out."
93. Lazo, "Some Uber Drivers Say Company's Promise of Big Pay Day Doesn't Match Reality."
94. Jim Nash and Ashley Soley-Cerro, "Uber Drivers Allege Unfair Wages, Protest Company's Rating System," *KTLA5,* September 10, 2014, http://ktla.com/2014/09/09/uber-drivers-protest-unfair-wages-harsh-rating-system/ (accessed March 31, 2015).
95. Kosoff, "Uber Drivers Protest."
96. Mike Isaac and Natasha Singer, "California Says Uber Driver Is Employee, Not a Contractor," *New York Times,* June 17, 2015, http://www.nytimes.com/2015/06/18/business/uber-contests-california-labor-ruling-that-says-drivers-should-be-employees.html (accessed June 18, 2015); Joshua Brustein, "Uber's Other Legal Mess: Drivers Sue over Missing Tips," *Bloomberg,* April 29, 2013, http://www.bloomberg.com/bw/articles/2013-08-29/ubers-other-legal-mess-drivers-sue-over-missing-tips (accessed March 31, 2015); and Bob Egelko, "Uber Drivers' Suit over Tips Clears Hurdle," *San Francisco Chronicle,* December 7, 2013, http://www.sfgate.com/business/article/Uber-drivers-suit-over-tips-clears-hurdle-5044858.php (accessed March 31, 2015).
97. See Teamsters, "Raising Standards," *CADA,* http://www.cadateamsters.org/ (accessed March 31, 2015); and the Uber Drivers Network NYC Facebook page, https://www.facebook.com/uberdriversnetwork?fref=nf (accessed March 31, 2015).
98. Kosoff, "Uber Drivers across the Country Are Protesting Today—Here's Why."
99. Scott Lucas, "Surge Pricing in Sydney Is Uber's Worst PR Nightmare Since Its Last PR Nightmare," *San Francisco Magazine,* September 15, 2014, http://www.modernluxury.com/san-francisco/story/surge-pricing-sydney-ubers-worst-pr-nightmare-its-last-pr-nightmare#sthash.hAxV7nb7.dpuf (accessed March 31, 2015).
100. Michael Carney, "Uber Seeing Deja Vu as Riders Complain of Rate Gouging Following Caltrain Fatality," *PandoDaily,* October 1, 2014, http://pando.com/2014/10/16/uber-faces-deja-vu-as-riders-complain-of-rate-gouging-following-caltrain-fatality/ (accessed April 3, 2015).
101. Aly Weisman, "Jerry Seinfeld's Wife Spent $415 during Uber's Surge Pricing to Make Sure Her Kid Got to a Sleepover," *Business Insider,* December 16, 2013, http://www.businessinsider.com/jerry-seinfelds-wife-spent-415-during-ubers-surge-pricing-2013-12 (accessed April 3, 2015).

102. Kim Hjelmgaard, "Uber Draws Criticism for Sydney Siege Pricing," *USA Today,* December 15, 2014, http://www.usatoday.com/story/news/world/2014/12/15/sydney-hostage-uber-pricing/20422427/, (accessed March 31, 2015).
103. Nina Golgowski, "Uber Customer Outraged over $539," December 3, 2014, http://www.nydailynews.com/news/national/uber-customer-outraged-billed-539-18-mile-ride-article-1.1997960 (accessed March 31, 2015).
104. Adam Uran, "Woman Hit with $411 Bill for 10-Mile Uber Ride, as 'Surge Pricing' Complaints Increase," *Bring Me the News,* December 4, 2013, http://bringmethenews.com/2014/12/04/woman-hit-with-411-bill-for-10-mile-uber-ride-as-surge-pricing-complaints-increase/ (accessed March 31, 2015); Sam Biddle, "The $357 Uber Ride," *Gawker,* December 17, 2013, http://valleywag.gawker.com/the-357-uber-ride-1485175707 (accessed March 31, 2015); Lauren Ohnesorge, "Uber Defends Price Surge That Charged Durham Man $455 on Halloween," *Triangle Business Journal,* November 4, 2014, http://www.bizjournals.com/triangle/blog/techflash/2014/11/uber-defends-price-surge-durham-man-455-halloween.html (accessed March 31, 2015).
105. Kelly Dessaint, "Gouge Away: Uber's Surge Pricing from a Driver's Perspective," *disinformation,* December 23, 2014, http://disinfo.com/2014/12/gouge-away-ubers-surge-pricing-drivers-perspective/#sthash.otfMq8Qg.dpuf (accessed April 1, 2015). For tips from a ridesharing coach, see The Rideshare Guy, "Consulting & Coaching," *Therideshareguy.com,* http://therideshareguy.com/consulting-coaching/ (accessed April 1, 2015).
106. Nicholas Diakopoulos, "How Uber Surge Pricing Really Works," *Washington Post,* April 17, 2015, http://www.washingtonpost.com/blogs/wonkblog/wp/2015/04/17/how-uber-surge-pricing-really-works (accessed May 8, 2015).
107. Swisher, "Man and Uber Man."
108. Bob Sullivan, "Uber Is a Danger to Itself, Its Customers, Mass Transit," *Daily Finance,* January 31, 2015, http://www.dailyfinance.com/2015/01/31/uber-endangers-itself-customers-mass-transit/ (accessed May 4, 2015).
109. Sarah Kessler, "Gett's Alternative to Uber-Style Surge Pricing," *Fast Company,* April 23, 2015, http://www.fastcompany.com/3045261/getts-alternative-to-uber-style-surge-pricing (accessed May 8, 2015).
110. Johana Bhuiyan, "Here Is Where Uber and Lyft Are Facing Regulation Battles in the United States," *Buzzfeed News,* December 15, 2014, http://www.buzzfeed.com/johanabhuiyan/here-is-where-uber-and-lyft-are-facing-regulation-battles-in?utm_term=.cveoOYoZN&sub=3544682_4617758%20-%20.mv21QQenv#.ck43zRzdPB (accessed April 1, 2015).
111. Rory Mulholland, "Uber Protests Sweep Europe," *Telegraph,* June 11, 2014, http://www.telegraph.co.uk/news/worldnews/europe/france/10892458/Uber-protests-sweep-Europe.html (accessed April 1, 2015); Carol Mattack, "Paris Cabbies Slash Tires, Smash Windshields in Protest against Uber," *Bloomberg,* January 13, 2014, http://www.bloomberg.com/bw/articles/2014-01-13/paris-cabbies-slash-tires-smash-windshields-in-protest-against-uber (accessed April 1, 2015).
112. Mark Scott, "Uber Suspends Operations in Spain," *New York Times,* December 31, 2014, http://bits.blogs.nytimes.com/2014/12/31/uber-suspends-operations-in-spain/?_r=0 (accessed April 1, 2015).
113. Dave Smith, "Report: China Bans Uber," *Business Insider,* January 8, 2015, http://www.businessinsider.com/uber-china-ban-2015-1 (accessed April 1, 2015).
114. Murad Ahmad, Jeevan Vasagar, Tim Bradshaw, and Duncan Robinson, "Uber Drives in to European Tech Backlash," *Financial Times,* September 2, 2014, http://www.ft.com/intl/cms/s/0/bec0f56e-32b8-11e4-93c6-00144feabdc0.html#slide0 (accessed April 1, 2015).

115. Greg Muender, "Uber vs. Lyft: A Former Driver Compares the Two Services," *PandoDaily,* December 3, 2014, http://pando.com/2014/12/03/uber-vs-lyft-a-former-driver-compares-the-two-services/ (accessed April 1, 2015); Heather Smith, "Uber, Lyft, and the Growing Problem of Temp Jobs," *Grist,* March 4, 2015, http://grist.org/business-technology/uber-lyft-and-the-growing-problem-of-temp-jobs/ (accessed April 1, 2015).
116. Lyft Blog, "Lyft Launches 24 Cities in 24 Hours (on the 24th)," *Lyft Blog,* April 24, 2014, http://blog.lyft.com/posts/2014/4/23/lyft-launches-24-cities-in-24-hours-on-the-24th (accessed April 1, 2015).
117. Cushing, "The Smartest Bro in the Room"; J. P. Mangalindan, "San Francisco Cab Drivers Are Uber's Latest Pickup," *Fortune,* January 15, 2014, http://fortune.com/2014/01/15/san-francisco-cab-drivers-are-ubers-latest-pickup/ (accessed April 1, 2015).
118. Laura M. Holson, "To Delete or Not to Delete: That's the Uber Question," *New York Times,* November 21, 2014, http://www.nytimes.com/2014/11/23/fashion/uber-delete-emil-michael-scandal.html?_r=1 (accessed April 1, 2015).
119. Comment in Michael Carney, "Boston Uber Driver Charged with Rape. Is It Time for Some Real Changes Yet?" *PandoDaily,* December 17, 2014, http://pando.com/2014/12/17/closer-to-home-boston-uber-driver-charged-with-rape/ (accessed April 1, 2015).
120. Holson, "To Delete or Not to Delete."
121. DeleteUber, "Results for #deleteUber," *Twitter,* https://twitter.com/search?q=%23deleteuber&src=tyah (accessed April 1, 2015).
122. Peter Sims, "Can We Trust Uber?" *Medium,* September 26, 2014, https://medium.com/@petersimsie/can-we-trust-uber-c0e793deda36 (accessed April 1, 2015); Cushing, "The Smartest Bro in the Room."
123. Andrew Leonard, "Why Uber Must Be Stopped," Salon, August 31, 2014, http://www.salon.com/2014/08/31/why_uber_must_be_stopped/ (accessed April 1, 2015).
124. Rosalind Helderman, "Uber Pressures Regulators by Mobilizing Riders and Hiring Vast Lobbying Network," *Washington Post,* December 13, 2014, http://www.washingtonpost.com/politics/uber-pressures-regulators-by-mobilizing-riders-and-hiring-vast-lobbying-network/2014/12/13/3f4395c6-7f2a-11e4-9f38-95a187e4c1f7_story.html (accessed April 1, 2015).
125. Neil Irwin, "Uber Scandal Highlights Silicon Valley's Grown-Up Problem," *New York Times,* November 19, 2014, http://www.nytimes.com/2014/11/20/upshot/ubers-latest-scandal-and-silicon-valleys-grown-up-problem.html?mabReward=RI%3A8&action=click&contentCollection=Arts®ion=Footer&module=Recommendation&src=recg&pgtype=article&abt=0002&abg=0&_r=0 (accessed April 1, 2015).
126. Juliet Schor, "Debating the Sharing Economy," *Great Transition Initiative,* October 2014, http://www.greattransition.org/publication/debating-the-sharing-economy (accessed April 1, 2015).
127. Aswath Damodaran, "A Disruptive Cab Ride to Riches: The Uber Payoff," *Forbes,* June 10, 2014, http://www.forbes.com/sites/aswathdamodaran/2014/06/10/a-disruptive-cab-ride-to-riches-the-uber-payoff/ (accessed April 1, 2015).
128. "Ride-Sharing in San Francisco," *What's the Fare,* October 8, 2014, http://blog.whatsthefare.com/2014/10/ride-sharing-in-sf.html (accessed April 3, 2015); "Wow! Sidecar Drivers Earn 20% More per Mile," *SherpaShare,* November 3, 2014, https://www.sherpashare.com/share/wow-sidecar-drivers-earn-20-more-per-mile/ (accessed April 3, 2015).

129. Megan Rose Dickey, "Uber Rival CEO: Uber Is for the Rich, We're for Everyone Else," *Business Insider,* March, 2014, http://www.businessinsider.com/sidecar-versus-uber-versus-lyft-2014-2 (accessed April 3, 2015); Carmel DeAmicis, "In Sidecar's New Business Model, People and Packages Share Rides," *Gigaom,* February 9, 2015, https://gigaom.com/2015/02/09/sidecar-rolls-out-local-delivery-a-big-departure/ (accessed April 3, 2015).
130. "BlaBlaCar Makes Ride-Sharing Work at Large Scale," *Wall Street Journal,* December 2, 2013 (see video interview with Nicolas Brusson), http://www.wsj.com/video/blablacar-makes-ride-sharing-work-at-large-scale/A902279D-F3C4-461D-93EA-247AACA1257C.html (accessed April 3, 2015).
131. Joshua Brustein, "Helsinki's Uber for Buses Is Stuck in First Gear," *Bloomberg Business,* May 16, 2014, http://www.bloomberg.com/bw/articles/2014-05-16/helsinkis-uber-for-buses-is-stuck-in-first-gear (accessed June 29, 2015).
132. Jay Cassano, "Could La'Zooz Be the Ride-Sharing App We've Been Waiting For?" *Fast Company,* January 2, 2015, http://www.fastcoexist.com/3041403/could-lazooz-be-the-ride-sharing-app-weve-been-waiting-for (accessed April 3, 2015).
133. Patrick Hoge, "Executive of the Year 2014: Travis Kalanick Steers Uber through Controversies into Fast Lane," *San Francisco Business Times,* December 2, 2014, http://www.bizjournals.com/sanfrancisco/print-edition/2014/12/26/executive-of-the-year-travis-kalanick.html (accessed April 3, 2015).

CHAPTER 4

1. Kevin Roose, "The Sharing Economy Isn't about Trust, It's about Desperation," *New York,* April 24, 2014, http://nymag.com/daily/intelligencer/2014/04/sharing-economy-is-about-desperation.html (accessed March 31, 2015).
2. "Hire Design Freelancers," *Upwork,* https://www.Upwork.com/o/profiles/browse/c1/design-creative/sc1/logo-design-branding/fb/45/max/5/rhrs/1/?q=design (accessed March 31, 2015).
3. "Hire Writing Freelancers," *Upwork,* https://www.upwork.com/o/profiles/browse/fb/45/skill/writing/?q=writing (accessed March 31, 2015).
4. Aymeric G., "So, Is Odesk a Scam?" *TaskArmy,* May 2011, http://taskarmy.com/blog/44-so-is-odesk-a-scam (accessed March 31, 2015).
5. George Cook, "Freelance Job Sites," *Freelancers Union,* December 2014, https://www.freelancersunion.org/hives/freelance-job-sites/posts/4209/ (accessed March 31, 2015).
6. "Work Differently," Elance Annual Impact Report, June 2013, https://www.elance.com/q/sites/default/files/docs/AIR/AnnualImpactReport.pdf.html, pages 12–13 (accessed March 31, 2015).
7. Jessica Leeder, "Virtual Offices Are Altering the Future of Work," *Globe and Mail,* December 28, 2012, http://www.theglobeandmail.com/report-on-business/careers/careers-leadership/on-the-digital-job-in-a-virtual-manner/article6789402/ (accessed March 31, 2015).
8. Carolyn Said, "Elance-oDesk Links Freelancers to Jobs Worldwide," *San Francisco Chronicle,* June 10, 2014, http://www.sfgate.com/technology/article/Elance-oDesk-links-freelancers-to-jobs-worldwide-5539951.php (accessed March 31, 2015).
9. "Global Online Work Report," Elance-oDesk, January–May 2014, http://elance-odesk.com/sites/default/files/media_coverage/reports/global-online-work-report-2014-ytd.pdf (accessed March 31, 2015).
10. Said, "Elance-oDesk Links Freelancers to Jobs Worldwide."

11. Ibid.
12. Jamie Keene, "How Facebook Stems the Deluge of Pornography, Violence, and Cruelty," *Verge,* February 17, 2012, http://www.theverge.com/2012/2/17/2804234/facebook-porn-violence-content-filtering-odesk (accessed March 31, 2015).
13. Adrian Chen, "Inside Facebook's Outsourced Anti-Porn and Gore Brigade, Where 'Camel Toes' Are More Offensive Than 'Crushed Heads,'" *Gawker,* February 16, 2012, http://gawker.com/5885714/inside-facebooks-outsourced-anti-porn-and-gore-brigade-where-camel-toes-are-more-offensive-than-crushed-heads (accessed March 31, 2015).
14. Sara Halzack, "Elance-oDesk Flings Open the Doors to a Massive Digital Workforce," *Washington Post,* June 13, 2014, http://www.washingtonpost.com/business/freelancers-from-around-the-world-offer-software-developing-skills-remotely/2014/06/13/f5088c54-efe7-11e3-bf76-447a5df6411f_story.html (accessed March 31, 2015).
15. Michael Carney, "'Work Is No Longer a Place'—oDesk Launches Private Workplace to Better Manage Freelance Talent Online," *PandoDaily,* September 25, 2013, http://pando.com/2013/09/25/work-is-no-longer-a-place-odesk-launches-private-workspace-to-better-manage-freelance-talent-online/ (accessed March 31, 2015).
16. Halzack, "Elance-oDesk Flings Open the Doors to a Massive Digital Workforce."
17. Michael Carney, "The 'Gig Economy' Is Growing Up. Elance and oDesk Just Merged to Dominate It," *PandoDaily,* December 18, 2013, http://pando.com/2013/12/18/the-gig-economy-is-growing-up-elance-and-odesk-just-merged-to-dominate-it/ (accessed March 31, 2015).
18. "World—Online Staffing Revenue Could Reach $46 Billion," *Staffing Industry Analysts,* January 6, 2014, http://www.staffingindustry.com/Research-Publications/Daily-News/World-Online-staffing-revenue-could-reach-46-billion-28527 (accessed March 31, 2015).
19. Carney, "The 'Gig Economy' Is Growing Up. Elance and oDesk Just Merged to Dominate It."
20. "The Looming Talent Crisis: Research Shows Companies Unprepared for Future of Work," *SAP,* September 10, 2014, http://www.news-sap.com/workforce-2020-looming-talent-crisis-research-shows-companies-unprepared-future-work/ (accessed March 31, 2015).
21. Said, "Elance-oDesk Links Freelancers to Jobs Worldwide."
22. Alexia Tsotsis, "TaskRabbit Turns Grunt Work into a Game," *Wired,* July 15, 2011, http://www.wired.com/2011/07/mf_taskrabbit/ (accessed March 31, 2015).
23. "In the News," *TaskRabbit,* https://www.taskrabbit.com/press (accessed March 31, 2015).
24. "About TaskRabbit/About Us," *TaskRabbit,* https://www.taskrabbit.com/about (accessed March 31, 2015).
25. Casey Newton, "Temping Fate: Can TaskRabbit Go from Side Gigs to Real Jobs?" *Verge,* May 23, 2013, http://www.theverge.com/2013/5/23/4352116/taskrabbit-temp-agency-gig-economy (accessed March 31, 2015).
26. Bureau of Labor Statistics, "Labor Force Statistics from the Current Population Survey," U.S. Department of Labor, Databases, Tables & Calculators by Subject, Civilian Labor Force, 1982–2015, http://data.bls.gov/pdq/SurveyOutputServlet (accessed March 20, 2015).
27. Sarah Kessler, "Pixel & Dimed: On (Not) Getting By in the Gig Economy," *Fast Company,* May 2014, http://www.fastcompany.com/3027355/pixel-and-dimed-on-not-getting-by-in-the-gig-economy (accessed March 20, 2015).

28. "How Task Rabbit Works," TaskRabbit, https://www.taskrabbit.com/how-it-works (accessed March 31, 2015).
29. CJ, "TaskRabbit Review," *Yelp,* October 11, 2012, http://www.yelp.com/not_recommended_reviews/taskrabbit-san-francisco?removed_start=20 (accessed March 31, 2015).
30. Alexia Tsotsis, "TaskRabbit Gets $5M from Shasta Ventures, First Round and Others to Help People Get Stuff Done," *TechCrunch,* May 4, 2011, http://techcrunch.com/2011/05/04/taskrabbit-gets-5m-to-help-people-get-stuff-done (accessed May 12, 2015).
31. One rabbit wrote, "When you make an offer on Task Rabbit, you have no idea what price they display to the job posters. A client's confusion led me to discover that he was paying $23+ for the task while I was earning $15. A more than 50% markup made me feel extremely taken advantage of." P. Ryan, "When You Make an Offer on Task Rabbit . . ." *Reviewopedia,* July 13, 2012, http://reviewopedia.com/workathome/taskrabbit-com-reviews-legit-or-scam/ (accessed March 31, 2015).
32. Cathy P., "I've worked as a task rabbit and it's basically blind . . . ," *SiteJabber,* May 29, 2012, http://www.sitejabber.com/reviews/www.taskrabbit.com#5 (accessed March 31, 2015).
33. Alyson Shontell, "My Nightmare Experience as a TaskRabbit Drone," *Business Insider,* December 7, 2011, http://www.businessinsider.com/confessions-of-a-task-rabbit-2011-12?op=1 (accessed March 31, 2015).
34. "TaskRabbit Terms of Service," *TaskRabbit,* November 12, 2014, https://www.taskrabbit.com/terms (accessed March 31, 2015).
35. Kessler, "Pixel & Dimed."
36. Robyn McIntyre, March 2014, from the comments section at ibid.
37. Newton, "Temping Fate: Can TaskRabbit Go from Side Gigs to Real Jobs?"
38. Shontell, "My Nightmare Experience as a TaskRabbit Drone."
39. Joshua Brustein, "In the Future We'll All Be TaskRabbits," *Bloomberg Business,* May 24, 2013, http://www.bloomberg.com/bw/articles/2013-05-24/in-the-future-well-all-be-taskrabbits (accessed March 31, 2015).
40. Shontell, "My Nightmare Experience as a TaskRabbit Drone."
41. Kessler, "Pixel & Dimed."
42. Sam Biddle, "If TaskRabbit Is the Future of Employment, the Employed Are Fucked," *ValleyWag,* July 23, 2014, http://valleywag.gawker.com/if-taskrabbit-is-the-future-of-employment-the-employed-1609221541 (accessed March 31, 2015).
43. Carolyn Said, "TaskRabbit Makes Some Workers Hopping Mad," *San Francisco Chronicle,* July 18, 2014, http://www.sfgate.com/technology/article/TaskRabbit-makes-some-workers-hopping-mad-5629239.php (accessed March 31, 2015).
44. Casey Newton, "TaskRabbit Is Blowing Up Its Business Model and Becoming the Uber for Everything," *Verge,* June 17, 2014, http://www.theverge.com/2014/6/17/5816254/taskrabbit-blows-up-its-auction-house-to-offer-services-on-demand (accessed March 31, 2015).
45. Colleen Taylor, "TaskRabbit Debuts Tools for Hiring Ongoing Temp Work as It Hones Focus on Business Users," *Tech Crunch,* May 23, 2013, http://techcrunch.com/2013/05/23/taskrabbit-for-business-temp-workers (accessed March 31, 2015).
46. William Alden, "The Business Tycoons of Airbnb," *New York Times,* November 25, 2014, http://www.nytimes.com/2014/11/30/magazine/the-business-tycoons-of-airbnb.html (accessed March 31, 2015).
47. Sarah Perez, "TaskRabbit for Business Service Portal Quietly Disappears," *Tech Crunch,* April 1, 2014, http://techcrunch.com/2014/04/01/taskrabbit-for-business-service-portal-quietly-disappears (accessed March 31, 2015).
48. Newton, "TaskRabbit Is Blowing Up Its Business Model."

49. Brustein, "In the Future We'll All Be TaskRabbits."
50. Todd Wasserman, "Walgreens Taps TaskRabbit to Deliver Cold Medicine to Shut-Ins," *Mashable,* January 6, 2014, http://mashable.com/2014/01/06/walgreens-taskrabbit/ (accessed March 31, 2015).
51. Liz Gannes, "Instant Replay: The Second Coming of On-Demand Delivery," *Re/Code,* August 7, 2014, http://recode.net/2014/08/07/instant-replay-the-second-coming-of-on-demand-delivery/ (accessed March 31, 2015).
52. Jill Lepore, "The Disruption Machine," *New Yorker,* June 23, 2014, http://www.newyorker.com/magazine/2014/06/23/the-disruption-machine (accessed March 31, 2015).
53. Silicon Prairie News, "Big Omaha 2011—Bo Fishback, Zaarly," speech by Bo Fishback, *Vimeo,* 2012, https://vimeo.com/24878946 (accessed March 31, 2015).
54. "Workers on Tap," *Economist,* January 3, 2015, http://www.economist.com/news/leaders/21637393-rise-demand-economy-poses-difficult-questions-workers-companies-and (accessed March 31, 2015).
55. Kessler, "Pixel & Dimed."
56. Jenna Wortham, "Handybook Buys Exec in a Deal for the On-Demand World," *New York Times,* January 15, 2014, http://bits.blogs.nytimes.com/2014/01/15/exec-an-errand-service-exits-with-an-acquisition/ (accessed March 31, 2015).
57. Kessler, "Pixel & Dimed."
58. Justin Kan, "What I Learned about Online-to-Offline," Justin Kan blog, March 11, 2014, http://justinkan.com/exec-errands-post-mortem (accessed March 31, 2015).
59. "There's an App for That," *Economist,* January 3, 2015, http://www.economist.com/news/briefing/21637355-freelance-workers-available-moments-notice-will-reshape-nature-companies-and (accessed March 31, 2015).
60. Gannes, "Instant Replay."
61. Julia Carrie Wong, "Codependent Contracting: Couriers Demand App Company Accountability," *SF Weekly,* April 22, 2015, http://www.sfweekly.com/sanfrancisco/san-francisco-freelance-contractors-couriers-app-companies-postmates-caviar-instacart-uber/Content?oid=3550851 (accessed June 3, 2015).
62. Sara Horowitz, "Welcome to Middle-Class Poverty—Does Anybody Know the Way Out?" *Atlantic,* September 23, 2011, http://www.theatlantic.com/business/archive/2011/09/welcome-to-middle-class-poverty-does-anybody-know-the-way-out/245447/ (accessed March 21, 2015).
63. Richard Florida, "The Geography of America's Freelance Economy," *Atlantic Citylab,* February 25, 2013, http://www.citylab.com/work/2013/02/geography-americas-freelance-economy/4118/ (accessed March 21, 2015).
64. Arun Sundararajan, "Trusting the 'Sharing Economy' to Regulate Itself," *New York Times,* March 3, 2014, http://economix.blogs.nytimes.com/2014/03/03/trusting-the-sharing-economy-to-regulate-itself (accessed April 4, 2015).
65. Farhad Manjoo, "Uber's Business Model Could Change Your Work," *New York Times,* January 28, 2015, http://www.nytimes.com/2015/01/29/technology/personaltech/uber-a-rising-business-model.html (accessed March 21, 2015).
66. Nick Wingfield, "How I Made—Instead of Spent—26 Cents with a Mobile App," *New York Times,* December 7, 2014, http://bits.blogs.nytimes.com/2014/12/07/how-i-made-26-cents-with-the-latest-in-sharing-economy-apps/ (accessed May 5, 2015).
67. Kessler, "Pixel & Dimed."
68. Wingfield, "How I Made—Instead of Spent—26 Cents with a Mobile App,"
69. Ibid.
70. Evgeny Morozov, "Out of the Clouds," *The Berlin Journal* (Spring 2015): 15.

71. Manjoo, "Uber's Business Model Could Change Your Work."
72. Brustein, "In the Future We'll All Be TaskRabbits."
73. Erin Hatton, "The Rise of the Permanent Temp Economy," *New York Times,* January 26, 2013, http://opinionator.blogs.nytimes.com/2013/01/26/the-rise-of-the-permanent-temp-economy/ (accessed March 31, 2015).
74. Hatton, "The Rise of the Permanent Temp Economy."
75. Charlie Warzel, "The Danger of Calling Uber a 'Tech Company,'" *BuzzFeed,* January 7, 2015, http://www.buzzfeed.com/charliewarzel/the-danger-of-calling-uber-a-tech-company (accessed March 31, 2015).
76. Jon Zerolnick, "Couch Surfers and Billionaires: On the Sharing Economy," interview with Tom Slee, *Capital and Main,* April 23, 2014, http://capitalandmain.com/latest-news/issues/labor-and-economy/couch-surfers-and-billionaires-on-the-sharing-economy/ (accessed March 31, 2015).
77. Avi Asher-Schapiro, "Against Sharing," *Jacobin,* September 19, 2014, https://www.jacobinmag.com/2014/09/against-sharing/ (accessed March 31, 2015).
78. "There's an App for That," *Economist.*

CHAPTER 5

1. Steven Greenhouse, "Day Laborer Battle Runs Outside Home Depot," *New York Times,* October 10, 2005, http://www.nytimes.com/2005/10/10/national/10depot.html (accessed March 31, 2015).
2. James Surowiecki, "The Underground Recovery," *New Yorker,* April 29, 2013, http://www.newyorker.com/magazine/2013/04/29/the-underground-recovery (accessed March 31, 2015).
3. Ibid.
4. Laurie Udesky, "ESPRIT: Sweatshops Behind the Labels," *Nation,* May 16, 1994, http://foundsf.org/index.php?title=ESPRIT:_Sweatshops_Behind_the_Labels (accessed March 31, 2015).
5. Mark Koba, "$2 Trillion Underground Economy May Be Recovery's Savior," *CNBC,* April 24, 2013, http://www.cnbc.com/id/100668336 (accessed March 31, 2015).
6. Ibid.
7. Robert E. Hall, "Testimony before the U.S. Senate Committee on Finance," Senate Committee on Finance, January 22, 2015, http://www.finance.senate.gov/imo/media/doc/Hall%20testimony.pdf, (accessed March 31, 2015), pages 4–6; also see appendix, Robert E. Hall and Nicolas Petrosky-Nadeau, "Changes in US Household Labor-Force Participation by Household Income," January 19, 2015.
8. Tim Fernholz, "Chilled-Out Rich Teens Are a Big Part of the Drop in the American Labor Force," *Quartz,* January 30, 2015, http://qz.com/336101/chilled-out-rich-teens-are-a-big-part-of-the-drop-in-the-american-labor-force/ (accessed March 31, 2015).
9. Surowiecki, "The Underground Recovery."
10. Ben Shapiro, "America's Black Market May Be Exploding," *Breitbart,* March 19, 2013, http://www.breitbart.com/big-government/2013/03/19/america-black-market-growing/ (accessed March 31, 2015).
11. Ibid.
12. Surowiecki, "The Underground Recovery."
13. Koba, "$2 Trillion Underground Economy May Be Recovery's Savior."
14. Surowiecki, "The Underground Recovery."
15. Andy Greenberg, "Why the Silk Road Trial Matters," *Slate,* January 13, 2015, http://www.slate.com/articles/technology/future_tense/2015/01/ross_ulbricht

_and_silk_road_the_trial_everyone_should_watch.html (accessed March 31, 2015).

16. Andy Greenberg, "Collected Quotations of the Dread Pirate Roberts, Founder of Underground Drug Site Silk Road and Radical Libertarian," *Forbes,* April 29, 2013, http://www.forbes.com/sites/andygreenberg/2013/04/29/collected-quotations-of-the-dread-pirate-roberts-founder-of-the-drug-site-silk-road-and-radical-libertarian/2/ (accessed March 31, 2015).
17. Rachel Swan, "The Obsolete Crime Lord: S.F. Tech Culture Begat the Silk Road and Its Replaceable Founder," *SF Weekly,* November 20, 2013, http://www.sfweekly.com/sanfrancisco/the-obsolete-crime-lord-sf-tech-culture-begat-the-silk-road-and-its-replaceable-founder/Content?oid=2828197&showFullText=true (accessed March 31, 2015).
18. Adrian Chen, "The Underground Website Where You Can Buy Any Drug Imaginable," *Gawker,* June 1, 2011, http://gawker.com/the-underground-website-where-you-can-buy-any-drug-imag-30818160 (accessed March 31, 2015).
19. Greenberg, "Collected Quotations of the Dread Pirate Roberts."
20. James Ball, "Silk Road: The Online Drug Marketplace That Officials Seem Powerless to Stop," *Guardian,* March 22, 2013, http://www.theguardian.com/world/2013/mar/22/silk-road-online-drug-marketplace (accessed March 31, 2015).
21. Chen, "The Underground Website Where You Can Buy Any Drug Imaginable."
22. *United States of America vs. Ross William Ulbricht a/k/a "Dread Pirate Roberts,"* Sealed Complaint, United States District Court, Southern District of New York, https://www.cs.columbia.edu/~smb/UlbrichtCriminalComplaint.pdf (accessed March 31, 2015), page 15.
23. James Ball, "Online Tools to Skirt Internet Censorship Overwhelmed by Demand," *Washington Post,* October 21, 2012, http://www.washingtonpost.com/world/national-security/online-tools-to-skirt-internet-censorship-overwhelmed-by-demand/2012/10/21/390457a2-082d-11e2-858a-5311df86ab04_story.html (accessed March 31, 2015).
24. Ibid.
25. Chen, "The Underground Website Where You Can Buy Any Drug Imaginable."
26. Swan, "The Obsolete Crime Lord."
27. Greenberg, "Collected Quotations of the Dread Pirate Roberts," page 3.
28. Ibid., page 2.
29. Swan, "The Obsolete Crime Lord"; Andrew Dalton, "Obscenely Rich Tech Folk Are Still Building Their Island Utopia Off the Coast of San Francisco," *SFist,* May 9, 2012, http://sfist.com/2012/05/09/obscenely_rich_tech_folk_are_still_building_their_island_utopia_off_the_coast_of_san_francisco.php (accessed March 31, 2015).
30. See the Captain Nemo–like plans for a high-tech Love Boat and floating city-islands at the website of the Seasteading Institute, http://www.seasteading.org/ (accessed March 31, 2015).
31. Swan, "The Obsolete Crime Lord."
32. Greenberg, "Collected Quotations of the Dread Pirate Roberts," page 3.
33. Associated Press, "Silk Road Founder Ross William Ulbricht Denied Bail," *Guardian,* November 21, 2013, http://www.theguardian.com/technology/2013/nov/21/silk-road-founder-held-without-bail (accessed March 31, 2015).
34. Swan, "The Obsolete Crime Lord."
35. "How Common Is Informal Employment?" Organization for Economic Cooperation and Development, http://www.oecd.org/dev/poverty/isinformalnormalmessagesfiguresanddata.htm (accessed March 31, 2015), excerpt from *Is Informal Normal? Towards More and Better Jobs in Developing Countries,*

Organization for Economic Cooperation and Development, March 31, 2009, ISBN 978-92-64-05923-8.

36. "Overview: Data on Informal Employment and Self-Employment," Organization for Economic Cooperation and Development, table 1, http://www.oecd.org/dev/poverty/42863997.pdf (accessed March 31, 2015), excerpt from *Is Informal Normal? Towards More and Better Jobs in Developing Countries,* Organization for Economic Cooperation and Development, March 31, 2009, ISBN 978-92-64-05923-8.
37. Robert Neuwirth, "The Shadow Superpower," *Foreign Policy,* October 28, 2011, http://foreignpolicy.com/2011/10/28/the-shadow-superpower/ (accessed March 31, 2015).
38. The French use a word, *débrouillards,* that describes particularly effective, resourceful and motivated people. The former French colonies adopted this word to their own social and economic reality, saying that inventive, self-starting and entrepreneurial merchants who are doing business on their own, without registering or being regulated by the bureaucracy, are part of "*l'economie de la débrouillardise.*" On the street, that became shortened to "*Systeme D.*" Neuwirth, "The Shadow Superpower."
39. Koba, "$2 Trillion Underground Economy May Be Recovery's Savior."
40. "Executive Summary," Organization for Economic Cooperation and Development, http://www.oecd.org/dev/poverty/42528353.pdf (accessed March 31, 2015), page 12, excerpt from *Is Informal Normal? Towards More and Better Jobs in Developing Countries,* Organization for Economic Cooperation and Development, March 31, 2009, ISBN 978-92-64-05923-8.
41. Neuwirth, "The Shadow Superpower."
42. "Executive Summary," Organization for Economic Cooperation and Development, page 12.
43. Surowiecki, "The Underground Recovery."
44. Grover Norquist and Patrick Gleason, "How Uber Can Help the GOP Gain Control of the Cities," *Reuters,* July 7, 2014, http://blogs.reuters.com/great-debate/2014/07/07/how-uber-can-help-the-gop-gain-control-of-the-cities/ (accessed March 31, 2015).

CHAPTER 6

1. Karin Rush-Monroe, "New UCSF Robotic Pharmacy Aims to Improve Patient Safety, University of California, San Francisco, March 7, 2011, http://www.ucsf.edu/news/2011/03/9510/new-ucsf-robotic-pharmacy-aims-improve-patient-safety (accessed March 31, 2015).
2. Farhad Manjoo, "Will Robots Steal Your Job?" *Slate,* September 26, 2011, http://www.slate.com/articles/technology/robot_invasion/2011/09/will_robots_steal_your_job_2.html (accessed March 31, 2015).
3. "Occupational Employment and Wages, May 2014: 29-1051 Pharmacists," Bureau of Labor Statistics, May 2014, http://www.bls.gov/oes/current/oes291051.htm (accessed March 31, 2015).
4. Robert Hof, "Still Can't Figure Out How Programmatic Advertising Works? Watch This Video," *Forbes,* June 11, 2014, http://www.forbes.com/sites/roberthof/2014/06/11/still-cant-figure-out-how-programmatic-advertising-works-watch-this-video/ (accessed March 31, 2015).
5. Paul A. Baran and Paul M. Sweezy, "The Quality of Monopoly Capitalist Society: Culture and Communications," *Monthly Review* 65, no. 3 (July–August 2013), http://monthlyreview.org/2013/07/01/the-quality-of-monopoly-capitalist-society-culture-and-communications/ (accessed March 31, 2015).

6. Hof, "Still Can't Figure Out How Programmatic Advertising Works?"
7. Mike Shields, "AOL Layoffs Reflect Rise of Programmatic," *Wall Street Journal,* January 30, 2015, http://blogs.wsj.com/cmo/2015/01/30/aol-layoffs-reflect-rise-of-programmatic/ (accessed March 31, 2015).
8. Graham Bowley, "Lone $4.1 Billion Sale Led to 'Flash Crash' in May," *New York Times,* October 1, 2010, http://www.nytimes.com/2010/10/02/business/02flash.html (accessed March 31, 2015).
9. Tom Lauricella and Peter A. McKay, "Dow Takes a Harrowing 1,010.14-Point Trip," *Wall Street Journal,* May 7, 2010, http://www.wsj.com/articles/SB10001424052748704370704575227754131412596 (accessed March 31, 2015).
10. Simone Foxman and Matt Phillips, "Markets Briefly Plunge after AP's Hacked Twitter Account Falsely Reports White House Explosions," *Quarts,* April 24, 2013, http://qz.com/77413/markets-briefly-crash-after-aps-hacked-twitter-account-falsely-reports-white-house-explosions/ (accessed March 31, 2015).
11. David Leinweber, "Avoiding a Billion Dollar Federal Financial Technology Rat Hole," *Journal of Portfolio Management* 37, no. 3 (Spring 2011), 1–2.
12. Eleni Himaras, "Equities Bear Brunt of Wall Street Job Cuts on Volume," *Bloomberg Business,* January 14 2013, http://www.bloomberg.com/news/articles/2013-01-14/equities-bear-brunt-of-wall-street-job-cuts-as-volume-drops-18- (accessed March 31, 2015).
13. Ibid.
14. Matthew Phillips, "How the Robots Lost: High-Frequency Trading's Rise and Fall," *Bloomberg Business,* June 6, 2013, http://www.bloomberg.com/bw/articles/2013-06-06/how-the-robots-lost-high-frequency-tradings-rise-and-fall#p4 (accessed March 31, 2015).
15. Aaron Smith and Janna Anderson, "AI, Robotics, and the Future of Jobs," Pew Research Center, August 6, 2014, http://www.pewinternet.org/2014/08/06/future-of-jobs/ (accessed April 1, 2015).
16. Kevin Kelly, "Better Than Human: Why Robots Will—and Must—Take Our Jobs," *Wired,* http://www.wired.com/2012/12/ff-robots-will-take-our-jobs (accessed April 1, 2015).
17. Steven Pearlstein, "Review: 'The Second Machine Age,' by Erik Brynjolfsson and Andrew McAfee," *Washington Post,* January 17, 2014, http://www.washingtonpost.com/opinions/review-the-second-machine-age-by-erik-brynjolfsson-and-andrew-mcafee/2014/01/17/ace0611a-718c-11e3-8b3f-b1666705ca3b_story.html (accessed April 1, 2015).
18. Manjoo, "Will Robots Steal Your Job?"
19. Nouriel Roubini, "Will You Find Work Once the Robot Revolution Hits?" *MarketWatch,* January 6, 2015, http://www.marketwatch.com/story/will-you-find-work-once-the-robot-revolution-hits-2015-01-05 (accessed April 1, 2015).
20. Smith and Anderson, "AI, Robotics, and the Future of Jobs."
21. Paul Krugman, "Is Growth Over?" *New York Times,* December 26, 2012, http://krugman.blogs.nytimes.com/2012/12/26/is-growth-over/ (accessed April 1, 2015).
22. "News Release: Oxford Martin School Study Shows Nearly Half of U.S. Jobs Could Be at Risk of Computerisation," University of Oxford, September 18, 2013, http://www.futuretech.ox.ac.uk/news-release-oxford-martin-school-study-shows-nearly-half-us-jobs-could-be-risk-computerisation (accessed April 1, 2015); Carl Benedikt Frey and Michael A. Osborne, "The Future of Employment: How Susceptible Are Jobs to Computerization?" Oxford Martin School, Programme on the Impacts of Future Technology, University of Oxford, September 17, 2013, http://www.futuretech.ox.ac.uk/sites/futuretech.ox.ac.uk/files/The_Future_of_Employment

_OMS_Working_Paper_1.pdf (accessed April 1, 2015); Andy Mukherjee, "Robots May Spell 'Control-Alt-Delete' for Workers," *Reuters,* October 23, 2014, http://blogs.reuters.com/breakingviews/2014/10/23/robots-may-spell-control-alt-delete-for-workers/ (accessed April 1, 2015). According to the Oxford study, among the occupations most susceptible to automation are: loan officers, receptionists, paralegals, store clerks, taxi drivers, security guards and computer programmers.

23. Smith and Anderson, "AI, Robotics, and the Future of Jobs."
24. John Markoff, "Armies of Expensive Lawyers, Replaced by Cheaper Software," *New York Times,* March 4, 2011, http://www.nytimes.com/2011/03/05/science/05legal.html (accessed April 1, 2015).
25. "Consensus: 97 Percent of Climate Scientists Agree," National Aeronautics and Space Administration (NASA), http://climate.nasa.gov/scientific-consensus/ (accessed April 1, 2015).
26. Eric Brynjolfsson and Andrew McAfee, *The Second Machine Age: Work, Progress, and Prosperity in a Time of Brilliant Technologies* (New York: W. W. Norton, 2014), 10–11.
27. Stephen Hawking, "Stephen Hawking: 'Transcendence Looks at the Implications of Artificial Intelligence—But Are We Taking AI Seriously Enough?'" *Independent,* May 1, 2014, http://www.independent.co.uk/news/science/stephen-hawking-transcendence-looks-at-the-implications-of-artificial-intelligence—but-are-we-taking-ai-seriously-enough-9313474.html (accessed April 1, 2015).
28. David Autor, "U.S. Labor Market Challenges over the Longer Term," MIT Department of Economics and NBER, October 5, 2010, http://economics.mit.edu/files/6341 (accessed April 1, 2015).
29. Sue Halpern, "How Robots and Algorithms Are Taking Over," *New York Review of Books,* April 2, 2015, http://www.nybooks.com/articles/archives/2015/apr/02/how-robots-algorithms-are-taking-over/ (accessed April 1, 2015).
30. Robert Atkinson, "Renaissance in American Manufacturing? Not So Fast," *Globalist,* February 2, 2015, http://www.theglobalist.com/renaissance-in-american-manufacturing-not-so-fast/ (accessed April 1, 2015).
31. Edward Luce, "Obama Must Face the Rise of the Robots," *Financial Times,* February 3, 2013, http://www.ft.com/intl/cms/s/0/f6f19228-6bbc-11e2-a17d-00144feab49a.html (accessed April 1, 2015).
32. Roubini, "Will You Find Work Once the Robot Revolution Hits?"
33. Charlie Warzel, "Meet the Man Who's Trying to Predict and Fight Tech's Future Battles," *BuzzFeed,* June 11, 2014, http://www.buzzfeed.com/charliewarzel/meet-the-man-whos-trying-to-predict-and-fight-tec#.onyznn7gl (accessed April 1, 2015).
34. Manjoo, "Will Robots Steal Your Job?"
35. David Autor, "The Polarization of Job Opportunities in the U.S. Labor Market," *Center for American Progress and The Hamilton Project,* April 2010, http://economics.mit.edu/files/5554 (accessed April 1, 2015).
36. "The Low-Wage Recovery and Growing Inequality," National Employment Law Project, August 2012, http://www.nelp.org/page/-/Job_Creation/LowWageRecovery2012.pdf (accessed April 1, 2015), p. 2.
37. "Heavy and Tractor-Trailer Truck Drivers," Bureau of Labor Studies, U.S. Department of Labor, Occupational Outlook Handbook, http://www.bls.gov/ooh/transportation-and-material-moving/heavy-and-tractor-trailer-truck-drivers.htm (accessed April 1, 2015); Cristen Conger, "Women Are Secretaries, Men Are Truck Drivers," February 8, 2013, http://www.stuffmomnevertoldyou.com/blog/women-are-secretaries-men-are-truck-drivers/ (accessed April 1, 2015).

38. Alex Ward, "Mechanic Masterchef: Robots Cook Dumplings, Noodles and Wait Tables at Restaurant in China," *Daily Mail,* January 13, 2013, http://www.dailymail.co.uk/news/article-2261767/Robot-Restaurant-Robots-cook-food-wait-tables-Harbin.html (accessed April 1, 2015).
39. Tom Meltzer, "Robot Doctors, Online Lawyers and Automated Architects: The Future of the Professions?" *The Guardian,* June 15, 2014, http://www.theguardian.com/technology/2014/jun/15/robot-doctors-online-lawyers-automated-architects-future-professions-jobs-technology (accessed June 6, 2015).
40. Manjoo, "Will Robots Steal Your Job?"
41. Markoff, "Armies of Expensive Lawyers, Replaced by Cheaper Software."
42. Manjoo, "Will Robots Steal Your Job?"
43. Greg Satell, "What to Do about the Rise of the Robots?" *Forbes,* February 9, 2013, http://www.forbes.com/sites/gregsatell/2013/02/09/what-to-do-about-the-rise-of-the-robots/ (accessed April 1, 2015); Brian Bergstein, "With Watson, IBM Seeks to Sell Medical Knowledge," *MIT Technology Review,* September 21, 2011, http://www.technologyreview.com/news/425490/with-watson-ibm-seeks-to-sell-medical-knowledge/ (accessed April 1, 2015).
44. A clear example of this is in the diagnosis of breast cancer. Radiologists improve the accuracy of mammographic diagnoses by "double reading"—the number of cancers detected increases substantially when two radiologists independently examine the same mammograms. However, one study found that a radiologist who uses a machine called R2 ImageChecker CAD can skip the second reading. A computer and a human are just as good as two humans, so half as many radiologists are needed for mammograms.
45. Manjoo, "Will Robots Steal Your Job?"
46. Ken Schwencke, "Earthquake Aftershock: 2.7 Quake Strikes near Westwood," *Los Angeles Times,* March 17, 2014, http://www.latimes.com/local/lanow/earthquake-27-quake-strikes-near-westwood-california-rdivor-story.html (accessed April 1, 2015); Aviva Rutkin, "Rise of Robot Reporters: When Software Writes the News," *New Scientist,* March 21, 2014, http://www.newscientist.com/article/dn25273-rise-of-robot-reporters-when-software-writes-the-news.html (accessed April 1, 2015).
47. Manjoo, "Will Robots Steal Your Job?"
48. Scott Klein, "How to Edit 52,000 Stories at Once," *ProPublica,* January 24, 2013, http://www.propublica.org/nerds/item/how-to-edit-52000-stories-at-once (accessed April 1, 2015).
49. Christer Clerwall, "Enter the Robot Journalist," *Journalism Practice* 8, no. 5 (February 25, 2014), http://www.tandfonline.com/doi/abs/10.1080/17512786.2014.883116#. (accessed April 1, 2015).
50. Markoff, "Armies of Expensive Lawyers, Replaced by Cheaper Software."
51. Ibid.
52. Satell, "What to Do about the Rise of the Robots?"; Bergstein, "With Watson, IBM Seeks to Sell Medical Knowledge."
53. Roubini, "Will You Find Work Once the Robot Revolution Hits?"
54. George Leef, "Will Online Education Render Traditional College Obsolete?," *Forbes,* October 29, 2013, http://www.forbes.com/sites/georgeleef/2013/10/29/will-online-education-render-traditional-college-obsolete/ (accessed April 1, 2015).
55. Ryan Blitztein, "Triumph of the Cyborg Composer," *Pacific Standard,* February 22, 2010, http://www.psmag.com/books-and-culture/triumph-of-the-cyborg-composer-8507 (accessed April 1, 2015); Greg, "Creative Intelligence," *Digital Tonto,* December 16, 2012, http://www.digitaltonto.com/2012/creative-intelligence (accessed April 1, 2015).

56. Stacey Vanek Smith, "What's Behind the Future of Hit Movies? An Algorithm," *Marketplace,* July 19, 2013, http://www.marketplace.org/topics/business/whats-behind-future-hit-movies-algorithm (accessed April 1, 2015).
57. Tom Whipple, "How Algorithms Are Doing a Number on You," *Financial Review,* April 20, 2013, http://www.afr.com/lifestyle/arts-and-entertainment/film-and-tv/how-algorithms-are-doing-a-number-on-you-20130424-j0wc8 (accessed April 1, 2015).
58. Vanek Smith, "What's Behind the Future of Hit Movies? An Algorithm."
59. Junji Tsuda, "Robots Are Not Going to Steal Your Job," *Financial Times,* February 22, 2015, http://www.ft.com/intl/cms/s/0/d0769e82-b8da-11e4-b8e6-00144feab7de.html (accessed April 1, 2015).
60. Brynjolfsson and McAfee, *The Second Machine Age,* 251.
61. Jeremy Rifkin, "The Zero Marginal Cost Society: The Book," http://www.thezeromarginalcostsociety.com/pages/The-Book.cfm (accessed April 1, 2015).
62. See Trebor Scholz, ed., *Digital Labor: The Internet as Playground and Factory* (New York: Routledge, 2012); and Vasileios Kostakis and Michel Bauwens, *Network Society and Future Scenarios for a Collaborative Economy* (New York: Palgrave Pivot, 2014).
63. Janna Anderson and Lee Rainie, "The Internet of Things Will Thrive by 2025," Pew Research Center, May 14, 2014, http://www.pewinternet.org/2014/05/14/internet-of-things/ (accessed April 1, 2015).
64. Karl Marx, "Critique of the Gotha Programme," April or early May, 1875, *Karl Marx and Frederick Engels: Selected Works in Three Volumes,* volume 3 (Progress Publishers, Moscow, 1970), pages 13–30, https://www.marxists.org/archive/marx/works/1875/gotha/ch01.htm (accessed May 7, 2015).
65. "Research Priorities for Robust and Beneficial Artificial Intelligence: An Open Letter," Future of Life Institute, January 2015, http://futureoflife.org/misc/open_letter#signatories (accessed April 1, 2015); also see "Research Priorities for Robust and Beneficial Artificial Intelligence," January 23, 2015, http://futureoflife.org/static/data/documents/research_priorities.pdf (accessed May 7, 2015).
66. Matt McFarland, "Elon Musk: 'With Artificial Intelligence We Are Summoning the Demon,'" *Washington Post,* October 24, 2014, http://www.washingtonpost.com/blogs/innovations/wp/2014/10/24/elon-musk-with-artificial-intelligence-we-are-summoning-the-demon/ (accessed April 1, 2015).
67. Smith and Anderson, "AI, Robotics, and the Future of Jobs."
68. Robert Kuttner, "The Task Rabbit Economy," *American Prospect,* October 10, 2013, http://prospect.org/article/task-rabbit-economy (accessed May 7, 2015).
69. "Difference Engine: Luddite Legacy," *Economist,* November 4, 2011, http://www.economist.com/blogs/babbage/2011/11/artificial-intelligence (accessed April 1, 2015).
70. Michael Dobbs, "Ford and GM Scrutinized for Alleged Nazi Collaboration," *Washington Post,* November 30, 1998, http://www.washingtonpost.com/wp-srv/national/daily/nov98/nazicars30.htm (accessed April 1, 2015), page A01.
71. Hawking, "Stephen Hawking: 'Transcendence Looks at the Implications of Artificial Intelligence—But Are We Taking AI Seriously Enough?'"

CHAPTER 7

1. Ben Bernanke testimony, "The Financial Crisis Inquiry Report: Final Report of the National Commission on the Causes of the Financial and Economic Crisis in the United States," submitted by The Financial Crisis Inquiry Commission, *U.S.*

Government Printing Office, January 2011, http://www.gpo.gov/fdsys/pkg/GPO-FCIC/pdf/GPO-FCIC.pdf (accessed May 8, 2015), page 354.

2. Kathryn Anne Edwards, Anna Turner, and Alexander Hertel-Fernandez, "A Young Person's Guide to Social Security," Economic Policy Institute, 2012, http://www.nasi.org/sites/default/files/research/Young_Person%27s_Guide_to_Social_Security.pdf (accessed April 1, 2015), p. 6.
3. Bruce Bartlett, "GOP Cuts Budget with an Axe Instead of a Scalpel," *Fiscal Times,* February 11, 2011, http://www.thefiscaltimes.com/Columns/2011/02/11/GOP-Cuts-Budget-with-an-Axe-Instead-of-a-Scalpel (accessed April 1, 2015).
4. Barack Obama, "Remarks by the President on Economic Mobility," The White House, Office of the Press Secretary, December 4, 2013, https://www.whitehouse.gov/the-press-office/2013/12/04/remarks-president-economic-mobility (accessed April 1, 2015).
5. Angela Johnson, "76% of Americans are living paycheck-to-paycheck," *CNN Money,* June 24, 2013, http://money.cnn.com/2013/06/24/pf/emergency-savings (accessed May 9, 2015).
6. Sara Horowitz, "94 Percent of Millennials Want to Use Their Skills for Good," *Huffington Post,* July 24, 2014, http://www.huffingtonpost.com/sara-horowitz/94-of-millennials-want-to_b_5618309.html (accessed April 1, 2015).
7. Dan Schawbel, "Millennials vs. Baby Boomers: Who Would You Rather Hire?" *Time,* March 29, 2012, http://business.time.com/2012/03/29/millennials-vs-baby-boomers-who-would-you-rather-hire/ (accessed April 1, 2015).
8. Lindsay Van Thoen, "3 Ways Millennials Are Revolutionizing the World of Work," Freelancers Union, July 26, 2013, https://www.freelancersunion.org/blog/2013/07/26/3-ways-millennials-are-revolutionizing-world-work/ (accessed April 1, 2015).
9. Sara Horowitz, "America, Say Goodbye to the Era of Big Work," *Los Angeles Times,* August 25, 2014, http://www.latimes.com/opinion/op-ed/la-oe-horowitz-work-freelancers-20140826-story.html (accessed April 1, 2015).
10. Robert Kuttner, "Why Work Is More and More Debased," *New York Review of Books,* October 23, 2014, http://www.nybooks.com/articles/archives/2014/oct/23/why-work-more-and-more-debased.
11. Robert J. S. Ross, *Slaves to Fashion: Poverty and Abuse in the New Sweatshops* (Ann Arbor: University of Michigan Press, 2004), cited in Kuttner, "Why Work Is More and More Debased."
12. Kuttner, "Why Work Is More and More Debased."
13. Amanda Armstrong, "The Sharing Economy: 21st Century Technology, 19th Century Worker Protections," *In These Times,* October 28, 2014, http://inthesetimes.com/working/entry/17278/the_sharing_economy_21st_century_technology_19th_century_worker_protections (accessed April 1, 2015).
14. Ibid.
15. As one European businessman said to his American counterpart, "I believe in capitalism, but you believe only in making money. There's a big difference." Steven Hill, *Europe's Promise: Why the European Way Is the Best Hope in an Insecure Age* (Berkeley: University of California Press, 2010), page 64.
16. Nouriel Roubini, "Where Will All the Workers Go?" *Project Syndicate,* December 31, 2014, http://www.project-syndicate.org/commentary/technology-labor-automation-robotics-by-nouriel-roubini-2014-12 (accessed April 1, 2015).
17. Thomas Edsall, "Can Capitalists Save Capitalism?" *New York Times,* January 30, 2015, http://www.nytimes.com/2015/01/21/opinion/can-capitalists-save-capitalism.html (accessed April 1, 2015).

18. Martin Ford, "The Robot Revolution: Why You Should Worry," *Huffington Post,* March 25, 2013, http://www.huffingtonpost.com/martin-ford/robots-economy_b_2500617.html (accessed April 1, 2015).
19. Aaron Smith and Janna Anderson, "AI, Robotics, and the Future of Jobs," Pew Research Center, August 6, 2014, http://www.pewinternet.org/2014/08/06/future-of-jobs/ (accessed April 1, 2015).
20. Nick Timiraos and Kris Hudson, "How a Two-Tier Economy Is Reshaping the U.S. Marketplace," *Wall Street Journal,* January 28, 2015, http://www.wsj.com/articles/how-a-two-tier-economy-is-reshaping-the-u-s-marketplace-1422502201 (accessed April 1, 2015).
21. Barbara Garson, "Freelance Nation: When Good Jobs Turn to Bad," Salon, August 20, 2013, http://www.salon.com/2013/08/20/freelance_nation_when_good_jobs_turn_to_bad_partner/ (accessed April 1, 2015).
22. Timiraos and Hudson, "How a Two-Tier Economy Is Reshaping the U.S. Marketplace."
23. Barry Cynamon and Steven M. Fazzari, "Inequality, the Great Recession, and Slow Recovery," October 24, 2014, Social Science Research Network, http://ssrn.com/abstract=2205524, p. 30.
24. Thomas Piketty, *Capital in the Twenty-First Century* (Cambridge, MA: Harvard University Press, 2014).
25. Frederick Allen, "How Germany Builds Twice as Many Cars as the U.S. While Paying Its Workers Twice as Much," *Forbes,* December 21, 2011, http://www.forbes.com/sites/frederickallen/2011/12/21/germany-builds-twice-as-many-cars-as-the-u-s-while-paying-its-auto-workers-twice-as-much/ (accessed April 1, 2015).
26. Niall McCarthy, "Germany Is the World's No. 1 Automobile Exporter by Far," *Statista,* September 13, 2013, http://www.statista.com/chart/1451/germany-is-the-worlds-no-one-automobile-exporter-by-far/ (accessed April 1, 2015).
27. Will Hutton, "Which Will Be the Big Economies in 15 Years? It's Not a Done Deal," *Guardian,* December 29, 2013, http://www.theguardian.com/commentisfree/2013/dec/29/worlds-largest-economies-and-their-future (accessed May 8, 2015).
28. "Daron Acemoglu on Why Nations Fail," MIT News/ MIT Video, March 23, 2012, http://video.mit.edu/watch/daron-acemoglu-on-why-nations-fail-10628/ (accessed April 1, 2015).
29. Hutton, "Which Will Be the Big Economies in 15 Years? It's Not a Done Deal."
30. Martin Wolf, "The Wealth of Nations," *Financial Times,* March 3, 2012, http://www.ft.com/intl/cms/s/2/56f88be0-6213-11e1-807f-00144feabdc0.html (accessed April 1, 2015).
31. There have been many criticisms of Acemoglu and Robinson's thesis, and some of them have merit. Geographer Jared Diamond, while finding much of value in their work, took issue with their dismissal of geographic explanations for why nations fail. Would England have achieved global supremacy in the mid-19th century if it had been a landlocked country in central Asia, rather than a maritime nation that used its naval fleet to conquer a global empire (including North America)? And wasn't it a precondition for the countries that launched the industrial revolution in the late 18th century to have access to nearby sources of iron and coal, as well as bountiful amounts of running water? Other criticisms were based on the authors' dismissal of cultural factors as being crucial to the success or failure of nations. See Jared Diamond, "What Makes Countries Rich or Poor?" *New York Review of Books,* June 7, 2012, http://www.nybooks.com/articles/archives/2012/jun/07/what-makes-countries-rich-or-poor (accessed March 25, 2015). Whatever the

merits of those criticisms, they are not crucial to our understanding of what conditions will launch an Economic Singularity.

32. See Claudia Dale Goldin and Lawrence F. Katz, *The Race between Education and Technology* (Cambridge, MA: Belknap Press/Harvard University Press, 2008).
33. Roubini, "Where Will All the Workers Go?"
34. Josh Bivens et al., "Raising America's Pay: Why It's Our Central Economic Policy Challenge," Economic Policy Institute, Washington, D.C., June 2014.
35. Martin Wolf, "Enslave the Robots and Free the Poor," *Financial Times,* February 11, 2014 http://www.ft.com/intl/cms/s/0/dfe218d6-9038-11e3-a776-00144feab7de.html#axzz3W2imOMid (accessed April 1, 2015).
36. Smith and Anderson, "AI, Robotics, and the Future of Jobs."
37. Martin Ford, *Rise of the Robots: Technology and the Threat of a Jobless Future* (New York: Basic Books, 2015), http://www.amazon.com/Rise-Robots-Technology-Threat-Jobless/dp/0465059996 (accessed April 1, 2015).
38. Jaron Lanier, *Who Owns the Future?* (New York: Simon & Schuster, 2013).
39. Sue Halpern, "How Robots and Algorithms Are Taking Over," *New York Review of Books,* April 2, 2015, http://www.nybooks.com/articles/archives/2015/apr/02/how-robots-algorithms-are-taking-over/ (accessed April 1, 2015).
40. Michael Doherty, "When the Working Day Is Through: The End of Work as Identity?" *Work, Employment and Society* 23, no. 1 (March 2009).
41. Kuttner, "Why Work Is More and More Debased."

CHAPTER 8

1. Paul Carr from the Silicon Valley watchdog website PandoDaily has been particularly scathing—and insightful—in exposing this "cult of disruption," the "faddish Silicon Valley concept which essentially boils down to 'let us do whatever we want, otherwise we'll bully you on the Internet until you do.'" See Paul Carr, "Travis Shrugged: The Creepy, Dangerous Ideology behind Silicon Valley's Cult of Disruption," *PandoDaily,* October 24, 2012, http://pando.com/2012/10/24/travis-shrugged (accessed March 25, 2015).
2. Doug Henwood, "What the Sharing Economy Takes," *Nation,* February 16, 2015, http://www.thenation.com/article/196241/what-sharing-economy-takes# (accessed April 1, 2015).
3. Richard Barbrook and Andy Cameron, "The Californian Ideology," *Alamut,* August 1995, http://www.alamut.com/subj/ideologies/pessimism/califIdeo_I.html (accessed April 1, 2015).
4. Barry Goldwater, the Republican nominee for president in 1964, often stated that his primary goal was not to improve government, but to shrink it. As he put it at the time, in what was to become a familiar conservative trope adopted and popularized by Ronald Reagan, "I have little interest in streamlining government or in making it more efficient, for I mean to reduce its size. I do not undertake to promote welfare, for I propose to extend freedom. My aim is not to pass laws, but to repeal them. It is not to inaugurate new programs, but to cancel old ones that . . . impose on the people an unwarranted financial burden." Douglas Amy, "The Anti-Government Campaign," *Government Is Good,* 2007, http://www.governmentisgood.com/articles.php?aid=9 (accessed March 25, 2015).
5. Barbrook and Cameron, "The Californian Ideology."
6. Henwood, "What the Sharing Economy Takes."
7. Thomas Friedman, "How to Monetize Your Closet," *New York Times,* December 21, 2013, http://www.nytimes.com/2013/12/22/opinion/sunday/friedman-how

-to-monetize-your-closet.html (accessed April 1, 2015); Thomas Friedman, "Welcome to the 'Sharing Economy,'" *New York Times,* July 20, 2013, http://www.nytimes.com/2013/07/21/opinion/sunday/friedman-welcome-to-the-sharing-economy.html (accessed April 1, 2015). Tomio Geron, "Airbnb and the Unstoppable Rise of the Share Economy," *Forbes,* February 11, 2013, http://www.forbes.com/sites/tomiogeron/2013/01/23/airbnb-and-the-unstoppable-rise-of-the-share-economy/ (accessed August 1, 2015).

8. Rachel Botsman and Roo Rogers, *What's Mine Is Yours: The Rise of Collaborative Consumption* (New York: HarperBusiness, 2010), 69.
9. Ibid., 223.
10. Charlie Warzel, "The Danger of Calling Uber a 'Tech Company,'" *BuzzFeed,* January 7, 2015, http://www.buzzfeed.com/charliewarzel/the-danger-of-calling-uber-a-tech-company (accessed March 31, 2015).
11. Jeremiah Owyang, "Weekend Read: Liberals and Conservatives Both Love and Loathe the Sharing Economy," *New York Times,* February 20, 2015, http://blogs.wsj.com/accelerators/2015/02/20/weekend-read-liberal-and-conservatives-both-love-and-loathe-the-sharing-economy/ (accessed April 1, 2015).
12. Sara Horowitz, "How Do We Define True Wealth? (And How Do We Get There?)," Freelancers Union, Freelancers Broadcasters Network, January 11, 2014, https://www.freelancersunion.org/blog/dispatches/2014/01/09/q-juliet-schor/ (accessed March 20, 2015).
13. Rachel Botsman, "The Currency of the New Economy Is Trust," Subtitles and Transcript: Rachel Botsman Interview, TED talk, September 2012, https://www.ted.com/talks/rachel_botsman_the_currency_of_the_new_economy_is_trust/transcript?language=en#t-25652 (accessed April 1, 2015).
14. Kevin Roose, "The Sharing Economy Isn't about Trust, It's about Desperation," *New York,* April 24, 2014, http://nymag.com/daily/intelligencer/2014/04/sharing-economy-is-about-desperation.html (accessed March 31, 2015).
15. Steve Jones, "The Problem with the Sharing Economy," *SF Bay Guardian,* May 1, 2012, http://www.sfbg.com/2012/05/01/problem-sharing-economy (accessed April 1, 2015).
16. "Van Jones on the Sharing Economy," video, *Shareable,* September 9, 2011, http://www.shareable.net/blog/van-jones-on-the-sharing-economy-video (accessed April 1, 2015).
17. Annie Leonard, "The Story of Solutions," The Story of Stuff Project, October 2013, http://storyofstuff.org/movies/the-story-of-solutions/ (accessed April 1, 2015).
18. Ellen Cushing, "The Smartest Bro in the Room," *San Francisco Magazine,* November 21, 2014, http://www.modernluxury.com/san-francisco/story/the-smartest-bro-the-room (accessed April 1, 2015).
19. Catherine Rampell, "Who Will Win the Ridesharing War? Probably Not Consumers," *Washington Post,* October 2, 2014, http://www.washingtonpost.com/opinions/catherine-rampell-consumers-likely-to-lose-the-uber-lyft-ride-share-war/2014/10/02/f4810f74-4a6c-11e4-a046-120a8a855cca_story.html (accessed April 1, 2015).
20. Bob Sullivan, "Uber Is a Danger to Itself, Its Customers, Mass Transit," *Daily Finance,* January 31, 2015, http://www.dailyfinance.com/2015/01/31/uber-endangers-itself-customers-mass-transit/ (accessed April 1, 2015).
21. Tim Redmond, "Leap Buses Are Nice—Unless You Are in a Wheelchair," *48 Hills,* April 7, 2015, http://www.48hills.org/2015/04/06/leap-buses-are-nice-unless-you-are-in-a-wheelchair (accessed April 7, 2015).
22. Albert Canigueral, "In Spain, National Federation of Bus Transportation Denounces BlaBlaCar," *Collaborative Consumption,* March 21, 2014, http://www.col

laborativeconsumption.com/2014/03/21/blablacar-denounced-in-spain/ (accessed April 1, 2015).
23. Juliet Schor, "Debating the Sharing Economy," Great Transition Initiative, October 2014, http://www.greattransition.org/publication/debating-the-sharing-economy (accessed April 1, 2015).
24. Juliet Schor, "Getting Sharing Right," *Contexts* 14 (Winter 2015): 12–19, http://contexts.org/articles/on-the-sharing-economy/#schor (accessed April 1, 2015).
25. Schor, "Debating the Sharing Economy."
26. Philip Oltermann, "Berlin 'Borrowing Shop' Promotes the Benefits of Sharing," *Guardian,* March 17, 2014, http://www.theguardian.com/world/2014/mar/17/berlin-borrowing-shop-benefits-share-leila (accessed April 1, 2015).
27. Schor, "Getting Sharing Right."
28. SolidarityNYC, http://solidaritynyc.org (accessed May 9, 2015).
29. Schor, "Getting Sharing Right."
30. Ibid.
31. Schor, "Debating the Sharing Economy."
32. Schor, "Getting Sharing Right."
33. Daniel Pink, *Free Agent Nation* (New York: Warner Books, 2001), 26.
34. Jenna Goudreau, "The Best Freelance Careers," *Forbes,* January 28, 2013, http://www.forbes.com/sites/jennagoudreau/2013/01/28/the-best-freelance-careers-job-openings/ (accessed April 1, 2015).
35. Tomio Geron, "Airbnb and the Unstoppable Rise of the Share Economy," *Forbes,* January 23, 2013, http://www.forbes.com/sites/tomiogeron/2013/01/23/airbnb-and-the-unstoppable-rise-of-the-share-economy/ (accessed April 1, 2015).
36. Daniel Pink, personal interview with the author via email, February 15, 2015; also see Andy Epstein, "Business Thought Leader Dan Pink's Advice to In-House Designers," *AIGA,* December 8, 2011, http://www.aiga.org/business-thought-leader-dan-pinks-advice-to-in-house-designers (accessed May 9, 2015).

CHAPTER 9

1. Neal Boudette, "Union Suffers Big Loss at Tennessee VW Plant," *Wall Street Journal,* February 15, 2014, http://www.wsj.com/articles/SB10001424052702304434104579382541226307368 (accessed April 2, 2015).
2. Mike Elk, "After Historic UAW Defeat at Tennessee Volkswagen Plant, Theories Abound," *In These Times,* February 15, 2014, http://inthesetimes.com/working/entry/16300/after_uaw_defeat_at_volkswagen_in_tennessee_theories_abound (accessed April 2, 2015).
3. Steven Greenhouse, "Union Membership in U.S. Fell to a 70-Year Low Last Year," *New York Times,* January 21, 2011, http://www.nytimes.com/2011/01/22/business/22union.html (accessed April 2, 2015).
4. Cherrie Bucknor and John Schmitt, "Union Byte 2015," Center for Economic and Policy Research, January 2015, Table 1, http://www.cepr.net/documents/union-byte-2015-01.pdf (accessed April 2, 2015), p. 1.
5. Eisenhower said this just before his election, in a speech to the American Federation of Labor, New York City, September 17, 1952. Dwight Eisenhower, "Quotes," Dwight Eisenhower Presidential Library, http://www.eisenhower.archives.gov/all_about_ike/quotes.html (accessed March 25, 2015).
6. Jake Rosenfeld, *What Unions No Longer Do* (Cambridge, MA: Harvard University Press, 2014), http://www.hup.harvard.edu/catalog.php?isbn=9780674725119 (accessed April 2, 2015).

7. Kevin Drum, "Why Unions Matter: The Numbers," *Mother Jones*, August 5, 2011, http://www.motherjones.com/kevin-drum/2011/08/unions-and-wages (accessed April 2, 2015).
8. Harold Meyerson, "The Seeds of a New Labor Movement," *American Prospect*, Fall 2014, http://prospect.org/article/labor-crossroads-seeds-new-movement (accessed April 2, 2015).
9. David Rolf, "The Death of Trade Unionism, and toward the Birth of a Labor 3.0," self-published, 2012, p. 1. Meyerson, "Seeds of a New Labor Movement."
10. Joseph McCartin, "The Strike That Busted Unions," *New York Times*, August 2, 2011, http://www.nytimes.com/2011/08/03/opinion/reagan-vs-patco-the-strike-that-busted-unions.html (accessed April 2, 2015).
11. Jefferson Cowie, "How Ronald Reagan Broke the Air Traffic Controllers Union—And Why That Fight Still Matters," *Alternet*, March 25, 2012, http://www.alternet.org/story/154595/how_ronald_reagan_broke_the_air_traffic_controllers_union—and_why_that_fight_still_matters (accessed May 9, 2015).
12. Ibid.
13. Meyerson, "The Seeds of a New Labor Movement."
14. Ibid.
15. Rolf, "The Death of Trade Unionism," 14.
16. Meyerson, "The Seeds of a New Labor Movement."
17. Jake Whittenberg, "1 Year after $15 Minimum Wage, Little Impact in SeaTac," *King 5*, December 31, 2014, http://www.king5.com/story/money/2014/12/31/15-hour-minimum-wage-seatac/21097523/ (accessed April 2, 2015).
18. Ben Bergman, "Why Unions Lead the $15 Minimum Wage Fight, though Few Members Will Benefit," 89.3 KPCC, January 29, 2015, http://www.scpr.org/blogs/economy/2015/01/29/17859/why-unions-lead-the-15-minimum-wage-fight-though-f/ (accessed April 2, 2015).
19. Nelson Lichtenstein, "'Only One Thing Can Save Us,' by Thomas Geoghegan," *New York Times*, January 30, 2015, http://www.nytimes.com/2015/02/01/books/review/only-one-thing-can-save-us-by-thomas-geoghegan.html (accessed April 2, 2015).
20. Timothy Noah, "Why the Democrats Need Labor Again," *Politico*, January 3, 2015, http://www.politico.com/magazine/story/2015/01/democrats-need-labor-again-113583.html (accessed April 2, 2015).
21. Ibid.
22. Meyerson, "The Seeds of a New Labor Movement."
23. Rolf, "The Death of Trade Unionism," 13, 16, 17.
24. A few other freelancer-supportive organizations worth noting are Fractured Atlas, a New York City–based nonprofit that supports those working in the arts and creative industries, including offering assistance in finding health care; and PLSCI, which provides independent-contractor, sole-proprietor and qualified-group health-insurance coverage. Peers, which originally was established in 2013 as an advocacy group for the sharing economy, has now pivoted and also provides a Web-based platform of support services for freelancers. Ellen Huet, "Turning Sharing Economy Workers into Customers," *Forbes*, http://www.forbes.com/sites/ellenhuet/2014/11/12/peers-relaunch-gig-economy-workers (accessed March 19, 2015).
25. When it was founded in 1995, the Freelancers Union originally was known as Working Today.
26. Sara Horowitz, "The Dream of the 1890s: Why Old Mutualism Is Making a New Comeback," *Atlantic*, March 13, 2012, http://www.theatlantic.com/business/archive/2012/03/the-dream-of-the-1890s-why-old-mutualism-is-making-a-new-comeback/254175/ (accessed April 2, 2015).

27. Sara Horowitz, "Helping You Connect Together," Freelancers Union, February 8, 2011, https://www.freelancersunion.org/blog/2011/02/08/helping-you-connect-together/ (accessed April 2, 2015).
28. David Bornstein, "Safety Nets for Freelancers," *New York Times,* December 6, 2011, http://opinionator.blogs.nytimes.com/2011/12/06/safety-nets-for-freelancers/ (accessed April 2, 2015).
29. Horowitz, "Helping You Connect Together."
30. Steven Greenhouse, "Tackling Concerns of Independent Workers," *New York Times,* March 23, 2013, http://www.nytimes.com/2013/03/24/business/freelancers-union-tackles-concerns-of-independent-workers.html (accessed April 2, 2015).
31. Ibid.
32. Sara Horowitz, "A Jobs Plan for the Post-Cubicle Economy," *Atlantic,* September 5, 2011, http://www.theatlantic.com/business/archive/2011/09/a-jobs-plan-for-the-post-cubicle-economy/244549/ (accessed April 2, 2015).
33. Sara Horowitz, "The Freelance Surge Is the Industrial Revolution of Our Time," *Atlantic,* September 1, 2011, http://www.theatlantic.com/business/archive/2011/09/the-freelance-surge-is-the-industrial-revolution-of-our-time/244229/ (accessed April 2, 2015).
34. Horowitz, "A Jobs Plan for the Post-Cubicle Economy."
35. Sara Horowitz, "America, Say Goodbye to the Era of Big Work," *Los Angeles Times,* August 25, 2014, http://www.latimes.com/opinion/op-ed/la-oe-horowitz-work-freelancers-20140826-story.html (accessed April 1, 2015).
36. Freelancers Union, "Independent, Innovative, and Unprotected: How the Old Safety Net Is Failing America's New Workforce," 2010, http://fu-res.org/pdfs/advocacy/2010_Survey_Summary.pdf (accessed April 2, 2015), pages 1-2.
37. Theresa Riley, "Organizing Workers in the Freelance Economy," *Moyers and Company,* August 28, 2014, http://billmoyers.com/2012/07/06/organizing-workers-in-the-gig-economy/ (accessed April 2, 2015).
38. Horowitz, "The Dream of the 1890s."
39. Sara Horowitz, "Freelancers Are Building the Sharing Economy," Freelancers Union, October 24, 2013, https://www.freelancersunion.org/blog/dispatches/2013/10/24/freelancers-are-building-sharing-economy/ (accessed April 2, 2015).
40. Horowitz, "The Freelance Surge Is the Industrial Revolution of Our Time."
41. Horowitz, "Freelancers Are Building the Sharing Economy."
42. Karl Marx, *German Ideology,* 1845, http://marxists.anu.edu.au/archive/marx/works/1845/german-ideology/ch01a.htm#a4 (accessed May 9, 2015).
43. On the Freelancers Union website, they have numerous online forums called "Hives" and "Sparks," some of them organized by geography and others by area of craft, occupation or industry. I conducted a quick survey of the number of participants in these online forums in February 2015. In the 16 or so Spark Cities, which are designated as the most active locations, there were fewer than 900 online members and only around 200 online conversations (with many of the conversations fairly dated); in the other Hives, also arranged by geography, there were fewer than 250 members and 133 conversations. Those numbers were derived just before the Freelancers Union embarked on a campaign in 16 cities to boost participation. Several months later, the numbers of online participants were only marginally higher. So despite claims that the Freelancers Union has 250,000 (nonpaying) members, the number of active members participating on the FU website is significantly smaller, about 0.6 percent of the membership.
44. John Stoehr, "A New Hamiltonianism: An Interview with Michael Lind," *Boston Review,* June 13, 2012, http://bostonreview.net/michael-lind-john-stoehr-a-new-hamiltonianism-land-of-promise (May 9, 2015).

CHAPTER 10

1. "Inclusive Capitalism: Building Value, Renewing Trust," May 27, 2014, http://www.inc-cap.com/index.html (accessed May 10, 2015).
2. Paul Pohlman and Lynn Forester de Rothschild, "The Capitalist Threat to Capitalism," Project Syndicate, May 23, 2014, https://www.project-syndicate.org/commentary/paul-polman-and-lynn-forester-de-rothschild-call-on-companies-and-governments-to-unite-in-the-search-for-an-inclusive-and-sustainable-economy (accessed April 2, 2015).
3. Dean Baker, "Are We Really Giving Larry Summers the Most Important US Economic Post?" *Guardian,* July 29, 2013, http://www.theguardian.com/commentisfree/2013/jul/29/larry-summers-federal-reserve-chair (accessed April 2, 2015).
4. Lawrence H. Summers and Ed Balls, "Report of the Commission on Inclusive Prosperity," Appendix 1, U.S. Policy Response, p. 107, https://cdn.americanprogress.org/wp-content/uploads/2015/01/IPC-PDF-U.S.appendix.pdf.
5. Claire Gordon, "How Employers Can Legally Strip Your Job of Benefits," *AOL Jobs,* April 27, 2012, http://jobs.aol.com/articles/2012/04/27/how-employers-can-legally-strip-your-job-of-benefits (accessed March 30, 2015).
6. "What Is a Multiemployer Plan?" International Foundation of Employee Benefit Plans, 2015, http://www.ifebp.org/news/featuredtopics/multiemployer/Pages/default.aspx (accessed April 2, 2015).
7. Ibid.
8. "The IUOE," International Union of Operating Engineers (IUOE), June 7, 2012, http://www.iuoelocal9.com/about_us.html (accessed April 2, 2015).
9. "Welcome to Our Website," International Union of Operating Engineers (IUOE), September 27, 2010, http://www.iuoelocal9.com/ (accessed April 2, 2015).
10. Frances Denmark, "Can the Teamsters Save Union Pensions?" *Institutional Investor,* May 20, 2014, http://www.institutionalinvestor.com/article/3343595/investors-pensions/can-the-teamsters-save-union-pensions.html (accessed May 10, 2015).
11. "What is a Multiemployer Plan?"
12. Ibid.
13. Currently, paid sick days, vacations and holidays, as well as health insurance and retirement in some jobs, are the result of a contractual agreement between a single employer and an employee. But what if a worker has multiple employers? That makes it very difficult to figure out which employer is responsible for providing paid sick days, vacations and holidays. The multiemployer model for construction workers, in which the joint labor-management trust becomes the repository for any funds paid by the employer for these purposes, provides a template for this situation, but in this proposal the Individual Security Account would assume the joint trust's role for the individual 1099 worker.
14. Bureau of Labor Statistics, "Employer Costs for Employee Compensation—September 2014," U.S. Department of Labor, USDL-14-2208, December 10, 2014, Tables 1 and 5, pages 5, 10, http://www.bls.gov/news.release/pdf/ecec.pdf (accessed February 24, 2015).
15. That amount works out to about 21 to 25 percent extra above the worker's base hourly wage.
16. Ellen Huet, "What Happens to Uber Drivers and Other Sharing Economy Workers Injured on the Job?" *Forbes,* January 6, 2015, http://www.forbes.com/sites/ellenhuet/2015/01/06/workers-compensation-uber-drivers-sharing-economy/ (accessed April 2, 2015).

17. European Commission, "Equal Treatment for All Agency Workers," news release, October 22, 2008, http://ec.europa.eu/social/main.jsp?catId=89&langId=en&newsId=410&furtherNews=yes (accessed April 2, 2015); European Commission, "Working Conditions—Part-Time Work," http://ec.europa.eu/social/main.jsp?catId=706&langId=en&intPageId=203 (accessed April 2, 2015); "Part-Time Working," *Europa,* July 4, 2006, http://europa.eu/legislation_summaries/employment_and_social_policy/employment_rights_and_work_organisation/c10416_en.htm (accessed April 2, 2015).
18. "Agency Workers," *Citizens Information,* January 9, 2013, http://www.citizensinformation.ie/en/employment/types_of_employment/agency_workers.html (accessed April 2, 2015).
19. For a nice summary of the laws and regulations regarding temp workers in nations all over the world, see Michael Grabell and Lena Groeger, "Temp Worker Regulations around the World," *ProPublica,* February 24, 2014, http://projects.propublica.org/graphics/temps-around-the-world (accessed April 2, 2015). The U.S. has some of the least temp-friendly or supportive laws in the world.
20. Clare O'Connor, "Report: Walmart Workers Cost Taxpayers $6.2 Billion in Public Assistance," *Forbes,* April 15, 2014, http://www.forbes.com/sites/clareoconnor/2014/04/15/report-walmart-workers-cost-taxpayers-6-2-billion-in-public-assistance/ (accessed March 21, 2015).
21. Rebecca Smith, "Will Uber and Lyft Make Your Job Obsolete?" CNN, February 10, 2015, http://www.cnn.com/2015/02/10/opinion/smith-sharing-economy-uber-lyft (accessed April 5, 2015).
22. Michael Grabell, "U.S. Lags behind World in Temp Worker Protections," *Pro Publica,* February 24, 2014, http://www.propublica.org/article/us-lags-behind-world-in-temp-worker-protections (accessed March 21, 2015).
23. Claire Cain Miller, "From Microsoft, a Novel Way to Mandate Sick Leave," *New York Times,* March 26, 2015, http://www.nytimes.com/2015/03/26/upshot/26up-leave.html (accessed April 2, 2015).
24. Grabell, "U.S. Lags behind World in Temp Worker Protections."
25. Robert Reich, "The Rebirth of Stakeholder Capitalism?" Robert Reich blog, August 9, 2014, http://robertreich.org/post/94260751620 (accessed April 5, 2015).
26. On Standard Oil's worker representation, see "Every Employee Is a Partner," *Petroleum Age* 5, no. 4 (April 1918): 142, https://books.google.com/books?id=7jw6AQAAMAAJ&lpg=PA142&ots=BqW2K1O3XH&dq=Walter%20Teagle%20%20worker%20representation&pg=PA142#v=onepage&q=Walter%20Teagle%20%20worker%20representation&f=false (accessed April 6, 2015); and Robert Zieger, "The Wage-Earner and the New Economic System, 1919–1929," in *Herbert Hoover as Secretary of Commerce: Studies in New Era Thought and Practice,* ed. Ellis Wayne Hawley (Iowa City: University of Iowa Press, 1981), 96, https://books.google.com/books?id=8R4UmnJhxLoC&lpg=PA96&ots=IJDxu18K6N&dq=%22standard%20oil%22%20and%20%22worker%20representation%22&pg=PA99#v=onepage&q=%22standard%20oil%22&f=false (accessed April 6, 2015).
27. One way it would do this is by helping to ensure that all unemployed workers actually receive their benefits. A recent study by the National Employment Law Project found that an astounding 73 percent of unemployed workers did not receive unemployment compensation in 2014, a record low. The rules for qualifying are so archaic and out of date, and the barriers to filing erected by states have been so discouraging (including some states adopting online filing systems which have been too complex for some of the unemployed), that the number of people receiving benefits has been greatly reduced in recent years. This not only is a tragedy for those eligible workers, but the macroeconomy loses the stimulus effect from these

unemployed workers acting as consumers. Particularly during an economic downturn, maintaining levels of consumer spending ensures that the downturn is less deep and prolonged. Claire McKenna, "The Job Ahead: Advancing Opportunity for Unemployed Workers," National Employment Law Project, February 2015, page 3, http://www.nelp.org/page/-/UI/Report-The-Job-Ahead-Advancing-Opportunity-Unemployed-Workers.pdf?nocdn=1 (accessed March 23, 2015).

CHAPTER 11

1. "There's an App for That," *Economist,* January 3, 2015, http://www.economist.com/news/briefing/21637355-freelance-workers-available-moments-notice-will-reshape-nature-companies-and (accessed April 4, 2015).
2. "Work-Sharing: Averting Layoffs, Saving Jobs," National Employment Law Project, January 29, 2014, http://www.nelp.org/page/content/WORK-SHARING/ (accessed April 2, 2015).
3. Nelson Lichtenstein, "'Only One Thing Can Save Us,' by Thomas Geoghegan," *New York Times,* January 30, 2015, http://www.nytimes.com/2015/02/01/books/review/only-one-thing-can-save-us-by-thomas-geoghegan.html (accessed April 2, 2015).
4. Marcus Walker, "For the Danish, a Job Loss Can Be a Learning Experience," *Wall Street Journal,* March 21, 2006, http://online.wsj.com/news/articles/SB114290848917403735 (accessed March 27, 2015).
5. Employment and Training Administration, "Registered Apprenticeship National Results Fiscal Year 2013 (10/01/2012 to 9/30/2013)," U.S. Department of Labor, available at http://www.doleta.gov/oa/data_statistics.cfm (accessed May 10, 2015).
6. Robert Lerman and Felix Rauner, "Apprenticeship in the United States," in *Work and Education in America: The Art of Integration,* ed. Antje Barabasch and Felix Rauner (New York: Springer Press, 2012).
7. Marc Winterhoff, "German American Business Outlook 2014: Confidence Hits Five Year High, 98% of German Subsidiaries Expect Business Growth in 2014," German-American Chambers of Commerce, December 16, 2013, http://www.ahkusa.com/fileadmin/ahk_usa/publikationen/GABO_2014/GABO_results/GABO_2014_ppt.pdf (accessed April 2, 2015).
8. Justin J. W. Powell and Johann Fortwengel, "'Made in Germany'—Produced in America? How Dual Vocational Training Programs Can Help Close the Skills Gap in the United States," American Institute for Contemporary German Studies, June 2014, http://www.aicgs.org/site/wp-content/uploads/2014/06/IB-47-ERP-Dual-Training.pdf, page 6.
9. Ilker Subasi, "An Instructor's Perspective: Volkswagen Academy in Chattanooga, TN," presentation, AICGS conference, Washington, D.C., May 23, 2014.
10. Sebastian Patta, "Technical Skills Education: Volkswagen Chattanooga Implements Creative Solutions to Fill Skills Gap," in *Shaping Transatlantic Solutions* (Washington, DC: AICGS, 2013), 29–32.
11. South Carolina Chamber of Commerce, "Apprenticeships in South Carolina: Baseline Report and Recommendations" (2003).
12. Ben Olinksy and Sarah Ayres, "Training for Success: A Policy to Expand Apprenticeships in the United States" (Washington, DC: Center for American Progress, 2013), http://americanprogress.org/issues/labor/report/2013/12/02/79991/training-for-success-a-policyto-expand-apprenticeships-in-the-united-states (accessed May 10, 2015).

13. Debbie Reed et al., "An Effectiveness Assessment and Cost-Benefit Analysis of Registered Apprenticeship in 10 States" (Washington, DC: Mathematica Policy Research, 2012), http://wdr.doleta.gov/research/FullText_Documents/ETAOP_2012_10.pdf (accessed May 10, 2015).
14. Peter Baker, "Obama Opens U.S. Effort to Fill High-Paying Tech Jobs," *New York Times,* March 9, 2015, http://www.nytimes.com/2015/03/10/us/obama-kicks-off-us-effort-to-fill-high-paying-tech-jobs.html (accessed April 2, 2015).
15. Laura Tyson and Lenny Mendonca, "Inside the Training Revolution," *Project Syndicate,* January 31, 2015, http://www.project-syndicate.org/commentary/public-private-workforce-training-by-laura-tyson-and-lenny-mendonca-2015-01 (accessed April 2, 2015).
16. Lawrence H. Summers and Ed Balls, "Report of the Commission on Inclusive Prosperity," Appendix 1, US Policy Response, pages 104–105, https://cdn.americanprogress.org/wp-content/uploads/2015/01/IPC-PDF-U.S.appendix.pdf (accessed May 10, 2015).
17. "Every Employee Is a Partner," *Petroleum Age* 5, no. 4 (April 1918): 142, https://books.google.com/books?id=7jw6AQAAMAAJ&lpg=PA142&ots=BqW2K1O3XH&dq=Walter%20Teagle%20%20worker%20representation&pg=PA142#v=onepage&q=Walter%20Teagle%20%20worker%20representation&f=false (accessed April 6, 2015).
18. Robert Zieger, "The Wage-Earner and the New Economic System, 1919–1929," in *Herbert Hoover as Secretary of Commerce: Studies in New Era Thought and Practice,* ed. Ellis Wayne Hawley (Iowa City: University of Iowa Press, 1981), 96, https://books.google.com/books?id=8R4UmnJhxLoC&lpg=PA96&ots=IJDxu18K6N&dq=%22standard%20oil%22%20and%20%22worker%20representation%22&pg=PA99#v=onepage&q=%22standard%20oil%22&f=false (accessed April 6, 2015).
19. "Every Employee Is a Partner," 142.
20. Steven Hill, *Europe's Promise: Why the European Way Is the Best Hope in an Insecure Age* (Berkely: University of California Press, 2010), pages 54–58.
21. Jonas Pontusson, *Inequality and Prosperity: Social Europe vs. Liberal America* (Ithaca, NY, and London: Cornell University Press, 2005), 115, 117–18. I received much of this information from Klas Levinson, a researcher with the former National Institute for Working Life in Sweden, who is one of the world's experts on codetermination.
22. Lichtenstein, "'Only One Thing Can Save Us,' by Thomas Geoghegan."
23. The origins of German codetermination are fascinating and perhaps instructive. It was introduced in Germany after World War II, with the victorious Allied powers greatly encouraging of this policy since it decentralized economic power and shifted it away from the German industrialists who had supported the Nazis. Unlike the George W. Bush administration, which incompetently mangled governance in postinvasion Iraq, American planners in postwar Germany understood the importance of having the right institutions. They knew exactly what they were doing, and they "punished" the Germans with economic democracy, as a way of handicapping concentrations of German wealth and power. Interestingly, U.S. auto companies like Ford and General Motors, as well as oil companies like Standard Oil, had a lot of business interests and contacts with the Nazis and other fascist leaders prior to and during World War II. So it raises an intriguing possibility of cross-hybridization, and that perhaps Germany got the idea for worker representation from Standard Oil and other U.S. corporate leaders. Pontusson, *Inequality and Prosperity,* 115; also see Hill, *Europe's Promise: Why the European Way Is the Best Hope in an Insecure Age,* 54–58.

24. Timothy Noah, "Why the Democrats Need Labor Again," *Politico,* January 3, 2015, http://www.politico.com/magazine/story/2015/01/democrats-need-labor-again-113583.html (accessed April 2, 2015).
25. Margot Sanger-Katz, "Is the Affordable Care Act Working? Has the Percentage of Uninsured People Been Reduced?" *New York Times,* October 26, 2014, http://www.nytimes.com/interactive/2014/10/27/us/is-the-affordable-care-act-working.html?_r=0#uninsured (accessed April 2, 2015).
26. Michael Lind, Steven Hill, Robert Hiltonsmith and Joshua Freedman, "Expanded Social Security: A Plan to Increase Retirement Security for All Americans," *New America Foundation,* April 2013, http://www.demos.org/sites/default/files/publications/LindHillHiltonsmithFreedman_ExpandedSocialSecurity_04_03_13.pdf (accessed May 10, 2015), page 4.
27. "Policy Basics: Top Ten Facts about Social Security," Center on Budget and Policy Priorities, November 6, 2012, http://www.cbpp.org/cms/?fa=view&id=3261 (accessed April 5, 2015).
28. Social Security provides 90 percent or more of income for 55 percent of elderly Hispanic beneficiaries, for 49 percent of blacks, 42 percent of Asian Americans, but only 35 percent of elderly white beneficiaries. And women constitute 56 percent of Social Security beneficiaries aged 62 and older and 67 percent of beneficiaries aged 85 and older, and receive nearly half of Social Security benefits despite women paying only 41 percent of Social Security payroll taxes. See "Policy Basics: Top Ten Facts about Social Security."
29. Steven Hill, "Don't Cut Social Security—Double It," *Atlantic,* December 12, 2012, http://www.theatlantic.com/politics/archive/2012/12/dont-cut-social-security-double-it/266095/ (accessed April 2, 2015).
30. Steven Hill, "Secure Retirement for All Americans, Guaranteeing the American Dream with Expanded Social Security," New America Foundation, August 2010, page 11, http://newamerica.net/sites/newamerica.net/files/policydocs/Hill%20-%20Social%20Security%20-%2013%20Sept%2010.pdf (accessed May 10, 2015).
31. See ibid.; and Michael Lind, Joshua Freedman, Steven Hill, and Robert Hiltonsmith, "Expanded Social Security: A Plan to Increase Retirement Security for All Americans," New America Foundation, April 3, 2013, http://www.demos.org/sites/default/files/publications/LindHillHiltonsmithFreedman_ExpandedSocialSecurity_04_03_13.pdf (accessed May 10, 2015).
32. "The Cost of Staying Home Sick," *New York Times* editorial, May 4, 2009, www.nytimes.com/2009/05/05/opinion/05tue3.html?scp=3&sq=paid%20sick%20leave&st=cse (accessed May 10, 2015).
33. Brigid Schulte, "Voters Want Paid Leave, Paid Sick Days, Poll Shows. Obama, Too. Will Congress Oblige?" *Washington Post,* http://www.washingtonpost.com/news/local/wp/2015/01/21/voters-want-paid-leave-paid-sick-days-poll-shows-obama-too-will-congress-oblige (accessed March 27, 2015); and Jane Farrell and Joanna Venator, "Paid Sick Days" (Washington, DC: Center for American Progress, 2012), 2, available at https://cdn.americanprogressaction.org/wp-content/uploads/issues/2012/08/pdf/paidsickdays_factsheet.pdf (accessed May 10, 2015).
34. Statistics, "Employee Benefits in the United States—March 2012," cited in Farrell and Venator, "Paid Sick Days," 2.
35. Statistics, "Table 1. Wage and Salary Workers with Access to Paid or Unpaid Leave at Their Main Job by Selected Characteristics, 2011 Annual Averages."
36. Elise Gould and Doug Hall, "Paid Sick Days: Measuring the Small Costs for Connecticut Business" (Washington, DC: Economic Policy Institute, 2011), http://www.epi.org/publication/pm177/ (accessed May 10, 2015).

37. Tom W. Smith and Jibum Kim, "Paid Sick Days: Attitudes and Experiences" (Washington, DC: Public Welfare Foundation, 2010), http://www.nationalpartnership.org/research-library/work-family/psd/paid-sick-days-attitudes-and-experiences.pdf (accessed May 10, 2015).
38. "Child Care in America: 2014 State Fact Sheets," Child Care Aware, http://usa.childcareaware.org/sites/default/files/19000000_state_fact_sheets_2014_v04.pdf (accessed April 7, 2015), page 3.
39. "Parents and the High Cost of Child Care: 2014," Child Care Aware, http://cca.worksmartsuite.com/GetThumbnail.aspx?assetid=644, page 4 (accessed May 10, 2015).
40. Helen Russell, "Childcare Changes: Why the Danish Model Won't Work in the UK," *Guardian,* January 30, 2013, http://www.theguardian.com/money/the-womens-blog-with-jane-martinson/2013/jan/30/childcare-changes-danish-model-uk (accessed April 2, 2015).
41. Donna Ferguson, "The Costs of Childcare: How Britain Compares with Sweden," *Guardian,* May 31, 2014, http://www.theguardian.com/money/2014/may/31/costs-childcare-britain-sweden-compare (accessed April 2, 2015).
42. "The Price of Parenthood," *BBCNews.com,* February 6, 2002, http://news.bbc.co.uk/2/hi/europe/1804390.stm (accessed May 10, 2015).
43. For a long list of good ideas, see Jacob S. Hacker and Nate Loewentheil, "Prosperity Economics: Building an Economy for All," 2012, http://isps.yale.edu/research/publications/isps12-020#.VP5Yoth0zEg (accessed May 10, 2015); also see Summers and Balls, "Report of the Commission on Inclusive Prosperity," 107.
44. "Overview of Paid Sick Time Laws in the United States," *A Better Balance,* March 10, 2015, http://www.abetterbalance.org/web/images/stories/Documents/sickdays/factsheet/PSDchart.pdf (accessed April 2, 2015).
45. "San Francisco Labor Laws—City Contractors," City and County of San Francisco, Office of Labor Standards Enforcement, August 13, 2014, http://sfgsa.org/index.aspx?page=431 (accessed April 2, 2015).
46. Claire Cain Miller, "From Microsoft, a Novel Way to Mandate Sick Leave," *New York Times,* March 26, 2015, http://www.nytimes.com/2015/03/26/upshot/26up-leave.html (accessed April 2, 2015).
47. Louis Jacobson, "Barack Obama Says Taxes Are Lower Today Than under Reagan, Eisenhower," *PolitiFact,* September 22, 2010, http://www.politifact.com/truth-o-meter/statements/2010/sep/22/barack-obama/barack-obama-says-taxes-are-lower-today-under-reag/ (accessed April 2, 2015).
48. "Should Congress Limit the Mortgage-Interest Deduction?" *Wall Street Journal,* March 16, 2014, http://www.wsj.com/articles/SB10001424052702304709904579407111906612936 (accessed April 2, 2015).
49. Robert Kuttner, "The Task Rabbit Economy," *American Prospect,* October 10, 2013, http://prospect.org/article/task-rabbit-economy (accessed May 10, 2015).

CHAPTER 12

1. Paul Krugman, "The Insecure American," *New York Times,* May 29, 2015, http://www.nytimes.com/2015/05/29/opinion/paul-krugman-the-insecure-american.html (accessed May 29, 2015); "Report on the Economic Well-Being of U.S. Households in 2014," Board of Governors of the Federal Reserve System, May 2015, http://www.federalreserve.gov/econresdata/2014-report-economic-well-being-us-households-201505.pdf (accessed May 29, 2015), pages 1–3.
2. Alex Williams, "Maybe It's Time for Plan C," *New York Times,* August 12, 2011, http://www.nytimes.com/2011/08/14/fashion/maybe-its-time-for-plan-c.html (accessed May 15, 2015).

3. According to the Kauffman Foundation, which tracks statistics on entrepreneurship in the United States. Dane Stangler, "Infographic: Kauffman Index of Entrepreneurial Activity, 1996-2013," Kauffman Foundation, April 9, 2014, http://www.kauffman.org/multimedia/infographics/2014/infographic-kauffman-index-of-entrepreneurial-activity-1996-2013 (accessed May 15, 2015).
4. Alex Williams, "Maybe It's Time for Plan C."
5. Theodore Roosevelt, "First Annual Message," The American Presidency Project, December 3, 1901, http://www.presidency.ucsb.edu/ws/?pid=29542 (accessed April 8, 2015).
6. Daron Acemoglu and James Robinson, *Why Nations Fail: The Origins of Power, Prosperity and Poverty* (New York: Crown Business, 2012), 321–23.
7. Franklin Roosevelt, "First Inaugural Address," The American Presidency Project, March 4, 1933, http://www.presidency.ucsb.edu/ws/?pid=14473 (accessed April 2, 2015).
8. Franklin Roosevelt, "State of the Union Message to Congress," Franklin D. Roosevelt Presidential Library and Museum, January 11, 1994, http://www.fdrlibrary.marist.edu/archives/address_text.html (accessed April 2, 2015).
9. Acemoglu and Robinson, *Why Nations Fail,* 319.
10. Harold Bloom, *The Daemon Knows: Literary Greatness and the American Sublime* (New York: Spiegel & Grau, 2015), 1.
11. Robert Michel, *Political Parties: A Sociological Study of the Oligarchical Tendencies of Modern Democracy* (1911; New York: Free Press, 1966).
12. John F. Kennedy, "Yale University Commencement," Miller Center, University of Virginia, June 11, 1962, http://millercenter.org/president/speeches/speech-3370 (accessed April 2, 2015).

SELECTED BIBLIOGRAPHY

Acemoglu, Daron, and James Robinson. *Why Nations Fail: The Origins of Power, Prosperity, and Poverty.* New York: Crown Press, 2012.

Alesina, Albert, and Edward L. Glaeser. *Fighting Poverty in the U.S. and Europe.* Oxford, UK: Oxford University Press, 2004.

Alperovitz, Gar. *What Then Must We Do? Straight Talk about the Next American Revolution.* White River Junction, VT: Chelsea Green Publishing, 2013.

Appelbaum, Eileen, and Rosemary Batt. *Private Equity at Work: When Wall Street Manages Main Street.* New York: Russell Sage Foundation, 2014.

Barabasch, Antje, and Felix Rauner, eds. *Work and Education in America: The Art of Integration.* New York: Springer Press, 2012.

Baran, Paul, and Paul Sweezy. *Monopoly Capital: An Essay on the American Economic and Social Order.* New York: Monthly Review Press, 1966.

Barnes, Peter. *With Liberty and Dividends for All: How to Save Our Middle Class When Jobs Don't Pay Enough.* San Francisco, CA: Berrett-Koehler Publishers, 2014.

Benkler, Yochai. *The Wealth of Networks: How Social Production Transforms Markets and Freedom.* New Haven, CT: Yale University Press, 2006.

Berg, Mike. *Invisible to Remarkable: In Today's Job Market, You Need to Sell Yourself as "Talent" Not Just Someone Looking for Work.* Bloomington, IN: iUniverse, 2012.

Bivens, Josh, Elise Gould, Lawrence Mishel, and Heidi Shierholz. "Raising America's Pay: Why It's Our Central Economic Policy Challenge." Economic Policy Institute, Washington, DC, June 2014.

Botsman, Rachel, and Roo Rogers. *What's Mine Is Yours: The Rise of Collaborative Consumption.* New York: HarperCollins, 2010.

Brynjolfsson, Erik, and Andrew McAfee. *Race Against the Machine: How the Digital Revolution Is Accelerating Innovation, Driving Productivity, and Irreversibly Transforming Employment and the Economy.* N.p., 2011.

———. *The Second Machine Age: Work, Progress, and Prosperity in a Time of Brilliant Technologies.* New York: W. W. Norton, 2014.

Carley, Mark. "Board-Level Employee Representatives in Nine Countries: A Snapshot." In *Transfer,* ed. Kevin O'Kelly and Dr. Norbert Kluge. Brussels: European Trade Union Institute, 2005.

CGP Grey, *Humans Need Not Apply,* August 13, 2014, YouTube video, https://www.youtube.com/watch?v=7Pq-S557XQU.

Chase, Robin. *Peers Inc: How People and Platforms Are Inventing the Collaborative Economy and Reinventing Capitalism.* New York: Public Affairs, 2015.

Cheng, Denise Fung. "Reading Between the Lines: Blueprints for a Worker Support Infrastructure in the Peer Economy." Master's thesis, Massachusetts Institute of

Technology, Department of Comparative Media Studies, June 2014. http://p2pfoundation.net/Worker_Support_Infrastructure_in_the_Emerging_Peer_Economy.

Clinton, Bill. *Back to Work: Why We Need Smart Government for a Strong Economy.* New York: Alfred A. Knopf, 2011.

Cowen, Tyler. *Average Is Over: Powering America beyond the Age of the Great Stagnation.* New York: Penguin Group, 2013.

Crain, Marion, and Michael Sherraden. *Working and Living in the Shadow of Economic Fragility.* Oxford, UK: Oxford University Press, 2014.

Dahl, Robert. *How Democratic Is the American Constitution?* New Haven, CT, and London: Yale University Press, 2002.

Davis, Gerald. *Managed by the Markets: How Finance Re-Shaped America.* Oxford, UK: Oxford University Press, 2009.

Diamond, Jared. *Collapse: How Societies Choose to Fail or Succeed.* New York: Penguin Group, 2004.

———. *Guns, Germs, and Steel: The Fates of Human Societies.* New York: W. W. Norton and Company, 1997.

Diamond, Patrick, et al. *The Hampton Court Agenda: A Social Model for Europe.* London: Policy Network, 2006.

Downes, Larry, and Paul Nunes. *Big Bang Disruption: Strategy in the Age of Devastating Innovation.* New York: Portfolio/Penguin, 2014.

Downs, Anthony. *An Economic Theory of Democracy.* New York: Harper and Row, 1957.

Easterly, William. *The Elusive Quest for Growth: Economists' Adventures and Misadventures in the Tropics.* Cambridge, MA: MIT Press, 2002.

Faux, Jeff. *The Global Class War.* Hoboken, NJ: Wiley and Sons, 2006.

Ferguson, Niall. *Civilization: The West and the Rest.* London: Penguin Press, 2011.

Ford, Martin. *The Lights in the Tunnel: Automation, Accelerating Technology and the Economy of the Future.* United States: Acculant Publishing, 2009.

———. *Rise of the Robots: Technology and the Threat of a Jobless Future.* New York: Basic Books, 2015.

Frank, Robert, and Phillip Cook. *The Winner-Take-All Society: Why the Few at the Top Get So Much More Than the Rest of Us.* New York: Free Press, 1995.

Frauenheim, Ed. "FedEx Loses Driver-Classification Legal Skirmishes." *Workforce Magazine,* April 4, 2008, http://www.workforce.com/articles/fedex-loses-driver-classification-legal-skirmishes.

Friedman, Thomas. *The Lexus and the Olive Tree: Understanding Globalization.* New York: Anchor, 2000.

———. *The World Is Flat: A Brief History of the 21st Century.* New York: Farrar, Straus and Giroux, 2005.

Friedman, Thomas, and Michael Mandelbaum. *That Used to Be Us: How America Fell Behind in the World It Invented and How We Can Come Back.* New York: Farrar, Straus and Giroux, 2012.

Fukuyama, Francis. *The End of History and the Last Man.* New York: Avon Books, 1992.

———. *The Origins of Political Order.* New York: Farrar, Straus and Giroux, 2011.

———. *Political Order and Political Decay.* New York: Farrar, Straus and Giroux, 2014.

Gansky, Lisa. *The Mesh: Why the Future of Business Is Sharing.* New York: Portfolio Penguin, 2012.

Garson, Barbara. *Down the Up Escalator: How the 99% Live in the Great Recession.* New York: Doubleday, 2013.

Geertz, Clifford. *The Interpretation of Cultures: Selected Essays.* New York: Basic Books, 1973.

Geoghegan, Thomas. *Only One Thing Can Save Us: Why America Needs a New Kind of Labor Movement.* New York: New Press, 2014.

———. *Which Side Are You On? Trying to Be for Labor When It's Flat on Its Back.* New York: New Press, 2004.

Goldin, Claudia Dale, and Lawrence F. Katz. *The Race between Education and Technology.* Cambridge, MA: Belknap Press/Harvard University Press, 2008.

Gore, Al. *The Future: Six Drivers of Global Change.* New York: Random House, 2013.

Hacker, Jacob. *The Great Risk Shift: The Assault on American Jobs, Families, Health Care and Retirement and How You Can Fight Back.* New York: Oxford University Press, 2006.

Hacker, Jacob, and Paul Pierson. *Winner Take All Politics: How Washington Made the Rich Richer—And Turned Its Back on the Middle Class.* New York: Simon & Schuster, 2010.

Hamilton, Alexander, James Madison, and John Jay. *The Federalist Papers.* New York: New American Library, 1961.

Hatton, Erin. *The Temp Economy: From Kelly Girls to Permatemps in Postwar America.* Philadelphia: Temple University Press, 2011.

Hill, Steven. *10 Steps to Repair American Democracy: 2012 Election Edition.* Boulder: Paradigm Publishers, 2012.

———. *Europe's Promise: Why the European Way Is the Best Hope in an Insecure Age.* Berkeley: University of California Press, 2010.

———. *Fixing Elections: The Failure of America's Winner Take All Politics.* New York and London: Routledge, 2002.

Horowitz, Sara, and Toni Sciarra Poynter. *The Freelancers Bible: Everything You Need to Know to Have the Career of Your Dreams—On Your Terms.* New York: Workman Publishing Company, 2012.

Hull, Thomas. "The Sharing Economy: Why Even the Mainstream Wants a Piece of the Pie." *Wharton School of Business at the University of Pennsylvania,* November 27, 2013, https://knowledge.wharton.upenn.edu/article/sharing-economy-even-mainstream-businesses-wantpiece-pie/.

Hutton, Will. *The World We're In.* London: Little, Brown, 2002.

James-Enger, Kelly. *Six-Figure Freelancing: The Writer's Guide to Making More Money.* New York: Random House, 2005.

Jones, Van. *The Green Collar Economy: How One Solution Can Fix Our Two Biggest Problems.* New York: HarperCollins, 2008.

Kahlenberg, Richard, and Moshe Marvit, *Why Labor Organizing Should Be a Civil Right: Rebuilding a Middle-Class Democracy by Enhancing Worker Voice.* New York: Century Foundation Press, 2012.

Kaletsky, Anatole. *Capitalism 4.0: The Birth of a New Economy in the Aftermath of Crisis,* New York: PublicAffairs, 2010.

Kauffman, Bruce, and Daphne Gottlieb Taras, eds. *Nonunion Employee Representation: History, Contemporary Practice, and Policy.* New York: Routledge, 2001.

Kennedy, Paul. *The Rise and Fall of the Great Powers.* New York: Random House, 1987.

Khanna, Parag. *How to Run the World: Charting a Course to the Next Renaissance.* New York: Random House, 2011.

Kluge, Dr. Norbert, and Michael Stollt, eds. "The European Company—Prospects for Worker Board-Level Participation in the Enlarged E.U." Brussels: Social Development Agency and European Trade Institute for Research, Education and Health and Safety, 2006.

Kostakis, Vasileios, and Michel Bauwens. *Network Society and Future Scenarios for a Collaborative Economy.* New York: Palgrave MacMillan, 2014.

Kotkin, Joel. *The City: A Global History.* New York: Modern Library, 2005.

Landes, David. *The Wealth and Poverty of Nations: Why Some Are So Rich and Some So Poor.* New York: W. W. Norton and Company, 1999.

Lanier, Jaron. *Who Owns the Future?* New York: Simon & Schuster, 2013.

———. *You Are Not a Gadget.* New York: Alfred A. Knopf, 2010.

Lee, Ed, Michael A. Nutter, Antonio R. Villaraigosa, Rahm Emanuel, Francis G. Slay, Jonathan Rothschild, Charlie Hales, Thomas M. Menino, and Carolyn G. Goodman. "Resolution No. 87: In Support of Policies for Shareable Cities." In U.S. Conference of Mayors, *Proposed Resolutions,* 240–42. Proposed Resolutions. Las Vegas, Nevada, 2013. http://usmayors.org/81stAnnualMeeting/media/proposedresolutions.pdf.

Lee, Frances E., and Bruce L. Oppenheimer. *Sizing Up the Senate: The Unequal Consequences of Equal Representation.* Chicago and London: University of Chicago Press, 1999.

Levinson, Klas. "Codetermination in Sweden: Myth and Reality." *Economic and Industrial Democracy* 21 (2000): 457–73.

———. "Employee Representatives on Company Boards in Sweden." *Industrial Relations Journal* 32, no. 2 (2001): 264–74.

Levy, Frank, and Richard Murnane. *The New Division of Labor: How Computers Are Creating the Next Job Market.* Princeton, NJ, and Oxford, UK: Princeton University Press, 2005.

Liddell, Stephen. *How to Get Rich Using Airbnb.* Lulu.com, 2013.

Lijphart, Arend. *Patterns of Democracy: Government Forms and Performance in 36 Countries.* New Haven, CT, and London: Yale University Press, 1999.

Lind, Michael. *Land of Promise: An Economic History of the United States.* New York: Harper, 2013.

Longman, Phillip. *Best Care Anywhere: Why VA Health Care Is Better Than Yours.* Sausalito, CA: PoliPoint Press: 2007.

Lynn, Barry C. *End of the Line: The Rise and Coming Fall of the Global Corporation.* New York: Doubleday, 2005.

Lynn, Richard, and Tatu Vanhanen. *IQ and the Wealth of Nations.* Westport, CT: Praeger, 2002.

Madrick, Jeff. *The Case for Big Government.* Princeton, NJ: Princeton University Press, 2009.

———. *Seven Bad Ideas: How Mainstream Economists Have Damaged America and the World.* New York: Alfred A. Knopf, 2014.

McCartin, Joseph. *Collision Course: Ronald Reagan, the Air Traffic Controllers, and the Strike That Changed America.* New York: Oxford University Press, 2011.

Meisel, James H. *The Myth of the Ruling Class: Gaetano Mosca and the Elite.* Ann Arbor: University of Michigan Press, 1962.

Michel, Robert. *Political Parties: A Sociological Study of the Oligarchical Tendencies of Modern Democracy.* 1911; New York: Free Press, 1962.

Morozov, Evgeny. *The Net Delusion: The Dark Side of Internet Freedom.* New York: Public Affairs, 2011.

———. *To Save Everything, Click Here: The Folly of Technological Solutionism.* New York: Public Affairs, 2013.

Mosca, Gaetano. *The Ruling Class.* 1939; New York: McGraw Hill Book Company, 1989.

Mumford, Lewis. *The City in History.* New York and London: Harcourt, 1961.

Neff, Gina. *Venture Labor: Work and the Burden of Risk in Innovative Industries.* Cambridge, MA: MIT Press, 2012.

Neuwirth, Robert. *Stealth of Nations: The Global Rise of the Informal Economy.* New York: First Anchor Books, 2012.

Noah, Timothy. *The Great Divergence: America's Growing Inequality Crisis and What We Can Do about It.* New York: Bloomsbury Press, 2012.

Owyang, Jeremiah, Alexandra Samuel, and Andrew Grenville. "Report: Sharing Is the New Buying, Winning in the Collaborative Economy." *Vision Critical* and *Crowd*

Companies. March 3, 2014, http://www.web-strategist.com/blog/2014/03/03/report-sharing-is-the-new-buying-winning-in-the-collaborative-economy.

Petroleum Age 5, no. 4 (April 1918).

Piketty, Thomas. *Capital in the Twenty-First Century.* Cambridge, MA: Harvard University Press, 2014.

Pink, Daniel. *Free Agent Nation.* New York: Warner Business Books, 2001.

———. *To Sell Is Human: The Surprising Truth about Moving Others.* New York: Riverhead Books, 2012.

Pontusson, Jonas. *Inequality and Prosperity: Social Europe vs. Liberal America.* Ithaca, NY, and London: Cornell University Press, 2005.

Poo, Ai-Jen. *The Age of Dignity: Preparing for the Elder Boom in a Changing America.* New York: New Press, February, 2015.

———. 2011. "A Twenty-First Century Organizing Model: Lessons from the New York Domestic Workers Bill of Rights Campaign." *New Labor Forum* 20 (1): 50–55. http://muse.jhu.edu/journals/nlf/summary/v020/20.1.poo.html.

Reich, Robert. *Aftershock.* New York: Vintage, 2013.

Reich, Robert, and Jacob Kornbluth, *Inequality for All.* Film. September 27, 2013, http://inequalityforall.com/.

Restakis, John. *Humanizing the Economy: Co-operatives in the Age of Capital.* British Columbia: New Society Publishers, 2010.

Rifkin, Jeremy. *The End of Work: The Decline of the Global Labor Force and the Dawn of the Post-Market Era.* New York: Tarcher/Putnam, 1994.

———. *The Zero Marginal Cost Society: The Internet of Things, the Collaborative Commons, and the Eclipse of Capitalism.* New York: Palgrave Macmillan, 2014.

Rosenfeld, Jake. *What Unions No Longer Do.* Cambridge, MA: Harvard University Press, 2014.

Ross, Robert J. S. *Slaves to Fashion: Poverty and Abuse in the New Sweatshops.* Ann Arbor: University of Michigan Press, 2004.

Schmidt, Eric, and Jared Cohen. *The New Digital Age: Transforming Nations, Businesses, and Our Lives.* New York: Knopf, 2013.

Scholz, Trebor, ed. *Digital Labor: The Internet as Playground and Factory.* New York: Routledge, 2013.

Schwenninger, Sherle, and Joshua Freedman. "America's Debt Problem: How Private Debt Is Holding Back Growth and Hurting the Middle Class." New America Foundation, June 16, 2014, http://newamerica.net/publications/policy/americas_debt_problem_0.

Schwenninger, Sherle, and Samuel Sherraden. "The U.S. Economy after the Great Recession: America's Deleveraging and Recovery Experience." New America Foundation, March 4, 2014, http://newamerica.net/publications/policy/the_us_economy_after_the_great_recession.

Shirky, Clay. *Here Comes Everybody: The Power of Organizing without Organizations.* New York: Penguin Press, 2008.

Simons, Rolf, and Dr. Norbert Kluge. "Workers' Participation at Board Level in the EU-15 Countries." Brussels: Hans Boeckler Foundation/European Trade Union Institute, 2004.

Slaunwhite, Steve, Pete Savage, and Ed Gandia. *The Wealthy Freelancer: 12 Secrets to a Great Income and an Enviable Lifestyle.* New York: ALPHA Books, 2010.

Slee, Tom. "Sharing Economy and Informal Economy." *Whimsley . . . where Tom Slee Writes about Technology and Politics,* 2014. http://tomslee.net/2014/01/sharing-economy-and-informal-economy.html.

———. "Why the Sharing Economy Isn't." *Whimsley,* 2013. http://tomslee.net/2013/08/why-the-sharing-economy-isnt.html.

Smith, Adam, *The Wealth of Nations* 1776; Oxford, UK: Oxford University Press, 1993.

Smith, Hedrick. "When Capitalists Cared." *New York Times,* September 2, 2012.

Stiglitz, Joseph. *The Price of Inequality.* New York: W. W. Norton, 2012.

Stiglitz, Joseph E., Amartya Sen, and Jean-Paul Fitoussi. *Mismeasuring Our Lives: Why GDP Doesn't Add Up: The Report by the Commission on the Measurement of Economic Performance and Social Progress.* New York: New Press, 2010.

Stone, Katherine V. W. *From Widgets to Digits: Employment Regulation for the Changing Workplace.* New York: Cambridge University Press, 2004.

Sullivan, Bob. *Gotcha Capitalism: How Hidden Fees Rip You Off Every Day—And What You Can Do about It.* New York: Ballantine Books, 2007.

Sundararajan, Arun. *Peer-to-Peer Businesses and Sharing (Collaborative) Economy: Overview, Economic Effects, and Regulatory Issues.* Written testimony. Washington, DC: United States House of Representatives, 2014. http://smallbusiness.house.gov/uploadedfiles/1-15-2014_revised_sundararajan_testimony.pdf.

Thiel, Peter, and Blake Masters. *Zero to One: Notes on Startups, or How to Build the Future.* New York: Crown Publishing Group, 2014.

Tocqueville, Alexis de. *Democracy in America.* New York: New American Library, 1956.

Weil, David. *The Fissured Workplace: Why Work Became So Bad for So Many and What Can Be Done to Improve It.* Cambridge, MA: Harvard University Press, 2014.

Wilensky, Harold L. *Rich Democracies: Political Economy, Public Policy and Performance.* Berkeley and London: University of California Press, 2002.

Wilkinson, Richard, and Kate Pickett, *The Spirit Level: Why Greater Equality Makes Societies Stronger.* New York: Bloomsbury Press, 2009.

Zieger, Robert. "The Wage-Earner and the New Economic System, 1919–1929." In *Herbert Hoover as Secretary of Commerce: Studies in New Era Thought and Practice,* ed. Ellis Wayne Hawley. Iowa City: University of Iowa Press, 1981.

Websites of "truly sharing/solidarity" economy companies and organizations:

The People Who Share, www.thepeoplewhoshare.com/

Shareable, www.shareable.net/

Peerby, www.peerby.com/

Yerdle, www.Yerdle.com

Loconomics, www.loconomics.com

Loomio, www.loomio.org/

Enspiral, www.enspiral.com/

Peers, www.peers.org

INDEX